The Big Muddy

An Environmental History of the
Mississippi and Its Peoples
from Hernando de Soto
to Hurricane Katrina

CHRISTOPHER MORRIS

OXFORD
UNIVERSITY PRESS

OXFORD
UNIVERSITY PRESS

Oxford University Press is a department of the University of Oxford.
It furthers the University's objective of excellence in research, scholarship,
and education by publishing worldwide.

Oxford   New York
Auckland   Cape Town   Dar es Salaam   Hong Kong   Karachi
Kuala Lumpur   Madrid   Melbourne   Mexico City   Nairobi
New Delhi   Shanghai   Taipei   Toronto

With offices in
Argentina   Austria   Brazil   Chile   Czech Republic   France   Greece
Guatemala   Hungary   Italy   Japan   Poland   Portugal   Singapore
South Korea   Switzerland   Thailand   Turkey   Ukraine   Vietnam

Oxford is a registered trademark of Oxford University Press
in the UK and certain other countries.

Published in the United States of America by
Oxford University Press
198 Madison Avenue, New York, NY 10016

Library of Congress Cataloging-in-Publication Data
Morris, Christopher (Christopher Charles)
The Big Muddy : an environmental history of the Mississippi and its peoples,
from Hernando de Soto to Hurricane Katrina / Christopher Morris.
p. cm.
Includes bibliographical references and index.
ISBN 978-0-19-531691-9 (hardcover : acid-free paper)
1. Mississippi River—Environmental conditions.
2. Mississippi River Valley—Environmental conditions.
3. Stream ecology—Mississippi River—History.
4. Human ecology—Mississippi River—History.
5. Mississippi River—History.   6. Mississippi River Valley—History.
I. Title.
GE155.M57M67 2012
304.20977—dc23
2012003182

ISBN 978-0-19-531691-9

1 3 5 7 9 8 6 4 2
Printed in the United States of America
on acid-free paper

For my parents, Carole and Charles,
and my children, Farley and Emily

It was a monstrous big river down there....
—MARK TWAIN

Mud, mud, mud.
—BENJAMIN H. B. LATROBE

Lord, the whole round country, man, is overflowed.
—CHARLEY PATTON

Contents

Acknowledgments

FOR THEIR PATIENCE, comments, and suggestions when I presented very rough sketches of early chapters and discussed a lot of half-baked ideas at professional conferences, symposia, and in informal meetings, I would like to thank the audiences and panel commenters, and in particular Amita Baviskar, Juliana Barr, Brad Bond, Gordon Cotton, Pete Daniel, Ron Davis, Tycho de Boer, Tom DiPiero, Don Doyle, Richard Francaviglia, Patricia Galloway, Pat Gill, Paul Greenough, Richard Hoffmann, Walter Johnson, Ari Kelman, Ed Lyon, Bob Markley, Stephanie McCurry, Andrew McMichael, Chris Merrill, Viv Nelles, Steve Noll, David Rumsey, Myra Rutherdale, Beth Schweiger, and Dave Tegeder.

I completed a first draft while a fellow at the Stanford Humanities Center, then under the directorship of John Bender. It was a remarkable year and I cannot mention everyone who made it so, the list would be too long, but I can mention a few fellows and others from the Stanford community who in addition to John lent me their ear, insight, and friendship after hours and beyond the lunch table: Ned Blackhawk, Jon Christensen, Chi Elliott, Jared Farmer, John Felstiner, Akhil Gupta, Teri Nava, Brad Pasanek, Erica Peters, Jim Sheehan, and Brett Whalen.

My year at Stanford was made possible by the generosity of the University of Texas at Arlington, and in particular by former Provost Dana Dunn. My university has been supportive in so many ways, but special thanks go to History Department chairs Don Kyle, Bob Fairbanks, and Marvin Dulaney, and to College of Liberal Arts deans Ben Agger, Ruth Gross, and Beth Wright.

Colleagues in and around Dallas, over lunch, at meetings of the Dallas Area Social History Group (DASH), and on the tennis court never stopped giving me more to think about or asking me why the book wasn't done yet, even at moments when all I wanted to do in life was put my serve in the court. My thanks to Stacy Alaimo, Sophie Burton, Gregg Cantrell, Stephanie Cole, Guy Chet, Jeanne Hamming, Sam Haynes, Ben Johnson, Todd Smith, and Dan Wickberg.

There are some whose influence on me and this book is far greater than they know, owing to what they said, or when they said it, or when I at last understood what they were saying. In some cases it was simply a few valuable words of encouragement offered when I needed them most. My thanks to Craig Colten, Ed Countryman, Bill Cronon, Paul Mapp, Larry Powell, Pat Ryan, Dan Usner, Richard White, and two anonymous readers. Jared Farmer helped crystallize my argument for me when he observed that I was writing about a place that was wet and then was dry. He knows about such places. Susan Ferber of Oxford University Press took a bloated manuscript and pushed me to reduce it, and then went at it herself, brilliantly, all the while reminding me that less is so much more. I think I get it now. Bert Wyatt-Brown offered valued advice and encouragement. He is convinced his students are the best in the world, which does keep us trying ever harder to be better historians and to make him proud. Steve Maizlish read and commented on the entire draft, offering gentle criticism and enthusiastic endorsement. I trust he will allow me to return the favor.

Dear friend Michael Fellman championed this book from the beginning. Late into its final stage of production, he generously offered to blurb it or to do whatever else I thought might help it reach as wide an audience as possible, because he believed the book deserved it, and because, he said, that's what friends are for. And then suddenly he was gone, before he could see it in print or read these inadequate words of acknowledgment. Shalom Michael. Shalom, chaver.

Rajani Sudan was the first to read the entire manuscript, and has read large portions of it since, some several times, and if she reads it again I hope she will recognize some of herself in it. But if she can't stand to read it once more, I understand.

The Big Muddy

Introduction

THERE ARE TWO Mississippi Valleys. One is wet, the other dry. The river made the wet valley by flooding it with dirty water and filling it with mud. People made the dry valley by draining it of water and hardening mud into dirt. The two valleys exist in uneasy tension, the wet valley always ready to burst into the dry valley that holds it down.

In the sixteenth century, Hernando de Soto and his small army searched for dry land in a wet valley, imagining that only dry land could sustain the thousands of people they encountered and the rich empires they hoped to conquer. They found little of it. In the eighteenth century, their French successors managed to dry a very small portion of the valley for agriculture, specifically, but more generally because a wet place to their way of thinking was incapable of sustaining a French colony. In the nineteenth and early twentieth centuries, the United States, whose citizens also believed wetlands did not suit their purposes, continued what the French had begun and eventually succeeded in drying the valley almost entirely. The wet valley persisted, however, behind the levees and beneath the fields and city streets. In each era, Spanish, French, and American, it pushed back by asserting its essentially wet nature against the dry nature people imposed upon it.

This is a history of how Europeans and their American descendants dried one of the world's greatest natural wetlands. They did so by first imagining the valley as a dry place, and then by technologically separating land and water. They dried the valley because they believed they had to if they were going to live there in the manner in which they lived elsewhere. For French to live as French in the Mississippi Valley, they believed they had to dry it. So too the Americans. Both nations had to show themselves and the world they could master their environment. Profits were also important, and the most profitable agricultural commodities would only grow in dry soil. In time, the most compelling reason for drying the valley became the investment already made in the effort. The effect over several centuries has been an incalculable cumulative investment of material and human resources into an effort that cannot be sustained because the valley remains wet, despite claims and appearances to the contrary. There may be less water in fields where cotton and soybeans now grow, but there is more water in and around New Orleans, where coastal marshes are eroding and the city is sinking. The structures that keep the valley dry in one place cause inundation elsewhere. Water has been displaced, not removed. There are other indirect but nevertheless real and serious ways a wetland repressed beneath an imposed human-made dry land occasionally emerges and makes its presence known. The disaster that followed Hurricane Katrina may indicate that the effort of repression is becoming more than the nation can bear. Much of the last 500 years of history in the valley may have to be undone; indeed, the recent growth of wetland rice cultivation and commercial aquaculture suggest the process may have already begun. *Big Muddy* elucidates how this process between humans and environment has unfolded over the centuries.

The history of the wet valley is old. About 2 million years ago, the same tectonic collision that created the Appalachian Mountains buckled the continent at its center, creating the depression through which Big Muddy runs. Over the last million years, several episodes of glacial formation and deterioration sent torrents of water down that depression, alternately filling and cutting it, fashioning the valley that people came to know. The ocean's cycles contributed to the river's work. High sea levels shortened the river by flooding much of the valley and smoothing out the lines between cuts and fills. Low levels lengthened the river and helped it to build deltas at its mouth.[1]

The lower Mississippi Valley is an alluvial valley constructed over millennia by the mixing of water and dirt. Over 600,000 cubic feet of fresh water flow down the valley to the salt water of the gulf every second, an amount equal to what would be sent to the nation's sewers if 53 million people—roughly the total population of the ten states that border the Mississippi River from Louisiana to Minnesota—were to flush their toilets twice a minute, all day, every day. Within all that water are 150 million tons of insoluble sediment, 230 million tons including the Atchafalaya River distributary, plus another 50 to 70 million tons of dissolved matter, for a total of 200 to 300 million metric tons of dirt. The river deposits some of it along the way. A portion of it ends up in the sea, where it falls to the bottom or is sculpted by currents to form the coastline.[2]

The lower Mississippi River along which humans first built permanent settlements took shape 6,000 or 7,000 years ago, with the formation of the meander zone, a subsystem within the entire Mississippi River system that is responsible for sustaining the lower valley environment of lakes, swamps, and bottomland hardwood forests. In this region, the Mississippi's slow, broad, and shallow stream deposited a tremendous amount of silt. Today the lower river flows up to five or six miles per hour during flood stage but is normally about half that speed. Between Cairo and Baton Rouge, the Army Corp of Engineers maintains a shipping channel 300 feet wide and a minimum of nine feet deep, but before engineers modified it, the river ran slower, wider, and shallower. According to the United States Department of Agriculture, in some areas of the valley the fine silt loam topsoil is five feet deep.[3]

The history of the dry valley is not nearly so old. When Hernando de Soto arrived in 1541, water was everywhere across the vast floodplain, and when La Salle arrived in 1682, it was still soggy. The valley was wet in 1803, when Napoleon Bonaparte sold it as part of the Louisiana Purchase to Thomas Jefferson and the United States. By 1862, when Ulysses S. Grant's army marched into the valley, a significant portion of it along the river lay dry and blooming with cotton, but the depredations of the Civil War allowed water to reclaim most of its former wetland, and by 1865 most of the valley still lay under water. However, the idea of a dry Mississippi Valley began with the Spanish and their quest for dry land. This book begins with them and traces the struggles of their successors to transform an ancient wet land into a new dry land, which they ultimately accomplished by disconnecting Big Muddy from its floodplain, by separating mud into water and dirt, and by dividing what was wet from what was dry.

As *wetland* became *wet* between the levees and *land* everywhere else, water largely disappeared from the daily consciousness of the area's residents. It became an enemy to be quietly contained so they would not have to deal with it. The levees in time became naturalized features of a valley so dry that by the latter half of the twentieth century about 5,000 square miles of former floodplain were set aside for automobile usage and urban development and were utterly impermeable to water. Created initially to effect the separation of land and water, levees became barriers between natural opposites. It was a landscape memorialized in a line from a popular song, about driving a Chevy to the levee and finding the levee dry. All the water was on the other side. Water's periodic return to the land was a "disturbance," sometimes a disaster, always unnatural because water did not belong in city streets or cotton fields. Forgotten was a past in which land and water mixed freely and productively rather than destructively, a past written out of a narrative of progress in which water, not earthen and concrete levees, was seen as a troublesome material obstacle to be overcome. This book recovers that forgotten past when land and water freely mixed.[4]

The mingling of water and dirt—mud—is, or was, the essential building block of the Mississippi Valley. Mud was the substance that held together all the pieces and components—animal, vegetable, human—of the floodplain's wetland ecology. In its upper portions, the Mississippi and its tributaries moved quickly, accumulating sediment along the way. In the lower valley where the slope to the sea eases considerably, the river's stream broadened and slowed. Unable to push its way directly across the land, the river meandered, searching out paths of least resistance. As it meandered, it dropped sediment, which added to the resistance of the land by adding to the land itself, but it did so unevenly, depositing sediment along the inside banks of river bends, while eating away at outside bends. Sites of erosion and deposition, if near to each other, which they were in meander loops, pushed the river away from places it shored up and toward, and eventually through, places it undermined. At the river bottom, accumulations of sediment gradually raised the bed and further reduced its slope, further affecting patterns of erosion and deposition. When the river flooded, it dropped sediment atop its banks, forming natural levees that held the river in its channel, until squeezed by land of its own making—a rising bottom, or sand bars on the inside of its bends—it burst or topped its levees and spread out across the land, leaving trails of lakes and swamps. The Mississippi River system in the meander zone was one of constant dam building and dam breaking, and the dams were made of mud, and the river was full of it.[5]

The appearance of wetlands can be deceiving. From a distance the Mississippi River delta looks like dry prairie. Up close it looks like a weedy lake. The water may appear to be a few inches deep but may in fact be many feet deep, as anyone can attest after stepping into an apparently shallow marsh and sinking to the hip. Where suspended mud becomes bottom is not always clear. Biologists and ecologists have found that wetlands are difficult to define—they have identified thirteen types in all—and their boundaries hard to discern. They may be permanently inundated, seasonally inundated, intermittently inundated, or seasonally waterlogged. They may be part of larger aquatic systems, as with coastal estuaries, or they may be independent systems. What they all have in common is inundation, whether sustained, recurrent, or near surface saturation, and they all have the physical, chemical, and biological features of wet conditions. In particular, they have anaerobic soil (soil that lacks oxygen) and yet have macrophytes (trees, shrubs, grass, etc.) that generally require aerobic or oxygenated soil. In other words, wetlands exhibit the characteristics of both aquatic systems (such as algae) and terrestrial systems (such as trees), yet they are unique because they combine both.[6]

The Mississippi Valley is no longer the muddy wetland it once was. The borders between what is wet and what is dry are quite clear. Water is not welcome on the land except under completely controlled circumstances and for specific purposes. When it is no longer wanted, it is removed by pumps and canals. Upon the land the soil is aerobic and the plants are macrophytes, predominantly cotton, corn, and soybeans. What mud remains is either drying into dirt or eroding away to the sea. Increasingly the Mississippi River delta, formerly an expanse of mud, is either river and gulf water or city pavement.[7]

Nevertheless, river and land have found new ways of interacting. Deforestation has altered the rhythm of change in water volume and velocity, which tend to swing more quickly from high and fast to low and slow. In the meander zone and delta, patterns of erosion and deposition have changed, as have the way the river constructs natural levees, channels, lakes, bayous, and much of the Louisiana coastline. The river still carries a heavy load of sediment, but sediment does not end up where it once did. Environmental change has somewhat increased the speed of the Mississippi River by narrowing it—the same effect as putting a thumb over the end of a garden hose. Sediment carried by the river, rather than collecting along the coast is shot out into the Gulf of Mexico, where it drops to the sea floor. Gulf waters erode coastal marshes and inundate brackish areas with higher concentrations of saline, killing cypress trees and destroying bird and oyster habitat. Louisiana has been losing its coastal marshes almost as quickly as it has been losing its interior wetlands.[8]

Moreover, the water and sediment are not what they used to be. For a time the sediment load probably increased with deforestation and the spread of agriculture, although it has decreased in recent times, a consequence of dams put in place in many of the Mississippi's tributaries. As important as the change in quantity of runoff has been the change in its quality. Agricultural runoff is full of nitrogen from fertilizer and synthetic chemicals from herbicides and pesticides. Runoff from hard surfaces carries with it all sorts of debris, including paper, plastic, and motor oil, where it mixes in the river with the runoff from farmland. Much of this runoff is toxic to people and other animals; it has been found to contain endrin, nitrogen, phosphorous, nitrate, nitrite, benzene, carbon tetrachloride, hexachlorobenzene, polychlorinated byphenols, styrene, arsenic, cadmium, lead, zinc, copper, mercury, and uranium.[9]

It might be argued that the reconfiguration of the lower valley from wet to dry was not so different from the environmental reconfiguration that followed the final melting away of the glaciers and the emergence of the meander zone. Natural environments certainly undergo tremendous change without the intervention of people. However, many human-induced alterations to the river's physical system stem from the separation of land and water, which created systemic change that denies the existence of a natural system. People have sought to change certain aspects of it while struggling mightily to keep others unchanged. They have tinkered with it piecemeal, as if it were not a whole system but a series of discrete parts loosely connected and patched together.[10]

It is not only land and water that have been separated. Within the context of the lower Mississippi Valley there has been a separation of change and continuity. To facilitate change on the land, the river has been put into a state of suspended animation. Levees hold it in place, preventing it from going where it wants to go. It is as if the progress of human history in the lower valley has necessitated the denial of the river's history. The land has been cleared, dried, and planted so that people can take advantage of the rich soil, and yet clearing, drying, and planting has deeply disrupted the system that created and maintained the land in the first place, necessitating all sorts of countermeasures to maintain the richness of the land.

The Mississippi River remains a system, from top to bottom. Sediment in the river offers evidence that land and water continue to interact. Indeed, the river's toxic sediment load acknowledges what the levees repress, that land and water have remained in constant interaction in ways people do not entirely control. Levees facilitate pollution, and when they fail, water returning to the land can bring undesirable substances with it. For thousands of years, much of what is on the land has eventually ended up in the river, and every so often, the river ends up on the land; but for the last several centuries, people have lived in the lower valley as though the two can and ought to be kept apart.

These pages trace the process of drying the land both literally and figuratively. Through all the years that people have been draining the floodplain and constructing levees to keep water off it permanently, a very fluid indigenous social order predating European arrival and lasting through much of the eighteenth century was solidifying. Material and social transformations were connected. The French brought enslaved West Africans to Louisiana and put them to work constructing levees, and later, in the Jim Crow era, the Army Corps of Engineers and their contractors used indebted and impoverished African Americans as a kind of corvée labor to segregate land and water. Pushed further, the concept of drying explains a hardened approach to the natural environment, in which humans are thought to stand apart from nature—that is, so long as the levees hold—and to explain as well the clear, cut, and "dry" solutions to the "problems" posed for humans by the natural environment. In drawing attention to the imagined and manufactured space between wet and dry, between water and land, between reality and perception, and between society and nature, this book seeks to re-wet and reconstitute the history of the lower Mississippi Valley.[11]

Just as a river flows at several speeds, faster at the top and center, slower at the sides and bottom, history moves at several paces at once. Natural history moves more slowly than human history, which itself moves at several speeds simultaneously, political history more quickly than, say, demographic history. As with rivers, layers of differently paced motion can rub against each other and cause friction between human and natural history, and their intersections can create moments of turbulence, when the continuity of several layers of forward motion is disturbed or broken. At the risk of losing its chronological bearings, this book purposely travels in several layers of history at once.

Chapters 1 and 2 describe the "wet" lower Mississippi Valley, its geophysical and human histories prior to the arrival of Europeans, and early Spanish and French encounters with it. By some measures—species diversity, biomass production, regenerative capacity—the valley was one of the richest and hardiest environments in the world. Indeed, so productive was it that people living there, until the eighteenth century, had little need to practice much agriculture. They lived largely off fish, shellfish, and small animals that abounded in an ecology based on the interaction of land and water. Their ruins, huge earthen structures, some of them larger than the Great Pyramid of Egypt, remain. Rich as this land was, Europeans struggled to survive in a place they perceived as too wet and too resource-poor for human habitation. The Spanish entrada failed, the French nearly so, because they misunderstood the nature of the lower Mississippi Valley. Nearly two centuries after Hernando de Soto, nearly forty years after La Salle, Bienville succeeded in establishing New Orleans, and the process of drying the land and repressing the water began.

Chapters 3 and 4 recount French adaptations to the wetlands and their small but instructive successes with drying them, as well as the implications of their activities for the native inhabitants of the valley. Chapter 5 covers the interlude between the French defeat in the Seven Years' War and the US acquisition of Louisiana forty years later, when the Spanish governed the valley. While they continued the work of the French, the Spanish also witnessed some of the first consequences of drying the valley, which gave them pause. The United States did not hesitate.

Chapters 6 through 8 describe the drying of the valley to make it suitable for cotton planting and the construction of a system of flood control based almost entirely on giant levees, maintained by a bureaucracy of experts armed with a new scientific understanding of the ways of Big Muddy. The cotton kingdom and the flood control system that propped it up began to fail in the twentieth century, most visibly during the 1927 flood, but there were telling signs of trouble earlier, although few recognized them as such.

Chapters 9 and 10 explain why the long struggle to dry the valley began to fail and how some valley residents responded by allowing water to return to the land.

The lower Mississippi Valley is coming full circle and becoming a "wet" place once again. Since the collapse of the plantation economy in the twentieth century, valley residents have been struggling to reinvest in and to reinvigorate the lower valley environment, so that they may live off its natural abundance and regenerative capacity—for example, as catfish and crawfish farmers. Even some in the Army Corps of Engineers suggest it might be time to take down levee structures and permit the river to nourish the land and rebuild the rapidly eroding Louisiana coastline. The book ends with the Katrina disaster, when water returned to the land with a vengeance, and its implications for the future of New Orleans and the valley in light of the past 500 years of struggle to turn wetland into dry land. In this history, I hope readers will detect a nature that is trying to tell us something about the way we understand the natural environment and our place within it.

I

Valley of Mud

THE MISSISSIPPI RIVER has always been big and muddy. That was how Hernando de Soto found it, in May 1541, big with runoff from winter snows and spring rains, muddy with sediment worn away from much of the continent's face. Floods are a certainty in the lower Mississippi Valley, as certain as the laws of physics that pull water downhill against the resistance of a broad, flat plain. Until recent times, floods occurred every spring. In the spring of 1541, the river had, as usual, topped its banks to cover most of the valley with several feet of silted water. Over the next few months, Soto's army of 700 or 800 soldiers, retainers, and captives waded through water, and when the river receded that summer and fall, they marched through mud. The next spring found them still there, with the river back on the land, muddying the valley once more.

Off and on for a million years before Soto arrived, melting glaciers sent torrents of water laden with glacial sediment down the center of North America, gradually filling the valley with sand and dirt, and building the Louisiana coastline up and out into the sea. After the glaciers melted away, runoff kept the river muddy and the land wet. The lower Mississippi Valley was always wet. Numerous crescent or oxbow-shaped lakes lined the river, the remains of channels abandoned by a stream prone to erratic shifts and jumps in the course of its meander to the sea. Water from annual floods, trapped by ridges of sediment formed often during the same season, collected in pools and marshes that eventually overflowed into the many creeks and bayous that ran parallel to Big Muddy in search of a spot where they could re-join it.[1]

In Soto's time the lower Mississippi Valley comprised a vast wetland, one of the largest in the world, 35,000 square miles of water and dirt mixed

in various proportions ranging from the wet dirt of the floodplain to the
dirty water of the Mississippi River, a liquid earth never entirely one or the
other. Much of the lower valley lay permanently wet, and what passed for
dry land were the few places that stayed clear of water for a mere ten days of
each growing season, which was sufficient time for certain species of hardwood trees to take root. Water and dirt—mud—nourished a forest of water
oak, ash, elm, willow, cottonwood, tupelo, cypress, and sweet gum, to name
only the most prominent trees. Lakes, swamps, and sandy islands thickly
matted with cane broke up the forest cover into a quilt stitched of blue and
light-green patches. Numerous species of animals lived in this wet environment. Lakes and streams teemed with fish, shellfish, reptiles, and amphibians. They were food for raccoons, otters, muskrats, opossums, and other
small mammals that also ate grubs, insects, and the eggs of waterfowl.
Great flocks of birds nested in the valley. Many more passed through, making the valley the primary flyway for North America's migratory bird populations. A few larger animals also moved through the wetlands. Although
they lived much of the year in upland forests, deer sought the safety of
the lowland marshes and cane thickets in the spring, when they dropped
their fawns. Black bears populated the upland forests, but they were just as
at home lumbering through the lowlands. Being omnivores, they mostly
left smaller mammals alone, except to compete with them for many of
the same wetland foods. The lower valley was a haven for small creatures,
which thrived in a wet environment not favored by large predators such
as panthers and wolves. Humans, a million or more of them when Soto
arrived, were almost the only large predators. They ate fish and turtles;
dressed in furs, skins, and feathers; slept in shelters made of saplings and
thatched marsh grasses; and constructed giant mounds of mud.[2]

Hernando de Soto was a veteran of other expeditions of conquest,
including the one led by Francisco Pizarro against the Andean empire of
the Inca. He hoped his Mississippi expedition would be the greatest conquest of all, greater even than the one led by Hernán Cortés against the
Aztecs. Soto had set out from Cuba, landed at Tampa Bay, and from there
made his way north to the Savannah River region before turning westward and marching toward the Mississippi River. His official charge was
to claim for Spain the southern portion of North America from Florida to
Mexico, and to subjugate all people in that territory to the Spanish mon-
arch, converting the willing to Catholicism and enslaving or slaying the
unwilling. Gold, jewels, and other riches he plundered along the way were
to fill royal coffers, although Soto and his soldiers were permitted portions

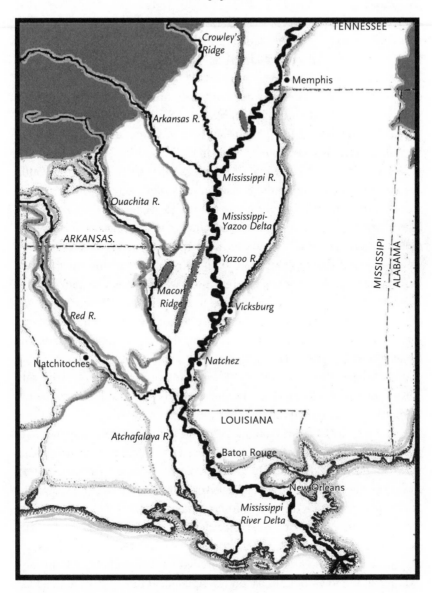

FIGURE I.I The Lower Mississippi Valley. (Drawing by author.)

as compensation. The Spaniards found no golden empires, but they did find many fiercely resistant people. When they arrived in the Mississippi Valley and discovered large populations thriving amid the wetlands, their spirits improved. If there were people, especially urbanized people, there might be powerful kings or chiefs, and where there was power there was sure to be wealth. There might even be gold.[3]

The Mississippi Valley was a rich land, though not in Soto's estimation. It was the richest and wettest land in North America and perhaps the world, if measured in environmental terms. The topsoil was many feet deep. There was no shortage of fresh water. Plant and animal species were highly diverse. Most important, the wetland ecology produced astonishingly high volumes of plant and animal life, or biomass. Some lakes, for example, supported 800 pounds of fish per surface acre of water, and there were over 35 million acres of water and wetlands in the lower Mississippi Valley.[4]

Hernando de Soto and his army entered the valley just to the southeast of present-day Memphis. For seven days they slogged through dense woods and marshes sometimes too deep to wade even on horseback before arriving at the village of Quizquiz near the Mississippi River. It took the soldiers a month to build the barges they needed to ferry themselves across the river, then more than two miles wide and moving fast. On the west bank they encountered more wetlands, which they tried to avoid as well as they could by keeping to the riverbank. Where water had pushed its way over or through the bank, and the resulting channel or crevasse was impassable, they made circuitous detours through wetlands that delayed their progress. They encountered in the Mississippi River floodplain of present-day Missouri, Arkansas, and Louisiana many towns with names foreign to modern ears because they disappeared long ago, before Europeans could record their precise locations.

On their way to Casqui, Soto and his soldiers spent one long day wading through water sometimes waist deep. From Casqui they marched to Pacaha, and from there to Quiguate, most likely in present-day eastern Arkansas, very near the Mississippi River. Between Pacaha and Quiguate, Soto's army trudged "through large pathless forests," pathless because they were inundated. For a week they slept each night "amid marshes and streamlets of very shallow water," too shallow for boats, yet too deep for easy walking. From Quiguate they marched nearly another week through swamps to the town of Caligoa, on the uplands at the western edge of the Mississippi Valley. In all, the Spaniards journeyed over 200 miles through wetlands as they traversed the lower valley from east to west.[5]

Everywhere Soto's army went in the lower valley there were fish to eat. In ponds and marshes, fish of various kinds "were so plentiful in them that they were killed with blows of cudgels...when as many were taken as were desired." Products of the woodlands and wetlands—animals skins, fur shawls, and fish—comprised the standard gifts of diplomacy in each village. The Aquixo ruler presented Soto with three boatloads of fish.

Casqui's leader several times sent him "a present of skins, shawls and fish." All the towns of the Casqui kingdom gave the Spanish "skins, shawls, and fish." Pacaha also made "a large gift of fish, skins, and shawls." One of Soto's chroniclers wrote of the abundance of fish: "as many were taken as need required; and however much might be the casting, there was never any lack of them." Catfish weighing over 100 pounds, "with large spines like a shoemaker's awl at either side of its throat and along its sides," buffalofish, paddlefish, large-mouth bass, bluegill sunfish, freshwater drum the size of hogs: as summed up by expedition member Rodrigo Ranjel, "there was no end of fish."[6]

Soto had hoped to find much more than fish. He and his soldiers associated agriculture with wealth and power, and fish with poverty, or worse, with an indolent complacency with poverty. In his experience, powerful armies fed on grain, carefully defending their own supplies while targeting those of their enemies. Thus Soto burned fields and robbed garners wherever he felt the need to make a show of force. Yet, nearly everywhere he turned in the lower Mississippi Valley he found not only farmers but also fishers. Dried corn filled garners in Pacaha, and fields of new corn stretched for two or three miles, but there was also an artificial pond and canal, connected to a nearby river and outfitted with weirs, in which villagers kept fish. In wartime, fields of corn might be burned, forcing those who depended on them to do without for that year. Not so with ponds of fish. Enemies might destroy weirs, releasing all the fish, but there were always more fish in the river.[7]

The fields around Pacaha proved to be exceptional. Many other people Soto encountered raised little or no corn at all. At Quizquiz, Soto found little, although he learned of an affiliated town nearby where there was plenty. At Casqui the Spanish found stores of nuts, probably a mix of acorns, pecans, and hickory, as well as what they identified as plums but were probably persimmons—but no corn. The Calusi, observed the Spanish, "paid little attention to sowing, because they maintained themselves on this fish and meat." All during the march from Florida, Soto had found plenty of cornfields. In contrast, while there was some corn to burn and steal within the valley, it was not nearly so prevalent there. Not until the Spanish left the valley did they once again meet truly agricultural people. At Caligoa, for example, corn supplies struck the Spanish as so abundant "the old was thrown out in order to store the new." Moreover, at Caligoa, corn grew in fields along with beans and pumpkins, a very common combination in dry, upland areas, but not noted by the Spaniards as they traveled through the lower valley's wetlands.[8]

In the Mississippi Valley, Hernando de Soto waded through water and into a human-environmental history already 8,000 years in the making. The valley was a landscape in motion: people trading and warring, building towns and abandoning them for new locations, hunting, gathering, fishing, planting. All the while, water advanced then receded, and mud collected and washed away, in what river ecologists call a flood-pulse pattern. Floods discouraged some but not all people from planting, and the distinction between agriculturalists and hunter-fisher-gathers was probably the most significant legacy of the valley's ecological pattern. Exhausted cornfields had forced Chickasaws to relocate, putting them in Soto's path. Crop failure may have weakened defenses at Quizquiz. Perhaps because they depended less on agriculture and more on the resources of the wetlands, some towns put up an especially stiff resistance to the Spanish intrusion. Their history of adaptation to wetlands led them to depend on the fleets of small vessels filled with warriors that Soto tried so hard to avoid. Currents of water and history pushed Soto's intrusion in particular directions. For example, if the Spanish brought diseases never encountered by lower valley populations, which he most likely did, not all populations were equally exposed to them. Contagions followed preexisting networks of communication, which extended primarily along waterways. They devastated the more centralized, urbanized populations near the river, leaving decentralized tribes and bands of hunter-gathers farther away relatively unscathed. Moreover, some of the valley's agriculturalists suffered from their own diseases, most of them associated with the physical demands of agricultural labor and a steady diet of maize, which lacked the nutrients needed for a balanced diet and may have left them weakened and vulnerable.[9]

The specific point of Soto's entry into the Mississippi Valley lay between two environmental zones and between two corresponding cultural zones. North from the mouth of the Arkansas River, the floodplain narrows, and there is more high ground near the river bottom. This was the Mississippian cultural zone. Southward, down the widening floodplain to the Gulf of Mexico, were the Plaquemine settlements. Mississippians and Plaquemines were similar in many respects, but in one very important way they differed. Mississippians were farmers, perhaps the most advanced corn cultivators east of the Great Plains. Plaquemines lived by other means, principally by hunting, fishing, and gathering from the abundant wetlands of the lower valley. Soto probably met representatives of both cultures.[10]

At its height, Mississippian culture reached northward into present-day Wisconsin, and southeastward into parts of present-day Alabama and Georgia, its trade connections reaching still farther afield. However, its purest expression was achieved during the Middle Mississippian period, 800 years ago, in the central Mississippi Valley, between the Missouri and Arkansas rivers. The culture was distinguished by, among other traits, a rather loosely connected network of villages organized as chiefdoms, a distinctive style of shell-tempered ceramics, large platform mounds built of earth, and an economy based on the intensive cultivation of corn. The largest and most impressive Mississippian settlement was Cahokia, which lay across the Mississippi River from present-day St. Louis. More than 20,000 people lived there among a cluster of over 100 mounds, the grandest of which was the largest prehistoric structure in North America.[11]

Within the entire region of the eastern woodlands the proportion of daily diet supplied by corn varied from people to people, but on the whole

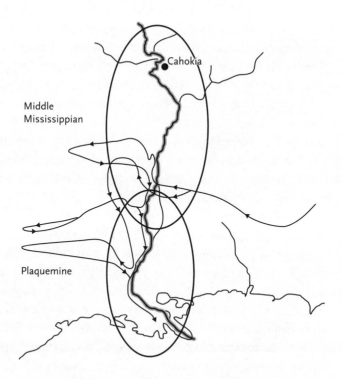

FIGURE I.2 Two possible routes for Hernando de Soto's expedition bisect the overlapping Middle Mississippian and Plaquemine cultural areas. (Drawing by author.)

it accounted for about 50 percent of caloric intake. Corn, particularly in combination with pumpkins and beans, was essential to this population's way of life and their primary point of intersection with their natural environment. Of all the corn cultivators east of the Great Plains, the Mississippians were the most sophisticated.[12]

The Mississippians of Soto's time were heirs to a tradition of agriculture and horticultural experimentation. Their central valley predecessors began cultivating gourds 5,000 years before any people did in the lower valley. They domesticated goosefoot, a grain akin to quinoa, which encouraged other horticultural experiments, and within a 500-year period middle valley settlements added three other plants to their repertoire: marsh elder, squash, and sunflower. Somewhat later they learned about corn. Agriculture reduced middle valley Mississippians' dependency on the resources of the floodplain. They continued to hunt for meat, but their fields often attracted upland animals, such as bison, which they grew to prefer over the smaller animals more typical of the bottomlands, so much so that during times when bison were scarce, they either ventured upland to find them or sought to trade corn for bison procured by upland peoples. Mississippians, through their agriculture, lived in but not off of the muddy bottom lands, at least in some very important respects, although they continued to collect shells, clay, and stones from the floodplain, fashioning them into containers for storing corn and weapons for hunting deer and bison.[13]

By AD 1400, Mississippian agriculture was struggling to feed its growing population. Corn depleted the soil of nutrients, for which cultivators compensated by churning the ground thoroughly with hoes to bring new soil to the surface, and perhaps by fertilizing fields with fish or waste. Such intensive agriculture, however, demanded an ever-greater commitment of time and labor, leaving less time for hunting, which only made agriculture more essential and people more vulnerable to crop failures. The culture was in trouble when Hernando de Soto arrived. By then Cahokia had been abandoned. Other once substantial settlements were losing population, as people left fields and took to hunting. Having invested so much in corn, there was no going back once they reached the limits of their ability to grow enough food in the central valley environment to sustain their current rate of population growth. No new crop, technology, or method of organizing labor presented itself to lift agricultural production to new heights. Mississippian settlements farther down the valley, such as Pacaha, persisted by supplementing corn with fish and other wetland resources.[14]

The Plaquemine people of the lower valley differed from the Missis-sippians of the central valley in that they had no long-standing tradition of agriculture. The earliest evidence of any kind of cultivation of plants in the lower Mississippi Valley dates back a mere 2,000 years at most. Maize cultivation apparently began much more recently. Whereas the Mississippians were heirs to an agricultural tradition in their portion of the valley, the Plaquemines of Soto's time were practically agricultural pio-neers in their valley. In 1541, the year Soto arrived at the Mississippi River, people in the lower valley had been cultivating large quantities of maize for only 300 years.[15]

The Plaquemines and their lower valley predecessors lived primarily off fish and wetland animals, as well as nuts, fruits, and wild grains gathered from the forest; only secondarily did they depend on corn. They fished with twine nets weighted with stone plummets and suspended, perhaps, with floats made of wild gourds. They fashioned lightweight boats that moved through waterways quickly and which they maneuvered skillfully. Their earthen mounds provided refuge during floods, emphasizing their incor-poration of the wetlands into their cultures. The mounds were not used as dry land for crops; they were staging areas from which they launched forays into the swamps. Indeed, in light of the remarkable architectural achievements in the lower valley, earthen embankments and other flood control technologies were conspicuously absent. Instead of developing technologies to keep themselves and their settlements dry, native peoples in the lower valley adapted to the wetland environment.[16]

Lower valley people also incorporated the wetland environment into their spiritual universe. Their most sacred symbol was the serpent, which represented the life-destroying and life-giving power of water. Later gen-erations of native people expressed both fear and reverence for water in ways perhaps similar to those of their predecessors. For example, they venerated water creatures, including the alligator and the crawfish. Floods represented for them a force for purification and regeneration. In a Caddo flood myth, all the people and animals climb into the sky upon a giant reed, while rising waters drown four giants that have been terrorizing the people. When the waters recede, the land blossoms like never before. In a Tunica myth, villagers dance, unafraid, as the rising waters of the Mississippi River slowly engulf them. One terrified man runs. When he returns months later to the site of his village he sees nothing but water and leaping fish—fish with human heads. The villagers had magically adapted themselves to the water, sprouting tails and fins, so they could continue to live where they had always lived. In the Choctaw, Taensas, and Natchez universes, water harbored dangerous, chaotic forces. In the native spiritual universe, only the power of the sun equaled the power of water, which is why, when Soto tried to intimidate the great Plaquemine chief, Quigualtam, by claiming that he was the son of the Sun, the chief demanded that Soto prove himself by drying up the river.[17]

The first permanent settlement in all the Mississippi Valley was established over 7,500 years ago along a lower valley bayou. Among the oldest earthen structures in all the Americas are the mounds built some 5,500 years ago near present-day Monroe, Louisiana. But the best example of complex cultural development based on the wetland ecology is Poverty Point.[18]

Poverty Point was an independent, terminal development not connected to any later cultures, other than its being a complex society with an economy based on the wetlands environment. Four thousand years ago, near present-day Tallulah, Louisiana, the people of Poverty Point constructed a semicircular arrangement of earthen mounds atop a piece of high ground known as Maçon Ridge. The town abutted a lake and was nearer then to the Mississippi River, which has since moved eastward. The earthworks are the oldest of their size in the western hemisphere. The giant "bird" mound, so called because its shape appears to be that of a bird on the wing, was built to a height of over seventy feet.[19]

Poverty Point may have been what anthropologists classify as a "simple" chiefdom. It had a population of perhaps several thousand, at least during certain times of the year, a system of graduated ranking to organize both mound construction and ceremonies involving thousands of people, and economic, political, and cultural networks that reached as far as the Appalachian Mountains and the Great Lakes.

It may also be classified as a "complex" hunter-gatherer society structured by kinship and guided by a "head man." The architecture suggests chiefdom; the absence of any indications of agriculture indicates hunter-gatherer society. Poverty Point was both, but at its height it verged on becoming a full-blown chiefdom.[20]

The first Plaquemine settlements appeared long after the abandonment of Poverty Point. The two cultures were not connected except environmentally, appearing in the same area of the Mississippi Valley and developing into chiefdoms without first establishing agricultural economies.

The origins of Plaquemine culture are still debated. It was similar to the earlier Coles Creek culture of the Tensas River region on the west side of

FIGURE 1.3 Poverty Point, as it appeared in this 1938 aerial photograph taken for the Corps of Engineers. The image clearly reveals the arrangement of mounds and ridges. The bird mound has trees and is center left. The creek on the right marks an ancient lake and the edge of Maçon Ridge, on which the mound complex sits. (Courtesy of the US Army Corps of Engineers.)

the Mississippi in that both had a pattern of villages built around platform mounds by people who preferred to hunt, fish, and gather rather than practice agriculture. But it also shared some Mississippian traits, leading some archaeologists to classify Plaquemine as a Mississippianized varia-tion of Coles Creek culture. However, on the east side of the Mississippi River, along the Natchez Bluffs, were settlements clearly recognizable as Plaquemine yet which appear to have developed independently of any other cultures. Regardless of origins, the Plaquemine culture was dis-tinctly of the lower Mississippi Valley, in that it relied much more on the resources of the wetlands than on cultivation of dry lands.[21]

Lower valley peoples were not actively avoiding agriculture. They sim-ply had little need for it in a wet environment that provided so much natu-ral plant and animal food. Agriculture on the floodplain, certainly on a large scale, was difficult. Dry land was limited to small scattered patches, and wetland, if it was to be transformed into reliably dry farmland, had to be drained and secured against inundation with embankments and drain-age canals, a difficult though not impossible undertaking for people who constructed large mounds. Nevertheless, farming wetlands entailed risks. The Casqui chief complained to Soto of drought, which, in the midst of the spring rise in the river, indicated serious problems of water and soil management. The bottomlands around the town were black and rich but too wet to plant. Casqui's cultivators probably looked to the higher ground upon terraces and natural levees, even though the soil in such places would have been sandy and incapable of holding much moisture through a dry summer.[22]

Lower valley cultures did eventually take up agriculture. However, even the Plaquemine people Soto encountered developed their culture so fully in the absence of agriculture that by the time they took up planting corn, its economic impact was largely superficial. Why they bothered with it at all remains something of a mystery. They may have been impressed by the Mississippian fields, just as Soto was. Moreover, their proximity to Mississippian settlements may have facilitated exchanges of ideas, styles, and cultural traits across the environmental boundaries that separated the central and lower Mississippi Valleys.[23]

Where there was little or no agriculture, nevertheless, the accumulated legacies of hunter-fisher-gatherers left lasting marks upon the land. Soto did not find a pristine wilderness. Along the river, native people burned canebrakes and forests to clear land for settlements and small gardens, which pushed some mammals and birds away even as it attracted others.

They cleared open areas beneath pecan and other fruit and nut trees to facilitate gathering. They collected plants, dropped seeds, and otherwise disrupted plant ecologies. They dredged massive amounts of dirt from river bottoms, which created ponds, and piled it into tremendous mounds that when abandoned became dry island refuges for hardwood trees, and for animals in times of flood. Their fishing practices, without threatening the sustainability of freshwater ecologies, nevertheless, set parameters for marine life as surely as did water temperature fluctuations, dissolved oxygen levels, and algae growth. Not all human adaptations to the wetlands were sustainable. For example, native peoples in the lower valley may have pressed to near extinction the population of the ivory-billed woodpecker, the beaks of which they prized and traded.[24]

The wet natural environment of the lower valley, marked by centuries of human occupation of it, subsequently shaped the development of European colonial society and the efforts of Europeans to impose intensive agriculture on a land that had avoided it for so long. Burn zones and clearings became cotton fields and grazing land for cattle. Soto's army encamped and planted crosses upon mounds. Later Europeans stripped mounds of timber and set their homes upon them. They mined midden mounds for lime and shells from which they made bricks for buildings and surface material for streets. "Hills of shells are found there,—a singular thing for that region," observed Jesuit Father Vivier in 1750. He had no idea they had been made by people. He saw them as anomalies because he thought of them as dry, even though all the mounds in the lower valley were made of shells taken from wet estuaries near the river's mouth or of wet earth taken from marshes. They were patches of dry land made by people who endeavored not to escape the wetlands, but to adapt to them.[25]

The more dramatic—the more singular, in Father Vivier's sense— environmental changes occurred in the central valley and stemmed from the rise and fall of Mississippian agriculture, although agriculture's effects reached far and wide. Cahokia's collapse in the fifteenth century was brought on by unsustainable agricultural practices. When the Spanish arrived in the next century, other Mississippian settlements were failing for similar reasons. People were abandoning settlements of long standing in search of new sources of food, which disrupted trade networks and affected the livelihood of Mississippians elsewhere. Populations declined in the Mississippi Valley and in other river valleys when people moved into upland hunting grounds that were often claimed by others. For example, the Chicasa of Soto's time left their gardens along the Tombigbee

River and wandered into hunting grounds near the Upper Yazoo River region east of present-day Memphis, where they collided with the ailing Mississippian chiefdom of Quizquiz. At first there was something of a standoff, but as Quizquiz weakened and withdrew, the Chicasa moved in and in time evolved into the Chickasaw culture familiar to the French and English in the seventeenth and eighteenth centuries. The chiefdoms of the Arkansas River region, themselves in trouble, prevented Quizquiz refugees from moving west, forcing them to the south, near present-day Vicksburg, where the French later encountered them as the Tunica. By the time the French established a presence in the lower valley, native peoples were moving because of European pressure elsewhere in the continent. In the mid-1600s, the Quapaw arrived from the Ohio River region and settled at the mouth of the Arkansas River in the empty space left by the chiefdoms witnessed by Soto a century earlier. The lower Mississippi Valley became a "shatter zone" of refugees and warriors out of which emerged new nations such as the Choctaw and the Chickasaw.[26]

Soto's arrival contributed new elements to the Mississippi Valley environment, with further consequences for people living there. His army destroyed whole towns, assisted some in battles with others, stole and burned food, and in general altered intertribal power structures. The Spanish introduced new animals and food sources into the environment, including hogs, chickens, and peaches. They probably brought diseases, malaria most likely, although they did not touch off any wildfire epidemics, as happened elsewhere in the Americas and later in the Mississippi Valley. Nevertheless, populations declined dramatically between 1541, when the Spanish arrived, and 1699, when the French established Louisiana.[27]

The Plaquemines did not escape the disruptions caused by the Mississippians' troubles and the arrival of the Spanish. In Soto's time, the Plaquemine heartland was certainly located below the mouth of the Arkansas river and was perhaps below the mouth of the Yazoo River. The impressive Winterville mounds near Greenville, Mississippi, as well as the Anna and Emerald mounds near Natchez, Mississippi, were Plaquemine settlement and ceremonial sites. Over the 150 years following the Spanish intrusion into the lower valley, the primary seat of Plaquemine culture moved several times, from Anna to Emerald to the Grand Village of the Natchez, indicating political instability associated with the successive rise and fall of particular chiefly personalities and their seats of power. That instability may have been both cause and effect of a general turn inward. As the Mississippian culture declined, the traffic in ideas and objects diminished along the river. Travel and intertribal exchange must have become less predictable and more dangerous in a context of disruption and relocation. Plaquemine villages responded by withdrawing into themselves, even going so far as to relocate their mound sites back from the Mississippi River. Eventually, they isolated themselves not just from distant and fading Mississippians, but also from some of their affiliated tribes and chiefdoms. The culturally related people who lived along the Pearl River abandoned their mound site and moved east, away from the Natchez area, into empty territory along the Leaf River. There they joined the refugees of other societies and eventually formed the Choctaw nation. And yet the Plaquemines survived into the colonial era as the Natchez Indians, a mound-building chiefdom upon the bluffs along the eastern edge of the river that lived off the wetlands of the valley below.[28]

In April 1542, near the town of Guachoyo, located in present-day Louisiana or Arkansas, Soto learned of the powerful Quigualtam. In the sixteenth century, Quigualtam was probably the most feared chief in the lower valley. He was Plaquemine and ruled from a town located near or to the south of the Yazoo River. Soto never visited Quigualtam, although he saw the chief's fleet of war canoes and exchanged communications with him. Weakened by illness, Soto had the audacity to claim he was a god and to demand Quigualtam's surrender. Soto died before he could confront the chief directly. To conceal their leader's mortality and their own vulnerability, several of Soto's officers secretly wrapped and weighted his body and dropped it into the Mississippi. Then, to avoid Quigualtam and his archers, they tried to reach Mexico overland, and when that effort failed, they returned to the Mississippi and floated down river as fast as possible. Arrows rained down upon them as they made their escape, and warriors in canoes harried them all the way to the gulf. To authorities in Mexico, survivors of Soto's army reported that in eastern North America there was no gold or great civilization or anything of value, and so the Spanish did not return.[29]

When the French arrived, nearly a century and a half later, they found many different cultures hunting, gathering, and fishing in the wetlands, although one of particular significance remained. The Natchez chiefdom, which was Plaquemine, avoided the fate of the Mississippians and survived Hernando de Soto's invasion. Indeed, the Natchez culture may still have been waxing when the French arrived, their strength and endurance deriving in part from a long history of living off the rich environment of the lower valley wetlands.

Knee Deep in Water and Snakes

IN 1673, 130 years after the survivors of Hernando de Soto's army exited the valley to the south, a French-speaking group of men entered the valley from the north. They set out from the Jesuit mission at Michilimackinac, at the head of Lake Michigan, traveled a water route that took them south and west, and slipped their canoes into the Big Muddy near present-day Prairie du Chien, Wisconsin. Only seven in number, they hardly constituted an army, and as they approached the Gulf of Mexico they understandably grew fearful of encountering opposing forces. At the Arkansas River, their leader, Louis Jolliet, turned his party around, pleased to take back to Canada and France the knowledge that the great river he had found west of Lake Michigan was Hernando de Soto's river. A few years later, in 1682, René-Robert Cavelier, Sieur de la Salle, completed Jolliet's journey. As he stood in the mud at the head of the passes near the mouths of the Mississippi River, he declared the entire Mississippi Valley to be La Louisiane, a possession of France.

La Salle did not come to the lower Mississippi Valley in search of civilizations to conquer, nor did he come looking for gold. His plan was much less grandiose: to establish a few forts supported by small settlements of farmers at strategic locations in the valley, including at or very near the mouth of the Mississippi River. A permanent, self-sufficient presence along the river would help expand France's existing fur trading empire from the St. Lawrence and Ottawa river valleys far into the center of the continent, into the *pays d'en haut*—the upper country—by giving it a second passage to the sea. French *coureurs de bois*, fur trappers and traders living in the interior of the continent, could bring furs down the Mississippi River to the Gulf of Mexico, skirting Dutch, English, and Iroquois interference with the eastbound route to Montreal. In addition, a permanent presence in the lower valley would position France to challenge Spain for control of the Mexican silver trade. Claiming and then holding their continental empire required a permanent and self-sufficient French presence in the wetlands of the lower valley, particularly in the Mississippi River delta.[1]

The Mississippi Valley was, of course, already claimed from end to end by native peoples. Seventy thousand people lived in the lower valley, far fewer than in the previous century, yet they easily outnumbered the French, of whom there were only a few thousand in all of North America, and who had therefore to proceed with caution. Decades of experience in Canada had left the French skilled at avoiding conflict when surrounded by overwhelming numbers of potential enemies. However, little in their Canadian experience prepared them for the lower Mississippi Valley environment. Nevertheless, for the French to hold Louisiana, they had to understand the environment for what it was, and adapt themselves to it.[2]

Below the meander zone, at the edge of the continent, the river had more room to spread out and move around. From here to the sea, all land existed because of the river. This was the Mississippi River's delta. Each year since the end of the last ice age the river had deposited hundreds of millions of tons of dirt on the coastal shelf, building the lower quarter of Louisiana. The delta was the largest marshland in what became the United States, salty toward the edges where the sea pushed in, sweet toward the center where the river pushed out, and brackish in between, full of alligators, turtles, fish, shellfish, birds, and small mammals, a vast expanse of cypress swamp and cord grass savannah dotted by a few ridges and islands of slightly higher ground. The delta's shape was never fixed. It moved continually, pushed and pulled by water, gravity, tides, and winds, including frequent hurricanes, east and then back west, extending into the gulf only to reverse itself and retract toward the coastline, rising in one spot while sinking in another, heaving when the ocean floor exhaled under the weight of accumulated sediment through tubes of mud pushed above the water's surface.[3]

Within the present delta are the remains of six former deltas, recalling a history of river shifts and land formation and erosion. La Salle's delta was, in 1684, only the most recent. It took a few thousand years following the last ice age before the oceans settled at their more or less current levels, and for the Mississippi River to settle into a single meandering stream and to begin to build its first delta. About 2,000 years later the river jumped to the east and began a new delta. It jumped three more times before Europeans arrived—back to the west, down Bayou La

Teche, far to the east where it left the Chandeleur Islands, west again, this
time down Bayou La Fourche, and at last down its current route through
Plaquemines Parish and beyond, building what is known as the Balise
(or Balize) Delta. The shifts have occurred regularly, about every 2,000
years, but from the human perspective they are unpredictable. Overnight
the stream can jump its bank and begin to fill bays with sediment, adding
mass to the delta, and then just as abruptly stop, abandoning the new land
to the sea. Off and on in the late seventeenth and early eighteenth centuries part of the river leaped back to its old La Fourche channel, creating
what some members of La Salle's party called The Fork. Iberville could not
find it, but it was back twenty years later in personal accounts and maps.
Today there is a seventh delta emerging, in Atchafalaya Bay, the same location as the first delta built 7,000 years ago.[4]

In 1542, when the remnants of Soto's expedition reached them, the
passes of the Plaquemine Delta had only just begun to form. Since then
the head of the passes, where the river divides into several channels—mile
zero, as it is known today—has moved steadily southeastward. In 1733, La
Balise, a fort and pilot station, sat on an island one mile out to sea from

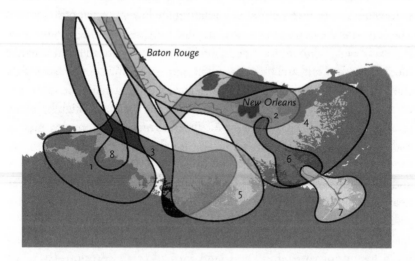

FIGURE 2.1 Historic deltas of the Mississippi River. 1. Maringouin/Sale Cypremort
Delta, 7,500–5,000 years before present (YBP). 2. Cocodre Delta, 4,000–3,500
YBP. 3. Teche Delta, 3,500–2,800 YBP. 4. St. Bernard Delta, 2,800–1,000 YBP.
5. Lafourche Delta, 1,000–300 YBP. 6. Plaquemine Delta, 750–500 YBP. 7. Balize
Delta, 350–0 YBP. 8. Atchafalaya Delta, 50–0 YBP. (Drawing based on J. M.
Coleman, "Dynamic Changes and Processes in the Mississippi Delta," *Geological
Society of America Bulletin* 100 (1998): 1000.)

the mouth of East Pass. Twenty-five years later the island was attached to the delta, and the channel had grown a mile and a half beyond it. By 1784 the fort, two miles up the channel, was abandoned, replaced by a new Balise at the channel entrance on a new island that did not exist fifty years earlier. By 1796, East Pass had shifted again and the new Balise sat several hundred yards up a small creek "in the midst of a morass" of mud, insects, and reptiles, where it slowly sank, as did much of the delta, at a rate of about one foot every twenty years. A century after the fort was built, water lapped at the arch atop its main doorway. East Pass eventually silted up and gave way to Pass a l'Outre. Meanwhile, Southwest Pass grew to a length of nearly twenty miles. As the river mouths have stretched farther and farther out into the gulf, the adjacent coastline has receded over the last two centuries at a rate of fifteen to twenty-five feet per year. The barrier islands, too, have shifted, chasing the retreating shoreline. The combined effect is the unmistakable long finger of land easily recognizable today on any map of the Gulf of Mexico as the mouth of the Mississippi River. As for the extenuated delta, it is thinner than it once was, owing to channel reconfigurations of more recent history. It was probably widest during the early eighteenth century when a substantial portion of the river flowed down Bayou Lafourche. In the mid-eighteenth century, twenty-five outlets distributed sediment broadly over a wide delta. In 2001, control structures designed to keep the channel deep and clear of debris confined much of the river and its sediment load to the primary shipping channel.[5]

La Salle and his countrymen had never seen anything like the Mississippi River delta. It was too big to comprehend from the crow's nest of a ship. Its behavior defied their imagination. They did not understand it as an amorphous place of land and water. Rather, they saw it as set dry land that periodically flooded, a misconception that caused no end of troubles as they tried to build on it or, in La Salle's case, as he tried to find it.

On December 18, 1684, La Salle's three ships weighed anchor off Cape Saint Antoine at the western tip of Cuba and headed north. Having demonstrated the existence of a water route from Quebec through the interior of the continent to the gulf, La Salle had gone to France to solicit official and financial support for a colony in the lower Mississippi Valley. His stay in France was brief but successful. With support in hand, he returned to the Mississippi River. While still in deep water, La Salle's ships entered seas clouded with sediment. Spanish sailors knew this place as Cabo de Lodo (Cape of Mud), which referred to the sediment plume streaming from the river mouth's southwest pass.[6] By evening they were beyond the

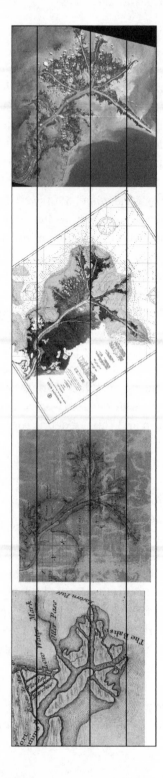

FIGURE 2.2 The passes at the end of the Mississippi River delta in 1796, 1853, 1906, and 2001. Over time the shape and thickness of the delta has changed. Some of the passes have grown farther out into the gulf, while others have receded. (The 1796 image is from Georges Henri Victor Collot, "General Map of North America," Courtesy of the David Rumsey Historical Map Collection. The 1853 image is from John La Tourrette, "La Tourrette's Reference Map of the State of Louisiana, 1853," Courtesy of the Library of Congress, Geography and Map Division. The 1906 image is from "Mississippi River from the Passes to Grand Prairie, Louisiana," Courtesy of the National Oceanic and Atmospheric Administration, Department of Commerce. The 2001 image is courtesy of NASA Earth Observatory.)

FIGURE 2.3 The passes at the end of the Mississippi River delta on May 24, 2001. (Courtesy of NASA Earth Observatory.)

sediment plume and into clearer waters when soundings indicated a bottom of "grayish muddy sand" at forty fathoms, then twenty-five, then seventeen. The coast was near. The crew had been sailing day and night, but as they entered shallow waters in the darkness of a lunar eclipse they grew cautious. At midnight the ships turned into the wind and dropped their anchors into the muddy bottom. The next day they proceeded. Sometime after noon a lookout spotted land, fifteen miles to the northeast, and La Salle ordered anchors set. The following day the group headed west-north-west, into slightly deeper water, and then approached land again. They made little headway in gusts that kept shifting direction. Frustrated by the wind, and with shores of Barataria Bay on three sides, La Salle ordered his captains to stop and await the first steady breeze from the north, at which time they were to set sail immediately, no matter the time of day or night, and head due south into deeper, safer water. At 2 A.M. they were on the move. The wind remained somewhat unsteady, but they managed to hold course through the darkness. At daylight they looked once again for land, which they spotted midmorning. The weather cleared, and there lay the coast, stretching from northeast to southwest. The ships stopped while La Salle and a small party went ashore. There they found a coastline littered with huge dead trees, some of them perhaps a hundred feet long, and beyond it "a large and vast country, flat, full of pasture land and marsh"[7] They found no river. Two years after La Salle's voyage, Enriquez Barroto, a Spanish navigator, recorded in his logbook a description of the coastline at Bayou Lafourche that precisely matches the description in the La Salle accounts. Barroto observed "much driftwood upon the oyster banks," and a shore that was "very flat and low," so low that at a safe depth it could be seen from the masthead "only with difficulty." He also observed that much driftwood exited the Mississippi River's southwest pass.[8] Spanish maps eventually labeled this location Ensenado de Palos, the literal translation being "covered with woods," which English charts translated as Bay of Loggs and Bay of Woods.[9] La Salle and his party stayed ashore briefly until, with the wind picking up, they returned to their vessels and moved westward along the coast. Henri Joutel, one of the crew, recognized that the dead trees indicated the close proximity of the Mississippi River, although whether to east or west he could not say. As the ships continued west, the men who took soundings continued to note a muddy bottom, but then abruptly found sand and gravel. They had probably reached what is known today as Trinity Shoal, a large sand bank off Atchafalaya Bay, 150 miles west of the Mississippi River. In any case, sand and gravel indicate the ships were well beyond the sediment plume. They continued westward, away from the Mississippi River and toward Matagorda Bay.[10]

Historians have offered several explanations for what Francis Parkman in 1869 called La Salle's "fatal error," his failure to relocate the mouth of the Mississippi, and which Parkman blamed on an "exaggerated idea of the force of the easterly currents." Some explanations blame La Salle's arrogance, incompetence, or faulty navigational tools. Others assert that he harbored a plan to get his hands on Spanish silver and intended to land on the Texas coast. Yet, the navigational records strongly indicate that LaSalle sailed a true course to the river but once at its mouth failed to recognize it for what it was, leaving him confused and somewhat at a

FIGURE 2.4 Satellite image taken March 16, 2001, of the Mississippi River sediment plume, or *cabo de lodo*, like that through which La Salle's ships passed. Had La Salle known about the plume, he would have recognized it as a sign of his proximity to the mouth of the river. Note the clear water behind the plume, in Barataria Bay. (Courtesy of Liam Gumley and NASA Earth Observatory.)

loss for what to do or where to go next. Not the sediment plume, not the encircling shoreline of Barataria Bay, not the log-strewn beach told him he had found the Mississippi River delta, because La Salle did not know there was a delta. This was not a case of a weak personality, faulty technology, or clandestine plan; this was a case of a failure to see or comprehend the nature of the Mississippi River delta.[11]

To be sure, La Salle and his sailors were in unfamiliar territory. "No one among us had knowledge of these waters or had sailed there," wrote Joutel. Their charts told them they were looking for a bay. They knew to look for passes, or jetties as La Salle called them, protruding from the coastline, which they had observed on the earlier expedition down the river from Canada. However, their idea of what they were looking for was not matched by what they found. They had no concept of a river delta, at least not one so huge. Just two years earlier La Salle had canoed through the delta. He had stood on it. Yet he had no idea where he was, directionally but also environmentally. He utterly failed to comprehend the delta's size, shape, location, and mechanics. One can imagine La Salle standing on deck, consulting with his captain, knowing what his various instruments told him, compensating for their errors, as an experienced navigator would do, and then looking at the coast but not seeing the river where it was supposed to be, where he knew it had to be. But the river was there. He had sailed right to it; he just could not see it. And so he groped his way westward.[12]

As La Salle and his crew approached the Texas coast, the men debated the nature of the water lying behind the barrier islands. They referred to the bays and channels as lakes and thought they might contain some fresh water, a sure sign of their lost river. They presumed that freshwater rivers such as the Mississippi fed the lakes, which collected the water until it overflowed into the gulf. The openings between the islands were, they assumed, river mouths. When they sailed closer they were quite surprised to find that the "lakes" were at sea level. When they discovered the water to be salty, they reasoned it was either because stormy seas sometimes spilled over the coastal islands and into the lakes behind them, or because there was no large river nearby to supply the lakes with fresh water. Three years earlier, when La Salle and his party of Canadians first arrived at the mouth of the Mississippi River, a similar debate occurred. As they canoed a stretch of river about halfway between the future sight of New Orleans and the gulf, one of La Salle's men spotted in the distance a large bay. Some, La Salle among them, were convinced they had found the Gulf of Mexico. Others, including La Salle's able partner, Henri de Tonti (Tonty), thought they had stumbled upon a large freshwater lake or sea. Clearly, they had no good understanding of gulf coast hydrography. Nor did they grasp the extent of the delta. La Salle estimated that the entire delta reached perhaps fifteen miles into the sea. In fact, it extended over fifty miles, a full degree of latitude, which meant that as he searched for the river along the coast of Barataria Bay, its mouth was miles behind him to the south.[13]

La Salle was not the first to misapprehend the delta. In 1519, as he sailed the northern rim of the Gulf of Mexico, Alvarez de Pineda encountered a strong current that he took to be the discharge of a great river. Rio del Espiritu Santo, he called it, without ever seeing it. Cartographers subsequently added the river, but not a delta, to their charts and maps. In 1528, the survivors of a failed expedition to Florida, the Narvaez expedition, attempted to enter one of the passes on the east side of the delta but were pushed to sea by the current. They, too, never comprehended the delta. When the survivors of Hernando de Soto's expedition reached the gulf, probably through the southwest pass, they thought they had entered a large bay, perhaps because they glimpsed coastline on their right, at Barataria Bay, and another pass on their left. Their bay, the existence of which was seemingly confirmed by the later "discovery" of Mobile Bay, found its way onto most charts, including those used by La Salle nearly a century and a half later, but charts still showed no delta.[14]

Jean-Baptiste Minet, who traveled with La Salle, sketched the mouth of the river based on descriptions given to him by members of the earlier expedition from Canada, in which he did not participate. His drawing shows the river dividing at the coastline into three short passes separated by several islands, which must have been how La Salle imagined the Mississippi's mouth. Cartographer Jean-Baptiste Louis Franquelin incorporated Minet's sketch into his map of North America, placing it erroneously on the Texas coast, perhaps because La Salle told him to, or perhaps because he deduced from the sketch's southeasterly angle that it had to be attached to a north-south coastline. Minet was with La Salle on the voyage to the gulf coast, and when he first saw Matagorda Bay he immediately recognized it as the place he had sketched, and as the place on Franquelin's map.[15]

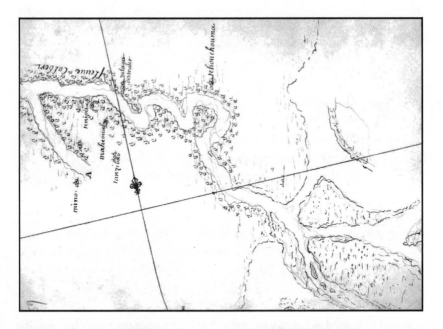

FIGURE 2.5 Jean-Baptiste Minet's drawing of the mouth of the Mississippi River was based on descriptions from members of La Salle's expedition in 1682. (Jean-Baptiste Minet, Journal de Jean-Baptiste Minet, p. 59, R7971-0-7-F, Library and Archives of Canada, Ottawa, accessed March 3, 2012, data2.archives.ca/e/e083/e002069763.jpg.)

FIGURE 2.6 Jean-Baptiste Louis Franquelin's map, completed in 1684, incorporated Minet's drawing of the Mississippi River's mouth and situated it on the
Texas coast. Note the large bay at the true location of the river's mouth. (Courtesy
of the Library of Congress.)

La Salle shipwrecked at Matagorda Bay. For two years he wandered
nearby, looking for evidence of silver mines, trading with native peoples,
and always searching for his river. Or at least he said he was searching
for his river. His men were not always so sure. La Salle kept suspiciously
quiet about his plans. Initially, his men read into such reticence a supreme
confidence and felt encouraged, even after it was clear they were not at all
where they wanted to be. In time, as they marched around in snake-filled
swamps, with mosquitoes swarming about their heads, and surrounded
by enemies, that air of confidence seemed more like arrogance. La Salle
treated his men as many European officers would have done in such
circumstances, with callous disregard. For some of the men, it was too
much. In March 1687, several mutinied. The man who actually shot La
Salle dead claimed to be avenging the death of his brother, which he attributed to La Salle's carelessness. Others joined the revolt simply because
they had had enough. More died, however. Mutiny was the most serious of
offenses, mutineers the most desperate of criminals. There was no surrender. Fearful of everyone, the mutineers began to kill indiscriminately and

eventually turned on each other. Only a few members of La Salle's original expedition survived the ordeal. Most were captured or killed by coastal peoples. Some ended up in Spanish hands, from which a few escaped. A small party journeyed all the way to Canada, where they told the story of La Salle's fatal error.[16]

In 1699, Pierre Le Moyne d'Iberville took up La Salle's unfinished mission. Landing well east of the Mississippi River delta, so as not to repeat his predecessor's mistakes, Iberville established a base, Fort Maurepas, at Biloxi Bay, before proceeding cautiously along the coast and up what he hoped was the Mississippi River. Confirmation of his location came when some Mougoulacha people who lived in the delta revealed a letter written in French. It was addressed to La Salle, dated thirteen years earlier, and signed by Henri de Tonti, who had come down the river from Illinois looking for his friend, unaware of his fate.[17]

Only after Iberville's reconnaissance of the river mouth did cartographers put a delta on their maps of the Mississippi River. Early in 1700, Guillaume Delisle, the most respected French cartographer of his day, completed a new map of North America. By this time everyone knew that La Salle had erred in thinking the river emptied into the gulf on the western coast. Delisle put the Mississippi where it belonged, but he drew no delta. Just as he began to print his map, he received new information from Iberville's reports. He stopped printing, added a delta to his drawing, and began to print again. Thus, the delta entered the consciousness of European explorers and mapmakers.[18]

To twenty-first century eyes, most early sketches of the delta appear wildly inaccurate. It took time to learn of its full size and shape. Delisle drew a fat stub of land with very short jetties at the mouths, and an advancing, not a receding, coastline. Yet Delisle's delta is a surprisingly accurate rendition of the delta as it probably was over three centuries ago, the delta Iberville found, the delta La Salle would have found had he known to look for it.

Iberville's caution and good luck paid off. However, finding the delta solved only the first problem. Living on it presented more challenges. La Salle's reports to his financial backers had fancifully described a dry land eminently suited to agriculture, silk production, and settlement. The banks of the Mississippi River were dry and stable, he promised. "They consist of a hard soil, covered with pretty large trees following regularly the banks of the river." Iberville was among those who believed La Salle's reports, for he sailed to Louisiana with a list of objectives that included the establishment

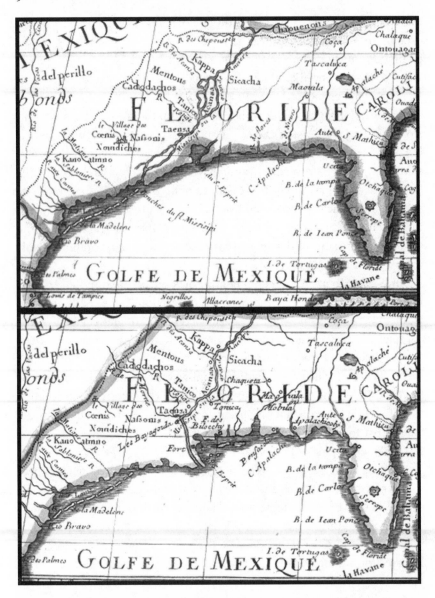

FIGURE 2.7 Two versions of Guillaume Delisle's map of 1700, one without and one with a Mississippi River delta. (Top, courtesy of the Historic New Orleans Collection, accession no. 1985.230: Detail; bottom, courtesy of the David Rumsey Historical Map Collection.)

of cotton and indigo plantations in the lower valley. However, once in Louisiana he realized all was not quite as he had expected. "Both banks of the river," he wrote in his journal, "almost the entire distance above the sea, are so thickly covered with canes of every size—one inch, two inches, three, four, five, and six in circumference—that one cannot walk through them. It is impenetrable country, which would be easy to clear." The apparent contradiction in Iberville's observation—impenetrable but easy to clear—expresses an emerging awareness of the realities of the environment in which he found himself, and his unrealistic hopes for the ease with which that environment might be transformed.[19]

In the winter of 1700, Iberville's brother, Jean-Baptiste Le Moyne de Bienville, supervised the first attempt at building a settlement near the mouth of the Mississippi River. Hastily erected on a small ridge, Fort de la Boulaye was a wretched place. The origin of the fort's name is not certain but it suggests that, like La Salle before them, Iberville and Bienville saw the delta environment in terms of their experiences in Canada. In French, *la boulaie* refers to a stand of birch trees. Birch are abundant in the Canadian Shield, the great arc of exposed granite that dips down from west of Hudson's Bay to the Great Lakes and east into Quebec, a land the Le Moyne brothers knew well. They are scrappy trees, growing where many other species cannot, and are typically found on the edges of bogs, where the top soil is thin though often rich and always wet. Iberville or one of the other Canadians in his group may have seen something familiar: small, scrappy trees and water. In any case, the Mississippi River near its mouth was no place for a fort. The spot was too wet. Vegetable gardens washed out. Wildlife was scarce. Hunters had to travel to Baie St. Louis, east along the Gulf Coast, to find game. There was precious little timber suitable for construction, and no stone. A thin strip of forest fifty paces deep did contain hardwoods and some cedars, although few of much size. There was plenty of cane, but that is a rather flimsy building material, especially for a fort. Shifting sand bars in the passes frequently blocked the ships that attempted to bring supplies, which had to be portaged in from Lac Borgne. Soldiers lived surrounded by water and clouds of gnats and mosquitoes that descended on them whenever the breezes died.[20]

At almost every turn, the delta thwarted French efforts to establish themselves in the unfamiliar delta environment. It helped when they found anything that reminded them of home, such as dry fields, and peach trees, which had come to the Americas with the Spanish and spread to the Mississippi Valley from Mexico. After grousing about swamps,

FIGURE 2.8 Mississippi River delta savannah, like that where Fort de la Boulaye was constructed. (Courtesy of Terry McTigue and the National Oceanic and Atmospheric Administration, Department of Commerce.)

FIGURE 2.9 Mississippi River delta cypress swamp, upriver from the savannah, near the location of New Orleans. (Courtesy of Terry McTigue and the National Oceanic and Atmospheric Administration, Department of Commerce.)

mosquitoes, and lazy Indians, Father Paul du Ru wrote of his visit to the Natchez village, high on the bluff above the floodplain: "The plains of the Natchez which I observed a little more attentively to-day are even more beautiful than I had realized. There are peach, plum, walnut and fig trees everywhere. It is unfortunate that this place is so remote from the mouth of the Mississippi." Du Ru did not know that the beautiful fields of the Natchez supplemented game, fish, and shellfish taken from the vast wetlands.[21]

What was not directly familiar became so through analogical reasoning. The buffalo *were* North American animals, but they were *like* European cattle: they grazed on the wet savannahs, which to the French were like dry "plains," and they possessed "a wool quite as fine as Spanish sheep," a reference to merino sheep prized in Europe. Cane and thatch temples at a Bayogoula village recalled for one of the priests who accompanied Iberville the portal of the Collège de Plessis, a Jesuit school in Paris. A member of La Salle's 1682 expedition thought the square in the Coroa village was "like the square in front of the Royal Palace in Paris." Even the river could seem familiar through comparison with well-known rivers elsewhere. The Mississippi was in some places "as wide as the Seine at the bank by the Gobelin," in others "scarcely broader than the Seine in front of L'Hotel de Mars." Some features of the lower valley suggested other colonies with which the French were familiar: the soil of Louisiana was as fertile as that of English Virginia. The abundance of mulberry trees reminded them of China. Such comparisons imagined the wetlands were dry and controlled—plains, city plazas, Virginia tobacco fields. Assigning names to unfamiliar features of the landscapes and waterscapes was another way of gaining some control over the wet delta environment, beginning with the naming of Louisiana for the king, and subsequently Lac Pontchartrain for the Minister of Marine who supported the colonial venture, Lac Maurepas for his son and successor at the ministry, and Nouvelle Orléans after the city on the flood plain of the Loire River in France.[22]

As French and native names claimed the Louisiana countryside, names the Spanish had assigned many landmarks, which appeared on the maps the French initially used, disappeared. The Spanish were never serious rivals to the French in the lower valley and many of their names were easily forgotten. By contrast, the English, who posed the most dangerous threat to the French in North America, were recalled at Detour des Anglois (English Turn), a bend in the Mississippi River that memorialized the successful rebuffing by the French of an English warship.

Not all the names assigned to landmarks were French. A list of places along the river reads like a census of native peoples for the year 1700: Bayogoula, Chitimacha, Tchuopitoulas, Natchez. Even after native inhabitants abandoned these sites, the names persisted. They were used by the French who encountered them and the people who inhabited them, and thus they memorialized their own history primarily, although that clearly intersected with local histories. Non-French place names also kept alive the competing claims of others who knew these places as wetlands.[23]

The permanent association of a name with a place is an assertion of control over history and environment. Consider, for example, how the Mississippi River got its name. Accounts from the Hernando de Soto expedition record that native peoples knew the river by various names, including *Chucagua*, *Tamaliseu*, and *Tapatu*. An early map based on the 1519 Alonso Álvarez de Pineda expedition named it Rio del Espiritu Santo. That name persisted on European maps for the next 180 years, a clear acknowledgment by other Europeans of Spain's claim to the river. The accounts of the Soto expedition refer to the Rio del Espiritu Santo, although they also use Rio Grande, indicating that they were not sure that their river was Pineda's river.[24]

The Spanish approached the Mississippi River from the south, from Havana, the Florida peninsula, and Mexico. The French approached the river from the north, from New France in Canada. They explored the river's upper region first as they extended their direct interest in the fur trade from Montreal all the way to the foothills of the Rocky Mountains. At the same time, the Five Nations Iroquois, working with the Dutch and then the English at Albany, were pushing their own trade into the west. A water route to the Gulf offered the French a way to ship northwestern furs around their rivals, who had seized control of water routes between Ontario and Kentucky. Europeans thus came to know the river by two names. The lower river kept its Spanish name. In its upper region, however, the French called it by its Ojibwa and Ottawa name, *Michi Zeebee*, which means great or greatest river. It was as if there were two rivers, which indeed there were on many European maps and minds until Joliet demonstrated otherwise. Even after Joliet, who turned around before reaching the gulf, La Salle, who did reach the gulf, doubted the Mississippi of the Great Lakes region was the Rio del Espiritu Santo of Pineda and Soto, because he was not sure where he was once he reached the river's end. He thought he just might be in Texas, on the Rio Escondido, known today as the Nueces River. Until Iberville received Tonti's letter, no European knew for sure that the Ojibwa

Mississippi and the Spanish Rio del Espiritu Santo were one and the same. That "discovery" of a single river created a need for a single name, but only for the French. The Spanish had never cared what the river was called at its headwaters, far beyond their reach. No native people claimed the entire river, and so called it what they wished on the stretches of river they knew. The French were the first to claim the entire river, which they managed in part by giving it one name.

But what name? La Salle had tried to name the river Le Fleuve Colbert, after Louis XIV's powerful minister, whose favor La Salle had curried; but the name did not stick, perhaps because Colbert died the next year. At some point in the early eighteenth century, La Riviere St. Louis appeared on some maps. But the name everyone used was Mississippi, which the French took from the Ojibwa. While La Salle and Iberville groped their way around the lower valley, missionaries, fur traders, soldiers, and diplomats quickly established themselves among the Algonquian-speaking people of the upper valley; and as French influence seeped southward, the Algonquian name for the river went with it. The native peoples of the lower valley, who did not speak Algonquian, had their own names for the river. To the Muskogean-speaking Bayogoula it was Malbanchaya, a name that Iberville used until he could be certain Malbanchaya and Mississippi were the same. Mississippi was the name that stuck because Louisiana was established as an extension of Canada. By 1699, when the Louisiana colony was founded, the French and their Algonquian allies had broken the Iroquois stranglehold on water routes to the east, rendering the lower river much less relevant to the interests of the fur trade, a development underlined by the French establishment of Detroit two years later. As Louisiana's founders struggled to give the colony a new raison d'etre, by looking west to Spanish silver mines, across the gulf to the West Indies, and to the emerging threat from the English at Charles Town, the northern name, the Ojibwa name, persisted.[25]

The many names given to the river reflect the history of the valley as contested terrain. Its final and lasting name recalls the history of French-Indian relations in the Great Lakes region, when the French depended on native peoples for trade and defense in the face of English and Iroquois power, and so accepted the Ojibwa name for the river. French activities in the lower valley were more recent and were regarded as an extension of their long-standing interests in Canada and on the French-Algonquian middle ground of the pays d'en haut. For French coming down the river, the familiar name was Mississippi, maybe the only thing familiar about the river as it flowed through the broad floodplain of the lower valley. Given the protracted struggle of La Salle, then Iberville, and finally Bienville, founder of New Orleans, in establishing a new colony that would advance French interests as they spread west and south from New France, it is understandable that when at last they succeeded, the name of the big muddy river that ran through their colony was neither French nor native to the region.[26]

Assigning a name to a foreign landscape may have helped the French to domesticate it. Still, a wetland, regardless of its name, is a wet land, and as such it posed a problem for people who preferred dry land. As they navigated their way through the delta and coastal estuaries the French frequently found themselves at the mercy of native guides. Iberville selected the site for his Mississippi fort upon the full assurances of his Bayogoula guide that the place never flooded. According to one member of Iberville's party, the guide, an old man "more dried up even than the bear meat and the venison" jerky he fed on, had been "sent by his tribe, as one of the most expert of the country, to show us a good place on the Mississippi." This "dried up" expert, however, soon had the French living knee deep in water. On another occasion, a party of French set out for the gulf from a Colapissa village, where they had destroyed a native religious icon and replaced it with a cross. Somewhere near Lake Pontchartrain they got lost. Reluctantly, they decided to heed the advice of the Indians accompanying them. They soon lost faith in their guides, however, and in the middle of a swamp the party stopped. As the Frenchmen bickered over which way to go, their primary guide abandoned them. After many hours of aimless wandering, the French, once again, turned to a native person for help. They put themselves in the hands of a man who took them a painfully roundabout way to the coast. On yet another occasion a native guide leading Father Gravier from Fort Biloxi to the Mississippi River apparently lost his bearings, turning what should have been in Gravier's estimation a three-day excursion into an eleven-day survival trip, though they traveled an old trail very familiar to the native peoples of the Gulf Coast. If the guides were intentionally misleading the French, it may have been to assert their authority within this environment, or perhaps they only sought to teach the newcomers a thing or two about it.[27]

Further contributing to their sense of being lost in the wetlands, the French could not easily account for the apparent ease with which native peoples lived in them. To the French, the people of the lower valley seemed to be ignorant of work. One Frenchman wrote of the Ouma, "As they rest satisfied with their squashes and corn, of which they have plenty, they are indolent and seldom go hunting." The Ouma may not have hunted, but they fished. They presented Iberville with a large catfish, and on another occasion fed the French a "mess of brill." Another Frenchman wrote about the Bayogoula, Mougoulacha, and Chitimacha: "I am struck by the dominant preference of these tribes for indolence. They will go without things that we regard as absolutely necessary, merely because it would require a little effort to get them. If they have more corn than they actually need for food, this is due less to the quantity they sow than to the fertility of their soil, which, alone, is responsible." Fishing and planting corn did not, according to the French, count as work. It was too easy. "All the Savages undertake," the observer continued, "is to raise enough Indian corn to maintain life. As for hunting, it is hardly worth mentioning. The buffalo and deer eat the crops and the people do not have enough spirit to kill them for food." This was an environment that, as the French saw it, made "docile savages" of a local population ignorant of work yet eager to learn all about it. It is ironic that in an environment so rich that one could apparently live without working, the French could only dream of what they might do by working the land. Rather than let the environment work for them, they would transform it so they could work it on their terms, by planting dry land crops such as wheat, building a fort, and living in it as proper French. Unable or unwilling to see the environment as it was, as a wet land, they privileged their own methods and technologies for intervening in the relationship between water and land, wet and dry.[28]

For the native peoples of the Mississippi delta, life was far from easy. Villages annually flooded, necessitating seasonal relocations. Large animals such as bear and deer also relocated, sometimes permanently. Raccoons and other smaller animals took to the trees. Still, the valley after a flood could be a desert, but for the pools full of fish and the birds they attracted. Fields flooded, too, and if the water was deep and stayed on the land long enough, crops died and people went hungry. By and large, however, people adapted. They knew how to live in their wet land, where to go when the water rose, and where to find food when stored supplies washed out. They knew, for example, that floods might leave people short on corn, but not short on fish.

Native peoples of the delta and valley wetlands may also have had their own notions of what constituted wet and dry land. The Bayogoula guide who showed Iberville a patch of land that he promised never flooded, but which flooded as soon as Iberville built his fort upon it, may have been neither ignorant nor deceitful. Given the extent of flooding possible along the Mississippi River, the inundation of the fort might have been, in the Bayogoula guide's experience, comparatively minor. A foot of water on the ground during spring perhaps did not, to the guide, constitute a flood. Native peoples had to contend with floods, which they did by packing up and moving to higher ground only to return once the water receded. They shifted with the shifting relationship between land and water. The French wanted a fixed settlement, which required finding a permanently dry location or creating one. Iberville considered relocating his Mississippi River fort upriver to the Bayogoula village but decided that spot, too, was prone to flooding, even though people had been living there for a long time. Similarly, the French may have thought that swamps were easily avoided by anyone who knew the terrain and possessed a competent sense of direction. The French saw swamps as water, as purely wet places, and so searched for their opposite, perfectly dry land. Had they seen swamps as a mixture of land and water they might have understood that there were few perfectly dry places and the valley environment was a continuum of wet and dry. Native peoples, however, would have known that marshlands lay all around and that even the best guide could not avoid them.[29]

However wet or dry the land selected for the fort was, the fort itself would have made the land wetter, since the soldiers altered the terrain in ways that affected flooding patterns. The fort sat on a low rise, "the nearest to the sea that was not swampy," Iberville wrote. Upon the ridge stood a small collection of hardwoods—oak, ash, elm, but no birch—broken by open areas, or plains. Iberville ordered that the trees be cut down to supply wood for construction, and perhaps to clear any possible obstruction to the fort's view of the river and its approaches. For intruders to be intimidated by a French fort, they would have to know it was there and recognize it as such. Cutting down trees and cane would have accelerated the pace of erosion. Trees held sediment upon ridges whenever the river inundated them, thus raising their height with each flood. Moreover, trees helped hold soil against rainfall. Iberville unwittingly subjected the fort to greater inundations.[30]

Less than a year after building it, the French were ready to abandon their miserable little fort in the midst of the Mississippi River delta. In December of 1700, Jesuit Father Gravier visited it and recorded a rather horrifying account of the garrison's ordeal of the past year: "I observed, on arriving, that the men were commencing to suffer from hunger, and that flour was beginning to fail. This compelled me to live on the same food as do the Savages, so as not to be a burden upon any one; and to content myself with Indian corn, without meat or fish, Until the arrival of the ships, which are not expected here before the end of march." High waters flooded the place, Gravier continued, "to such an extent that the men spent four months in the water; and frequently had to wade mid-Leg deep in it outside of their Cabins, although the savages had assured them that this spot was never inundated. The wheat that had been sown was already quite high, when the inundation caused by a heavy sea, in the month of August, carried it away. The Garden did not succeed any better; and, besides, there are great numbers of black snakes that eat the lettuce and other vegetables down to the roots."[31]

The French did not come to Louisiana to place themselves at the mercy of the natural environment, or its native populations. They believed themselves superior to both. They planned to transform the lower valley environment into a dry land suitable for French habitation. In the short term, however, the French had to learn from the native peoples how to survive in this wet land. Gravier's remark, about living on Indian corn after French wheat failed, indicates as much. The new location Iberville and Bienville had in mind for a second settlement was at the one-time location of a Bayogoula village. Time would prove many of their most successful settlements to be those established on the sites of former villages. From the lower valley people the French learned about the portages that linked the many waterways, including one that enabled them to bypass the big river's mouth they had sought so hard to find in the first place. They eventually gave up on wheat and planted maize, successfully, preparing the ground for planting by burning and clearing canebrakes in the manner of the native peoples they had observed. By observing others, the French learned how to adapt, which eventually gave them the means and the confidence to begin a process of transforming wet land into dry land, and a foreign land into French land.

Constant threat from imperial rivals told the French they needed to hold on to their fort. Constant assault from water told them they needed to let it go. In 1707 the French conceded that water was more troublesome than the British and Spanish, and they abandoned La Boulaye and the delta. Bienville, who by then had succeeded his older brother as the colony's commander, explained the situation to his superiors in France: "This last summer I examined better than I had yet done all the lands in the vicinity of this river. I did not find any at all that are not flooded in the spring. I do not see how settlers can be placed on this river." Bienville moved his headquarters to Fort Louis on Mobile Bay, where the land was dry and where he could observe and guard against any attacks out of Spanish Pensacola or British

Carolina. The small bastion on the Mississippi River delta remained a periodic place of rendezvous until the founding of New Orleans over a decade
later, after which it was left to sink beneath into the marsh. Twenty-five
years after La Salle claimed it for France, ten years after Iberville began to
colonize it, the wet and muddy delta was home to five French settlers.[32]

In 1714 the French established a post up the Red River, at Natchitoches,
as far into Spanish territory as they dared to go. Two years later, the French
established a post at Natchez. Below the arc that connected Natchitoches,
Natchez, and Mobile Bay stretched the wetlands of the Mississippi River
delta, for the time being set aside, because the French could not figure out
how to live there. Unable to situate themselves comfortably in the coastal
and river marshlands, the French built their first permanent settlements on
its edges, on the geographical and environmental frontier between upland
and lowland, between forest and marsh, between dry land and wetland.[33]

Mobile, Natchez, and Natchitoches proved to be easier for the French
to settle. The locations were forested, providing plenty of timber for

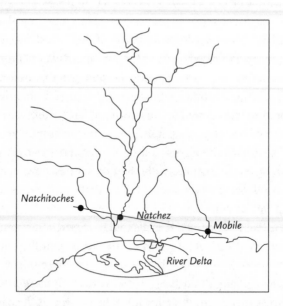

FIGURE 2.10 Until French colonial administrators gained confidence that they
could build a settlement in the delta wetlands, they avoided it, preferring the
higher ground on the edge of the continental plate. Prior to the establishment
of New Orleans in the delta, the primary directional axis of French activity in the
lower valley was east-west. New Orleans shifted that axis to north-south, making
the Mississippi River the primary artery of communication and transportation in
colonial Louisiana. (Drawing by author.)

construction and fortification. The land was fertile and dry enough for European-style agriculture. There was plenty of pasture for cattle. The locations were strategically useful, with Mobile and Natchitoches abutting Spanish territories, and Natchez checking the Chickasaw and their English allies. However, in 1717, with the English active in "the land of the Alabamas," the French looked to relocate their colonial capital and gave serious thought to returning to the delta. When war broke out between France and Spain, the garrison at Mobile acted quickly and seized Pensacola. Meanwhile, the commander at Natchitoches marched into the nearby Spanish fort of Los Adaes and arrested his counterpart. Upon resumption of peace in Europe the immediate threat to Louisiana dissipated, and the French returned Pensacola and Los Adaes to the Spanish. Long-term threats remained, however, and the French moved their capital again, from Mobile to Biloxi, site of Iberville's original base. Meanwhile, they renewed efforts to establish a permanent settlement near the mouth of the Mississippi River, buoyed by recent successes with rice cultivation in the delta wetlands.[34]

3

Rice

IN LATE SPRING of 1712, naval commissioner Martin d'Artaguette sent a rather gloomy report to the French Ministry of the Marine on the state of affairs in Louisiana. As he despaired over the failure of yet another wheat crop, he managed to offer one hopeful observation. He had seen stalks of Indian corn standing in fields of water, and it occurred to him that rice might grow well in the wetlands of the lower Mississippi Valley. Antoine Crozat, who in 1713 received proprietary control of Louisiana from the king, picked up on D'Artaguette's idea, asserting that "One is able to cultivate in Louisiana as much rice as one wants." On the basis of these observations, colonial administrators arranged to transform the lower valley into rice farms. In 1716, the first seed rice arrived in Louisiana, likely shipped from West Africa by way of the West Indian island colony of Saint-Domingue. Later that year Crozat imported a large shipment of rice from Nantes, on the Loire River near the west coast of France, which may have originated in West Africa, India, Valencia in Spain, the British colony of South Carolina, or even the south of France. Meanwhile, surveyors divided the wetlands along the lower Mississippi River and its branches and tributaries into private farms. In 1718, two ship captains delivered barrels of seed rice purchased directly from West African producers, along with several enslaved Africans familiar with its cultivation. By 1719, rice fields planted by French and West Africans lined several miles of the Mississippi River in the delta wetlands. That year floods destroyed all the crops along the Mississippi except rice, which saved the colony from disaster. Thereafter rice became the staple food for French Louisiana. In 1733, Governor Bienville reported that "Three-fourths of the inhabitants live on [rice] and have forgotten wheat bread."[1]

The French built Louisiana on rice. Through its successful cultivation, they learned that wetlands could sustain a colony. Rice fed colonists who previously had depended on imported wheat and on locally grown corn, which they did not much like. In time, rice fed the development of an export trade in indigo, sugar, tobacco, and cotton, principally by feeding field laborers, including slaves. As it provided the colony with the means to sustain itself, rice helped convince kings, ministers, and financiers in France to invest in Louisiana. Rice fed the people of New Orleans, the officials, merchants, sailors, artisans, priests, nuns, dock workers. Rice fed the soldiers who defended Louisiana against native peoples frustrated and angered by the encroachment of French fields on their lands. In short, rice transformed a foreign environment into a familiar environment, one the French, with West African assistance, understood and knew how to work.

Until they started planting rice, the lower valley seemed almost uninhabitable, despite the fact that it was very much inhabited. The French struggled just to find enough to eat, or so some of their memoirs suggest. Of his first trip down Big Muddy, Father Gravier wrote, "we lived entirely on Indian corn and a few squashes, since for some time back we met in these parts neither buffalo, deer, nor bear; and if we found any bustards or wild geese, they were so lean that they were tasteless as wood, which makes all our canoe men sigh often for the river of the Illinois and the beauty of the country and landings and its plenty of buffalo and deer and all sorts of fat and excellent game." In the watery lower valley, he continued, the currents were more violent, the selection of campsites "wretched," the shallows and beaches made of potter's clay, and dry land reached only after hard slogs through dense thickets of cane. Several in the party killed an alligator. "It is said that the tongue is good to eat, but I have never had the curiosity to taste any of it, or any other part of the body, which most of the Savages consider a great treat." Members of La Salle's first expedition, which also had found the hunting tough in the lower valley, surprised three lower valley people, who ran off leaving behind two large pieces of meat they were smoking. The French greedily devoured smoked alligator and a piece of meat they suspected of being human flesh. "The human meat was better than that of the alligator," one wrote. "We left an awl as payment in the canoe." Meat was scarce at the Tensas village Gravier visited. Below the Arkansas River he found no peaches. He and his companions lived off what little they could acquire from the native population. There are not, wrote Father Paul du Ru, "anywhere between Illinois and the sea, pears, oranges, hemp, flax, pigs, or sheep. As for fish, which are said to be so numerous in the rivers that one can seize them with one's hand, this is an exaggeration. If it has any foundation at all, we shall not fare so badly during Lent." "Biscuit and sagamité again," Du Ru sighed. "Praise heaven, we lack many things, both to eat properly or to sleep comfortably. We have fallen back upon the sagamité, that is to say good meal of Indian corn soaked in the water of the Mississippi." According to Du Ru, two hunters, lost in the forest lived for six days, barely surviving on laurel leaves and berries.[2]

The scarcities can be explained. Several early expeditions occurred during the spring when the river was high, dry land was scarce, and most wildlife and people had gone elsewhere. When the river was low, large animals such as buffalo avoided the dense canebrakes. The scarcity of fat fowl, noted by Gravier, was seasonal. For the most part, however, the French suffered from inexperience with the wetland environment. Education came with as much difficulty as a good meal. For example, the French were convinced that the climate and soil along the Mississippi was suitable for planting wheat. Every spring they would plant it, and every summer the crop would mold from excessive moisture. The next year they tried again, certain that the previous year's floods and rains were rare exceptions.[3]

With rice, the French adapted to the wetlands. That is not how they saw matters, for they never really thought of rice as a wet crop naturally different from a dry crop such as wheat. Rather, they considered rice to be like a hardy wheat, able to withstand wet soil. Planting rice, therefore, entailed no concession to the environment. In Louisiana, rice fields became wheat fields, and sterile wetlands became fertile dry lands. Rice flour mixed with some wheat flour became French bread. Over time, rice cultivation encouraged and underwrote the environmental transformations necessary for the cultivation of truly dry land crops.[4]

Like wheat, rice is a true grass and at least its domesticated varieties are Old World. The French were certainly familiar with *Oryza sativa*, an Asian domestic, and by the eighteenth century they may also have been familiar with *Oryza glaberrima*, a West African domestic. Like cattails and water lilies, rice can germinate in anaerobic soils that are low in oxygen from sustained submersion, soils that wheat cannot abide. Moreover, both Old World domestics were closely related to American wild rice (*Zizania aquatica*), another wetland grass. Nevertheless, the French did not think of rice as wet and new. Rather, they thought of it as familiar and dry, which in their mind made the lower Mississippi Valley environment a little more familiar and a little less wet.[5]

In the early spring, Louisiana rice farmers prepared ground for seeding, using mattocks and sharp hoes, the ground often being too muddy to support the weight of oxen and plows. They sowed their fields by hand and then waited for the river to flood them. Water, so long as it moved slowly over the land, did not carry away seeds or sprouts or otherwise hurt the crop. To the contrary, water covered the land with a fertilizing layer of sediment and stimulated germination. As floodwaters slowly receded, roots dried and stems gained strength. Late season flooding and summer rains smothered weeds and shielded plants from pests. Crawfish were a nuisance during the early stages of plant growth, although they were also a source of food for rice farmers. In general, successful harvests followed wet summers. In dry years farmers sought ways to keep water on their fields, and over time methods of manipulating water became more sophisticated and labor intensive. Following harvest, rice was bundled, stacked, threshed, hulled, and stored until eaten.[6]

As the French adapted to the lower valley wetlands by cultivating rice, they also adapted to rice as a food. Wheat had long been their grain of choice. Wheat bread distinguished Europeans from Native Americans and was a marker of European identity, perhaps for the French most of all. In December 1700, as the French were busy establishing themselves on the coast of the Gulf of Mexico, they received a visit from the commander of the Spanish fort at Pensacola. The ostensible reason was to retrieve deserters. "But in Reality," remarked Jesuit Father Jacques Gravier, who was present on this occasion, "it was only an excuse to visit the Fort...for the purpose of procuring linen and clothing Because they [the Spanish] lack everything." The French were not much better off, although they were not about to reveal as much. According to Gravier, "Although we are already short of provisions,—at least of french flour," the governor "caused the Indian corn to be concealed, and displayed French bread all over the Fort." This display signaled prosperity, that supply and communication lines with Europe were secure.[7]

The hidden corn was as meaningful as the prominently displayed wheat bread. Corn was not a French grain, food, or commodity. It signaled dependence on others, principally native peoples. Because the French found corn distasteful, they rejected it, even though corn plants withstood moderate inundation and were therefore somewhat adaptable to the wet environment of the lower Mississippi Valley.

In 1699, André Pénicaut watched some Pascagoulas prepare fields on a small ridge along the Mississippi River, noting how they used hooked sticks to pull up cane by its extensive root systems, and then dried and burned the cane before planting the cleared ground with corn and beans. The cane ridges of the lower valley could be sufficiently high for planting, and though a poor quality soil of sand and gravel lay just below the surface, a thin layer of good soil collected on top, held by the cane, permitting a season or two of planting. In time, topsoil washed away and cultivators abandoned fields to the river and to resurgent cane, and a natural re-wilding process began. Native peoples dried corn for storage and prepared it for eating by grinding it and cooking it in broth, a dish of corn grits that the French called *sagamité*, for which they never acquired a taste. In 1704, twenty or so French women recently recruited to Louisiana became "indignant at being fed corn" and threatened insurrection. The very name Indian corn (*blé d'inde* in French, sometimes abbreviated as *bléd*), which was often mistranslated as turkey corn (*blé dinde*) or even Turkish corn (*blé de Turquie*), marked it as foreign. Gravier described being "compelled" by a shortage of wheat flour "to live on the same food as do the Savages" and "to content myself with Indian corn," which he found hard to do. Whereas they might have built Louisiana on corn, the French instead built it on rice, which was firmly established in French culture and a good substitute for corn in Louisiana fields and on Louisiana tables.[8]

Since Roman times, southern Europeans had eaten rice imported from India. By the start of the eighteenth century, rice was a dietary staple throughout much of Western Europe, including France, Germany, the Netherlands, and Belgium. Rice cultivation in Europe dated to the thirteenth and fourteenth centuries, when Moorish farmers brought their methods to Majorca and Valencia. In the fifteenth century, estate owners in the Po Valley of Lombardy were earning their living off rice cultivation and marketing, just as French farmers began to turn the salt marshes of the Rhone River delta, the Camargue, into productive rice fields. Since the Middle Ages when it served as a substitute for meat on Fridays and during Lent, rice had made inroads into French cuisine. It was an essential ingredient in the delicacy known as *blancmange*, a kind of savory sweet white pudding. By the seventeenth century, rice was fast becoming an essential grain in the French diet, second only to wheat on the table, and as a starchy side dish second to none. Cookbooks from the period do not mention potatoes, or pasta, except occasionally vermicelli. By the time Iberville landed at the mouth of the Mississippi River, rice was standard fare on many French tables, served in *potages* alongside capons and pullets. By the end of the eighteenth century, rice could be found in cakes, casseroles, soufflés, and beignets. It never entirely shook its association with poor and working people. The church distributed it whenever the wheat crop fell short. On board French ships, officers ate bread, but crewmen often received rice. In Louisiana, as in France, officers, administrators, and the affluent got first dibs on the wheat bread supply. Still, though déclassé, rice was an accepted substitute for wheat. Rice was French, especially in Louisiana, where wheat was always in short supply, and the only other alternative was undeniably American.[9]

In France rice was typically cooked first in water, then dried into a hard clump, and in the manner of dried bread, stored until needed, when it was easily reconstituted in hot broth or milk. This was how French in Louisiana cooked rice, although according to one observer they preferred it "boiled much thicker" than was common in France. Dumont de Montigny described rice as "a kind of wheat," the proper plant for Louisiana, where fields lay inundated for three months of every year. Rice bread, in his view, made "a good manna for settlers." Marie Madeleine Hachard and her Ursuline sisters mixed rice and wheat flour for their bread, just as many in France stretched wheat flour supplies by mixing it with grains and nuts. Louisiana rice bread, Antoine Simon Le Page Du Pratz observed, "is very white and of a good relish; but they have tried in vain to make any that will soak in soup." Because rice lacks gluten, bread made entirely of rice flour differs in texture and will not rise properly; for this reason Louisiana rice bread typically included some wheat flour.[10]

The ability of rice to approximate flour, particularly in *potages*, but eventually in baked goods, made it appealing. Today *potage* is, simply, soup. Originally, however, it was meat and/or vegetables cooked in broth thickened with dried bread crusts but sometimes egg yolks, and sometimes rice. The dish was "the basis of the French national diet," wrote Jean-Anthelme Brillat-Savarin in his treatise on food and taste, "and the experience of centuries has inevitably brought it to perfection." The variations were almost limitless, consisting of combinations of meats, poultry, fish, and vegetables, but they all started with a broth thickened with dried bread or bread crumbs. Raw flour easily spoiled or became infested with vermin unless baked into bread and dried. *Sagamité* was a kind of *potage*, but gumbo served over rice in lieu of bread was a better approximation of *potage*.[11]

The incorporation of rice into French cuisine was an adaptation to Louisiana's environmental conditions. In time, however, the development of rice agriculture became an imposition forced upon the wetlands as well as upon many of those who worked the fields. Between 1719 and 1731, the Company of the Indies brought nearly 6,000 enslaved Africans, some of them already experienced rice planters, to Louisiana. The company transferred most of them to the owners of the larger concessions, as the French plantations were called. For example, the directors of the Sainte-Catherine concession at Natchez requested, paid for, and received 1,500 Africans. The company also offered small allotments of enslaved laborers to soldiers as an incentive to settle down and farm. During his tenure as director of Louisiana, Crozat proposed sending France's poor to the colony to work as *engagés*, indentured servants, to be freed after a term of three years. John Law followed up on Crozat's proposal and arranged for a large group of German *engagés* to be settled on the Mississippi River. Most died en route or soon after arriving, but some outlived their terms and settled on what became known as the German coast, a stretch of the Mississippi River where they planted rice and vegetables for residents of nearby New Orleans. Law also sent convicts to his colony. The French purchased captives of Indian wars, predominantly women, from native allies and passed them along to single Frenchmen who promised to take up farming. Overall, fewer than 200 native people were held in bondage in the lower Mississippi Valley, most of them women. "I bought an Indian female slave," a Chitimacha war captive, "in order to have a person who could dress our victuals," recalled Le Page Du Pratz. Shortly after acquiring the Chitimacha woman, Le Page Du Pratz bought an African man and woman. Etienne Dubuisson of the Bayagoulas concession managed a typically mixed labor force of sixteen enslaved Africans, six indentured French, and one enslaved Indian. Whether on concessions or farms, landowners and company officials applied the energy of bound human labor to the land and water to produce the rice that sustained the colony.[12]

Many of the slaves brought to the valley were very familiar with rice. West Africans had been cultivating an indigenous variety for 2,000 years when European sailors arrived, using methods devised to suit local environments. In the uplands of Sierra Leone, farmers banked their rice fields to capture rainwater, which they channeled down adjacent hillsides. Along the Niger, Senegal, and Gambia rivers, herders planted rice in small plots on the floodplain, using manure to fertilize seeds and hold them in place against the gentle flood current. In the mangrove tidal estuaries at the mouth of the Gambia River, farmers rebuilt the landscape, constructing a complex infrastructure of banks, dikes, and canals to manipulate tidal and rain waters. West African methods of rice farming approximated those of European farmers in wet environments. For example, Italians in the Po Valley raised rice using methods that resembled those of farmers in upland areas of West Africa. Rice farming in the Camargue, the Rhone River delta in southern France, resembled the floodplain methods developed along the Gambia River, where rainwater was captured and used to wash saline from the soil deposited by tidal floods. In North America, the English planted rice in Carolina, where they probably relied on West African expertise. In Louisiana, though the flood recession *décrue* method practiced up the Gambia and Niger rivers closely resembled techniques applied to the floodplain of the lower Mississippi River, the French could have drawn on their own experiences in America, India, and France, as well as on those of enslaved West Africans and the methods of lower valley wetland corn farmers. Louisiana rice planting methods evolved out of the accumulated experiences of many different wetland cultivators.[13]

In early Louisiana, gumbo resembled African rice stews, such as Wolof *thebouidienne (ceebu Jĕn)*, just as it resembled French *potage* thickened with rice instead of bread, and Native American *sagamité*. In the eighteenth century, many of the ingredients considered today to be essential for an authentic gumbo—okra, red pepper, filé, wheat flour for a roux—were not always available. But gumbo was always made with a stock, usually of fish, and served over rice. One visitor to Louisiana in 1802 observed, "The dish they Call Gumbo which is made principally of the Ochre [okra] into a Thick kind of Soop [sic] & Eat with Rice, it is the food of every Body for Dinner & Supper." Just as basic to gumbo as the blending of foods uniquely European, American, and African—flour, filé, okra—was the practice common to all of eating a stock thickened with grain. What made gumbo gumbo was rice, fish, and shellfish, products of the lower valley's wet environment. "Our most common food is rice with milk, little wild beans, meat, and fish," wrote Ursuline Sister Marie Hachard, "fish is very abundant and very good." There is "an incredible quantity of fishes in this country," wrote Le Page Du Pratz of early eighteenth-century Louisiana. There were oysters "large and delicate," and "excellent mussels." "The whole lower part of the river abounds in crayfish," he noted, all the more so as spreading rice fields provided crawfish with additional forage. Whatever the disadvantages of settling in the wetlands along the river, they were compensated for, wrote Dumont du Montigny, by the excellent fish easily caught from the river and nearby lakes and bayous. Shrimp filled the nets of fishermen on Lake Pontchartrain and the river for hundreds of leagues up. Fish was the mainstay of the native peoples' diet long before there was an abundance of rice to go with it. For native peoples, fish was fish, whether eaten alone, with corn, or with rice. But French and West Africans used rice to turn Louisiana fish into French and West African dishes.[14]

By the 1730s in Louisiana, everyone ate rice. However, some ate more than others. Rice raised in the lower valley wetlands thus delineated social

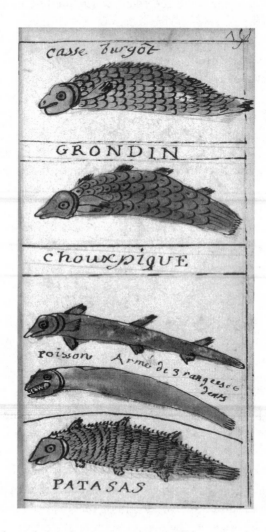

FIGURE 3.1 Fish were abundant in the rivers and lakes of the lower Mississippi Valley, and they were a dietary staple of the native peoples and of French and African newcomers. From "Poissons de Louisiane," p. 158, Jean François Benjamin Dumont de Montigny, *Poême en Vers touchant l'établissement de la province de la Loüisiane*, 1744. (Courtesy of the Bibliothèque Nationale de France, Paris.)

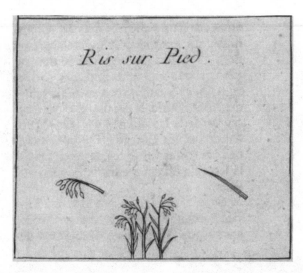

FIGURE 3.2 By planting rice, French colonists adapted themselves to the wetlands of the Mississippi River delta, which gave them the confidence to invest in a permanent settlement. Rice, often eaten with fish, was a familiar food to both French and West Africans. From Antoine Simon Le Page du Pratz, *Histoire de la Louisiane*, 1758.

boundaries. For example, rice signified ethnicity and class when lower class French farmers raised it as a primary crop for their own consumption and for local markets, while French concessionaires, who could afford imported wheat, raised rice to feed West African slaves. When an enslaved Indian ate rice, she was more fully a captive, eating her owner's food, than when she ate corn. When the master ate rice he was French, and when he ate wheat bread he was privileged French and ate in contrast to slave and servant, African and French, respectively. As rice thickened the social stew within households, outside in the fields rice thickened wetlands, joining solid earth and liquid water in a creole landscape that was French, West African, and Native American.[15]

Initially, rice gave the French a foothold in the wet land of the lower Mississippi Valley. Very soon, however, rice facilitated efforts to transform wet land into dry land. The individual most responsible for showing how the lower valley could be dried was Joseph Villars Dubreuil.

Dubreuil arrived in the lower Mississippi Valley from Dijon. At thirty, he had money to invest in a large concession of land at Tchoupitoulas, not far above New Orleans. He also received an allotment of slaves. He brought with him his wife and children, carpenters, coopers, joiners, domestic servants, a shoemaker, and a tailor. Intending to be an indigo

FIGURE 3.3 In this illustration, the artist presents not a scene but an assemblage of portraits that suggest the variety of non-French found in and around early New Orleans. Represented are an enslaved woman of the Fox Nation, with whom the French were at war, an African boy, presumably enslaved, an Atakapa man from the coastal region west of the town, and several Illinois people from the north. Behind them is what appears to be a rice field, and before them is the Mississippi River. Not visible but certainly present is the artist, a Frenchman from Picardy. Desseins de Sauvages de Plusieurs Nations, N.ᴵˡᵉ Orleans 1735. By Alexandre de Batz. (© President and Fellows of Harvard College, Peabody Museum of Archaeology and Ethnology, 41-72-10/20.)

planter, he set his woodworkers to building a large house. His slaves he put to the back-breaking work of clearing, draining, and leveeing, driving them urgently until they completed nearly ten miles of canals and drained over 400 acres of cleared land. Observed Governor Périer in 1731, "the lands can be drained and freed from water only by those who have negroes, since the work on levees and drainage is difficult and hard. Even though a man were not sick, no matter how good a settler he may be, in an entire year he would not put one arpent [0.84 acres] of land in condition to be planted." By 1744 Dubreuil was the wealthiest property owner in Louisiana, with several estates and over 500 slaves to do the work of freeing his land of water.[16]

The levee system put in place by Dubreuil and others who followed his lead became much more than a wall separating land and water.

Landowners and colonial administrators considered it essential technology for productive agriculture in the lower Mississippi Valley, as in France, where levees lined the Canal du Midi and were being erected in the Loire Valley. For the fields that stretched out behind them, levees were a mechanism of protection, irrigation, drainage, and fertilization. These dikes gave humans more control of the land and subjected them less to the vicissitudes of the river. Unlike modern structures reinforced with concrete, colonial levees were earthen and reinforced with timber. Barricaded from the land, water nevertheless returned to it and recreated wet land. During flood stages, water seeped through embankments into a network of drainage ditches that channeled it to low-lying cypress swamps at the back of the lots, where it would collect and eventually drain back into the river downstream. Landowners learned to use seepage to irrigate fields and to replenish them with deposits of fertile silt. Some concession managers stored water within reservoirs so they could flood fields later in the growing season, after the river had receded. By constructing levees, they endeavored not merely to keep the river at bay but to control the interaction between land and water so as to advance their interests as farmers who worked dry land that they irrigated and fertilized with muddy water.[17]

The construction of levees changed the geography of individual farms and plantations. Initially, landowners cleared, planted, and built their houses and out-buildings on the high ground that fronted the river. To make room for levees, they had to move buildings and fields sometimes twenty or thirty feet back from the river and into lower lying areas, placing them at greater risk of inundation from behind, necessitating still higher levees along the front as well as at the back of lots, and more elaborate networks of drainage canals. They planted indigo and sugar in drier areas, rice in wetter areas, switching out rice for one of the other crops as they drained and leveed. Cypress swamps lay at the back of plantations, receding before advancing fields. Ditches moved water from front to back, and conveyed cypress trees from back to front to be milled upon the levee and shipped downriver to market. Meanwhile, the river rose higher because it was being contained within ever higher and longer artificial walls.[18]

Dubreuil's first levee had been two feet high. In 1725, the directors of the Company were assured that "a levee three feet high will always give protection against the river." What was meant by the word "protection" is not clear, although it likely meant that the land would be safe from the worst effects of flooding. In any case, flooding continued and probably

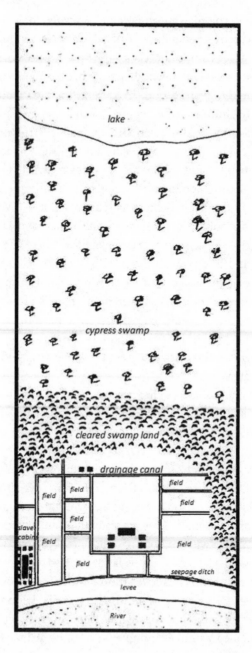

FIGURE 3.4 The French surveyed riverside property into long lots. Landowners situated their homes close to the river, on the natural levee, a little farther back if they constructed their own levee. Ditches channeled water downhill to the cypress swamp at the back of the lot and moved cut cypress forward to the river. (Drawing by author.)

worsened because of the levees. Longer, higher, wider levees necessitated still longer, higher, wider levees.[19]

Dubreuil's success almost immediately brought him into conflict with neighbors, particularly Nicolas, Joseph, and Louis Chauvin of the St. Reyne concession. In regulating the Mississippi River's access to his land, Dubreuil put more pressure on adjoining plantations. The Chauvins had a levee at the front of their land, but not at the back. They also had a mill powered by water running through an opening in the levee at the front of their concession, through a ditch that ran the length of their lot, and out into the swamp behind. To their dismay they discovered that as Dubreuil's construction proceeded at Tchoupitoulas, more water filled the swamp behind La Reyne, reversing the normal direction of flow. Suddenly, their indigo fields were in jeopardy and their mill inoperable. The Chauvin brothers took their case to court, the first of many lawsuits between neighbors over levees and liability for flood damage. The Louisiana Superior Court ordered that a continuous levee be built, with no openings to the river, not even for mill troughs. All area concessions placed a total of 150 slaves in the command of army engineer Captain Boutin who designed and supervised the project. The solution to flooding caused by leveeing and draining was more leveeing and draining, which seemed to work for all. By the time Boutin completed construction, the concessions at Tchapitoulous and St. Reyne were the most prosperous in the valley, each with sixty or more slaves raising rice, corn, indigo, and tobacco.[20]

Arguments like the one between Dubreuil and the Chauvin brothers were repeated wherever farmers attributed floods to the more substantial levees of neighbors. By 1732, levees lined both sides of the river for nearly fifty miles. By 1752, the network was extended perhaps another ten miles. If the levee walls were unbroken, which they probably were not until the later date, they could not have been uniform in height and composition. Eventually, all landowners along the lower Mississippi River bought or hired laborers to build embankments. Beginning in 1727, government edict began to force landowners to construct levees to uniform specifications, in the interest of better flood control, but also to minimize neighborly bickering.[21]

Using slaves to free the land of water encouraged other environmental transformations. Agriculture fully occupied slaves only at certain periods of the year, planting and harvest times in particular. During the winter lull, owners put slaves to work on levees and ditches, and at clearing timber from back lots. Cutting and milling cypress into lumber developed

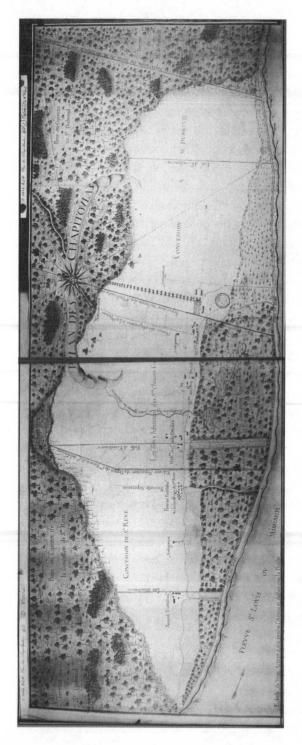

FIGURE 3.5 The Chapitoulas and St. Reyne concessions of Joseph Dubreuil and the Chauvin brothers, upriver from New Orleans, showing cleared and drained land near the river, surrounded by cypress swamp. From "Plan des Chapitoulas. Concession à M Dubreuil, terroir de Mde Bienville, etc. Aquarelle figurant les bois ou ciprières, les indogoteries." 1724. Karpinski Collection of the Harvard Map Collection. From the original, cote SH 210 60, Service Historique de la Défense, Département Marine, Cartes et Plans, Vincennes, France. (Courtesy of the Harvard Map Collection.)

into a prosperous off-season industry on Louisiana plantations, providing the colony with another valuable export. By 1729, however, officials expressed concern about the shrinking forests. Le Page Du Pratz wrote that "cypresses were formerly very common in Louisiana: but they have wasted them so imprudently, that they are now somewhat rare. They felled them for the sake of their bark, with which they covered their houses, and they sawed the wood into planks that they exported at different places. The price of the wood now is three times as much as it was formerly." The most accessible cypress trees were found in places that flooded part of the year, so that they could be cut when the ground was dry, and floated to mills when the ground was inundated. Dragging cut timber by man or animals was time-consuming and expensive. Cutting trees while balancing in a pirogue or skiff was next to impossible. The disappearance of only the most accessible timber would have caused the price of lumber to rise, as Le Page Du Pratz noted.[22]

The cypress forests of Louisiana remained abundant, notwithstanding official expressions of concern for their depletion. Only the most accessible stands had been cleared. Nevertheless, authorities encouraged farmers to preserve one third of the timber on their lots, although they granted that this guide would be difficult to follow in the lower delta, where wooded land was but a "tongue" between the river and several lakes. They feared that once the timber nearest the river was gone, it would have to come at greater cost from sources much farther upriver or in more inaccessible swamps.[23]

If the French put only a small dent in the total cypress forest of the lower Mississippi Valley, it was enough to change the relationship between land and water. As they cleared their lots, landowners made more room for water otherwise displaced by tree trunks. Clearing increased the water storage capacity of the floodplain, lowering flood levels. However, once they cleared land, landowners were sorely tempted to drain, levee, and till it. If they did, the land no longer stored water but instead contributed to the growing problem of rising flood levels. Moreover, deforestation increased rain runoff by reducing the land's ability to absorb water, and accelerated the pace at which water flowed over the land and downriver, reducing flooding where the land was cleared but greatly increasing flooding downstream, where water backed up, especially in areas not yet cleared. This in turn necessitated more clearing, more levees, more ditches.

Sometimes the French reshaped the environment in ways that defeated their purposes. Levees and drained fields meant that timber had to be dragged, not floated, out by teams of men and oxen. Sawmills and gristmills also contradicted the general direction of environmental transformation. The river's descent through the lower valley was too gradual to make water-powered mills feasible. In addition, some expressed fears that the large trees that came down in the current would smash mills located too near the river's edge. Some landowners, however, placed mills near their levees. Using the levee as a mill dam, they released high floodwater over the levee to the mill wheel. The more ingenious captured water that ran from the river over the mills, holding it in swamps or reservoirs—provided, of course, they had not turned all their swamp land into fields—so it could be used to power mills in the reverse direction after flood waters receded. Late-season milling, however, infuriated landowners downstream, whose fields received much of the sluice. A skillful plantation manager had to manipulate the environment with the precision of a watchmaker: flooding and draining rice fields and timber stands to ensure a timely harvest; allowing sufficient water over the levee to turn mill wheels, but no more than existing swamps could safely hold. Even the most carefully constructed and tended mill could weaken levees, which were built to keep water off the land. Openings in levees, even if intended to power mills, were nevertheless leaks that weakened the entire structure.[24]

Rice cultivation and timber cutting proved to be a middle stage in the development of a dry lower Mississippi Valley. To a point rice did not need levees, because it could withstand and even benefit from a certain amount of inundation, and to a point water facilitated timber removal. However, successful harvests of wetland rice from land cleared of timber invited farmers to manipulate the movement of water over the land, if only to achieve more bountiful harvests of rice and to make more timber accessible, and to power mills for finishing both. They did not risk much, for if their manipulations failed, rice was likely to survive anyway, and there was plenty of timber and there were animals to turn mills. In time, successful water control suggested the possibility of drying the land completely and planting it with dry land crops, such as indigo and sugar. At this point levees ceased to be mechanisms for harnessing the natural flooding power of the river and became barriers against the river. Rather than manipulate the natural flow of water over the land, land owners kept water off the land. Thus did rice encourage the transformation of wet land into dry land. Once in place, levees and drainage systems made the cultivation of indigo and sugar—dry land crops—easier and natural.[25]

Colonial authorities encouraged the cultivation of indigo for the valuable dye extracted from its leaves. Native to Asia, the plant grows anywhere
there is loamy soil and warm air, both of which the lower valley had in
abundance. But indigo fields had to be well-drained, which was impossible to guarantee in a floodplain. Even with the river blocked from the
land by levees, water from summer rains could stand in pools upon fields
for days. Damp air impeded the process by which the dye was extracted.
Insects could be a problem. Caterpillars fed on the plant's leaves, and flies,
drawn in swarms to the foul smelling vats full of decomposing plants,
annoyed workers and often damaged the cakes of processed dye. Some
planters kept turkeys in their fields to keep caterpillars down. Flies had to
be manually fanned away. Despite difficulties, indigo production increased
steadily during the French era, in the region around New Orleans. During
the Spanish period, at the end of the eighteenth century, indigo cultivation
spread up the valley to Natchez and along some of the western tributaries and forks of the Mississippi River, including the Ouachita River and
Bayou Teche. Indigo became such a dependable export that British fur and
deerskin traders from upriver who could not legally ship their merchan-
dise through Spanish New Orleans (authorities could be bribed, of course,
but that entailed risks) exchanged their loads for indigo, which they could
export more easily. Louisiana indigo was of good quality, and it cut into
English markets, forcing the English to subsidize their own producers. It
also competed with indigo raised in other Spanish colonies.[26]

By 1800 indigo cultivation in Louisiana was on the wane, its demise
brought about by climate, insects, competition from producers in India,
and the emergence of sugar as a viable staple crop. Indigo's longest-lasting
legacy in the lower valley derived from its toxicity. Its leaves were processed into dye in vats of water that contained lye, a caustic substance;
the plants themselves contained rotenone, a naturally occurring poison.
Runoff from the vats polluted streams, endangering cattle and killing fish.
The problem was sufficiently serious to elicit the lower valley's first pollution regulations and restrictions. It was not clear that fish populations in
some places had recovered even by the 1850s.[27]

Joseph Dubreuil first adapted West Indian sugar cane to the cooler climate of Louisiana. By 1760, he and several Louisiana planters harvested,
milled, and exported sugar for profit. "It must suffice for me to add," wrote
commissaire ordonnateur Vincent-Gaspard-Pierre Rochemore in 1760, "that
nobody here doubts any longer the profitable success that is expected from
this new crop, which alone would be sufficient to wipe out the defects that

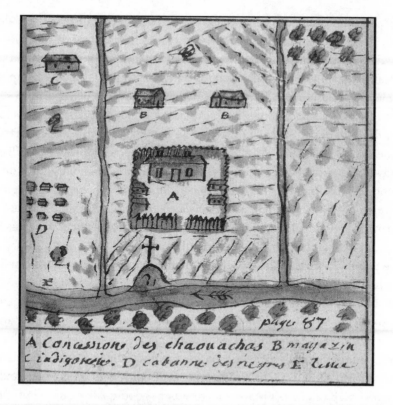

A Concassions des chaouachas B magazin
C indigoterie. D cabanne des negres E luue

FIGURE 3.6 The Chaouachas indigo plantation downriver from New Orleans. From "Forts et campements de l'armée française en Louisiane" p. 148. Jean François Benjamin Dumont de Montigny, *Poème en Vers touchant l'établissement de la province de la Loüisiane,* 1744. (Courtesy of the Bibliothèque nationale de France, Paris.)

originate from the natural poverty in Lousiana." In the 1790s, Spain loosened the restriction on sugar production. Someone introduced Tahitian sugar cane, which ripened in eight to ten months, faster than the West Indian variety, and production in Louisiana began to take off. By the start of the new century sugar had largely supplanted indigo, and according to one observer, the owners of all the sugar plantations were French.[28]

Tobacco was one staple crop not grown on the floodplain, the soil being too wet. John Law had tried to make tobacco the primary commercial staple of Louisiana, but it was more difficult to plant and cure than he anticipated. Initially, planters struggled with varieties not well suited to the soil and climate. Attempts to cultivate it in the floodplain failed. Through trial and error, landowners discovered a seed capable of thriving on the bluffs between Baton Rouge and Natchez, and thereafter production steadily increased, becoming by mid-eighteenth century Louisiana's most valuable export crop. Spain profited from France's success when it granted to Louisiana the exclusive right to sell tobacco to Mexico. Overnight, Natchez became the largest tobacco-producing region west of the Appalachian Mountains. Within a decade, however, the district's tobacco planters were feeling stiff competition from Kentucky growers and turned their energy to raising cotton.[29]

Only a few French planters, Dubreuil foremost among them, experimented with cotton. Crops were small at first. Dubreuil's gin had a capacity to clean a mere five pounds per day. But by the end of the eighteenth century, overseas demand caused cotton prices to soar, and it quickly became the dominant staple crop from Pointe Coupée north to the mouth of the Yazoo River, and west across the floodplain to the Ouachita River.[30]

Experiments with other crops once deemed eminently suitable for the lower valley went the way of wheat, which itself was tried again from time to time. In the 1790s a few farmers raised wheat in the Ouachita Valley not far from Poverty Point. In the 1720s, efforts at raising mulberry trees and silk cultures were begun and quickly abandoned. Dubreuil processed candle wax from myrtle berries, but after several years gave up. It was too much work for too little return at a time when he and others had begun to have some success with indigo.[31]

From the indigo plantations of the lower delta wetlands to the tobacco farms of the higher and drier lands at Natchez to the cotton farms of the moderately wet lands in between, rice supported them all. "Great quantities of rice grow in the swamps belonging to almost every habitation in Lower Louisiana," observed George-Henri-Victor Collot in 1796. François Marie Perrin du Lac found rice everywhere there were wetlands, from the vicinity of New Orleans in the Mississippi River delta to more than one hundred miles north, up the Ouachita River, and as far to the west as Natchitoches, up the Red River. Though small amounts of rice were exported, and an unknown quantity must have been used to replenish the stores of outbound ships, rice grown in the lower valley was largely consumed in the lower valley. However, rice fed laborers who grew indigo, sugar, and cotton for export. Rice reduced the risk of developing alluvial land, permitting landowners to secure a source of food before they invested in production for the export market, which was always risky.[32]

The transformation of cypress swamps, savannahs, natural levees, and canebrakes into rice fields and an ever-expanding network of levees and ditches turned Iberville's impenetrable countryside into a fertile and productive colony. Indeed, the environment that had once given the French pause became the flower of Louisiana. "There will not be any grain this year," wrote Governor Périer in 1730, "except in the lower part of the colony, since the drought has burnt everything in the upper lands. It was only by irrigating from the river that we have saved the greater part of the rice, which proves that the lower part of the colony will always be more fertile than the upper part, since the fields are easy to drain because of their natural slope; so whether it rains or does not rain, we shall always be assured of the crop when the fields are prepared for bringing the water from the river to them." The fluctuating mix of wet and dry, river and land, made for the rich environment that supported the Plaquemine culture and so many others indigenous to the lower Mississippi Valley. In the rice fields of the concessions, water and land continued to mix, but in ways the French tried to control. The French had become masters of the environment, or so they liked to think. But what they had done was to raise the stakes in their contest with nature. The year after Périer expressed his satisfaction with the landscape the French had constructed, severe floods broke through the low wall of levees, submerging more than half the farm land. "If this high water does not withdraw very soon," wrote Bienville in the spring of 1734, "we run the risk of having a shortage of provisions. This would be the third bad year that we should have experienced." He continued, "This country is subject to such great vicissitude that one can almost not count on the crops at all. Now there is too much drought, now too much rain." The French conceived of land and water as separate entities. Water was like a fertilizer, which if applied to dry land in proper proportions, made the land fecund. They did not conceive of wet land, a substance that fluctuated between wet and dry but which was always both. The same "great vicissitude" that powered their mills, or made possible the flooding of rice fields, frustrated them when they sought to keep land and water separate for the most part, allowing them to mingle only on occasion and under controlled circumstances.[33]

If the levees and the fields behind them gave the French a sense of control over the wet environment, they also left them more vulnerable when water returned to the land, as it always did. Severe floods occurred in 1734, 1735, and 1737, when crevasses, as the French called breaks in the levee, first became a problem. They occurred with regularity thereafter. In the spring of 1779, Robin de Logny managed at least to maintain a sense of humor in the face of a broken levee at the front of his farm. "I myself have 60 arpents of grain fields under water, in addition to a portion of my indigo fields. I can grab ducks from my window and fish in my back yard." In 1795 the river spilled onto sixty miles of leveed floodplain. In 1802 severe flooding convinced authorities in Louisiana that the levees needed to be heightened, and so they were, but the river continued to rise, reaching a new high in 1813. Many new highs followed.[34]

A tremendous investment in remaking the landscape by separating land and water had been made by individuals such as Dubreuil and Logny and by several colonial regimes. There was no going back. Having initially sought ways to, as Iberville put it, penetrate an impenetrable environment by adapting to it, the French slowly adapted the environment to them. By cultivating rice, the French colonizers of Louisiana initially made the mixing of water and land—wetland—their servant. In time, they separated water and land, putting water on one side of the levee line and dry land on the other. In the lowest and wettest part of the lower Mississippi Valley, in the Mississippi River delta, the French built levees that put the river and its valley into an unstable relationship. Upon this they hoped to build a stable society.

4

The Rise of New Orleans and the Fall of Natchez

WHEN THE COMPANY of the Indies ordered the establishment of a port town as near to the mouth of the Mississippi River as feasible, some advised against the idea, fearing the delta was too wet for a town. Bienville pressed ahead anyway. He selected a stretch of ground upon a natural levee at a sharp bend in the river, in a partial clearing where a Quinipissa village once stood. No place was ideal, and this location was prone to flooding, although perhaps not so much as most places. The nearest truly dry land was more than a hundred miles north, at Manchac. Bienville compromised, trading dry land for ocean proximity.[1]

In the spring of 1718, work on the town named in honor of the French Regent, Phillipe II, Duke of Orléans, officially began with a ceremonial first cutting of the cane by Bienville. He then stepped aside while thirty convict laborers went to work. The cane that had reclaimed the native village site was easier to clear than the cypress forest that surrounded it. Progress was slow. In 1723, five years after clearing began, Pierre Mousel received an uncleared lot near the planned intersection of Bourbon and Toulouse Streets. Mousel, a company carpenter, received the lot for his services, on the condition that he clear his land and the street in front of all trees and stumps, and erect a fence, within three months. More than cane and forest, water inhibited the construction of New Orleans. When, in 1719, a flood brought work to a standstill, landowners at Manchac and Natchez urged that the site be abandoned. Bienville responded by ordering "a great many slaves" to dig drainage ditches and build a levee to keep New Orleans dry. In 1722, a severe hurricane leveled two thirds of the town. For the most part, the ruined buildings were rickety affairs arranged haphazardly and not on the symmetrical grid then being surveyed, and so they would have been torn down in any case. Whipped up by the hurricane, the Mississippi River overcame the levee. Work on a better one began later that year. Undaunted by high winds and water, Bienville confidently declared New Orleans the capital of Louisiana and congratulated himself for not giving in to pressure to locate the town elsewhere. "It appears to me," he wrote, "that a better decision could not have been made in view of the good quality of the soil along the river suitable for producing all sorts of products." The colonial council agreed, "New Orleans is the place," the center of trade for all Louisiana. In 1724, about 380 people lived in New Orleans. That spring, a flood "greater than in preceding years" inundated the town with water that lingered until the end of June.[2]

At almost at the same time the first cane was cut, French concessionaires commenced their first experiments at tobacco planting 300 miles up Big Muddy, near Fort Rosalie on Natchez Indian land. The land, which was fertile and drained easily, proved to be well suited to tobacco. Flooding was not a problem at Natchez. But a profitable tobacco business required a port from which the harvest could be shipped overseas. The port of New Orleans encouraged tobacco planting at Natchez. The creation of dry land in the delta brought the dry but distant land at Natchez within reach of the gulf coast and into the world market. As Governor Bienville watched the rise of his colonial capital in the midst of the delta swamp, the Great Sun of the Natchez watched the slow but steady spread of French tobacco fields upon his bluff.[3]

Throughout the French colonial era, New Orleans remained a small, damp, smelly, and often dangerous place to live. City engineers struggled to respond to increasingly higher flood levels, replacing their small, earthen levee with a structure eighteen feet thick and reinforced with timber and masonry. In addition, they raised the city. In the 1720s buildings sat one foot off the ground. In later years they were elevated several times until by the 1760s piers held them eight feet off the ground.[4]

Even when the levee succeeded at keeping Big Muddy out of New Orleans, it remained a wet place. What the levee actually did was to change the nature of the wet land on the side of the levee that was ostensibly, though rarely in fact, dry. Water from rain ran off roofs into streets and toward low-lying areas back of town, where it pooled. Into these stagnant ponds trickled the contents of chamber pots carelessly dumped into streets, manure deposited by the horses, cattle, and pigs that wandered about the town, the filth from the rabbits, chickens, and doves kept in hutches in nearly every yard, and the rotting remains of dead animals and people. It is common for communities prone to flooding to bury their dead on hilltops. In New Orleans, dry land was reserved for the living. The dead, buried in low-lying areas toward the back of town, ascended to the earth's surface whenever the water rose. While water moved quickly past New Orleans on the river side of the levee, on the other side, water lay quite still. Buildings displaced surface water into smaller, deeper pools that were slow to evaporate and became breeding ground for deadly pathogens, such as malaria, dysentery, cholera, and yellow fever. In building a dry colonial capital amid the wetlands of the Mississippi River delta, Bienville unwittingly constructed a disease environment. All in all, building a dry city in such a wet place was downright unnatural and begged for trouble.[5]

A 1726 watercolor by Jean-Pierre Lassus presents a view of New Orleans from the opposing riverbank. A village consisting of a church on a central square near the river and surrounded by numerous small cabins stands in the midst of a cypress forest that stretches across the paper and recedes to the vanishing point. The land is flat. In the foreground, on the West Bank, men cut and burn timber while one man keeps an alligator at bay. Five rowboats head up and down the river. Uprooted trees drift with the current, whose direction of movement is indicated by arrows. Across the river, people gather in the square and along the river's edge. On the left at the upriver end of New Orleans a windmill turns. But for the three schooners moored in front of the village, all is motion: birds, boats, water, wind, people. The river carries millions of tons of water and dirt in one direction, building the delta and the natural levee upon which the forest stands. Men and machines work against the river, rowing into the current, pumping water uphill, cutting down the forest, and erecting buildings that impede the flow of water downhill over the land. The painting does not depict the work of people drying the land up and down river, nor does it reveal the ways in which water and dirt mingled, despite human efforts to separate them: the erosion of soil from the newly cleared banks, the sediment in the water, the ponds in the streets that fostered deadly pathogens. The wet environment was no static backdrop to human activity. It was nature's work and the work of people, much of it against moving water, that produced the historical moment Lassus's painting captures.

Construction and urban growth offered opportunities for people such as Pierre Mousel, a carpenter and early resident of New Orleans. In turn, town dwellers such as Mousel offered opportunities for farmers. Rice growers along Bayou St. Vohn and up the Mississippi River supplied the growing New Orleans market with rice, as well as fresh milk, poultry, sweet

(a)

(b)

FIGURE 4.1 (a) & (b) This painting of early New Orleans by Jean-Pierre Lassus is a picture of motion and labor. The Mississippi River moves from left to right, men row in the opposite direction. In the foreground, men cut trees. Across the river (see the close-up image) people work to construct the new town. From "Veüe et Perspective de la Nouvelle Orléans, 1726," by Jean-Pierre Lassus. (FR.ANOM. Aix-en-Provence. 4 DFC 71A.)

potatoes, beans, peas, peaches, leeks, pumpkins, melons, onions, and figs. Small Native American nations, including the Acolapissa, Chitimacha, and Ouma, supplied the townsfolk with corn, game, and most of all, fish. But for native peoples, wrote Bénard de La Harpe, New Orleans would have had "neither a flesh nor a fish market." While the French dried the wetlands, native peoples brought the wetland environment back in the form of game and fish.[6]

Bienville considered other, drier locations for the colonial capital. Mobile was too close to English and Spanish settlements in Florida and Carolina. Biloxi offered a good harbor surrounded by fertile land at a safer distance from France's imperial rivals, but it was too remote from the Mississippi River. Serious consideration was given to Manchac and Natchez, but they lacked easy access to the coast. Sand bars at the mouth of the Mississippi prevented all but the smallest of ocean vessels from entering and exiting the river. Most people moving between Biloxi and the river took the Bayou St. John canoe route, which included a portage that substantially raised shipping costs. The price of transporting a single barrel of grain or tobacco between Natchez and Biloxi was 60 livres. Bienville decided to build his city on the river where it intersected with the Bayou St. John canoe route, which would provide primary access to the coast until his engineers made the river more accessible at its mouth. Making the river wetter at its mouth was essential to the long-term success of New Orleans as a dry city.[7]

The rise of New Orleans reconfigured the relationship between the wetland environment, colonization, and administrative bureaucracy in Louisiana. The construction of an earthen rise between city and river—a levee—appeared to raise New Orleans up and out of the delta wetlands. In actuality, the city was very near sea level, and often many feet below river level. In addition, the dry land below the new buildings began to sink, albeit very slowly—nearly two centuries passed before subsidence become a serious problem—as it dried, contracted, and compacted. Nevertheless, most of the time New Orleans's residents thought of their city as a dry place.

The establishment of New Orleans as the administrative and economic center of French Louisiana accelerated change in the surrounding countryside by facilitating trade with Europe and the West Indies in slaves, rice, beef, timber, later indigo, and eventually sugar. New Orleans also became a market in its own right. The moment Bienville decided to locate the colonial capital at New Orleans, the chief engineer of the colony contracted with several landowners in the lower valley to supply planks, boards, and beams—on one occasion he ordered 10,000 cypress boards eight feet long—to construct new buildings and erect fortifications. Meanwhile, the administrative council requisitioned 2,000 cypress piles eighteen feet long for La Balise, the fort built in the marshes at the mouth of the eastern pass. The city also needed meat and dairy products, which came from cattle that grazed on the levees along the river outside of town. Colonial officials understood that the progress of New Orleans depended on progress in the countryside. In 1728, when the directors of the Company of the Indies expressed concern that enslaved plantation laborers might be drafted to work on the town levee, Governor Périer assured them that completion of public works at New Orleans would not be allowed to interfere with drainage and levee projects under way on the plantations. Administrators also regulated grazing to minimize damage to levees. Landowners cleared timber from swamps to make way for rice fields protected by levees that shielded fields and offered pasture for livestock. They sent timber, beef, and rice to New Orleans to house and feed the people who collected, counted, stored, and shipped indigo, tobacco, sugar, and cotton raised in the same surrounding countryside. Environmental change in the surrounding wetlands facilitated and even pushed the development of New Orleans to become a point of intersection with a world market that in turn pulled commodities from the wetlands.[8]

By winning some control over the land, the French put themselves in a better position to win some control over the Indians. New Orleans gave the colony a vital administrative center from which to plan, protect, populate, and supply its outposts at Biloxi, Natchez, Natchitoches, and elsewhere. The presence of New Orleans reoriented the material and administrative flow of Louisiana, adding a north-south orientation to its existing east-west axis, which enhanced the strategic importance of Natchez, the mouth of the Arkansas River, and the Illinois country. Louisiana's administrators began to make the case that Illinois needed to be brought into the purview of New Orleans, rather than of Montreal. Illinois, they argued, could provide wheat for Louisiana. It helped Louisiana's case for Illinois that as beaver were trapped out, Montreal merchants lost interest in the region. They were never very interested in deerskins, which they let go to merchants in Mobile, Biloxi, and New Orleans. In 1719, Louisiana's governors, not Canada's, established Fort de Chartres on the Mississippi River just below the mouth of the Missouri River. Natchitoches in the west remained important to the colony as a whole, developing into a supplier of food, beef especially, and raw resources for New Orleans. In the 1720s, the cattle herds of Opelousas and Natchitoches grew along with the population of the new capital, soon surpassing the herds in the vicinity of New Orleans. As wheat, meat, and vegetables flowed into New Orleans, men, manufactures, and directives went out.[9]

The rise of New Orleans changed relations between French officials and native peoples. From the dry city, colonial administrators who designed and oversaw its construction, projected outward over that environment and colony an emerging French national identity bolstered by Enlightenment notions of citizenship. The French state sought to transform a foreign land into a French land and the native Mississippi Valley peoples into foreigners on French soil. The assistance of native nations was no longer so essential to France, and in some cases their presence, like water on the land, became an obstruction in need of removal. Colonial administrators planned and staged war first against the Natchez, then against the Chickasaw.[10]

Through the 1720s, the decade following the establishment of rice agriculture and New Orleans, France's relations with lower valley native populations began a new chapter. Only after the lower river had been turned into rice and indigo plantations—an economy and natural environment that did not include native societies—did the company start to pressure Natchez villagers for their land. Only after the French had learned how to provide for and protect themselves on the river independently of the Natchez could they think about destroying such a powerful nation.

The Natchez uprising began with an argument over land held by the Natchez but coveted by French tobacco planters. The Company of the Indies did not merely decide one day to plant tobacco at Natchez. Environmental change made it possible to respond to overseas demand. Just as rice underwrote early experiments at indigo planting, rice underwrote development at Natchez by feeding those who administered plantations, shipped tobacco, provided refuge for the few who escaped the revolt, and organized and fought in the counterattack. Through New Orleans and its surrounding rice fields, the history of a global commodities trade merged with the histories of the river and of the people who lived along it.[11]

Relations between individual French and Natchez had always been volatile, especially after 1716 when the French constructed Fort Rosalie on the Natchez bluff. French traders, soldiers, and sometimes priests could easily irritate Natchez villagers. Whenever violence flared, however, authorities on both sides immediately acted to douse the flames. In 1716, several

Natchez killed five French they found particularly offensive. Louisiana Governor Bienville responded by executing three Natchez, including a chief, and negotiating for the head of another. In 1725, several Natchez killed Sieur Guenot and a slave at the St. Catherine Concession on the bluff. Bienville again bargained for the heads of the perpetrators, which he received for five bottles of brandy. The Natchez vicinity during these years was what historian Richard White has defined as a middle ground, a place culturally, economically, politically, and environmentally between Europeans and Native Americans. Both sides needed to maintain peace, in the interest of mutual trade and military alliance. The French wanted meat, fish, and corn from the Natchez, who in turn wanted powder, shot, and brandy from the French. As the exchange of the five bottles of brandy indicates, conflict was often quickly transformed into trade, and anger and hatred sublimated into commodities and profit, or else were projected toward other people, such as Chickasaws and their British allies.[12]

Rice began the transformation of French Louisiana from a colony based on trade with native peoples, as in Canada, into a colony based on agriculture, as in the French West Indies, a transformation that destroyed the middle ground. In 1719, the Company of the Indies granted two large tobacco concessions at Natchez. At first, the greater presence of French planters and bound field laborers was a boon to the Natchez, who hunted for them, and even helped them clear land in return for trade goods, but that presence—in plantations, cattle, technology, diseases, people—kept expanding. In 1725, the Company of the Indies opened a trading post at Natchez to receive the tobacco from the expanding plantations, signaling a shift in trade priorities away from the Indians and toward French planters. For the Natchez, more French meant more frequent contact with European disease, including smallpox. Between 1715 and 1721, the Natchez military force shrank from 4,000 to 2,000 warriors, although they still outnumbered nearby French more than ten to one. Depopulation made the Natchez people less valuable to their French allies on the middle ground, just as tobacco concessions made the Natchez land more valuable to the French. The Natchez had begun to increase their dependence on agriculture sometime before the arrival of the French, as numbers of deer and other animals diminished from over-hunting for the European fur and skin trade, and they would have felt French pressure on their farmland even more acutely. Over the course of the 1720s, French concessions encroached on more Natchez territory, including former mound sites, which were sacred lands.[13]

In the autumn of 1729, as the Natchez celebrated a corn feast, Captain Chépart of the French garrison abruptly interrupted festivities to read an order from the governor: the Natchez were to abandon one of their villages and yield the land to the French. In his account, Dumont de Montigny called the governor *le grand Chef des François qui étoit à la Nouvelle Orléans*, asserting his supremacy and that of his seat of power, namely, New Orleans. Chépart gave the Natchez two months to pack up and move, sufficient time he thought for them to find a suitable new location and to harvest their corn. In addition, the captain demanded a share of the harvest, plus chickens, several pots of bear oil, and furs. If the Natchez refused him, Chépart promised to send the chief to New Orleans with his feet and hands bound. The Natchez acquiesced, although several leaders planned to retaliate.

On the morning of November 28, over 25,000 pounds of tobacco sat in Natchez warehouses awaiting shipment to New Orleans. Several Natchez hunters asked to borrow French guns for hunting that day. They promised to pay with corn and meat. The French agreed and foolishly disarmed themselves, as though it were an earlier era and French and Natchez traded guns for game on the middle ground. By the end of the day the Natchez had killed well over 200 people, mostly French, including Chépart, and captured even more, mostly Africans. That day and over the next weeks, the tobacco, buildings, equipment, and livestock were destroyed, for a loss to the company of over 130,000 livres. Panic spread down the Mississippi River to New Orleans, where officials debated the likelihood of a general revolt of native peoples. Suddenly, all Indian nations began to look like potential enemies to the French. If such a pan-Indian uprising were to occur, combining the largest nations—Natchez, Chickasaw, and Choctaw—the French would be vanquished. But when the French struck back at the Natchez the next year the Chickasaw offered only minor assistance to retreating Natchez, while the Choctaw, after some negotiation, fought with the French. Smaller nations tried to stay out of the way, and if they could not, they supported whichever power held sway over them. The Yazoo joined with the Natchez, while the Tunica assisted the French.[14]

No sooner had they obliterated the Natchez villages and carried their prisoners to New Orleans, from where they shipped them to Saint-Domingue and sole them into slavery, than the French found themselves at war with the Chickasaws and also with the Fox in Illinois. Between 1733 and 1743, lower valley farmers and herders sent rice, cattle, and slaves with soldiers in campaigns against both nations. Meanwhile, they stepped up timber and indigo exports. Army officers took slaves off plantations and put them to work paddling pirogues, hauling artillery, building bridges, and performing various other tasks of menial labor, leaving landowners temporarily shorthanded. When slaves died in battle or more commonly suffered the cruelties of abusive French soldiers, slave owners despaired for the survival of their farms and beseeched authorities to pay compensation. They were told to produce still more rice and indigo and to clear more timber. Fox and Chickasaw warriors attacked convoys of canoes and pirogues plying the river between Illinois and New Orleans, putting additional pressure on farmers in both regions to produce.[15]

The French undertook two major campaigns against the Chickasaws, the first in the spring of 1736, the second in the winter and spring of 1740. The first set out from Mobile but failed. The second achieved partial

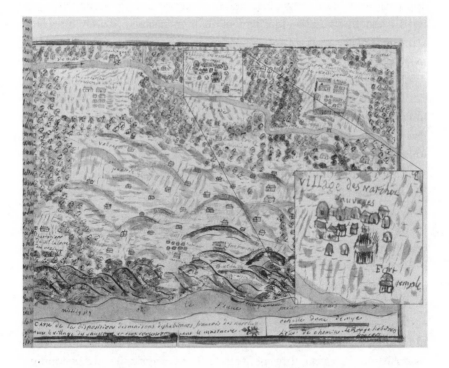

FIGURE 4.2 The Natchez bluffs are crowded with French buildings, in this illustration by Jean-François Benjamin Dumont de Montigny, who lived at Natchez until weeks before the revolt. The inset reveals what appear to be French structures in the midst of the primary Natchez village. From "Carte de la disposition des maisons des habitants français, des Natchez," Jean-François Benjamin Dumont de Montigny, *Poême en Vers touchant l'établissement de la province de la Loüisiane.* 1744. (Courtesy of the Bibliothèque Nationale de France, Paris)

victory, less in the field than in the impression it gave the British. The French assembled in New Orleans a European-style army of over a thousand soldiers and allied warriors, complete with artillery, horses, cattle, and hundreds of retainers. The plan of attack was utterly impractical. Soldiers rowed up Big Muddy to a base at the mouth of the St. Francis River, from where they launched their assault over roads partially constructed to convey artillery. Progress was painfully slow. Artillery got bogged down in mud. There was no hope of surprising the enemy. Indeed, the Chickasaws watched, prepared, and discussed options. When an exhausted French army finally arrived, the Chickasaws sued for a favorable peace, ending the conflict before it ever really began, walking away unscathed and in good shape to fight another day. The French turned around and slogged their way back to the river. Native allies were dumbfounded by the French approach to warfare. However, they mistakenly thought vanquishing the enemy was the ultimate objective. As the French saw it, mobilizing a large army with heavy artillery, as though the land were dry and solid, amounted to victory of sorts. It demonstrated that wet native ground had become dry French ground. The French may not have won the war, but they had nevertheless won the show. The British were greatly alarmed, and for the next several years worked to keep peace. They harbored the same belief that fighting Indian-style was a sign of weakness, whereas undertaking warfare European style was a sign of strength.[16]

With their rivals sufficiently intimidated, Governor Bienville and his successor restarted the deerskin trade. In 1743, the year Bienville left Louisiana, the colony sent 100,000 skins to France. The deerskin trade, however, revealed to French and Indians alike the shortage and inferior quality of French manufactured goods, compared to British goods, which opened a wedge for British interference once again. British meddling usually brought on war and a temporary recession in the skin trade, during which the deer population recovered.[17]

From the Natchez uprising in 1729 to the end of the Seven Years' War in 1763, hardly a year passed in peace. Shipments of skins and furs were inconsistent. However, through it all, the pace of agricultural development and environmental transformation in the lower valley held steady. The progress of war and agriculture were connected. The French saw both as necessary steps toward their permanent presence in Louisiana.

During these troubled times France reassessed its investment in Louisiana and all of Canada. On one hand, France dared not let go of its North American empire, for if they did the British would surely grab it all.

On the other hand, the colonies were bleeding the King's coffers dry. In 1748, Roland-Michel Barrin, comte de la Galissonière, Governor General of Canada, summed up matters: "We must not flatter ourselves that our Continental Colonies; that is to say this [Canada] and Louisiana, can ever compete in wealth with the adjoining English Colonies, nor even carry on any lucrative trade; for, except peltry, the amount of which is limited, and whose profits are and will be always diminishing, we shall scarcely ever have it in our power to furnish any but similar commodities to those of Europe." Only Louisiana held some promise, Galissonière believed, with its warm climate favorable to the cultivation of plants not grown in Europe, including indigo, tobacco, and sugar. Furthermore, its coastal location facilitated trade. However, the legacy of the fur and skin trade was that Louisiana had few settlers. Invest more in agriculture and husbandry, Galissonière recommended, and Louisiana's population would swell with immigrants, if not from France, then from Quebec. A more populated Louisiana would keep the British at bay. An expanding agricultural economy would replace the deerskin and fur trade, which in turn would render unnecessary any alliances with native nations. No longer would officials anxiously await the next shipload of manufactures from France—blankets, guns, tools, liquor—the items native peoples demanded for their loyalty, though they always complained about their quality and quantity. Galissonière added that Illinois might become a supplier of food for Louisiana's agricultural export economy. One way or another, however, population and agriculture had to grow. Until that happened, the English, with their superior manufactures, lured Choctaw and other hunters away from the French, who could only respond with force and by discounting their own inferior trade items at substantial cost to the Crown. "But what merits most our attention," concluded the Ministry of Marine, "is the design of the English to push their settlements," their people and their trade "into the interior of the country so as to be able to interrupt the communication between the two Colonies of Canada and Louisiana."[18]

In the 1740s, Louisiana stepped up exports of tar, pitch, boards, furs, skins, sassafras, tobacco, indigo, and rice to defray the costs of imports. In October 1745, a British ship captured a French vessel loaded with 14,090 pounds of indigo which, at 3 livres per pound, amounted to one third the cost of the first expedition against the Chickasaw. The last eighteenth-century French governor of Louisiana wrote, "The Progress of agriculture shows remarkable results in the Mississippi Valley, when, in territories under English control, the harvest is disappointing." The year was 1757, in the midst of the Seven Years' War, and the Royal Navy had brought French shipping to a standstill. "Unfortunately, the French take no advantage from this success, no more being able to export their production." Not until 1760, when the war in North America had ended, did trade resume. Furs, skins, but more significantly, tobacco, indigo, and sugar led the way out of the lower Mississippi Valley through the port of New Orleans.[19]

In 1763, at the conclusion of the Seven Years' War, which was fought on several continents but not in Louisiana, the English nevertheless took the colony along with all other French claims in North America. Soon after, an Englishman named Gordon traveled down the Mississippi River to see what his nation had acquired, and there he found an empty land. "There are no Nations of Indians below the Illinois on the Mississippi, 'till You come to the Arkansas, they live up the Branches of the Arkansas River near the French Post, which is Half way to New Orleans. They consist of 150 Men. The Next Nation of Indians, is the Tonicas below the Natchez [i.e., the former site of the Natchez villages], a small Nation of about 30 men; Then the Oumas and Alibamons of about 150 both; The last has settled here lately, having withdrawn from the River of that Name, when we [the British] took Possession of West Florida [from the Spanish]." Of course, Gordon did not see everyone he passed by. Historian Daniel Usner estimates there were approximately 3,000 native people living along the Mississippi River at the end of the French colonial era. However, approximately 29,000 native people, mostly Choctaws, Chickasaws, and Upper Creeks, lived in Louisiana. They kept their villages well away from the river, in the uplands or up major tributaries, such as the Red River, but often hunted in the remaining wetlands along it. Taking the place of native people along Big Muddy were European farmers and African enslaved laborers, perhaps 10,000 of them, all the way up to Natchez. Soon they would be at the mouth of the Yazoo River near present-day Vicksburg, and competing with Chickasaw hunters for territory in the vicinity of present-day Memphis.[20]

The Natchez uprising is usually depicted as a high water mark of French colonization in Louisiana, after which the French increasingly turned their attention and resources to places elsewhere in their empire, until the inevitable transfer of the colony to Great Britain. In 1733, the Company of the Indies handed Louisiana back to the king, who appointed Bienville governor for a fourth time but wished to devote no more attention to the failed colony. In 1730, outgoing governor Périer wrote what might have been an epitaph for the period: "The least little [Indian] nation thinks itself our protector, whereas if we had forces to sustain ourselves by our own efforts the greatest nations would respect us," a wry comment on France's dependence on the indigenous peoples who altogether so vastly outnumbered them. But the French did have the force to sustain themselves, as the Natchez War demonstrated. During the levee war between Joseph Villars Dubreuil and the Chauvin brothers at Tchoupitoulas, six years earlier, the Chauvins wrote of their planting efforts, echoing Iberville, "Out of an impenetrable forest, by force of labor they made a fine and fertile plain." They might have been referring to the entire New Orleans area.[21]

France lost Louisiana just as it was about to realize much of Iberville's vision. The French had cleared what Iberville had first described over six decades earlier as "impenetrable" cane and forest. They had drained swamps, erected levees to control the river, raised crops foreign to the lower valley environment, and built New Orleans, from which they launched a successful war against the lower valley's most powerful nation, the same nation whose ancestors had chased the Spanish from the valley nearly two centuries before. They adapted themselves to the floodplain environment, and then began to change it in ways that would alter natural and human history along Big Muddy. While much of the countryside remained as Iberville had found it, by 1763 the French had shown their successors how to dry the lower valley's vast wet land.

The French were not the only people capable of adaptation. If the wetland environment had been foreign and unfamiliar to the French, the dry environment of fields and cattle pasture they created was equally foreign to many native residents of the Mississippi Valley. In the 1720s, the Natchez regularly raided French cattle herds. In 1732, a party of Chickasaw raided the farms at Pointe Coupée, killing cows and calves. In 1748, several Choctaw attacked the German settlement above New Orleans, killing people and livestock. In the 1760s, Choctaw warriors struck again, slaughtering cattle grazing near Biloxi. Sometimes they butchered cattle on the spot and made off with fresh meat. On occasion they targeted crops in fields. Traditions of hunting and war-making thus persisted in the new environment. Native peoples also took up herding, incorporating livestock into their village economies.[22]

Similarly, the laborers who bore most of the physical burden of environmental transformation also adapted, by finding in the new environment ways of resisting its designers. The abundance of food resources in the wetlands hindered the efforts of landowners to hold laborers on their concessions and to keep them working on indigo or other commercial crops. On the edges of the concessions near New Orleans, slaves, native peoples, free blacks, and lower class whites hunted and gathered deer, wildcats, raccoons, opossums, rabbits, ducks, starlings, roots, and berries to feed themselves and their owners, as well as to sell at the market in town. Runaway servants and slaves hid in the woods and swamps but returned to plantations to steal what they could find and carry back to their hideouts, including rice, chickens, and, most worrisome for authorities, cattle. In the 1720s there were scattered reports of cattle killing by runaways who claimed in their defense that they were underfed. One had had his finger broken by an abusive owner and killed a cow in retribution. Caught stealing meat from plantation stores, the slave La Fleur ran away to escape punishment and to find something to eat, as he later explained. In February 1748, a soldier in the vicinity of the German Coast, a settlement of small farms upriver from New Orleans, stumbled upon six runaway Africans and one Native American. They were all armed and living well off of deer and ducks, and also chickens and sheep stolen from nearby farms. They were an audacious bunch, daring to milk cows as they grazed in open areas in the woods. Authorities caught several of the runaways in the woods where they were smoke-curing stolen beef.[23]

Water also adapted to the changes imposed by the French in ways the French did not always anticipate or appreciate. Flooding was a continuing problem, despite increasingly higher levees and more sophisticated drainage systems. Water pooled in areas that were supposed to be dry, providing breeding grounds for disease. The French saw such problems as arising externally rather than from their own actions. That was how they viewed the unwanted behavior of people, too. Choctaw attacked, enslaved Africans ran off, because it was their nature, not because they were responding to environmental change introduced by the French.

The changes in the lower valley over the course of the eighteenth century gave the French a new and positive perspective on the wetlands. Iberville had looked upon them with no small amount of trepidation, and with good reason. He had depended on native guides to find his way. After nearly seven decades, land and water had proven not to have been so impenetrable after all. However, possession and control of the lower valley and its peoples had only partially been achieved. Some of their successes also set the French up for failure, as when levees raised water levels, enemies attacked farms, and farm laborers ran into the still vast expanse of wetlands. Nevertheless, it seemed to the French that the place desperately needed them. Their alterations of the land left them poised, at long last, to overcome what *Ordonnateur* Rochemore had called "the natural poverty in Louisiana." The natural poverty? This was not a rich land that the French were harvesting, but a poor land that they were improving. The year 1730 proved a high water mark. From that point, the land became steadily drier. A wet and forested land of fish and game that had been home to the Plaquemine people and all their ancestors and descendants, including the Natchez, was fading before a dried and cleared land of fields and livestock that would be home to French, British, Spanish, West Africans, and their American descendants.[24]

The French were in the valley to stay, and no decision made in Paris in 1730, or 1763, or, for that matter, 1803, the year the United States purchased Louisiana, was going to change that. Despite the French government's loss of interest in Louisiana following the Natchez Revolt, French settlers continued the work of making the land theirs.

At the moment that France officially abandoned North America entirely, landowners along the lower Mississippi River produced their first successful and profitable crops of sugar. If agriculture is a marker of imperial power and success, then the French have not received their due. They built the apparatus for the transformation of the wet lower Mississippi Valley into dry farms and fields, but they had barely done so when they were forced to surrender Louisiana to Great Britain and Spain. Whether or not dry land agriculture in the wetlands of the lower Mississippi Valley was an environmental success remained an open question.

5

Consolidation, Transformation, Conservation

ON A SPRING day in 1773, Rufus Putnam climbed a tree. From his perch high above the cliffs where the city of Vicksburg now sits he surveyed the valley for miles around. The land rose "high north eastward, and S.S. eastward, bearing off from the river, but somewhat uneven, full of cane and rich soil, even on the very highest ridges, just below the cliffs, the bank is low, by which means the water on the *Mississippi* flows back and runs between the bank and high land which range near north and S.S.E. to the *Loosa-chitta*, forming much low land, cypress swamp, and dead ponds, without one brook, or running stream." To the southeast, along the Loosa Chitta, or Big Black River, lay high but broken lands, "good and full of springs of water." To the west, across Big Muddy, were the wetlands of the lower Mississippi Valley. It was now Spanish territory, and Putnam, who was from Massachusetts, had little to say about it.[1]

On another spring day seventy-some years later, Benjamin Wailes found a tree. He was locating places and collecting samples of archaeological and geological significance in the vicinity of Natchez, about seventy miles south of Vicksburg, on behalf of the newly established University of Mississippi, when he stumbled into a small stand of old growth forest. Upon and around some Indian mounds near Second Creek, as he put it, stood "the noble forest trees which have shaded them for centuries. Some of these measure more than fifteen feet in girth," that is, over four feet in diameter.

Upon the Natchez bluff, landowners and their slaves had turned forest into cotton fields. Across the river, in Louisiana, they were transforming wetland into cotton plantations. High ground or low, dry land or wet, it would all be the same. Louisiana was beyond Wailes's jurisdiction as a representative of the state of Mississippi, but no longer was it foreign territory, as it had been in Putnam's day.[2]

Men like Rufus Putnam transformed the lower Mississippi Valley from forest and swamp into fields and towns. They responded to global markets that offered high rewards for certain agricultural commodities that the valley's soil and climate seemed well suited to produce, such as tobacco, sugar, indigo, and above all, cotton. They also had their personal reasons for their undertakings. They were hardly the first to gaze at the untamed expanse of North America and project visions of great businesses and profitable ventures upon it, nor were they the last. As they pursued their ambitions, their societies encouraged them. Nevertheless, the decision to transform the valley into a vast field that they would plant and harvest, into an environment that they would control, was theirs to make. Rufus Putnam was present at the beginning of the lower Mississippi Valley's great transformation and could not have known how the process he helped initiate would play out over the next several decades. Later valley residents, such as Benjamin Wailes, saw many of the consequences of King Cotton's ascendancy, the good and the bad, but they boldly carried on what others began. A few, including some in positions of power, hesitated.

Between the time Putnam climbed his tree and the time Wailes found his, much of the lower Mississippi Valley was in the process of being transformed from wet land into dry farmland. What had begun early in the French colonial era would take another century to be completed, but the tipping point between wet and dry occurred during these years. During this time the full implications of drying the valley started to become apparent. On one hand, the valley's manifest destiny was to become the richest plantation land the world had ever seen. The only obstacle was Big Muddy, which seemed to assert itself with greater force the more people tried to contain it. On the other hand, there were clear signs of the financial, political, technical, and environmental costs of containing the Mississippi River and drying its valley. Transformation of the valley from wet to dry either would need to stop or at least proceed in a very different manner. As valley residents and their governments decided to invest more into drying the environment to make it suitable for dry crops, there emerged a tiny spark of concern for the conservation of the valley as a wet place.

Much more than seventy miles and seventy years separated the trees Putnam and Wailes found. A soldier and a self-taught surveyor, Rufus Putnam was the original proponent of a corps of engineers. He came to the lower Mississippi Valley following the Seven Years' War to scout the

territory on behalf of a group of Connecticut veterans who sought to establish a colony in former French territory along the Big Muddy. He recognized an "old field" at the Yazoo River, where "it is said the *French* formerly
had a fort and settlement." The French had been gone less than a decade,
but Putnam described a quiet, empty, timeless land. Indeed, many lowland
ponds and creeks in his estimation were dead. The Yazoo River was "a dead
streme, bad water,—with many Allegators." The bottomlands he described
as "very rich, with a very deep Soil," but "much injured by ponds, Cyprus
Swamps & overflowing of the river," which would "be very expencive to
drane." Only the occasional sound of spring waters breaking through the
high ground and trickling down hillsides interrupted the silence. Putnam
took careful note of the springs, for there he envisioned towns.[3]

Benjamin Wailes gazed upon the same land and saw layers of natural
and human histories, like the layers of silt upon the floodplain—Indian
mounds, rock formations, petrified trees, mastodon bones, fossils, old
growth forests, old plantations, cemeteries. Like Putnam, Wailes had practiced surveying as a young man, but he had more than a practical interest in the land. He had taught himself geology, paleontology, and botany;
befriended ornithologist John James Audubon; and hosted Sir Charles
Lyell when the distinguished English geologist visited Natchez. Much
of what Wailes found so fascinating had been present in the Mississippi
woods when Putnam made his visit, but Putnam had looked beyond them.
As he gathered his samples and jotted down notes, Wailes peered through
the cities and settlements, fields and farms, roads and bridges, and into
the layers of a much older natural history. As he translated the geographical record into a documentary record, he noted what had already been
done to the land. He knew that what his own civilization built on the valley
had been added to the work of other people with their own histories, and
to the work of winds, water, and soils through geological history. He knew
nothing was permanent, which was why he worked to collect, preserve,
and conserve what remained of the Mississippi Valley Rufus Putnam had
seen.[4]

In the decades following 1763, the lower Mississippi Valley changed
hands several times. At first, Britain took possession of the east side of
the river. The territory from Baton Rouge east along the north shore of
Lake Pontchartrain to Pensacola comprised the colony of British West
Florida. Spain claimed the west side of the valley, and both sides below
Manchac—the strip of land that included New Orleans—as *Luisiana*. In
1779, with Britain occupied with the American Revolutionary War, Spain

seized West Florida. The Spanish administered the territory from Natchez to the Yazoo River as a separate district with its own governor, who reported to the governor of all *Luisiana* in New Orleans. Following the signing of a 1795 treaty with Spain, the United States took possession of the east side of the river down to the thirty-first parallel. This included Natchez, but not Baton Rouge. In October of 1800, General Napoleon Bonaparte reclaimed Louisiana from Spain. *Luisiana* became *Louisiane* once again. Soon thereafter, Bonaparte entered into negotiations with representatives of President Thomas Jefferson's administration, and on December 20, 1803, after nearly a year of negotiation, the United States took possession of the colony. *Louisiane* became Louisiana. For the first time in forty years, the entire lower valley fell under the jurisdiction of a single power, and for the first time ever, under the jurisdiction of a power thoroughly committed to a North American empire.[5]

The parade of administrations may have altered the pace of environmental transformation, but not its trajectory. They all—French, English, Spanish, and American—wanted to dry the wet land of the lower Mississippi Valley. What the French began with the first rice fields the Americans completed with cotton plantations two centuries later. It matters little that Rufus Putnam was an eighteenth-century English colonial subject and Benjamin Wailes a nineteenth-century American, or that French and Spanish had come and gone between them. It mattered much more that from his perch Putnam looked across old growth forest broken by the river, oxbow lakes, and swamps and imagined how it might all be transformed, whereas Wailes looked across a more uniform landscape of cotton fields and was thrilled just to find one old tree. It also mattered that in the intervening years the valley was consolidated under the authority of a single nation-state. The Louisiana Purchase made it possible for the United States to apply far greater resources to the effort to dry the entire lower Mississippi Valley than any previous imperial power.

Environmental transformation in Putnam's time proceeded in the forests that covered much of the valley. Trees, wildlife, and the labors of people who cut and hunted subsidized agriculture, which supplanted the forest and wetlands, killed off the animals, and displaced the people. After 1763, Indian traders intensified their production of deerskins. They were no longer able to play one imperial power against another, and consequently they grew more dependent on whomever they did business with, be it Spanish or British. As Europeans and Euro-Americans grew less interested in the skin trade and more in the production of agricultural commodities they turned a seller's market into a buyer's market. Indian hunters were the sellers of fur and skins. During this time there were no wars during which large game animals could recover their numbers. The Revolutionary Wars barely touched the valley. Deer hunters roamed the Louisiana woods, from Opelousas to the Missouri River to Texas. In a tradition more often associated with the Rocky Mountain trappers of the next century, they gathered annually for a rendezvous on the St. Francis River. By the last decades of the eighteenth century European and Native American hunters were killing over 100,000 deer per year, many of them in Choctaw territory.[6]

European participants in the fur and deerskin trade redirected profits from that business into agriculture. John Joyce kept a plantation on the Sunflower River, in Chickasaw hunting ground, from which he supplied food to traders and to craftsmen who built canoes and other trade technologies. Joyce's partner, John Turnbull, started a plantation near Fort Nogales at the mouth of the Yazoo River where he also kept a post that supplied the garrison. Farmers moved up the Big Black River into Choctaw territory and traded for furs and skins while they cleared their first fields and awaited the returns on their first crops. If anything, the intensification of agriculture during the Spanish period only intensified the fur and skin trade that supplemented it, until there were few animals left to hunt, and agriculture and livestock were the only basis of the Louisiana economy. According to one observer, exports of peltries in 1796 matched the value of exports of agricultural and timber products. By 1802, the value of cotton and sugar exports was ten times that of peltries.[7]

The business of traders such as John Joyce linked a wide array of people, places, economies, and environments. Joyce arrived in the lower Mississippi Valley during the American Revolution. He fought for the British, but in 1782 left the army while in East Florida and opened a store in a St. Johns River settlement to trade in deerskins. When he hooked up with John Turnbull is unclear. Turnbull was from Charles Town, the entrepôt for the British deerskin trade that extended west from South Carolina to the Chickasaw and Fox villages, and Joyce may have known him there. By the time Joyce opened his store, Turnbull had moved west to avoid the disruption to his business caused by the Revolution. From his plantation at Baton Rouge, Turnbull conducted an extensive trade in furs and deerskins with the Chickasaws. Meanwhile, Joyce traveled. In October 1783 he and his guides set out from Mobile for Turnbull's camp at the forks of the Tallahatchie River, in Chickasaw territory, where several people were employed building boats and press-ing skins. From there Joyce took three boats loaded with skins down the Yazoo River toward New Orleans. Along the way he stopped in Natchez and sold most or all of his skins. In New Orleans he purchased supplies and headed back up river, stopping in Natchez again, on the way back to Chickasaw country. Before long, Joyce was again in Natchez, then Baton Rouge, then New Orleans. From New Orleans he sailed to Havana and Jamaica, where he and his partners had business interests in trade and plantations. Before the end of his second year on this circuit he traveled back to New Orleans, visited posts among the Choctaw, returned to the Tallahatchie River and the Chickasaw villages, Natchez, New Orleans, and finally Mobile. Throughout, Joyce traveled with a black servant, prob-ably a slave, someone he entrusted to conduct some business for him in the Cumberland settlement.[8]

Choctaw, Chickasaw, Tallapoosa, and other lower valley hunters extended the boundaries of their business, which brought them into con-flict with the Osage and Arkansas nations on the edge of the Great Plains. The Spanish Commissioner to the Choctaws and Chickasaws reported that the Indians "are in a most wretched condition" and "they are dying of hun-ger." To compensate for their dwindling supply of meat, made worse by the behavior of the Spanish, who proved to be as unreliable as the French at providing annual gifts of food in return for skins and military alliance, some Indians organized raiding parties against white settlers.

In the fall of 1792, a Tallapoosa party attacked the McFarland family on the Big Black River, in the same vicinity as Putnam's tree, killing the men and carrying off the women. The Spanish governor of Natchez reinforced his post at Fort Nogales and suggested that settlers construct blockhouses so that they might defend themselves. The 1795 transfer of the east side of the lower valley above the mouth of the Red River from Spanish to US authority left a temporary vacuum between regimes that provided native peoples with an opportunity to make further strikes. Winthrop Sargent, governor of the new Mississippi Territory, reported from Natchez to General James Wilkinson in April 1800, "Our situation at present is more than a little alarming and it is unnecessary for me to observe to you upon the present Disposition of the Savages, or that they have become much more assuming and Insolent since the evacuation [by the Spanish] of the Posts above—by one of your Officers I am very Credibly informed they have menaced to kill the Cattle of the Inhabitants at the Walnut Hills, and to burn the Buildings."

Where some native people attacked herds and burned fields, others took up herding and planting. Beginning in the 1780s, former Indian traders and especially people of mixed parentage were driving cattle into the Yazoo River region. As large game dwindled, and with it the skin trade, many native peoples simultaneously expanded and contracted their territories. They ventured farther afield in search of animals but also took up cattle herding and planting near their settlements.[9]

Domesticated livestock facilitated the advance of agriculture by enabling would-be cultivators, both native and newcomer, to live off the bounty of forest and marsh. They provided much more than meat and milk. They devoured and trampled much of the natural flora, creating openings for European grasses and weeds that eventually crowded out their American counterparts. They turned grass, nuts, roots, and cane shoots into manure for permanent fields. As stocks grew, they could be sold for cash for the purchase of tools and slaves to clear more land for planting. Animal husbandry entailed environmental change in ways few understood or cared about.[10]

In 1803, the total native and European population of Louisiana stood at about 50,000, half what it had been a century earlier. Over the eighteenth century the native population had declined dramatically, mostly from disease but also from war and malnutrition, the last a consequence of environmental and economic transformations. By century's end the population had stabilized and even began to grow, but it remained far below previous levels. Vast areas of the lower Mississippi Valley lay empty of people, into which a growing population of Europeans and Euro-Americans moved, many taking with them enslaved Africans and African Americans to build farms and plantations.[11]

Life on the farm in the lower Mississippi Valley could be uncomfortably close to nature. For example, Jacques Milhet and his family lived in the midst of a large canebrake on the shore of Lake Pontchartrain nine miles from New Orleans, in a small cabin filled with furniture homemade of cypress wood. Everyone slept under mosquito netting, the cabin walls providing a permeable boundary with the outdoors. His small herd of cattle wandered and grazed unattended. The family probably gathered and fished. Although there is no indication of cultivation at the Milhet place, there must have been a garden. What the family's two slaves did is unclear. Jacques Milhet's health was poor, in which case it was the slaves, along with the family, who gathered cypress wood, made furniture, gardened, fished, hunted, and butchered cattle.[12]

Death denied Jacques Milhet the time to put a greater distance or more solid barrier between him and the natural environment, but what he might have done was carried out on neighboring farms. Farmers cut cypress trees, milled them into planks, and sold them for the construction of solid houses in Louisiana and elsewhere. At the start of the Seven Years' War, Louisiana annually exported 180,000 livres of lumber, mostly to St. Domingue and Martinique, on top of the lumber consumed by construction within the lower valley. The Spanish continued to export lumber, cypress mostly, to Havana where it was manufactured into boxes used to ship sugar. As the sugar industry developed in Louisiana, the need for lumber increased. The streets of New Orleans were guttered with planks. During the Spanish era, the city burned twice. Each fire consumed approximately 300 buildings, and each time the town was rebuilt with wood, the first time entirely, the second time partially. After the second fire, builders made more use of lime, earth, tar, slate, tile, and oyster shells gathered from ancient midden mounds. Wooden floors remained common, however, and larger timbers offered the only material for the beams upon which houses sat. Cypress was the sole source for the many pirogues that conveyed people and produce up and down the river and through the marshlands.[13]

By 1800, dozens of saw mills turned along the Mississippi River and its tributaries, from below New Orleans to above Natchez. When Rufus Putnam and his party selected the location for their settlement, their first action was to plan the construction of a lumber mill so they could begin to finance their grand vision with the proceeds of timber sales in New Orleans. Turning trees into barrel staves provided William Dunbar with the steady income that helped him to build his first plantations near Baton Rouge.[14]

By 1860, nearly 40 percent of the five lower river counties in the state of Mississippi was cleared and planted. Compared to the rapid, industrialized deforestation of the lower valley, what occurred in the eighteenth and early nineteenth centuries was more of a patchwork clearing around farms, towns, and along the river, and a thinning of larger timber from stands elsewhere. Nevertheless, enough lower Mississippi Valley forest had been cleared to provoke Benjamin Wailes's delight upon encountering a stand of old growth trees. The operator of one rather large mill in the vicinity of New Orleans claimed to cut four twelve-foot logs per day, for a total of 700 feet of boards, each an inch thick. But if the pace and impact of deforestation were minor compared to what came later, when power mills spit out over a million board feet per day, it represented a tremendous leap from the past. To be sure, valley peoples and early French settlers made pirogues of large fallen trees, furniture and tools of small logs, and shelters of saplings, bark, and thatched leaves. In certain upland areas they burned forests to create open areas for corn cultivation and to draw deer to the edges where they liked to browse. Burning, however, hastened the natural process by which trees ultimately returned to the soil. What native people and the first Europeans took from the soil and forests, they took primarily for food and crude shelters. Felling trees at Baton Rouge for barrel staves for tobacco shipped to Europe represented a qualitatively different approach to the land and its resources. However, the drying of the valley's wet land was predicated upon pulling wet material elements out, such as trees, and reshaping them into something dry, such as planks for buildings.[15]

Trees did not have to be cut to underwrite agriculture. They could be slashed and burned. Over an area of several acres farmers would remove rings of bark from large trees to kill them. Then they would set fire to the land to clear underbrush and to defoliate the trees and to fertilize the land. The very largest trees remained standing, though dead, sometimes for several years. In this manner Europeans prepared land for planting just as native peoples had done for centuries. Initially, the land was incredibly fertile, producing thirty to forty bushels of corn per acre per year, but yields diminished quickly after a year or two of planting. William Dunbar, who prepared some of his fields in this manner, recorded that corn planted at the end of July stood four feet high just one month later. When yields declined, native peoples abandoned their fields for locations where they could repeat the process. European squatters followed the same pattern of slash and burn, plant, and move on. In time, grasses and briars reclaimed abandoned fields. Eventually, hardwoods returned, but the cycle took decades to complete. Private property, however, encouraged farmers to break this cycle. They developed and "improved" their land by pulling down dead trees and uprooting stumps, then plowing deeper into the topsoil, working it more intensively to compensate for declining fertility at the earth's surface.[16]

Landowners and their laborers felled trees, erected levees, dug ditches, raised houses, and raised them some more if levees proved inadequate. Drainage ditches ran along each property, so anyone traveling up or down the river knew where one lot ended and the next began. Houses were crude, small, leaky abodes roofed with cypress bark or palm thatch, but the levee in front of them put more than its four feet of earth between house and river. Levees reconfigured the human relationship with the environment, by separating land and water so as to enhance human control over both. Water touched land when people permitted it to do so, for example, when it flowed through man-made ditches and sluices, turning sawmills and irrigating fields, then exiting at the backs of lots into swamps and lakes. Levees protected land from the river. More than that, they transformed the river from a "destructive" power into a force for "improving" the land. At least, that is what landowners saw when they looked at a levee: human power triumphing over nature's power.[7]

Levees became legal evidence of landownership, just as clearing and fencing did in other settings. Once earthen barriers were in place, flooding was supposed to stop. Levees properly designed and carefully constructed were expected to be impermeable barriers between water and land, a little seepage notwithstanding. They might be surmounted or breached in years when the river reached extraordinary heights, but if they failed under normal conditions, someone was at fault. Even the Ursuline Sisters attributed the inundation of their plantation not to God, or the river, but to Monsieur St. Martin and his faulty ditch. Lorenzo Sigu charged David Munro for constructing a "faulty" drainage system that flooded Sigu's land. Later, when local governments began to organize individual landowners into levee districts, at the behest of those unable to persuade neighbors to build and care for their levees, the same sort of squabbling continued. The political issues involved tax collection and distribution for levee construction, but the environmental problems were the same. Newer, higher levees rendered older, lower structures inadequate, causing flooding on what had come to be thought of as *naturally dry* land, *dry* because it had not flooded in recent memory, and *naturally* dry despite a levee. In 1812 a group of residents in Warren County, Mississippi, petitioned their government to build a levee to hold back flooding waters that left "waste and desolate a vast body of most excellent Bottom Lands filling them with marshes and stagnant pools of water." Other residents of the county objected strenuously, on the grounds that the county had no right to collect a tax from them to pay for a levee that they did not need, and which in any case might redirect water onto their land. No one, however, put forth the argument that, left alone, the bottomlands were perhaps just desolate, stagnant waste.[18]

Civil disputes over levees and flooding reveal a slow process of change in the way the environment was seen. Contesting parties rarely used the word "nature," but when they did it was to reinforce the assumption that people controlled water. For example, when a plaintiff charged that an improperly placed levee *downriver* had caused his land to flood, the defendant responded that for a downriver levee to cause upriver flooding was not possible, "such a thing being against nature."[19]

The process in which levees became natural and floods unnatural unfolded hesitatingly and incrementally. Like the French before them, the Spanish administrators managed relief and repair operations along the river nearly every year. Indeed, the annual floods, which continued despite levees, gave them reason to reflect on the wisdom of barricading the river from the land, and of manipulating the river at all. There were still moments when some wondered if nature was not best left alone.

In 1797, Spanish governor Manuel-Luis Gayoso de Lemos entertained a proposal put before him by several of his engineers, on the feasibility of constructing a series of canals through meander loops to shorten the river, which would hasten river water to the gulf before it could backup and overflow. That the cut-offs would reduce transportation time between New Orleans and Natchez would be an additional benefit. The idea was not new. Thomas Hutchins, who surveyed the lower valley for the US Congress in 1784, thought the river could be shortened by 250 miles. At that time the US claim to the valley was partial and tenuous and so the Congress was not willing or able to act on Hutchins's recommendation. Gayoso had been governor of the Natchez District before being appointed governor of all Louisiana and moving to New Orleans. He maintained a plantation home in Natchez, so he had a personal reason to bring Natchez and its surrounding tobacco and cotton plantations closer to the colony's political, social, cultural, and economic center. The engineers examined the sites of the proposed canals, and consulted with local planters familiar with the river's behavior. Several potential consequences of the project required careful consideration. First, there was the question of where best to construct the canals. They might be started at places where the river was eating away at riverbanks anyway, in its own effort to reach the sea by the shortest possible route, or they could be placed where engineers deemed most efficient. There was the possibility of routing the canals through some existing lakes. Second, there was the matter of how the canals would affect the meander loops that would be abruptly severed from the mainstream. Third, serious consideration had to be given the possibility that the canals might divert the entire Mississippi River into the Atchafalaya River, or disconnect the Red River from the Mississippi River. The proposed canals were in the vicinity of the confluence of three large waterways, and how they would react to the engineers' modifications was anybody's guess. How certain were the engineers that they could predict the river's reaction to their canals? Concluding they were not certain enough, Gayoso opted to leave the Mississippi River to pursue its own course.[20]

As Spanish authorities deliberated over their canals, they also debated the wisdom of interfering with the natural flow of the Mississippi River. On one hand, Gayoso's engineers, like Hutchins before them, argued that rivers naturally flowed to the sea, and thus any obstacles that slowed them down and caused them to flood, whether logjams or meanders, were unnatural and ought to be removed. They were joined by civilian leaders such as Jacques-François Pitot, a prosperous New Orleans merchant, who recommended cut-offs. In addition, they urged that the Atchafalaya River and Bayou Plaquemines be cleared of logjams and opened as spillways to siphon off rising waters from within the Mississippi River before they overflowed or broke through levees. Drain the swamps, they proposed, and any overflow would be easily absorbed. As for the levees, they needed to be higher, standardized, and better regulated, to keep the river in its channel and on its way to the sea. Nature was too chaotic for its own good. On the other hand, Gayoso seemed inclined to share the view of British cartographer Thomas Jefferys that the river in fact had an order to it that included meanders, logjams, and floods, which levees and cut-offs would disturb. In 1760 Jefferys had recommended that rather than protecting fields by walling out the river, farmers instead simply avoid land that was prone to heavy flooding. Mild flooding would be beneficial, Jefferys argued. The annual inundation "renews and fattens" the soil and rebuilds natural levees, which were good locations for houses and outbuildings and perhaps for small fields of wheat.[21]

The debate came at an important moment of reflection upon decades of river management that had brought mixed results. Indeed, if anything was to be learned from the previous century of agriculture in the lower valley, it was that without levees no land was safe from inundation, but levees, while often helpful, could also be detrimental. The problem was that the river was unpredictable. Solving problems tended to cause other problems. The cut-offs proposed by Governor Gayoso's engineers might alleviate flooding and improve navigation, but they might also cause the river to turn disastrously down the Atchafalaya basin and abandon New Orleans. Then again, the river was so unpredictable, it might just turn down the Atchafalaya anyway, all on its own, unless engineers could somehow control it.

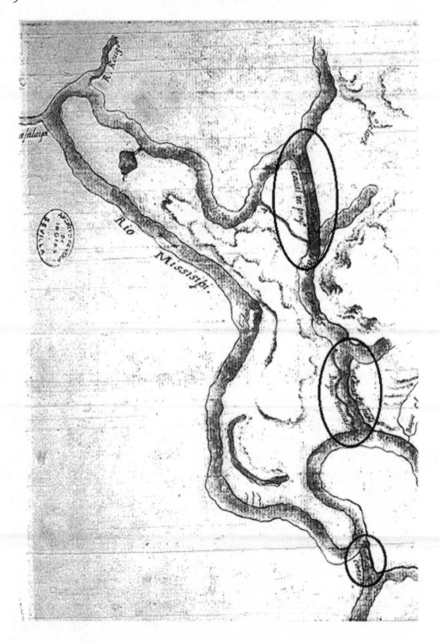

FIGURE 5.1 Spanish drawing of the Mississippi River, showing proposed cut-offs (circled). The Red and Atchafalaya rivers intersect with the Mississippi River in the upper left. From "Mapa de la parte del Mississippi situada a sur a confluencia del Rouge y Chafalaya, con proyecto de cortar lazo para abreviar la navegación entre Natchez y Nueva Orleans," 1796, Archivo General de India, Mapas y Planos, no. 180.

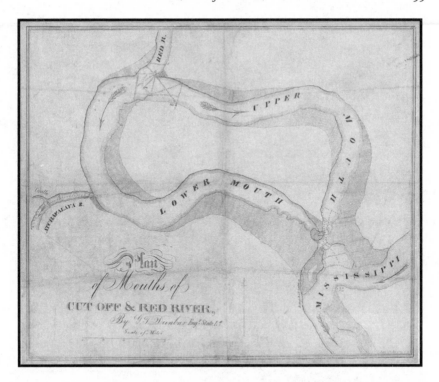

FIGURE 5.2 Henry Miller Shreve's cut-off of a Mississippi River meander loop that Spanish governor Manuel Gayoso had decided to leave alone. Shreve's cut-off led to problems at the intersection of the Mississippi, Red, and Atchafalaya rivers that engineers struggled with for decades. This 1839 illustration was made by one of those engineers, George T. Dunbar. (Courtesy of Barry Lawrence Ruderman.)

Six hundred years ago the Red and Ouachita Rivers merged to form the Atchafalaya, which flowed to the gulf independently of the Mississippi River. Four hundred years ago a Mississippi River meander loop cut into the intersection of the other rivers, and some portion of the Red River started flowing into the Mississippi while some portion of the Mississippi spilled into the Atchafalaya. In 1831, Henry Shreve and the US Army Corps of Engineers completed the cut-off Gayoso had refrained from undertaking.

Gayoso's trepidation concerning canals was typical of continental Europeans. French engineers, for example, believed in following courses laid out by nature and where feasible, exploiting them without really altering them. Shreve and the engineers who worked on behalf of the United States built on a British tradition that held that canals were vastly superior

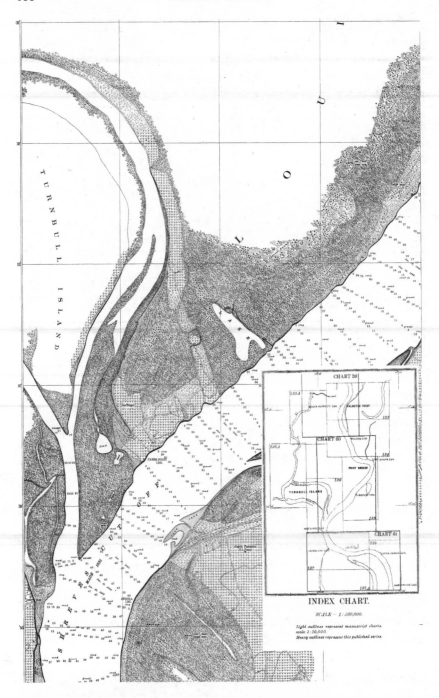

FIGURE 5.3 Shreve's Cut-off in 1879, by which time the intersection of the Red and Mississippi rivers was nearly closed with sediment. (Courtesy of the National Oceanic and Atmospheric Administration, Department of Commerce.)

to rivers because they were far easier to control. As Benjamin Franklin observed, canals were "quiet and very manageable but rivers were ungovernable things." French engineering had its American adherents, Thomas Jefferson most famously. While president, Jefferson arranged for the appointment of French engineers to the faculty at West Point, which led, in 1802, to the establishment of a permanent Army Corps of Engineers. Despite French influence, the Corps tended to prefer manageable canals and engineered rivers over unmanageable natural streams. Shreve's cut-off represented an attempt—mistaken, it quickly turned out—to canalize a section of the Mississippi River that had long been unpredictable.[22]

As a consequence of Shreve's cut-off, water from the Red River began to flow almost entirely into the Mississippi River. Meanwhile the entrance to the Atchafalaya River clogged with driftwood and silt, much of it loosened from upriver locations by landowners as they cleared forests for farms and plantations. A year after making his cut-off, Shreve set to work loosening a massive log jam known as the Red River raft, an accumulation of many centuries of driftwood, and in so doing sent tremendous amounts of driftwood downriver to lodge in the mouth of the Atchafalaya. Shreve had apparently solved two problems and created a third. Within a few years the mouth of the Atchafalaya was so clogged the river was reduced to a trickle and steamboat traffic upon it ceased, to the dismay of many people in lower Louisiana, who beseeched their political representatives for help. In 1839, engineers drew up plans to remove the debris at the mouth of the Atchafalaya, thereby fixing the problem Shreve had caused when he cut through a meander loop in the Mississippi and removed the raft in the Red River. Clearing the opening of the Atchafalaya caused more water from the Red River to flow freely down the Atchafalaya, filling the channel between the Red and the Mississippi rivers with silt and obstructing steamboat traffic. The great 1927 flood solved this problem, and when the Mississippi River pushed its way back into the Atchafalaya, it seemed very possible that the entire Mississippi might take its course.

Old River, the location where Gayoso refrained from making a cut-off and where Henry Shreve did not, has long been a trouble spot for engineers, steamboaters, and riverside planters and farmers who seek stability and predictability. Either too much of the Red River has flowed into the Mississippi, leaving the Atchafalaya dry, or too much Red River has flowed into the Atchafalaya, making for difficult riverboat passage between the Red and Mississippi rivers, or too much Mississippi has flowed down the

Atchafalaya, raising the possibility that Big Muddy might take the channel as its own and abandon its route past Baton Rouge and New Orleans.[23]

Big Muddy's erratic behavior was not the only environmental problem confronted by the Spanish and their successors. Toward the end of the eighteenth century visitors to the Natchez District began to notice evidence of soil erosion and exhaustion. Rufus Putnam noted that the land around the town of Natchez was "much worn out," but whether from Natchez Indian corn or French tobacco he did not say. Early in the nineteenth century more visitors reported seeing large areas of eroded land around Natchez. In the vicinity of Vicksburg, agriculturalist Solon Robinson observed: "It used to be celebrated as one of the best cotton-growing counties in the state, but a continuous cropping of the land, without manure, or even returning the cotton seed as manure to the soil, has so worn out much of the land that it hardly pays for cultivating." The land was, thought Robinson, "gone past all redemption, and worthless for every purpose except Bermuda-grass pastures." The same soil on which corn once grew four feet in one month exhibited "great ulcers," and was "gullied to death" from erosion caused by rain runoff as it raced unobstructed into nearby creeks and eventually into the Mississippi River, raising the river's level, increasing the risk of flooding, and adding incentive for yet another heightening of the levees, which prevented lowland plantations from benefiting from all the upland topsoil that flowed past them.[24]

The powdery dirt, called loess soil, was particularly vulnerable on the many hills between Baton Rouge and Vicksburg. While trees and plants protected it, rain and wind did not damage the soil. Canebrakes, with their extensive root systems near the surface, had been particularly effective at preventing erosion. In the mid-nineteenth century some farmers began to plant willow trees in an effort to stem erosion. A proponent of conservation, Solon Robinson recommended that Mississippians give up farming and raise sheep. Over the decade of the 1850s, the number of sheep doubled.[25]

Thoughts of conservation may be seen in the debate over levees and canals and in general over whether the river ought to be controlled or left to its own devices. Solon Robinson clearly had soil conservation in mind. Benjamin Wailes, if not an outspoken advocate of conservation, nevertheless was keenly aware of how much the land had changed in his own lifetime in the lower valley. The specimens he collected for display in his university's glass cases constituted conservation of a sort. Earlier generations of Europeans had thought agriculture "comes most naturally" to the lower valley. Robinson was not so sure, and Wailes lamented that progress had come with a price that was hard to measure financially but was real and significant nonetheless.[26]

It was in Europe, however, that efforts to conserve a disappearing lower valley environment first emerged. Europeans had begun to think about conservation a century or more before, when some of the same concerns that sent them overseas also caused them to reflect on their relationship with their own lands. In France, the government of Louis XIV addressed the issue of diminishing timber stores with a Forest Ordinance aimed at regulating timber cutting and use. Intellectuals in both France and England were struck by how quickly forests in overseas "new worlds" were destroyed. On the North American continent there always seemed to be more trees over the horizon, but on the island colonies, Europe's rapacious appetite for natural resources was downright destructive. Some were concerned about the Christian ethic of stewardship of the earth, whereas others foresaw a time when all timber stores would be gone and European economies would collapse. On one point eighteenth century conservationists agreed: there were lessons to be learned from the colonial experience, and from changes within industrializing Europe, about how human intervention in nature might be balanced with human dependence on natural resources and forces.[27]

The relationship between people and environment in the lower Mississippi Valley informed thinking in France most directly where the specific concern was marshland. France's concern with land and water predated the founding of Louisiana. In 1682, Louis XIV's engineers undertook several major canal projects, influenced by the model of the Dutch and Italian engineering. Dutch and Italian ideas also made their way to French Louisiana. For example, French engineer Bernard Forest de Belidor, whose *Architecture Hydraulique* (1737–1739) was read by engineers in Louisiana, built his argument for straightening rivers on the studies of Domenico Guglielmini. By the mid-eighteenth century, ideas were beginning to flow from Louisiana to France. In 1740, a company of land developers planned to turn marshes in the Loire Valley, in the vicinity of Orléans, into rice fields, just as had been done in the Mississippi Valley in the vicinity of Nouvelle Orléans. In addition to providing a source of food to supplement wheat, rice, it was thought, would help with flood control and prevent disease associated with wetlands. Unfortunately for these developers, an epidemic broke out the year after they first planted rice, confirming what many had suspected, that rice somehow encouraged disease. The project was abandoned.[28]

Concern with France's wetlands persisted, however, and so long as it did, Louisiana would be one source of information on how to manage them. In 1809, Simon-Louis Pierre de Cubières, at the urging of the Institute of France, published his treatise on the cypress tree of Louisiana. Drawing on the observations of Le Page du Pratz, Duhamel, Charlevoix, and others who had visited Louisiana, he argued that vast wetlands across France, in Flanders, la Bresse, and Saint-leger, could be easily and profitably reclaimed by planting them with Louisiana cypress. He claimed that this tree would dry up and purify wet, brackish, muddy, and generally unhealthy wetlands, while beautifying them and providing bird habitat. "When I reflect," Cubières wrote, "on the immense quantity of water that one tree draws up in the space of twenty-four hours, to restore the large part to vital area, I am struck by the great advantage which will result from the cultivation of cypress in the cesspools of stagnant water that surround so many villages and hamlets." Cypress trees, he believed, neutralize "the noxious miasmas that the mires exhale," thereby improving the "healthiness of the air, and the inhabitants of those rotting countrysides." For Cubières, the lower Mississippi Valley environment, not the French environment, was balanced and healthy.[29]

Cubières believed a vigorous America had much to teach a worn-out Europe, about wetland forest conservation. It was an argument for understanding nature on its own terms and as a whole system, and not merely as an object to be shaped by people or as a series of problems to be solved. People do change nature, as they ought to, he argued, but they needed to do so thoughtfully, or else nature would turn against them. Remarkably, nothing of the sort was practiced in Louisiana at that time. A few may have advocated a more systematic approach to land and water, but in the main valley residents charged ahead, cutting, clearing, draining, and planting. Governor Gayoso's hesitation was exceptional. Henry Shreve's blundering confidence was typical.

Abundance bolstered confidence, as did the launching of a new republic that seemed destined to roll westward across the continent. "The lands are so rich on the Mississippi," predicted Bernard Romans in the 1770s, that intensive cultivation of the most "impoverishing plants" would not exhaust them. That was prevailing wisdom through the nineteenth century. "It is generally believed in Europe," wrote George-Henri-Victor Collot, in 1796, that the United States can "by means of its vast forests, supply the marine of Europe with timber." In truth, Collot argued, timber supplies in the United States were running short. He blamed shipbuilding, farms, and fences, "which inclose fields from one end of the continent to the other." Collot blamed "waste of every kind made by an improvident people" who have "destroyed such a quantity of wood, that scarcely any is to be found within an hundred miles of the sea, or near navigable rivers." Thankfully, "the resources which are no longer to be found in the territory of the United States, are met with in abundance in the forest of Louisiana and the Floridas." In 1803, though, Americans got their hands on Louisiana.[30]

In 1811, government surveyors wrote officials in Washington, DC, to report widespread poaching of cypress timber from public lands along the lower Mississippi River. Gangs of men were cutting it down and floating it out in rafts, stripping the land of much of its value. They were, in short, robbing the United States Treasury. They threatened violence against anyone who tried to stop them. There was nothing the distant government could do.[31]

People transformed the landscape of the Natchez District in the half century that followed the American Revolution, as they had done in the region around New Orleans in the previous half-century, and as they would do to the entire lower valley over the course of the nineteenth century. Hogs, cattle, and fields filled formerly forested areas. Change was not abrupt, of course. In many ways, the Americans lived off the environment as the French had done, and the native peoples before them. Fish and game, including small fur-bearing animals such as raccoons, remained a dietary mainstay, served with beef, pork, lamb, corn, and rice. There remained plenty of trees for fuel and construction.

The grounds at Concord Plantation on the outskirts of Natchez, built by Governor Gayoso, offered a visible example of the changed landscape. At its center was an old field, unplanted and abandoned. Around it were newer fields planted in cotton and corn. At the far edge were woods, comprising about 15 percent of the plantation property. The stream that meandered through the fields helped control drainage. The mansion sat across the road. From the columned big house one could cross the road and stand in a new and very large cotton field. Walk across the field and into the forest on the far side and one stepped into the land of the Natchez Indians and their Plaquemine ancestors, the same land glimpsed by Hernando de Soto's men, as they hurried down Big Muddy to the Gulf of Mexico.[32]

What might seem to have been small changes in ecology had tremendous ripple effects in human society. The end of the deerskin trade led to Indian depopulation, but by the start of the nineteenth century to

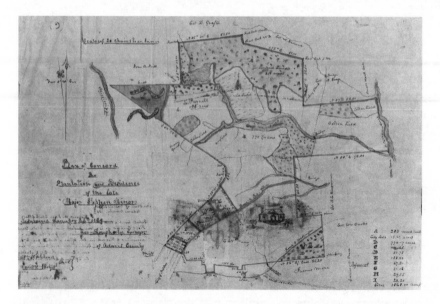

FIGURE 5.4 Concord Plantation, near Natchez, built by Spanish governor Manuel Gayoso de Lemos and passed along to his son-in-law, Stephen Minor. In 1829, the property was a landscape in various stages of transformation, with the manicured lawns near the house and the new fields of cotton and corn representing the most humanly altered areas, older fields lying fallow representing areas returned to nature, and patches of timbered acreage representing land unchanged. The property is bisected by streams and roads, and defined at its borders by survey lines. (Courtesy of the Mississippi Department of Archives and History.)

revitalization, as Choctaw, Chickasaw, and other nations took up cotton planting, much as native residents lower down the valley earlier had taken up farming and fishing for the New Orleans market. The expansion of intensive agriculture reinvigorated slavery, which provided labor for the construction of levees. Plantations and levees caused more destructive floods, which were met with more levees. The cycle might have been broken had the conservationists and hydrologists prevailed, and had not the Louisiana Purchase unleashed the force of hundreds of landowners with thousands of enslaved laborers, driven by world demand for cotton and backed by a state that hired men like Henry Shreve.[33]

On the evening of May 3, 1849, a swollen Mississippi River broke through the levee at the Sauvé plantation upriver from New Orleans. By midmonth the city's second ward was a lake, water surrounded the Dryades Street market, and concerned citizens were talking of breaking a hole in a public levee so water could escape. The city posted watchmen.

When flood levels rose above the doorsill, residents moved into their upper stories, if they had them, and fled if they did not. By early June, the seventh ward lay wet and deserted. The city's poor were hardest hit. The *New Orleans Bee* reported, "Others can pay for boat or carriage hire, or can move away from the vicinity of the overflow, but the poor have no choice. They must remain, and to wade through the water half a dozen times a day is to risk their health and life." "We have heard that in the back part of the 7th Ward, there are whole families almost literally in a state of starvation, having neither money to procure food, nor the means of reaching the markets." By the end of the month, volunteers with skiffs were evacuating the poor. Early June brought several days and nights of rain. As the water continued to rise it threatened more affluent neighborhoods on higher ground. "The situation of a large number of inhabitants who reside in the inundated district will become most distressing, as their lower doors will be invaded by the element, and thus compel them to seek for shelter in the upper stories of their houses, or look out for dry quarters elsewhere," the *Bee* predicted. Not until June 10 did the water begin to recede.[34]

The flood of 1849 stands as the worst of the nineteenth century. It lasted forty-eight days, during which time perhaps 12,000 residents of New Orleans, nearly one in ten, temporarily left home. It was not the greatest flood the valley had seen, in terms of crest height at New Orleans, but it was high enough to break through Sauvé's levee and drown New Orleans with water that came down the Mississippi, Red, Ouachita, and Tensas rivers, all rivers that had been leveed by cotton planters. Eighty years of clearing, draining, leveeing, and planting had transformed much of the lower Mississippi Valley. With less and less room to spread out, all the water converged on New Orleans. The Mississippi River in 1849 and 1851 was especially high below the mouth of the Red River, which brought water from the valley's newest plantation districts along the Red, Ouachita, Tensas, and Yazoo rivers. While many residents of New Orleans profited handsomely from the expansion of agriculture upriver, they and their city also paid a heavy price. Levees collected water between the Yazoo River in the east and the Red River in the west and funneled it all into the main channel at Shreve's cut-off. The 1849 flood at New Orleans began not with the crevasse at Sauvé's but with the transformation of wetland into dry land hundreds of miles up Big Muddy and its tributaries.[35]

6

King Cotton Meets Big Muddy

IN 1810, JACOB Bieller purchased a four-acre clearing on an island in the Mississippi River above Natchez, in Concordia Parish at a place then called Petit Gulf, from a squatter who had supported his family for three years on corn, pumpkins, and the proceeds from a little cotton. Bieller paid the man $120 for the small improvement and moved onto the island with his own family and fifty-one slaves. Thirteen years later Bieller was a prosperous cotton planter looking to expand his holdings. With the best lands on the Mississippi River taken, he looked inland, finding what he hoped would be a good location on a bluff along Bayou Maçon between the Tensas and Ouachita rivers in what was then Catahoula Parish. The task of managing the new plantation he handed to his son, Joseph.[1]

The area between the Ouachita and Tensas rivers was sparsely populated when Joseph Bieller arrived, although for several decades the population had been increasing. Wrote one visitor to the region, in 1786: "All vestiges which we discover daily everywhere announce that the nation which inhabited [this country] formerly must have been very populous. We do not know what became of it." Nevertheless, by the 1790s, Choctaws, Creeks, and other native peoples eager to escape encroaching white settlements east of the Mississippi River were trickling into the area. Meanwhile, the powerful Osage nation of the Missouri River was expanding its territory with several new settlements along the upper Ouachita River. These newcomers joined a hundred or so whites, mostly French and Spanish, who farmed, hunted, and worked the trade between Natchitoches and the Arkansas River. Fearful of losing control over the region, Spanish authorities built a fort near present-day Monroe and looked for ways to settle the region with more Europeans. The revolutions in France and Haiti provided them with an opportunity.[2]

Royalists, many of them aristocrats, were leaving France for corners of the world they believed safe and welcoming. The Marquis de Maison Rouge fled to New Orleans. He may have gone there because he was loyal and perhaps even related to the Bourbon monarchs, one of whom sat on the Spanish throne, or because he had friends there. He quickly ensconced himself with Louis Bouligny, one of New Orleans's most respected citizens, and his circle of friends.[3]

Maison Rouge struck a deal with Spanish Governor Francisco Luis Hector, Baron de Carondelet. In return for grants of land totaling over 200,000 Spanish acres, or arpents, he would help recruit and settle thirty white, royalist farmers and their families, and develop the region into one of thriving wheat farms and mills. Success with wheat cultivation would end the need for trade with Illinois, a U.S. possession. The marquis would have an estate befitting his status, and the governor would have a permanent settlement of royalists to block U.S. and Osage expansion. Neither man fully understood the nature of the land they agreed to transform. On the west bank of the Ouachita River the floodplain rose rather quickly, within a mile or less, to a ridge of poor, dry land covered with pine trees. It was no good for farming. At Sicily Island, for example, the land was high but the soil was a stony clay. Above Sicily Island, a strip of natural levee of about one quarter to one half mile in width bordered the east bank of the Ouachita, but beyond it an alluvial prairie of fertile soil gradually descended into a vast cypress swamp where water sat year-round at depths of fifteen to twenty-five feet. Across the swamp the land rose a little toward the Tensas River, then sank once more into permanent wetland before rising at the natural levee of the Mississippi. During flood season, the waters of Big Muddy often drowned it all, even the strip of high ground along the Ouachita and Tensas. This is where Maison Rouge tried to build his estate.[4]

The marquis arrived at his new home by boat, unmarried and without family, but accompanied by a gaggle of retainers that included clockmakers and jewelers. He also brought a fine carriage. There was, however, no road, only swamp. One observer noted, "he had to give up his plan of driving forth that all might admire his magnificence." Maison Rouge was not an old man, yet he was physically and mentally unable to adapt to his surroundings. Low on funds, having abandoned his estate in France, and suffering from gout, his mood was often foul, which did little to endear him to the settlers he managed to recruit to the Ouachita, who might have been able to help him. He constructed a small house on a few acres of high ground known as Prairie Ronde, and lived there with his Irish maid, Marie Faer.[5]

The clockmakers and jewelers departed when their employer could no longer pay them, but Marie remained. Together with the small neighborhood of French, Swiss, and American families, Maison Rouge built a feeble mill and planted wheat. When the wheat failed they turned to corn, potatoes, and cotton. Flooding was a problem. Fields and milldams washed away. Overland communication with New Orleans was impossible, and the rivers proved hard and occasionally treacherous to navigate. According to a neighbor, the marquis "brought into this country but two families and some single men; in all about fifteen persons. As for mills, I never knew of his having built any, except a horse mill for the use of his plantation." A list of recruits indicates twenty-two whites, one free person of color, and nine slaves, far fewer than the thirty families he had contracted with Carondelet to bring to the Ouachita settlement. Meanwhile, the marquis's health worsened. In 1799 he returned to New Orleans, where he died at the home of Louis Bouligny. The ensuing squabble over the estate revealed not only the failure of the Ouachita venture but the true nature of the relationship between Maison Rouge and his maid Marie. He left her his house and five arpents of land, and the rest of his estate of 200,000 arpents to Bouligny, or so Bouligny claimed, though there were no witnesses to the bequest. Almost immediately, Marie's four children, all of whom claimed the marquis as their father, but were illegitimate in the eyes of the law and therefore not legal heirs, put claims on the estate.[6]

The story of a fallen aristocrat struggling to rebuild himself in the wilderness of the American South and failing by his own overreach and temperament, if not his incompetence or decadence, is repeated throughout the lower Mississippi Valley. Near Prairie Ronde were the lands of another royalist refugee. Originally from Holland, the Baron de Bastrop fled Europe during the French Revolution and, striking a deal similar to the one made by Maison Rouge, received a tremendous Spanish land grant of nearly a million acres. When the United States acquired Louisiana, he relocated to Texas where he could continue his allegiance to the Spanish crown. He later worked with Stephen F. Austin to establish colonies of Anglo-American settlers in Texas and to press the Mexican government to keep Texas open to slavery. He died in Saltillo, Coahuila, in 1827, too cash poor to pay the expenses of his own funeral. As his estate was investigated, evidence surfaced that the Baron was perhaps not an aristocrat but an opportunist who had succeeded in playing Carondelet, Austin, and others for fools.[7]

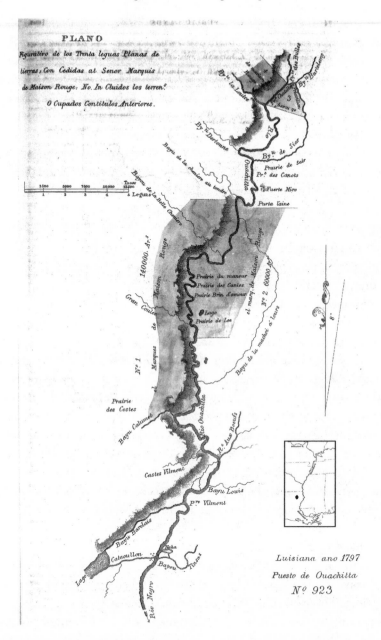

FIGURE 6.1 The Maison Rouge grant of 200,000 Spanish acres sprawled along the Ouachita River. The strip of high ground on the west side of the river was not good farmland, and the bottomlands on the east side, between the Ouachita and the Bayu de la machoi á lours (Bayou de la mâchoire á l'ours)where Maison Rouge built his home, were difficult to work and inhabit. From Luisiana ano 1797 Puesto de Ouachitta No. 923, *American State Papers: Public Lands*, vol. 1.

If the hunters, traders, and simple homesteaders of European, African, and Native American ancestry were wandering, idle, and unfit, as Carondelet and others described them, then the displaced aristocrats were just the sorts of men "with the temper, acquirements and peculiar views" to "transform those deserts into an enchanted land." Carondelet saw the Ouachita wetlands as uncivilized, dirty, and impoverished, which is why he invested in Maison Rouge and Bastrop. He could see neither the land nor the people he sent there for what they were but only as reflections of the same fantasy of wet land and "dry" people. In the 1820s, Americans such as Caleb Forshey regarded these aristocrats as decadent relics from a bygone era. Forshey preferred to populate the lower Mississippi Valley with enterprising men like Jacob and Joseph Bieller, who succeeded through effort and intelligence at transforming wet land into enchanted land, thereby exemplifying the republican spirit of Thomas Jefferson and Andrew Jackson.

At the time of Maison Rouge's death, the land between the Ouachita and Tensas Rivers remained a watery wilderness. The few people who lived there hunted deer and bear for a living, taking skins and oil into Natchez once a year and trading them for supplies. Some floated out timber and sold it, either at Natchez or New Orleans. Game and fish were the primary sources of food, supplemented with rice, which everyone grew. It was a red rice, perhaps of the West African variety, and did very well on the bottom or "craw-fish land." Some planted small patches of cotton for their own use, although the wet soil produced a rust, a type of fungus that killed the plants. According to one report on land applications made to the U.S. government after the Louisiana Purchase, most settlers "were afraid of the swamp, and located their grants in the pine woods," where the land was dry although not especially fertile. "They seemed not to be willing to trust the waters," and with good reason.[8]

In the name of progress, as hydrographic engineer Caleb Forshey explained, "surplus water" had to be controlled or removed and land reclaimed for civilization. Forshey associated the work of "improving" and "reclaiming" forests and swamps with the moral improvement and reclamation of humanity. Such Jeffersonian linking of land and morality was probably widely shared by educated Anglo-Americans, and it contributed to notions of a Mississippi Valley inhabited by indolent people. Forshey described its inhabitants as "fat," "greasy," "barefoot," "filthy," "immodest." If the lines between people and nature, land and water, and dry and wet were unclear, then so too were the lines between ethnicities and between genders. Women living in wetland settlements were large and masculine, even when nursing babies. Everyone was mongrelized. "Mongrel Indian, French, and Negro" lived together "in huts scattered among the black-oak forests," "hybrids with their gibberish—French Spanish Italian Congo & English mixed." Hunting parties of French, Italian, and African eating supper around the same campfire bordered on the outrageous. "The old settlers chiefly Canadian French," wrote George Hunter, "appear to have little ambition, few wants & as little industry, They live from hand to mouth & let tomorrow provide for itself," and "in want of almost every comfort, except what is absolutely necessary for subsistance." William Dunbar of Natchez estimated there were about 500 people in the area living in an "indian mode of life," hunting and planting small amounts of corn, "barely sufficient for bread during the year." Robert King and his gang of bandits were rumored to be hiding out there. It was home to Edward Lovelace, bear hunter of renown, and his brothers. It was land unfit for respectable men of enterprise, who could not abide water.[9]

In the summer of 1811, the United States surveyor for the Mississippi Territory wrote to the secretary of the Treasury to explain why surveys and land sales would be delayed that summer: "The whole face of the country between the Mississippi & Washita Rivers (about 40 miles in width opposite this place) has been Inundated to an uncommon depth this year. All the crops of cotton & corn &c in the low land have been wholly destroyd [and] with two or three solitary exceptions," conditions would not "admit even the Slaves return to those plantations." Nor would conditions improve immediately upon the recession of the water. "Few men can be found hardy enough to stand the poisonous effects of Half dried mud, putrid fish & vegetable matter—almost impenetrable cane brakes, and swarms of mosketoes—with which the lowlands abound after the waters are withdrawn." In a petition to Congress asking for extra time to make payments on land, a group of farmers and planters explained how, in addition to the disruption of commerce attributable to the war with Great Britain, geography added to their burden. It was necessary for them to purchase land they would never cultivate, land that would never bring an income: "To the fertile swamp-lands pregnant with disease," the petitioners explained "they were obliged to add barren pine-lands [i.e., sandy natural levees and ancient terraces] whose only recommendation was, that they afforded a healthful settlement." In 1815, with the end of the war with Great Britain, cotton planters from Natchez turned their eyes to this poisonous land, and surveyors got busy clearing, draining, and drying.[10]

What a job it was. Young Joseph Bieller and a portion of his father's slave force had cotton and corn in the ground very quickly. They likely slashed, burned, and planted the highest ground hastily to produce a quick first crop before getting down to the more time-consuming work of draining lower lands, pulling stumps, and raising levees. Getting the cotton crop to market was problematic, for there were few roads into the Ouachita region, none of them suitable for wagons. The crop from 1827 sat baled and on the ground in the spring of the next year, waiting the recession of floodwaters. Not until August did the last of the crop leave the landing, on barges carefully maneuvered down Bayou Maçon to Choctaw Bayou to within a few miles of the original Bieller home, then hauled over the broad natural levee that separated the Mississippi River from its tributaries. The last leg of the journey to Natchez and New Orleans was made by boat. As he struggled to get one crop to market, Bieller had to get another one in the ground. Inundation delayed that work, too, and for a moment it looked as though one wet spring might ruin two years of planting. Yet, he survived, much to his father's relief. "Please," the father wrote his agent when at last the cotton was at market, "send me one barrel of the best whiskey."[11]

Along Bayou Maçon there erupted something like a war between people and the natural environment. Always, there was the water advancing against earthen barriers, and all too often breaking through lines. Animals caused trouble, too. Bears stole hogs. Gnats attacked the eyes of livestock. Crows, raccoons, and squirrels ate corn from field and store. Mosquitoes attacked everyone. The Biellers, their neighbors, and slaves armed and stationed in fields fought back by shooting at anything that moved. "We have the bear verry plenty," Joseph wrote his father, "they are catching hogs daly I have killed too Arthur one Harris three the Wards one they are all hog catchers." Bears were not the only obstacle to plantation development. One Bayou Maçon resident confessed to Jacob Bieller of shooting indiscriminately. "Abrams tale is almost true, never since I was created did I Experience such a night of misery, alligators 12 feet long, prowling about the boat, a bear or panther lurking around us and to make bad worse the musketoes tormented us all night long." He persisted with his "gunning," however, killing "one alligator, one or two Racoons and Crows Blackbirds woodcocks woodpeckers pecker woods, etc. etc. in abundance. I cannot shoot a rifle good, but I can shoot a shotgun as well as any person on the Bayou."[12]

There also occurred something of a war between residents, as "industrious" cotton planters and their slaves pushed out "indolent" trappers, hunters, and subsistence farmers. William Dunbar and George Hunter described a Spanish settler and his family as living in "great misery," the result of "extreme indolence." Not only did the Spaniard live in a wetland, but he had been attracted to it by the abundance of fish and water fowl and had no intention of altering it in any significant way. By contrast, a more ambitious husband and wife team lived in "a Covered frame of rough poles without walls." Nearby, Dunbar related, "a Couple of acres of Indian corn had been cultivated, which suffices to stock their little magazine with bread for the year." The forest supplied the household with plenty of "Venison, Bear, turkey &c, the river fowl and fish," and "the skins of the wild animals and an abundance of the finest honey being carried to market enable the new settler to supply himself largely with all other necessary articles." In short order, settlers such as these arrive "at a state of independence," able to purchase "horses, cows & other domestic animals, perhaps a slave also." "How happy the contrast, when we compare the fortune of the new settler in the U.S. with the misery of the half starving, oppressed and degraded Peasant of Europe!" American settlers sought to live off the wetland while they transformed it. The separation of land and water, settlement and wilderness, civilization and savagery, Protestant and Catholic, white and nonwhite—it was all one process and it justified U.S. expansion into the West.[13]

Where the land had been improved, there was clear, Anglo-American, masculine intelligence, as well as Protestant industriousness and civic virtue. In 1860, James Carson of Carrol Parish had cleared two thirds of his 2,500 acres of cane and forest, beginning at the river front on the highest ground. A levee kept back the river. Ditches drained water to the swamp at the back of the lot. Every winter he cut, cleared, burned, and ditched more land, which he planted with cotton, corn, potatoes, oats, peas, watermelon, and pumpkins. Even in midsummer, when rainy days interrupted field work, Carson put his slaves to work on the ditches. Carson's neighbor, Judge Morgan, was also a picture of industriousness in the name of progress. "Here," Caleb Forshey exclaimed, "is wealth with an emphasis! Judge M[organ] holds here about 17,000 acres—& makes 1000 bales of cotton. He is a man of intelligence and talents."[14]

Living and working in the wetlands had a way of erasing differences between people. Whether one was of the "better sort," to use Forshey's term, or a low-down hunter-trader-squatter mattered less in the marshes of the lower valley. Of course, when out of the swamps and back in society, status, wealth, and ancestry mattered. Joseph Bieller would have been welcomed into Natchez's finest drawing rooms, while the slaves who worked his land would not have been free to go on their own to Natchez at all. Likewise, some of the buckskin-clad hunters would have made quite a sight among the finely dressed city folk on the streets of Natchez. In the lower Mississippi Valley, it was the natural environment, and in particular the work of making a living within it, that mattered. However, as work progressed at clearing, draining, and drying the land, and as the profits of that labor solidified into cash and credit, social differences emerged and hardened.

Bear hunters and squatters could not do to the land what Jacob and Joseph Bieller did. It took capital to transform wetland into dry land. Lacking the funds to purchase land and labor, they sold out or were otherwise chased away by men with resources. For $50, Jacob Bieller purchased 640 acres at a spot on Bayou Maçon known as Walnut Bluff. He bought this from a homesteader named Robinett and another tract from a man named Isaac Adair that included some small buildings, fences, an orchard, and a garden, but not much else. Robinett and Adair moved off the bluff and the Biellers moved on, with nearly eighty enslaved laborers at their command.[15]

Few had access to more capital than Joseph Davis, when he left his law practice in Natchez to take up planting along the Mississippi River about fifteen miles below Vicksburg. He acquired a large tract of land from the territorial government, to which he added acreage purchased from several homesteaders. With a small army of enslaved laborers, he cleared several hundred acres, barricaded it behind earthen levees, and planted cotton. The farmers who had been living there had planted small amounts of cotton on the natural levee near the river. Davis's operation was of a vaster scale: 5,000 acres and over 100 slaves.[16]

In the floodplain, men with little capital and labor built small farms on patches of high ground and hunted, trapped, and fished in the bottoms. They lacked the resources that would have allowed them to plant in the bottom lands without exposing themselves to inundation, crop loss, and bankruptcy. Hemmed in by water, they could not move off the natural levee, where the land was dry if overly sandy, suitable for small gardens but not for cotton; they were trapped unless presented with a chance to sell out for enough cash to enable them to develop some wetland elsewhere. It is likely that the Ouachita River farmer whom William Dunbar admired eventually sold out to a wealthier man. At his cabin on Sicily Island, Edward Lovelace tried his hand at cotton planting, building one of the first cotton gins in Catahoula Parish. But his land, while high and for the most part dry, was sandy and unproductive. When wealthier men moved into the region and began to drain and dry the rich bottomland, and as the bear and deer began to disappear, Lovelace sold out and moved to Texas.[17]

In time, levees divided people as they divided land and water, bottomland and upland. The embankments protected annual investments in slaves and cotton, and long-term investments in a particular place. The rich, black land, once dried, permitted uninterrupted cropping, year after year, unlike upland soil that was plagued by erosion and exhaustion. There is evidence of wealth stratification that corresponds to geography. Lewis Gray, in his classic study of the history of southern agriculture, observed of the entire cotton region the "most extreme concentration" of slaves and wealth "existed in the alluvial lands of the Mississippi and its tributaries, where conditions of commercial production were especially favorable. In spite of the difficulty of bringing the alluvial lands of the lower valley into cultivation, they were peculiarly suited to the production of cotton under a plantation economy." Gray, however, missed the paradox within his own observation. The valley was eminently suited to cotton planting only after plantations were established. Until the nature of the valley was transformed, it was most definitely not suited to agriculture, and that came at a heavy cost.[18]

Human labor became the principal shaper of the valley environment. The physical work was not done by men such as Jacob and Joseph Bieller or Joseph Davis, but by the Africans and African Americans they and so many others held enslaved. In 1860, the slave population of Louisiana stood at 331,726, in Mississippi at 436,631, and in Arkansas at 111,115. The parishes and counties most heavily populated by slaves were the new cotton districts along the river, from Baton Rouge to beyond Vicksburg and up the Yazoo River.[19]

The cost in human life, black and white, of clearing and draining the lower valley was high. During the first half of the nineteenth century, the life expectancy from birth for the white population of Warren County, Mississippi, was forty years. It is not likely that the black population lived longer. The mortality schedules for the 1850 census indicate that on the whole in Louisiana and Mississippi the deaths of blacks and whites, measured as percentages of the total black and white populations, were about even. In the parishes and counties of the wetlands, the mortality rate exceeded state averages, and the rate for the black population exceeded that of the white population. Higher mortality rates were a rough indicator of the physical toll of working at building dry plantations and farms in the wet floodplain. In 1849, for the river counties of Mississippi, there were on average twenty-three slave deaths per thousand slaves, with the figure reaching a high of fifty-one deaths per thousand in Bolivar County, but fewer than seventeen white deaths per thousand whites. In Louisiana's valley parishes, excluding Orleans, there were on average twenty-five slave deaths per thousand slaves, with the high figure of forty-nine deaths per thousand in Madison Parish, but fewer than eighteen white deaths per thousand whites.[20]

Hard work and inadequate diet may have been the leading cause of early death among the predominantly young, male population of the lower valley's new plantation districts, but infectious diseases took many lives, including several Biellers. In the spring of 1835, Joseph and his wife died of "billious pneumonia," most likely cholera. They left behind five children. How many slaves died on the Bieller plantations is not known. The 1850 census for Franklin Parish, formerly part of Catahoula Parish, where the Biellers lived, reported thirty-nine slave deaths per thousand slaves, and, inexplicably, fifty-six white deaths per thousand whites, considerably higher than for the state as a whole.[21]

Death did not disrupt work on the Bieller plantation. The orphaned children went to live with their grandparents, who administered the estate. Joseph's eldest son, once of age, may have taken on responsibilities of managing the Bayou Maçon lands. If so, it was not for long. He disappears from the record very quickly, gone and perhaps dead by 1853, when his younger sister, Clarissa, married a thirty-year-old "speculator" from Kentucky named Alonzo Snyder, who held possession of the Bieller estate for the next quarter century.[22]

Snyder's investments paid off. He transformed himself from speculator to planter-lawyer, as he transformed forested wetland into cotton fields. In the year Abraham Lincoln was elected president, Snyder was worth nearly $200,000 in real and personal property. He, too, won election to a seat in the state Senate in Baton Rouge, which he continued to hold after Louisiana left the Union. He was at the old Bieller home in the spring of 1863 when U.S. Army soldiers came to arrest him. Snyder spent three months in prison in Alton, Illinois. By war's end he was back in Louisiana with Clarissa.[23]

The Snyders continued their in-laws' struggle to transform the lower Mississippi Valley. At some point, probably in the 1870s, Alonzo Snyder began keeping inventories of his largest trees, those twenty-four or more inches in diameter. Totaling 289, they were primarily poplar, walnut, hickory, ash, and accounted for about one in five trees in his small forest. Sixty-six percent of the trees he inventoried were at least thirty inches in diameter, including three poplar trees over six feet in diameter, indicating a healthy forest. However, as with most inventories, what was being counted was being counted because its numbers were finite. If the Bieller family correspondence from the 1820s and 1830s are full of the abundance of nature, Snyder's tree inventories of fifty years later tell of depletion.[24]

After the Louisiana Purchase, cotton agriculture spread across the Gulf States and up the Mississippi Valley, including tributaries such as the Ouachita River. During the Civil War years plantation construction stopped and total farm acreage declined. However, by 1880 a clear pattern of farm settlement and development had emerged. Farms spread across the valley below Baton Rouge, with concentrations near Lafayette and at Ascension Parish, just below Baton Rouge. To the north, agricultural activity spread along high ground, along the natural levees that bordered the major rivers, and along the edges of the uplands at the sides of the valley. By century's end, cotton covered most of the high ground and much of the low land, and the work of clearing the lowest, wettest land in the heart of the Mississippi-Yazoo Delta and between the Mississippi and Ouachita Rivers was well under way. In a giant pincer movement, settlers first surrounded the valley and then began to attack it, from the outside in. Traveling down river in 1796, George-Henri-Victor Collot found cypress standing in every marsh below the mouth of the Arkansas River. In 1869, Eugene Hilgard descended the same stretch of river and noted acres of stumps standing in those same swamps, especially near Natchez. By 1900, almost the entire forest was gone from the lower Mississippi Valley.[25]

Over the same period, the lower Mississippi Valley's wetlands disappeared at a rapid rate. Figures for marshland drainage, commonly referred to as reclamation, are scattered but clear. According to the U.S. Department of the Interior, Louisiana, Mississippi, and Arkansas had lost between a third and a half of their wetlands by the 1920s. In 1820, naturalist John James Audubon noted that during spring floods, mail carriers traveled by boat through the Louisiana bottomlands for as much as forty miles west of Natchez. Much of the valley for much of the year was a lake. By the 1870s, "reclamation" was fast becoming industrialized. Animal-powered pumps had been used earlier in the century to drain marshes, but later in the century steam-powered pumps became more common.

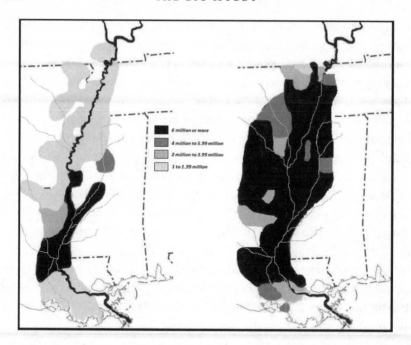

FIGURE 6.2 Cotton Production, 1840 and 1900, in pounds gathered. In 1840, cleared and drained cotton acreage lined the high ground along the Mississippi and Yazoo rivers north of the wetlands of the river delta. By the end of the nineteenth century, cotton fields covered the entire valley from Baton Rouge to north of Memphis. Based on U.S. Census Bureau, 1840, 1900 Census of Agriculture. (Drawing by author.)

In Terrebonne Parish, steam-powered dredges in short order emptied 13,000 acres of swampland. In the early twentieth century, conservationist Percy Viosca, expressed concern for the effect of wetland loss on Louisiana fish and wildlife. "Several million acres formerly suited to fish and other aquatic wild species have been made unfit for such creatures," he wrote in a report for the Louisiana Department of Conservation, and "it is chiefly the result of building levees." As with the spread of agriculture in general, swamp "reclamation" began first in the southern parts of the valley, in Louisiana, later in Mississippi, and later still in Arkansas.[26]

Continuing a trend begun by the French, rice and sugar replaced forests and swamps below Baton Rouge, along the Mississippi River and Bayou Lafourche. Above Baton Rouge, land was cleared and drained for cotton. As landowners dried land for cotton, they also dried it for corn, which was grown in some quantity just about everywhere, but much more so in cotton districts. In some parishes and counties, early settlers planted rice, but as they dried their fields for cotton, they switched their choice of grain from rice to corn.

Soil and moisture explain the ranges of rice and corn, as do the peculiar requirements of slave labor. In their effort to keep their slaves busy throughout the growing season, cotton planters raised corn, whose seasonal labor demands complemented rather than competed with those of cotton. Unlike earlier French and West African settlers, Anglo- and African Americans from the eastern seaboard states where corn was popular settled and dried the newer counties and parishes.

By the end of the nineteenth century, the woods and wetlands were nearly gone. What little remained, in the center of the Mississippi-Yazoo Delta and in the Ouachita Valley, disappeared over the next two decades. In its place was a new environment of largely treeless flatland segregated from the big river running through it. Acre after acre of cotton plants covered the land each summer. The lush, green carpet of sugar cane waving in the thick, humid air of the lowest regions of the valley, around New Orleans, must have seemed more natural to a nearly tropical climate and terrain. But the uniformity of sugar fields and indeed the sugar plant itself were as new to the land as was cotton. Rice was still grown and was spreading toward the southwestern corner of the lower valley, which the New Orleans *Times* predicted would become the China of America.[27]

It is tempting to think of a decline or an end to nature in the lower Mississippi Valley. The lateral movement of the river over the floodplain ended. Levees and drainage systems repressed the interaction between land and water. The days of bears and bear hunters ended. For a time, deer came to the edges of fields and began to grow in numbers until the forests were so diminished there were no edges, only fields, and then the deer began to disappear. Benjamin Wailes predicted in 1854 that deer, "like the Buffalo and Elk, is perhaps, destined to become extinct in our limits." Indeed, by the early twentieth century "deer can nowhere be said to persist in numbers justifying hunting," according to a wildlife inventory compiled by conservationist Aldo Leopold. If some creatures died with the old nature, new creatures moved in: cotton lice, army worms, and boll weevils. Otters and beavers, rare at the end of the colonial period, were by mid-nineteenth century quite abundant and troublesome to landowners. Opossums and raccoons flourished in the absence of wolves and cougars, feeding on shoots, vegetables, and earthworms exposed by overturned soil in plowed fields. Some bird species, turkey most notably, declined in number with the clearing of forests, but others thrived in new fields. Numbers of quail, once quite rare in the forests of the lower Mississippi Valley, steadily increased, feeding on grain at the edges of corn fields. They, along with the chickens that lived on every farm, left plenty of eggs for thieving mammals.[28]

The essential difference between the older and newer natures came down to the matter of who or what was doing the work of sustaining the natural environment. In the lower Mississippi Valley, the river once sustained the land and all that lived on it. By the end of the nineteenth century, people sustained the land. Even the rich black dirt of the Mississippi-Yazoo Delta was in need of added fertilizers by the 1920s. As people created a dry land environment suitable to agriculture, and then worked to sustain that environment, they cut the river off from the land. Just as the water came from some place else, from Ohio and Montana, most human laborers came from other places, and most, until the 1860s, were enslaved. After emancipation, many were tied to the land—land owned by someone else—by one means or another. Meanwhile, all the energy that was the Mississippi River ran to the sea. Its power was once used in conjunction with human labor to sustain an environment that also sustained human life. Over the nineteenth century, its power was relegated to the other side of the levee by people who labored to sustain a new, dry nature of their creation.[29]

By 1900, King Cotton's triumph over Big Muddy was complete, facilitated by the separation of land and water in a process that also hardened social boundaries. Victory's environmental costs, not recorded in the typical plantation's account books, included the loss of Big Muddy's restorative powers, followed by the steady depletion of plant and animal life, and eventually, of the soil that had attracted so many to the valley in the first place. Big Muddy rolled on in its confined space between the levees, while across the expansive valley, people transformed the land.

Transformation had been quick. Jefferson Snyder had been born two years before the Civil War, in St. Joseph, Louisiana, on the banks of the Mississippi River, when planters and slaves were still clearing land of cypress trees. His aunt Clarissa had spent much of her childhood on a new plantation, the original Bieller home. Before Snyder turned fifty, the home had largely been abandoned. It sat on the wet side of the levee, the wrong side of the new boundary line. In time, the river would claim it entirely. Like the Bieller place, Snyder's hunting cabin on Lake Bruin occupied a space out of time. Lake Bruin is an old meander loop, a remnant of days

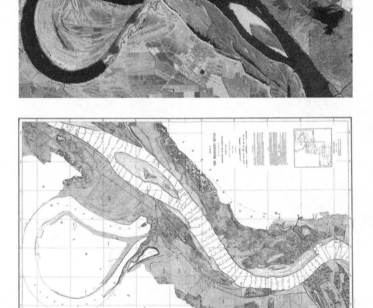

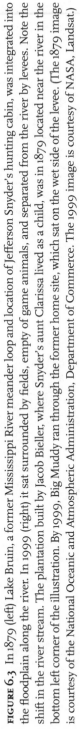

FIGURE 6.3 In 1879 (left) Lake Bruin, a former Mississippi River meander loop and location of Jefferson Snyder's hunting cabin, was integrated into the floodplain along the river. In 1999 (right) it sat surrounded by fields, empty of game animals, and separated from the river by levees. Note the shift in the river stream. The plantation built by Jacob Bieller, where Snyder's aunt Clarissa lived as a child, was in 1879 located near the river in the bottom left corner of the illustration. By 1999, Big Muddy ran through the former home site, which sat on the wet side of the levee. (The 1879 image is courtesy of the National Oceanic and Atmospheric Administration, Department of Commerce. The 1999 image is courtesy of NASA, Landsat.)

when the river ranged widely across its flood plain before levees caged it. In the 1870s, a levee severed the lake's connection with the river and it became an artifact of a former environment.[30] In April 1938, an eighty-year-old Jefferson Snyder and his friends, politicians, newspaper men, and businessmen, gathered at the cabin for a week of hunting and fishing, as they had done all their adult lives. But no hunting or fishing took place. There was poker. There was craps. There was a lot of whiskey drinking. But no hunting. The woods were too dry, they said. In truth, there was not much to hunt. The bear were gone. The deer were gone. Most of the trees were gone. Instead, Snyder and his friends got drunk and told stories about hunting in the old days. And then they all went home, back to Tallulah, Greenville, New Orleans, New York, and back to the business of planting and shipping cotton.[31]

7

The Cotton Kingdom's Edges
Made and Unmade

BETWEEN THE ADVANCING nature of the cotton plantations and the vanishing nature of the wetland forests appeared a third nature. Plantation development created new habitat for many species of flora and fauna, some of which had been scarce or unknown in earlier times, which in turn created spaces for slaves and lower class whites to hunt, gather, and mingle. For many who lived and worked on the new plantations in the lower Mississippi Valley, the edges provided the context for their experiences with and understandings of the natural environment, experiences and understandings not shared by the planters who inhabited the centers of the plantations.

The combined resources from adjacent ecological zones can significantly enhance the growth and diversity of planet and animal life, creating an intermediary third zone *ecologist* refer to as an ecotone. At a micro level in the lower valley, open areas left by dried lakes, savannahs, abandoned Indian fields, and burned-over zones created ecotones full of life. William Dunbar described one such place, a lake bed in the lower Mississippi Valley, near the Tensas River, that in the summer and fall months dried up, whereupon it "becomes covered with the most luxurious herbage; the bed of the lake then becomes the residence of immense herds of deer, of turkeys, geese, crane & which feed on the grass and grain." Similarly, the edges of fields, with their mixture of large trees, saplings, and grasses, attracted an abundance of insects and larger animals.[1]

Edges also attracted people. Slaves and some lower class whites spent much of their time on the margins of southern society, socially, politically, economically, intellectually, and environmentally. On the edges of the plantations were people who worked every day within nature, experiencing it with their bodies, principally through their labor but by consuming what they grew, hunted, and fished. For them, nature was not abstract, but sensual, palpable, inhabitable if often inhospitable, mundane.

Consider how slave owners and slaves experienced turtles, which abounded in the streams and marshes at the edges of the plantations. In his natural history of Mississippi, published in 1854, Benjamin Wailes catalogued seventeen varieties of turtles. "The shell of the largest of our turtles, the *Chelonura Temminicki*, sometimes measures three feet in its greatest diameter....The couter, or *Emys terrapin*, the second in size, is found to measure twelve or fourteen inches along the back, and the average size may be given at about eight to ten inches." The gopher turtle "attains considerable size, and possesses sufficient strength when full grown, it is said, to walk off with a man standing upon his back." Size was important to Wailes. But that was not all. Of the gopher turtle, Wailes observed that "Numbers of them are taken to the fashionable watering-places on the sea-shore, and find a ready sale, being in much demand by epicures," and the soft shell turtle "of all our turtles is esteemed the greatest delicacy," and finds "a ready sale to steamboats and restaurants." Wailes experienced turtles as a naturalist, when he measured their size and strength and catalogued them according to the Latin names of Linnaean taxonomy, and as a businessman, when he noted their market value as luxury foods.[2]

Ruben Fox, a slave in Washington County, Mississippi, provided a somewhat different perspective. "When ever I wanted to make bets," he recalled, "all I had to do was catch me a nice big terrapin. The white folks loved terrapin soup, and they would always buy them from me. All of us was allowed to keep any money we made." What Fox saw when he looked at a turtle was the means to enjoy a little wagering.[3]

Fox caught turtles for food and for the money that bought him leisure time, which for slaves was a rare luxury. Wailes studied and ate turtles for pleasure without acknowledging people such as Fox and the work they performed. Turtles mediated the relationship between the two men, not merely by bringing them together but in the process turning one into a wholesaler, the other into a scientist. Fox, when he collected and sold turtles, took the woods and wetlands into the more abstract world of commodities and prices. Wailes, when he collected turtles, brought the abstract world of science and markets into the woods and wetlands.[4]

In the lower Mississippi Valley, nature often mediated social relations, between slaves and slave owners, rich and poor, men and women, and

valley residents and the rest of the world. Mediation occurred most visibly when people exchanged natural objects, which they did regularly. The
exchange of natural objects also shaped one's perspective on nature. It is
easy to think of southern planters as deeply embedded in a natural world,
and indeed some were, but it was nature transformed into commodities
and objects of scientific observation and thought, nature in the abstract,
that men such as Wailes knew. Slave ownership made that possible by
enabling them to distance themselves from the land. In contrast, laborers
such as Ruben Fox maintained a more subjective, experiential, and practical relationship with and understanding of nature. Enslavement made
that certain, by keeping them close to the land.[5]

The distinction between those who *thought* about an abstract nature
and those who *labored* in a material nature tended to fall along class and
spatial lines. Professor Eugene Hilgard, like Benjamin Wailes before him,
was a State Geologist of Mississippi, and in that official capacity he traveled
the state in the summer of 1859, collecting information for the geological
and agricultural survey he would publish. His travels took him through
many small Mississippi towns where he sometimes struck up conversa-
tions with local farmers and working people about agriculture and soil,
and plumbed them for leads that might result in interesting geological
discoveries. At Fayette, Mississippi, however, Hilgard was clearly frustrated. "At Fayette I found nobody who knows anything; all they seemed to
care about was whisky and gambling." Most of the people of Fayette were
farmers, farm laborers, hunters, and fishers who made their livings off
the land, yet, since no one seemed interested in what he was interested in,
in Hilgard's estimation they knew nothing. The locals evidently gave the
visiting professor the brush-off.[6]

From the center of their plantations, planters measured and calculated
nature. They bought and sold the woods and the wetlands and the creatures within them. Some used their incomes to escape the forests and wetlands entirely, to live in town homes. Others used their incomes and the
time it bought to study the environment from the vantage point of objective observers. "The lands decline rapidly, as in all alluvial countries, from
the margin to the Cypress swamps, where more or less water stagnates
all the year round," wrote William Dunbar, in his account of a scientific
expedition up the Ouachita River taken at the behest of President Thomas
Jefferson. "Among the plants growing on the margin of the river is the
cheria root, used in medicine, and the cantac, occasionally used by the
hunters for food." During floods, the Mississippi River can advance "so far

as to be ready to pour over the margin into the Washita." Dunbar used the word "margin" to mean the dry land between bodies of water. It is an apt word to describe the boundary he maintained between himself and nature as he journeyed into the Ouachita country, recording landmarks and the distances between them, noting the height of the riverbanks, the locations of dry land, soil quality, mineral deposits, vegetation, and the standard of living of local inhabitants, always with the eye of an outside observer. In positioning himself outside of the natural environment, Dunbar was no different from Wailes, Hilgard, or any Natchez planter who calculated how he might turn Ouachita wetland into cotton plantation and financial gain.[7]

In January 1852, the trustees of the new university at Oxford, Mississippi, asked Benjamin Wailes to conduct a state agricultural and geological survey to document the quality and quantity of natural resources that might be used to the benefit of the state's citizens. Wailes commenced his survey in March, with a ten-day excursion to nearby Wilkinson County, which lay along Big Muddy in Mississippi's southwestern corner. By his side as he traversed the state over the next two years was his slave, Gabriel, who was about twenty years old, making him at least thirty-five years younger than Wailes, and who worked primarily as Wailes's personal servant and driver. As the slave owner burrowed into the natural history of Mississippi, the slave was made to follow. Gabriel appears to have known about collecting, preparing, and displaying specimens. On more than one occasion Wailes sent him in search of reptiles, which he pickled in whiskey, and fossils, which he cleaned and shellacked in preparation for display. Whether Gabriel had received specific instructions on what to look for or was scavenging on his own remains unclear, as is the matter of whether he acquired anything like his owner's interest in natural history. As a slave, Gabriel developed a relationship with nature along with his relationship to his owner.[8]

Wailes's relationship with nature also grew along with his relationship to Gabriel and other slaves. Many of the specimens he placed in his personal museum at his home in Washington, Mississippi, in the state capitol in Jackson, and in the collections of the Smithsonian Institution in Washington, DC, were acquired from slaves. Wailes bought turtles from slaves at the market in Natchez. His own slaves and those of his neighbors who knew about his interest in natural history brought him live rattlesnakes, moles, bats, and scorpions, for which Wailes usually paid cash. The slaves from the neighboring Ferguson plantation, where there were several Indian mounds, sold him "specimens of Indian implements."[9]

The most skillful of the slave naturalists and archaeologists was Horry. Wailes paid Horry nearly $30 for the mastodon bones he discovered encased in mud in a ravine. Wailes was thrilled by the find and he immediately sent several hands to confirm Horry's discovery. Then he went to see for himself. He put three slaves to work digging up the bones and carting them to his home, where he assigned Gabriel the task of varnishing them for display. Over the next several weeks Horry found more mastodon bones. In his final report Wailes made no mention of Horry. Instead, he used the passive voice: mastodon bones "have been obtained" and "are frequently found."[10]

Gabriel, Horry, and the numerous other slaves who gathered artifacts for Wailes knew what to look for when they went scavenging, and Wailes trusted some of them enough to have them verify stories of new discoveries. However sincerely interested they may have been in finding objects of nature and learning about them simply for the pleasure of it, any ambitions they may have had for what their endeavors as naturalists might bring them were necessarily different from those of Wailes. They might be able to escape the tedious chores of farming and to work with the master on his projects, perhaps even do some traveling. Nonetheless, they remained master and slave; the natural world at the plantation's edges that brought them together also kept them apart.

Earlier in the century, when wildlife was more abundant, owners gave slaves guns so they could defend herds and crops from human and animal predators, and so they could hunt for food for themselves and for the plantation community. They were a nuisance when they did not return from forays into the woods and remained at large, living off whatever they could catch. They brought back and sold meat and fish to planters or market vendors for cash, which allowed them to maneuver unsupervised. The woods also harbored and sustained runaways, who lived on the plantations' edges short and long term. Well into the nineteenth century, camps of runaways were discovered on Mississippi River islands and in marshes along the Ouachita River. What many people found foreboding about wetlands, their darkness and impenetrability, made them ideal hiding places. Wetlands were foes to anyone seeking control, and friends to anyone seeking to evade control.[11]

Most slaves experienced the plantations' edges temporarily and frequently, often with the permission of owners, some of whom saw advantages in looking the other way when some of their slaves went into the woods and swamps to forage and fraternize. Mark Oliver and other slaves fished Lake Washington and hunted in the woods of Washington and

Coahoma counties. "The Woods was full of game," Oliver recalled, "deer, bears, wild cows, panthers, turkeys, geese, ducks, possums, rabbits, squirrels, birds and everything." Isaac Potter, of Simpson County, hunted with "long flint guns" for pigeons and small game in the swamps and woods near his home. In the delta below New Orleans, slaves used steel and log traps, and pit traps hidden under mats of saplings and grass, to hunt for deer, opossum, and raccoon, and used muskets to shoot doves, blackbirds, and ducks. Peter Ryas recalled taking ducks and cranes from their nests in the sedge grass along Vermillion Bayou in St. Martinville Parish. Ryas and his friends also caught alligators for their tails, which they sliced into steaks and pan fried. At Fonsylvania Plantation in Warren County, Mississippi, which Benjamin Wailes sometimes managed for his wife's family, the slave Philip hunted deer that came to browse on the shoots and saplings sprouting along the farm's edges. "The biggest fun what the men had on the place was going hunting," recalled Ruben Fox of Washington County. "They could keep the kitchen supplied with everything such as coons, possums, squirrels, and rabbits," small game that thrived in the ecotone at the plantation border. Slaves also fished in the lakes and bayous on the edges of the plantations, catching garfish, perch, catfish, and crawfish with hook-and-string, net, and sometimes bare hands.[12]

Archaeological sites in the lower Mississippi Valley confirm the significance of fish and game in the diet of slaves. Excavations of a slave cabin at the edge of the Saragossa Plantation site near Natchez turned up the remains of deer, opossum, squirrel, raccoon, and rabbit. In contrast, at the plantation owner's home the only game animal archaeologists identified was rabbit. Investigators found no fish remains at the plantation house, but plenty at the slave cabin, where catfish and other fish accounted for 35 percent of all wild species recovered. Turtle shells turned up more often at the plantation home, confirming Ruben Fox's observation that "white folks loved terrapin soup." The remains of domestic animals, cows and pigs especially, made up the bulk of discoveries from both locations. For the slave owner and his family, and probably for the slaves who worked in his home and ate in his kitchen, domestic animals provided nearly all the meat in their diet. The slaves who lived in the cabins also consumed beef and pork, but they supplemented them with fish and game taken from the plantation's edges. Downriver at Nina Plantation, a sugar and cotton operation on the west bank of the Mississippi River near Pointe Coupée, the diets of slaves and slave owners diverged as at Saragossa. Archaeologists found evidence of deer, raccoon, rabbit, dove, and pigeon only at the slave cabin site. They found fish at both the cabin and plantation house, but in greater quantity at the cabin where they also found fishing weights and traps. As at Saragossa, turtle remains appeared at both sites, but more predominantly at the site of plantation owner's house.[13]

The dietary pattern of domestically raised meat supplemented with game and fish was probably typical of many southern plantations districts, if there remained edges of forests and wetlands. However, in the lower Mississippi Valley the pattern was a little different. Fish and wildlife were so abundant that they provided many people with the bulk of their diet of meat, just as they had for the Plaquemines and other precolonial indigenous peoples. The resources of the woods and swamps could be so abundant that some planters integrated them completely into the plantation economy, for example, by assigning slaves the full-time task of hunting for meat to supply the entire plantation population, black and white. In Lafayette Parish, a French-speaking planter named Duhon set one of his slaves "to hunt all the time." "He didn't do other things," recalled another slave, "The partridge and the rice birds [bobolink] he killed were cooked for the white folks. The owls and the rabbits and the coons and the possums were cooked for us." "Mos' ever' plantation kep' a man busy huntin' an' fishin' all de time," recalled Charlie Davenport, of Aventine Plantation, near Natchez. "If dey shot a big buck, us had deer meat roasted on a spit." Slaves on one Mississippi River plantation in Baton Rouge Parish relied entirely on game for their meat—they favored deer and turkey—supplemented only on rare occasions with hog meat from the master's store. Solomon Northup, a northern-born African American kidnapped and sold to a planter in the lower Red River region of Louisiana, recalled that it was customary "to hunt in the swamps for coon and opossum," and on some plantations slaves "for months at a time have no other meat than such as is obtained in this manner." According to Northup, planters encouraged slaves in their hunting "because every marauding coon that is killed is so much saved from the standing corn." Of course, it was the standing corn and the chicken coops and garbage near cabins that attracted an abundance of raccoons.[14]

Northup observed that while slaves considered raccoons a welcome source of food, planters considered them varmints, which points to the differences in the ways planters and slaves approached the natural world at the edges of the plantation. Many a planter enjoyed hunting large animals, while Benjamin Wailes observed that opossum was "much hunted and highly esteemed" among the African American population. He positioned himself outside of nature, as a scientific observer cataloguing, classifying, counting, and collecting. It all amounted to a form of control over the natural environment, similar to his activities as a planter and slave owner. Wailes was hardly unique. He conducted his agricultural and geological survey at the behest of peers, planters for whom the transformation of swamp and forest into fields by teams of enslaved laborers was the ultimate expression of the power to control one's environment.[15]

Slaves found themselves squarely within the natural world.[16] They and lower class whites let nature embrace them. This is evident in their culinary traditions, folklore, religion, indeed, their entire cosmology to the extent that we can know it. Most West African religions held that gods and spirits animated water, trees, and animals in their interactions with people. Belief in nature spirits could easily be transferred to the environment of the lower Mississippi Valley and reinforced by the experiences of working with and living off the woodlands and marshes at the edges of plantations. For example, a Mississippi River slave who claimed to have been born in a village near the Senegal and Niger rivers told of how the Niger rises in the west and flows east, coming very close to the Senegal before the two rivers abruptly diverge. For this reason, the man explained, water from the two rivers can never be mixed. One who drinks water from the Senegal cannot then cross the Niger, and vice versa. Collected in the same cup, the two waters would cling to opposite sides of the container and there would be a small gap between them. The consequence of drinking both would be a burst stomach. Whether this man transferred his belief in African water spirits to the waters of the Mississippi is not known. Such a transfer is clearer in the case of a Mississippi conjurer who believed, as many West Africans did, that trees could speak. Such casual mystification of nature shared little with the scientific and romantic notions of the planters, who saw nature as an obstacle to be removed, a place of leisure to be visited, or an object worthy of scientific inquiry.[17]

In the 1840s, Warren County, Mississippi, resident and former governor Alexander McNutt wrote a series of stories under the pseudonym "The Turkey Runner," for the popular magazine *Spirit of the Times*. McNutt told tales of fox chases, bear hunting, fishing, drinking, and boasting, set mostly in the swamps of the Mississippi Delta, the state's last wilderness, which men such as McNutt were busy cutting down and planting. Of course, he stayed in Vicksburg and wrote about this transformation, while his slaves did that work. Consider his story "The Chase in the South West," published in 1845:

Behold! how brightly breaks the morning!—how the twinkling stars pale before the crimson day! See where the breath of the night reposes in vapoury veils in the lap of the valley. All nature is calm and beautiful as the "rest of infancy". The matin hymn of the bubbling brook falls softly on the ear, it is nature's song of gladness and "the air freighted with the violet breath of spring", fans the feverish cheek and soothes the bitter thoughts and cares that corrode and destroy the finer sympathies of the heart.[18]

Clearly the writer is not immersed in nature and maintains a romantic distance from it. His use of humor also creates distance. This contrasts with the verses of slaves who sang of nature:

A hunting song:

> *Out from under the trees*
> *Our boat moves into the open water,*
> *Bring us large game and small game.*[19]

A spiritual:

> *I found free grace in de wilderness,*
> *in de wilderness, in de wilderness,*
> *I found free grace in de wilderness*
> *For I'm a-going home.*[20]

A work song:

> *A cold frosty morning*
> *the blacks feeling good*
> *Take your ax upon your shoulder*
> *Man, talk to the wood.*[21]

A lament:

> *Misery led this black to the woods,*
> *Tell my master that I died in the woods.*[22]

These are the verses of people who did not attempt to transcend nature, but who lived and worked within it. McNutt trivialized and mocked the

Mississippi Valley environment and the people who lived within it, justifying his control of them.[23]

During the Civil War, the edges between field and wetland forest
often fell between the spaces controlled by one army or the other. They
became "no man's land," even when they were in fact inhabited, as in the
lower Mississippi Valley. The ecological edges provided cover and food
for soldiers, white refugees, and liberated laborers. In the winter of 1862,
when Union gunboats shelled Baton Rouge, the town's residents packed
up their jewelry and silver and took to the woods. After three days "All
had suffered greatly from mosquitoes," recorded one of the residents.
"Several old persons and sick children died from exposure." Woods and
wetlands offered cover to Confederate guerrillas who interfered with US
Army efforts to restore the lower valley's cotton economy by burning
gins, capturing laborers, and trampling fields. It appeared the rebels had
nature on their side. Their efforts to thwart agriculture enabled weeds
to take over fields, which in turn may have touched off the plague of
army worms that consumed all sorts of grasses and grains, including
rice and corn. Worse than weeds and worms was the water. Untended
levees decayed during the war to such an extent that by war's end flooding was the single greatest obstacle to land reclamation and agricultural
restoration.[24]

The plantation edges offered cover to those who had reason to fear
both armies. Unspecified numbers of contrabands, as the former slaves
were called by the US Army, hid in the woods where they lived by hunting
hogs and cattle and by selling firewood to passing steamboats, civilian and
military. Their flight from former slaveholders and the Confederate Army
was understandable to Union Army correspondents, but their distrust of
Union soldiers pointed to a serious problem: some officers and soldiers
brutalized the people they claimed to have freed. One report told of a US
Army officer who punished a contraband laborer deemed insubordinate
by tying him up and leaving him in the woods to die of exposure to mosquitoes. The report did not treat this incident as isolated.[25]

By temporarily disrupting agriculture, war altered the environment at
the plantations' edges. The weeds, worms, and water that returned to former fields may have caused upswings in the population cycles of birds
and small animals. Abandoned and untended fields would have attracted
white-tailed deer, populations of which may have grown while war interrupted the hunting of sportsmen and deerskin traders. Soldiers needed to
eat and probably took advantage of rising wildlife populations. Refugees,

former slaves, and guerrilla fighters also would have pressured wildlife resources of the forests and swamps.[26]

The significance of the edges as a place of refuge hardly changed in the immediate aftermath of the war. Many former slaves found themselves in a political no man's land between competing forces, including land owners, the US Army, the Freedman's Bureau, the Republican Party, Southern Democrats, and the Ku Klux Klan, and sought refuge and sustenance in the plantations' edges. The resources in nearby forests and marshes provided plantation laborers with the means to sustain themselves while they held out for more favorable contracts from employers.[27] Some former slaves sought to escape the plantations entirely by moving into the edges to live permanently. In the heart of the Mississippi Delta, where the most extensive wetland forest stood, Isaiah Montgomery and a group of followers built the Mound Bayou colony where former slaves could live and work apart from white society.[28] Just as they had during the war, recalled Israel Jackson of Yalobusha County, freedmen and women "fed themselves by stealin' and getting things in de woods."[29]

Men caught opossum and raccoon, but as Wash Wilson recalled, it was women—in his case, his mother—who cooked them and served them. To enslaved women and lower class white women, many of whom also hunted and gathered, fell the additional chore of preparing and cooking game, fowl, and fish gathered from the plantation edges. The natural environment was for women, an especially palpable reality. "I don't know what my mother did in slavery. I don't think she did anything but cook," recalled Elizabeth Hines of Baton Rouge. Israel Jackson lived as a slave on a plantation in Yalobusha County, in the Delta in Mississippi. His master provided no meat whatsoever. To compensate, "My mother would go huntin' at night and get a possum to feed us and sometimes old master would ketch her and take it away from her and give her a piece of salt meat. But sometimes she'd bury a possum till she had a chance to cook it." Bess Mathis's mother cooked on the Hancock plantation in De Soto County, Mississippi, south of Memphis. When the master failed to provide meat, she and Mathis's father took their dogs and went hunting for raccoon and opossum. Recalled Mathis, "Game helps out lots." So too did plants and herbs. In the hunting camps along the Ouachita River, William Dunbar observed women pounding cantac root gathered from the marshes into a flour they mixed with corn meal to make a "wholesome and agreeable food."[30]

At the French Market in New Orleans, which attracted shoppers white and black, rich and poor, male and female, one could find nearly every

creature for sale. Game, fowl, and fish mediated relations between sup-
pliers, processors, and consumers. One amazed visitor to the market saw
vendors hawking "scores" of opossums, coons, crawfish, eels, minks, and
frogs, as well as Gulf oysters, Louisiana venison, and Mississippi bear.
"This is an unrivaled market," he declared. "Every fish that swims in the
Gulf, every bird that flies in the air, or swims upon the wave, every quad-
ruped that scours the plains or skulks in dens, which are usually eaten by
men, can be had in great abundance." A few items—elk from the Osage
River, buffalo from the Yellowstone River—were brought to market from a
great distance. However, most of the items were locally produced, caught,
and hauled from the swamps and forests around New Orleans by native
peoples, slaves, free blacks, and lower class whites. A portion of the game
sold at the French Market in New Orleans made its way to the tables of the
city's well-to-do and onto the menus of the city's finest restaurants, from
the margins of the plantation world to the center.

Until the end of the nineteenth century the market at New Orleans was
famous for its assortment of game, and its restaurants for their prepara-
tions of it: ducks of all sorts, snipe, woodcock, plover, robins, partridge,
grouse, wild turkey, squirrels, rabbits, venison, and bear. Two species of
birds were considered local specialties: the papabotte, a kind of plover
thought to imbue its consumer with amatory prowess, and the caille de lau-
rier, a kind of quail. However, early into the next century game had largely
disappeared from sight, its commerce severely restricted by the Migratory
Bird Treaty Act of 1918 and other legislation aimed at conserving species
then on the verge of extinction from over-hunting and habitat loss.[31]

Over the course of the nineteenth century, the spread of agriculture
across the lower Mississippi Valley consumed large tracts of wild area, creating a fragmented landscape of fields and edges. In time, even the edges
disappeared. The creatures of the edges, especially small mammals and
certain fowl, at first grew in numbers. Rabbits, for example, multiplied
as large predators disappeared. By the 1880s even rabbits began to disappear, when they lost nearly all forest cover across much of the lower valley.
Cotton fields offered nothing to rabbits. By the 1920s their population was
at a historic low. Their disappearance led to the final demise of remaining
smaller predators, such as the bobcat. Quail, which at first become numerous with the spread of agriculture and the creation of edges, also began to
decline in the twentieth century.[32]

The legacy of the edges between plantation and wetland forest persisted in the culture of the people who once lived there. Wild duck "should

not be stuffed, but cleaned well and seasoned with pepper and salt, inside and outside, and put into a hot oven. Ten minutes will cook it," advised Abby Fisher in her cookbook. She added, "Do not forget to baste all game and fowls while cooking, so as to make them juicy." Although not from the lower Mississippi Valley, Fisher lived much of her life, in slavery and in freedom, in an environmentally and culturally similar place, Mobile, Alabama. Her cookbook, *What Mrs. Fisher Knows about old Southern Cooking* (1881), was among the first published by an African American woman, and it documented a culinary tradition that had, until then, existed almost entirely off the written record and within African American oral tradition. What Mrs. Fisher knew about cooking was what Wash Wilson's mother and Bess Mathis's mother and Elizabeth Hines's mother and so many other women born into slavery in the lower Mississippi Valley and across the South knew about gathering and cooking food on the edges of plantations.[33]

Fisher intended her book for a white female readership whose experiences with nature would necessarily be less intimate than her own. She conveyed what she knew by abstracting her dishes from their personal and environmental contexts, and breaking them down into lists of ingredients, measurements, proportions, and temperatures to be reassembled in other kitchens, much as Benjamin Wailes abstracted Mississippi turtles by cataloguing them. Although readers may have been familiar with preparing some types of game, such as venison, among white folks of the sort who would purchase a cookbook, hunting was a masculine rite that was circumscribed by traditions, experiences, and expectations associated with race, class, and gender. White men of property and standing shot deer and bear. Blacks, poor whites, and boys learning to handle a rifle shot small animals. Fisher offered no suggestions on how best to prepare opossum or raccoon, although she surely knew how. Likewise, she offered no recipe for catfish. But she did provide recipes for venison and turtle soup. Middle-class white women probably heard about how some people hunted such creatures, and they saw the evidence of it when they strolled past the stands at the market, but opossum and raccoon stew was not for them.

Four years after Mrs. Fisher published her cookbook, the first truly Creole cookbook appeared from a New Orleans publisher. *La Cuisine Creole* (1885), by Lafcadio Hearn, claimed to be "A Collection of Culinary Recipes from Leading Chefs and Noted Creole Housewives, Who Have Made New Orleans Famous for Its Cuisine." The section on game was extensive and included recipes for wild duck, goose, partridge, pigeon, quail, rice bird, venison, rabbit, and squirrel, but no opossum or raccoon. When the author promised that squirrel and rabbit pie "is almost as good as venison pie," he presumed a limited culinary experience on the part of his readers. He may simply have known that his readers would never prepare squirrel but might be titillated by thoughts of squirrel pie. His neglect of opossum, a meat savored by many African Americans was perhaps a tacit recognition of a boundary his white readers were not likely to cross.[34]

If the boundary between plantation center and edge persisted in the minds and subcultures of residents of the lower Mississippi Valley, out of doors that boundary eventually disappeared, as the spreading plantations destroyed the edges they had at first created. Nearly all fell under the control of the planters, or else it was shut out and locked away. In 1904, Mississippi governor James K. Vardaman supervised the construction of Parchman Farm penitentiary out of 4,000 acres of Delta wetland forest in Sunflower County, where society's most marginalized and abject members would be sent and made to grow cotton. Two years earlier and a hundred miles to the south, the edges of the plantation world symbolically closed, with the fiasco that was President Theodore Roosevelt's bear hunt.[35]

The primary guide in the 1902 presidential hunt was Holt Collier, the lower Mississippi Valley's most famous woodsman. Born into slavery in Jefferson County, Mississippi, he was a young boy when taken by his owner to Washington County in the Delta. An expert tracker and hunter, he worked for the Confederate Army as a scout in the region along the river between Memphis and Natchez. After the war, in freedom, Collier traveled to Texas, Mexico, and Alaska, where he shot grizzly bear, or so he later claimed. When he returned to the Delta he made his living on the edges of the plantation world by hunting, black bears mostly. Near the end of his life he boasted of having killed over 2,000.[36]

In 1902, Roosevelt came to the Delta to shoot a bear at the behest of a group of notables led by John Stuyvesant Fish, president of the Illinois Central Rail Road, on whose land the hunt took place. In the months before the president's arrival in Mississippi, newspapers reported "that bears are unusually plentiful for this season of the year, and the swamps are filled with many fine specimens of the black bruin." Collier promised an impatient president a bear on the first day, and he made good on his word. However, the bear was not the fat 300 to 600 pound animal the president had been told to expect. It was a lean, graying animal with rotting teeth, one Collier recognized as the same bear that had killed one of his dogs on another occasion. Collier's dogs chased the animal to near exhaustion, at which point Collier was able to knock it half senseless with the butt of his rifle and put a rope around it. With the dazed animal tied to a tree, he signaled for the president and the rest of the party. When Roosevelt arrived he was disturbed by what he saw. At least one dog lay dead, and the bear was dazed and clearly in agony, wounded from dog bites and Collier's beatings. He refused to shoot it but asked that someone put the animal out of its misery. Collier and another man then knifed the bear. During the rest of the hunt, the party never saw another bear. The national press had great fun with the story of the president who refused to shoot a roped and wounded bear, and one enterprising toymaker capitalized on the publicity when he introduced the Teddy Bear.[37]

Collier and his stories, including aspects of the Roosevelt bear hunt, provided inspiration for William Faulkner's story of the last bear hunt in the disappearing wilderness at the edge of an expanding modern world of sawmills, railroads, cotton plantations, and towns. Sam Fathers, the guide in the novella, "The Bear," is clearly modeled on Collier, as is Boon Hogganbeck, who in the story knifes the old bear to death in a vain effort to save the dog he loves. However, it is the bear, Old Ben, who provides perhaps the strongest link between Faulkner's story and President Roosevelt's bear hunt. The animal that Collier caught, and which Roosevelt refused to shoot, may not have been the last bear in the Delta, but he was the last bear the hunting party saw, an indication of how few there were by that time. Within twenty years, according to the state wildlife inventory, there really were no bears left in the Delta. In Faulkner's story, Sam Fathers dies the moment Boon kills the old bear. Holt Collier outlived the last Delta bears by a decade or more. He died not in the forest, like Sam Fathers, but at his home in Greenville.[38]

8

Engineering the River of Empire

THE 1849 FLOOD sparked a vigorous debate over whether and how to control the Mississippi River. For every forceful advocate of cut-offs, levees, and outlet channels there was an opponent certain that such measures would fail and perhaps bring ruin to the lower valley. Over the next decade nothing much was settled. Then, in April of 1858, the river broke through a west bank levee a few miles upriver from New Orleans. By June, it had broken through the levee line in three dozen places. The Delta, in Mississippi, sat under three feet of water. So, too, did New Orleans suburbs, and all the land across the river from the city, extending west to Bayou LaFourche. According to one calculation, as the river crested that summer, each day for several days the equivalent of a lake a mile square and eighty feet deep poured through giant holes in the levees and onto cotton and sugar fields. When the waters receded, much of the valley lay in ruins. Planters within the four parishes that comprised the Tensas bottom, among them Biellers and Snyders, lost a cotton crop worth $5 million, the equivalent today of about $100 million dollars. Losses were equally great in the Delta and in the sugar parishes below Pointe Coupée. It was the fourth flood in a disastrous decade that began with the Sauvé Plantation crevasse and the terrible flooding of New Orleans. The 1850s were a bitterly divisive time in America, but in the fall of 1858 there was one subject on which all agreed: the flooding had to be stopped. But who should do it, and how?[1]

The French and Spanish colonial regimes had made levee construction an obligation of land ownership. Shirkers risked forfeiture. Individual landowners, however, undertook construction. The royal engineer might inspect the works, but he generally did not design, build, or maintain levees on private lands. Only when neighbors got to squabbling and their differences were clearly irreconcilable would the governor and his engineer step in and take charge. When the United States took control of the lower valley, government was even less active. Riverside planters and farmers did ask for assistance from county and state governments, but localized efforts at flood control were inadequate. In 1816, New Orleans flooded, even though the municipal levee held, because weaker private levees fronting plantations upriver gave way and water poured into the city from behind. In response, Benjamin Latrobe proposed to build a comprehensive levee system based on Prussian engineering along the Oder River that would integrate municipal and private sections to protect New Orleans from all directions. The city council declined Latrobe's offer and flood problems persisted. Taxpayers resisted paying for levees on anyone's land but their own, even if they understood that the chain of individual levees was only as strong as the weakest link. Municipal, county, and parish governments tried to coordinate private flood control efforts and to close holes in the levee line where it crossed public land, but that proved difficult to do. Only when the federal government relinquished unsold swamp lands to the states, on condition that they sell the land to raise money for flood control and swamp reclamation, did money begin to flow into the treasuries of county and parish, and eventually, state levee boards.[2]

The Swamp Acts of 1849 and 1850 comprised the first major steps taken by the United States government on the matter of flood control in the Mississippi valley, though they were intended to encourage states to act. State levees would be an improvement over county and parish and individual flood control efforts. When Mississippi, Louisiana, and Arkansas became states, unsold public lands remained federal property. With these acts, the United States government transferred unsold swampland to the state governments to sell to private interests, on condition that the revenues from their sale be used to fund flood control and wetland drainage. Flood control, however, was a secondary, if necessary, objective, the primary one being settlement and cultivation. The acts did not encourage the construction of a uniform and unbroken wall against the river, nor did they permit the use of funds from new land sales to build levees on lands already settled or surveyed. The states were to undertake surveys, administer sales, and supervise construction. Meanwhile, the federal government divested itself of the swamplands of the lower Mississippi Valley. It did, however, commission the Delta Survey, a study of the entire lower river valley, from Cairo to New Orleans, to provide information useful to the states in their efforts to control the river. Some congressmen argued in favor of greater federal involvement in flood control as well as in the construction of national roads and canals. Others argued for federal responsibility in developing the West, which in the antebellum era included the lower Mississippi Valley.[3]

The decision not to make flood control a federal responsibility was based on concerns about expenditures and distance. Good arguments were made for considering the Mississippi River an inland sea, like the Great Lakes, with implications for national defense. The Constitution also granted the central government jurisdiction over harbors and coastlines, in the interest of interstate and international commerce and navigation. Indeed, in 1852, as part of a $2.25 million appropriation for nationwide improvement projects on 100 waterways, Congress designated $150,000 for surveying, dredging, and removing snags from the Mississippi Valley. Moreover, until the transfer of swamplands to the states, much of the property that would have been protected was public, rendering moot the constitutional problem of using federal funds and authority to develop private property.[4]

The Swamp Acts encouraged state governments to take the lead in water control, to which Louisiana and Arkansas responded by establishing state levee boards and commissions. Mississippi delegated its business to county governments, thereby defeating the act's purpose. All three states sold land, disbursed funds, and built levees, which by 1858 lined the lowlands on both sides of the river for much of the stretch from the Arkansas River to the Gulf of Mexico. However, the system was far from watertight. Money leaked into corrupt hands. Big Muddy leaked onto cotton and sugar fields. The flood of 1858 demonstrated that the individuals and county governments had not been up to the task of controlling the river, and perhaps never would be. The state of Mississippi quickly set up a Board of Levee Commissioners that assumed responsibility for construction, but levee failures across the river, in Louisiana and Arkansas, called into question the reliability of state-regulated levees. The principal author of the Delta Survey, the Army's chief engineer, who in 1858 had not yet completed the assignment given him eight years earlier, used the flood as an opportunity to make the case that water control in the lower valley needed to be handed over to him. At the start of the Civil War the question of who should take responsibility for controlling the Mississippi River remained unanswered. After it was over, the levees were in ruins, the plantations under water, and state coffers empty. By that time the federal government was already in the business of subsidizing transcontinental railroads and undertaking other measures to integrate states and regions into a more centralized nation, which made it the obvious leader in the matter of controlling the Mississippi River. Even the states of Louisiana, Mississippi, and Arkansas agreed, despite having just fought a war in part to protect the rights of states from an overbearing central government. Resistance to federal flood control came largely from the North and from politicians concerned about the constitutional authority for federal action. By 1879, the year Congress created the Mississippi River Commission, nearly all agreed that effective flood control required federal leadership.[5]

The engineering and scientific question, of how the river should be controlled, if it indeed could be controlled, necessarily raised the political question of who should control the river. The argument for private individual and county responsibility assumed the river was nothing more than a stream of water capable of being redirected at any given point by earthen walls of sufficient dimension. The argument for federal control viewed the river as a hydraulic system that reached across state boundaries, from which viewpoint it followed that flood control should be systematic and interstate—that is to say, federal. State governments fell on one side or the other. In assuming responsibility for flood control from its river counties, Mississippi sought to address the political and administrative failures of county governments but did not change its view that floods and flood control were local matters. Louisiana, no doubt because it lay at the end of the river, tended to see the Mississippi and its floods as originating beyond its borders and pushed if not for federal control, at least for coordinated management with Mississippi and Arkansas. Political culture favored local control and development. Science favored regional development. The engineers who sought survey and design contracts knew where the money came from and were tempted to tell politicians in Washington, so long as they supported levee construction, everything they wanted to hear. Those same politicians in turn found in the authority of science a powerful argument to level against congressional opponents of federal flood control.[6]

There were two competing sciences of rivers and floods, and by mid-nineteenth century they were becoming hardened paradigms, locked in competition for the full support of the federal government. Hydrography described and mapped the river, its forms and features, identifying where banks were caving, bars building, cut-offs forming. The Delta Survey was a model hydrographic study. Hydrographers worked inductively, collecting mountains of data about a specific river to formulate theories about how it worked, and then perhaps to make theories about how rivers generally worked. Hydrographers might study one river to help them understand another, but typically they would explain why the specifics of one case made it inapplicable to another. Hydrologists were quite different. They worked reductively, using theories about slow, meandering rivers in general to make sense of the specific facts collected from a particular river. They offered theories for predicting river behavior, where banks were likely to give way, bars likely to build, bends likely to be cut-off. Hydrologists drew on case studies from one river to hypothesize about another.[7]

Hydrographers looked at the banks of the Mississippi and saw natural boundaries between water and land. To their thinking, floods were unnatural disturbances. Levees, whether built by the river or by engineers, were therefore natural. Caleb Forshey, for example, argued that the river was always building up its levees, confining itself in its channel, forcing itself to flow faster and straighter. If the lower valley were left alone, the self-taught engineer James Buchanan Eads is said to have remarked, in time it would create its own levees and cease to flood of its own accord. Human-made barriers merely hastened the natural process by which water and land were separated.[8]

The most famous American hydrographer of the nineteenth century was Andrew Atkinson Humphreys, chief of the Army Corps of Engineers and principal author of the Delta Survey report. Humphreys and his team required a decade to complete their 600-page study. Several times he had to explain to Congress why the assignment was unfinished and request further appropriations. In his introduction he wanted it understood "how absolutely essential it was in every division of the subject to collect fact upon fact, until the assemblage of all revealed what were and what would be the true conditions of the river in every stage that it had passed through or could attain, and thus to substitute observed facts and the laws connecting them for assumed or imperfectly observed data and theoretical speculations." The first half of the report dissected the river in mind-numbing detail. The final sections offered recommendations for flood control and for removing sand bars from the river's mouth. The author's confidence was absolute: "all knowledge requisite to accomplish the objects of the present investigation has been secured."[9]

Humphreys likened the lower Mississippi River to "an immense reservoir, into which the floods of the tributaries are successively poured." Know the volume of water dumped into the lower river any point in time and one can know the height of the levees necessary to contain it. The problem of flood control was that simple. And so he measured water volume and velocity, at various points in the stream and at different times of the year, and measured precipitation. He concluded the 1858 flood was an all-time high not likely to be repeated, using it as his guide for calculating the maximum amount of water that levees would have to contain. When the river reached new heights the very next year, Humphreys did not flinch. He simply added the new data to his tables and carried on. He flatly rejected the idea that levees worsened the problem of flooding on the grounds that levees added no additional water to the river. Flooding was all about water volume and nothing more, certainly not about the relationship between land and water. Not even the dirt in the water mattered to Humphreys. The Mississippi River, he declared, was so "undercharged" with sediment that it had no predictable effect on the flow of water, nor on the deposition of sediment. The interaction of water and sediment in an "undercharged" river "will follow no law," and therefore was of no concern to the scientist. This was quite a statement to make about the muddy Mississippi.[10]

Several hydrologists authored studies of the lower Mississippi River. One, Charles Ellet, found enough support in Congress for his approach to river science to win a research grant from the War Department. His report could not have been more different from Humphreys's. Completed in just two years and half its length, it never pretended to hold all requisite knowledge. While Ellet's study offered plenty of data, it also offered a very different perspective on the Mississippi and on rivers in general. For hydrologists such as Ellet, rivers were giant machines that moved water and earth, in some cases in great quantities, over thousands of miles, according to laws that predicted the effects of the many interactions of water and land. Ellet looked at the banks of the Mississippi and saw that the unceasing interaction of water and dirt connected the entire Mississippi River system, from the Rocky and Allegheny Mountains from whose hillsides dirt was eroded to the lowlands of the lower valley where dirt accumulated. Banks and natural levees were not barriers between water and land, in Ellet's view, but a kind of middle zone between the two, partly solid, partly liquid, hard yet porous, and always shifting, like the river itself. Floods, he argued, began and ended on the land, with run-off and inundation. Agriculture and deforestation along the river's upper regions, in Ohio and western Pennsylvania, caused flooding in the vicinity of New Orleans by altering the speed and volume of run-off. The spread of agriculture into the Far West, he predicted, would cause more devastating floods in years to come. Humphreys measured water; Ellet measured land. Humphreys could only see the water downstream as a reservoir for water upstream. For Ellet, land was reservoir for all water, and if it was to be removed from the land in one place, it needed to be stored on the land somewhere else. Humphreys sought to regulate the river. Ellet sought to assist "the river to regulate itself." Ellet concluded that levees were not the solution to flooding, but in fact contributed to the problem. "It is essentially the exclusion of this water of overflow from the swamps, that is now creating so much distress in lower Louisiana," he argued, "while to remove the water and reclaim these swamps has become a prominent object of National and State legislation." Ellet also opposed cut-offs. By hastening the flow of water they did indeed alleviate flooding upstream, but they rapidly passed water into the channel downstream and worsened problems there. Other hydrologists argued that at the very least, before one invested in a levee, one ought to be sure that the ground upon which it was to stand was indeed solid.[11]

A good example of the difference between Humphreys's hydrography and Ellet's hydrology can be found in their disagreement over the effect of levees on the riverbed in the lowest reaches of the river. Evidence from the Po River, in Italy, indicated that levees had raised the bed of the river, and so had raised the level of the water and the risk of flooding. Ellet explained the phenomenon as the natural result of the gradual elongation of the Po's delta into the Adriatic Sea, by continual sedimentary deposition. The same process would occur in the vicinity of New Orleans, Ellet agreed, but so gradually—in about twenty centuries—that the problem was not worth worrying about. Humphreys disputed the facts of the Po River, not so much because they mattered—Ellet had conceded they did not—but to advance his case that only he had provided a full study of the Mississippi River, whereas everyone else offered "supposed facts." Ellet and anyone else who failed to see the flaw in the studies of the Po could not be trusted on the subject of the Mississippi River. According to Humphreys, only he could rightly proclaim that "every river phenomenon has been experimentally investigated and elucidated," and "the great problem of protection against inundation...solved." Ellet viewed delta elongation as a natural process exacerbated, albeit slowly, by unnatural levees. Humphreys, who favored levees, would have none of that.[12]

The question of why the banks of the Mississippi so easily caved and eroded offers another example of the different scientific approaches to the river. Humphreys collected data on the banks and concluded that they eroded because they "are underlain by a [stratum] of nearly pure sand," which easily washed away. Hydrologist Raymond Thomassy concluded that the banks consisted of more than sand. Within them immense holes absorbed and hid incalculable amounts of water during flood stages and then released it. The movement of water through the banks, especially where sand was squeezed between strata of clay, shifted and undermined them. However, riverbanks stored water.[13]

Opposing sciences led to opposing political solutions for flood control. Hydrographers offered a patchwork approach to controlling the river. Build levees where water overflowed, do nothing where it did not. Problems along the river could be isolated and prioritized, which suited congressional budget-makers. Chief Engineer Humphreys encouraged Congress to take a greater hand in managing levee and reclamation projects, although his approach suggested that the river might be controlled locally, one problem at a time. Levees were all Humphreys recommended in an argument for federal supervision that was more political than scientific. Levees had thus far failed, he contended, "not from inherent difficulties in the construction of works of protection," but from inconsistencies between levee board jurisdictions. The embankments needed to be standardized, their construction regulated by congressional appointees, since the states could not work together. Humphreys advocated stronger federal involvement in local flood control. A majority of Congress continually disagreed. Ellet conceded that levee construction could remain primarily "a local measure, but one requiring state legislation, and official execution and discipline." Levees, however, were only one part of his proposal. Ellet prescribed a series of interdependent mechanisms, ranging from outlets for the releasing of water onto the flood plain, to reservoirs in the uplands and mountains that would hold rain and snow melt until the threat of flooding had passed, to levees. Another hydrologist went further and recommended not just ordinary levees but Haupt levees, independent structures placed on the outside of bends that would allow the river to meander naturally and encourage it to build its own levees on the inside curves. The problem of flood control required several mechanisms, Ellet argued, "that harmonize with each other." Ellet's hydrological science demanded congressional action on a grand scale, and so Congress overwhelmingly rejected it.[14]

Wartime neglect, conflict, and flooding damaged the levees, in many places beyond repair. When Benjamin Butler captured New Orleans and Baton Rouge, in April 1862, the river was on the rise. By the time the water crested that summer at yet another historic high, much of the riverside had been deserted by its human occupants. Slaves ran for Union lines, to

New Orleans especially. Confederate supporters ran for the edges of the valley, east and west. As Butler and his subordinates fought Confederate offensives and negotiated with former slaves, nothing was done to shore up the levees. The rise in the spring of 1863 was rather modest, and yet the embankments were in such a sorry state that the sugar fields of several of the lower-most parishes flooded. Captain Samuel Cozzens organized a labor force of former slaves and set them to work repairing levees in Ascension Parish, paying them with corn and pork. Hunger brought people back to the land. So, too, did the guns of the US Army, after General Nathaniel P. Banks began to implement his plan for "compulsory" free labor. Forced to work for wages on plantations supervised by whites, many of the 700,000 former slaves in the lower Mississippi Valley found themselves once again planting cotton, cutting sugarcane, and building levees. Progress on the levees was slow and uneven. Confederate guerrillas chased away workers, set fire to sheds and cabins, and sabotaged construction. As the Republican administration in Washington debated what to do with the former slaves, reports from Louisiana and Mississippi made it clear that in the lower valley, whatever the president and Congress decided to do, Reconstruction would depend on what could be done to protect land from inundation.[15]

During the war years, several efforts were made to put abandoned plantation lands into the hands of former slaves. In the Port Royal Sound area of South Carolina, which the Union Navy and Army had taken early in the war, agents of the federal government, along with missionaries, profiteers, and other nongovernment agents, settled former slaves on abandoned land and had them raise food to feed themselves and cotton to bring in revenue for the Union war effort. This was also to be an initial experiment in freedom and reconstruction. In January 1865, General William T. Sherman issued Special Field Order No. Fifteen, which directed that a stretch of Carolina and Georgia coastline be broken into forty-acre allotments for former slaves. In March 1865, Congress passed the Freedman's Bureau Act, which extended Sherman's idea to help freedmen across the South secure their independence and freedom.[16]

In the Mississippi Valley, a similar process of land confiscation, redistribution, and resettlement unfolded, first under the army and then under the Freedman's Bureau. The army needed to get the former slaves out of its way. The Treasury Department needed to increase revenues. Federal agents and officers worked with southern white landowners who proclaimed loyalty to the Union, and with northern civilian land speculators who moved onto abandoned plantations, to help them negotiate for the labor of former slaves. Where negotiations failed, the army compelled laborers to work. In many places, freed men and women did not wait to be told where to go and for whom to work; they simply took fields as their own and raised food crops for themselves and for market. The army also established what become known as home farms, to which they relocated African American laborers from around the lower valley and set them to planting, but the army also initiated various programs of education and indoctrination intended to help former slaves become free subjects and citizens of the United States.[17]

Before any of these social and economic experiments could succeed in the lower valley, land along the river had to be secured against flooding. The work of rebuilding the levees uniquely complicated Reconstruction, most acutely in the moments when the Union government and army became the overseers of county and parish construction projects built with corvée labor, that is, labor not attached or assigned to particular plantations but drafted and moved from place to place as project engineers and construction supervisors required. Such moments, deemed military necessities, belied the benefits of freedom and citizenship. In Pointe Coupée Parish, the provost marshal as "a military necessity" ordered all able-bodied hands to work at restoring decayed embankments. In St. John the Baptist Parish, farmers paid a tax to have the federal government, both military and civilian branches build a new levee, with former slaves providing the manual labor. In June 1864, reconstruction of the levees remained far from complete. Colonel Samuel Thomas, provost marshal of Freedmen, welcomed the dry spring, but worried that numerous breaks in the levee between Washington County, Mississippi, and Natchez, where he was redistributing over 25,000 acres of abandoned land, would not be repaired in time to save the next year's crop. Another dry spring would be too much to hope for. Indeed, the flooding in April 1865 not only interfered with planting but also stopped the redistribution of land to freedmen.[18]

The use of army resources to construct levees for the protection and advancement of private property interests resurrected an old debate over federal aid for internal improvements. Similarly, the government's power to confiscate land from disloyal citizens had long been debated. Confiscation and redistribution had its advocates among radical Republicans seeking to impoverish and embarrass southern planters as well as among those who believed land to be the only means to guarantee the freedom of the former slaves. Where the land in question required flood control there could be found support for federally financed levees. However, confiscation, redistribution, and thus federally sponsored flood control also had its opponents. Moderate Republicans, including Abraham Lincoln, recognized the justice of giving land to former slaves, but not the legality of confiscating land without due process. In his view, wartime confiscations, including emancipation, were temporary means of achieving military objectives, which would cease to be in effect once the war ended. While some argued that emancipation amounted to a justifiable confiscation of property from disloyal citizens, others pointed out that it would become permanent only upon the ratification of the Thirteenth Amendment.[19]

No proposal for a similar amendment regarding land confiscation and redistribution garnered much support. The president and members of Congress had reason for opposing such an amendment, which would profoundly alter the balance of power between state and citizen. While the federal government debated the legal abstractions of confiscation and federal flood control, in the lower valley thousands of acres sat abandoned and under water, and thousands of people sought land and work. Out of necessity, the army and other federal agents brought land and labor together. Once the war ended, however, the constitutional questions came to the fore. On August 16, 1865, President Andrew Johnson ordered the property of all pardoned Confederates restored to their possession. The Freedmen's Bureau commissioner hesitated to carry out the order. When Congress passed a bill to reauthorize the bureau and its program of land confiscation and redistribution, Johnson vetoed it. Another bill won sufficient support in Congress to override the veto, but only after it was stripped of a land provision. Congress did sell freedmen some public lands at a discount, but those along the Mississippi River entailed additional expenses for flood control structures, which few could afford.[20]

In the lower Mississippi Valley, most land ended up in the possession of whites, who also found levees prohibitively expensive, and state governments were in no position to help them. The magnitude of the task and of the valley demanded federal action. While landowners argued against federal land confiscation and redistribution on constitutional grounds, they pushed for federal flood control on behalf of private interests despite the Constitution. In time, however, lower valley landowners won congressional support for federal flood control by fashioning an argument that skirted the constitutional question entirely, when they redefined levees as instruments primarily for improving navigation, and only incidentally about flood control.

The new argument for federal leadership in controlling the Mississippi River had three parts: first, federal authority over navigation was clearly constitutional. Second, the nation's interests in financing transportation improvements on the Mississippi River and into the Far West along its tributaries were unrelated to the divisive politics of North and South and the question of federal aid and protection for the freedmen. Third, the objective authority of science proved that levees kept rivers open to navigation, and that the Mississippi River offered the most natural and therefore most efficient means of connecting West, East, and South into a continental empire.[21]

Louisiana, Mississippi, and Arkansas were in no position to shore up defenses by war's end. Louisiana tried, issuing bonds to raise money for levee repair and construction. The U.S. Army governed the state in accordance with martial law. In addition to the day-to-day struggles between landowners and laborers then playing out on every plantation, violent race riots made for an unstable economic climate. No smart investor was going to buy Louisiana bonds, and in fact very few did. Mississippi and Arkansas were bankrupt and their situation dire. Mississippi's state levee board delegated maintenance and repair responsibilities to the counties, which in turn delegated them to landowners, who had no funds and were struggling with laborers. With nowhere else to turn, senators and representatives from the three states began to coordinate their lobbying efforts in Washington.[22]

In 1865, the state of Mississippi sent a committee to Washington to ask for federal funds to rebuild levees. In addition, the committee sought out private investors. The members returned to Jackson empty-handed. In June 1866, the state of Louisiana submitted a memorial to Congress, requesting aid for reconstruction of levees. The House referred it to the Committee for Ways and Means. The Senate sent a similar petition to a new select committee to study the matter, which reported back a bill for appropriating funds. The bill never became law. Over the next year, the political climate in Washington shifted considerably. As Congress moved to impeach President Andrew Johnson, it also moved to punish the southern states. Taking up the question of appropriations for levees, in the summer of 1867, the House of Representatives resolved that the southern states would have to swear loyalty and accept harsher terms of reconstruction than those offered by Johnson. Once fully reconstructed, the southern states would be free to ask for appropriations, which Congress might still not be in a mood to grant. One Pennsylvania congressman indicated that he would not be inclined toward generosity under any circumstances. The subject was then referred to the Committee on Reconstruction.[23]

The House Committee on Reconstruction was at that moment considering confiscating all public land given to southern railroad companies before the war in order to grant homesteads to "poor men, white and black." The subject raised, again, the issue of "the rights of vested property" and the authority of the central government. When one representative asserted that rebels had forfeited their right to protection under the Constitution, another rebutted that stockholders in southern railroad companies "are to be found North, South, East, and West." Representative Fernando Wood, Democrat of New York, was more pointed. Everyone knows, he argued, that investors from Boston, New York, and Philadelphia built the South's railroads. When the discussion turned to appropriations for levees, the House remained divided between those who sought to punish the South and those who did not wish to do so if it undermined property rights. Representative Benjamin F. Butler of Massachusetts introduced a resolution authorizing the commanding general of the Fifth Military District, which included Louisiana, to issue bonds for levees, placing "a perpetual lien" on all lands protected by them. A lot of Northerners now owned riverside plantations, though not nearly so many as owned stock in southern railroads. A former Union Army general, Butler had governed New Orleans during the war, and many in the city loathed him. His resolution was purely punitive. Wood objected, in the interest of northern investors in southern lands, and in the interest of southern whites, with whom he had long sympathized, and the resolution was dropped without debate. But the point had been made. Congress would not take southern land, but neither would it assist in its development.[24]

Over the next two years, developments in the West increasingly took angry northern eyes off the South. The nation's infatuation with transcontinental railroads displaced concerns with waterways. It might have been the end of debate over federal involvement in flood control in the lower Mississippi Valley, and yet Republican Senator John S. Harris, a New Yorker who in 1863 acquired a cotton plantation in flood-prone Concordia Parish, saw an opportunity. On at least one earlier occasion Harris had introduced a resolution, requesting that the Senate Committee on Finance look into appropriating funds for rebuilding levees destroyed during the war. In a long speech delivered in June 1870, he explained the nation's interest in the lower Mississippi Valley, expanding on an idea articulated the previous year by James Alcorn of Mississippi at the commercial convention in Memphis. In a public statement, the members of the convention had acknowledged "the fact that 'Westward the Star of Empire has taken its way,'" and so "we declare in favor of the Crescent City as the seat of a commercial empire, whose scepter shall rule the world." Harris likewise spoke of commerce and the joining of East and West, rather than of flood control. "Build railroads as we may, a great navigable river will always be a highway," he declared. In the case of the Mississippi River and its tributaries, that highway stretched for 16,000 miles and carried an annual commerce in the valley estimated at over $2 billion. It was the principal highway for bringing the wealth of western forests and mines into the East, and for bringing eastern and overseas manufactures into the interior of the nation. The East-West connection was central to Harris's argument. The Ohio and Missouri rivers connected the Alleghenies to the Rockies. At the center of the axis lay the Mississippi and the most fertile agricultural land in the world—manufactures in the East, raw resources in the West, and agriculture in the valley between, with water connecting it all. "In this age of great engineering enterprises, when Pacific railroads and Suez canals dwarf the old Egyptian pyramids, it may well-nigh be said of such efforts 'nothing is impossible.' The civilization of our age undertakes nobler tasks and enterprises of wider and more lasting benefit than those of the pyramid builders. Its network of railroads, its steamships and telegraphs, and its clearing of forests are triumphs full of utility to all, and this changing a watery waste to a smiling expanse of cultivated lands unequaled in fertility is in accord with its other useful undertakings." The Civil War had ended only five years earlier, and yet here was a senator representing Louisiana, one of the most recalcitrant of southern states, arguing for the region's centrality to the creation of the American Empire.[25]

Harris gave slight nod to issues that dominated Reconstruction. He did not request federal assistance in protecting land from inundation. Although that was what he wanted, Congress had continually proven unreceptive to assisting southern landowners. When southern members of Congress argued that flood control would help black landowners and laborers, their northern colleagues thought them insincere. When they sought help in protecting their own land, Northerners thought they lacked contrition. The westward course of empire, however, took the nation across the Mississippi Valley, making these southern states into the middle ground between East and West.

The Mississippi River's central role in westward expansion was no mere political assertion but a known fact demonstrated "by careful scientific experiments." From East and West the river and its tributaries each year collected a bulk of sediment a mile square and 300 feet deep and deposited it over 32,000 square miles of floodplain, building the delta out into the sea. As flowed the silt, so would flow the commerce of the United States. The river was a force for destruction or it could be harnessed for the nation's interest. It was the same scientific argument that had helped convince Thomas Jefferson that control of the West was the key to control of the Mississippi River, and that control of the Mississippi River was squarely in the nation's interest.[26]

Harris asked for $50 million, the estimate arrived at by the southern commercial convention. The money could be expended entirely under government care and direction, or it might be invested in an incorporated company. "By such a course the Pacific railroad has been built and the development of the far West helped; but this [the Mississippi River] is to be far greater in results than that transcontinental road." He happened to have a corporation in mind, the Mississippi Valley Levee Company, but which option Congress exercised was less important to him than that Congress appropriate the funds and get on with the work of reconstructing the Mississippi River.[27]

Committees discussed bills and resolutions for several years, with no action resulting until the flood of 1874. That April, Congress debated three bills pertaining to the lower Mississippi Valley. One provided relief for flood victims, another proposed to establish a committee of engineers to report on the means and cost of permanently redeeming the flood plain, and a third sought to open the mouth of the Mississippi River to large oceangoing vessels, by canal or by permanent removal of the sand bars. The personalities and egos of rival engineers, northern resentment of southern planters and politicians, and real concerns about the state of the treasury enlivened debates. Nevertheless, they all raised the abstract constitutional question of the power and responsibility of the central government to control nature in the national interest.[28]

Representative Frank Morey of Louisiana, a Boston-born newcomer to the Deep South, introduced a resolution authorizing the president to issue army rations to flood victims, spurred by the president's earlier responses to national disasters in 1873. In that year, Chicago had burned, and yellow fever had taken 1,200 lives in Memphis. In both cases, with the Congress in recess, the president had authorized aid. Morey then made a case for further relief appropriations. As with the disasters of fire and disease, he argued, the flood in the lower valley "is confined to no class of people.

The colored laborer and the tenderly nurtured southern lady are alike suffering." There were some objections, but the bill passed quickly with the addition of a Senate amendment that would cause all relief operations to expire in September.[29]

Morey also introduced the bill "to provide for the appointment of a commission of engineers to investigate and report a permanent plan for the redemption of the alluvial basin of the Mississippi River subject to inundation." The bill was simple enough in its specifics. It directed the president to appoint a commission of two army and three civilian engineers and appropriated $10,000 for expenses and salaries. The preamble to the bill, however, stirred debate. The Mississippi River "is national in its character," fed by waters from twenty states and territories. Its reclamation would contribute to "the general welfare of the whole Union" and therefore "should be undertaken and accomplished by the General Government." Representative Charles W. Willard, Republican of Vermont, moved to strike the preamble and consider the bill itself. In his view, the bill, if passed, "is certain to inaugurate a new policy in respect to the levees of the Mississippi River...and perhaps in the end a large appropriation of money, of many millions of dollars, out of the Treasury of the United States for the levees of the Mississippi River." Willard conceded that the Mississippi River was "a great natural highway of commerce." Levees would benefit agriculture in Louisiana and Mississippi and might also facilitate the expansion of railroad networks in the floodplain, but they would be of local, not national value. Why should the taxpayers of one section of the country pay to improve another? Levees, Willard insisted, were about protecting and developing private property and local interests, and therefore the federal government must refrain from spending money on them. Willard had a point. Supporters of reclamation could wax poetic on the Mississippi River and westward empire, but they could not explain what levees had to do with that. The river may have belonged to the Republic, but the land along it belonged to local and private interests.[30]

Unfortunately for Willard, the general question of federal involvement in flood control and irrigation, in pursuit of both public and private interests, had already been conceded the previous year, when Congress authorized the establishment of a commission to investigate water control along the San Joaquin, Sacramento, and Tulare Rivers in California. The questions of public funds for private interests, federal authority in local affairs, and the state of the U.S. Treasury were all raised then, but in the end Congress approved the California commission quickly and easily. Morey asked for nothing more than the Californians had received, but in the debate of the previous year, the greatest concern among some representatives was whether investment might encourage the corruption thought rampant in Louisiana. Recalling an incident in Tangipahoa Parish, in which speculators secretly bought land along a bayou and then sought federal assistance in improving it, one senator warned that the government might be walking into a similar scam in the San Joaquin Valley.[31]

The debate soon turned personal and sectional, with Southerners challenging Northerners to be "manly" enough to rebuild levees that they, after all, had destroyed in the war. Such acrimony weakened the shaky coalition of Republicans and Democratic-Conservatives in Louisiana and elsewhere in the South, which had formed to pursue federal aid for internal improvements. But people were at that moment suffering from a devastating flood, and it was clear to most in Congress that only the federal government could provide adequate relief. Representative Fort of Illinois offered a compromise, with an amendment providing for a commission of army engineers, eliminating the need to appropriate funds specifically for a study of the lower Mississippi Valley. In the end, Washington would have direct control over the majority of the board, which consisted of army engineers. Unconstitutional or not, if there was going to be a board of levee commissioners, the central government would direct it.[32]

The third Mississippi River bill debated and passed in the spring of 1874 was very clearly about navigation and commerce, both squarely within federal jurisdiction. What divided members in both houses of Congress was the question of how the mouth of the Mississippi River could best be opened permanently to larger vessels. One proposal was for a canal that would bypass the mouth by connecting the river at Fort Saint Philip below New Orleans to the Isle au Breton Sound on the Gulf of Mexico east of the delta. The second proposal was to construct jetties at the end of one of the passes, which would constrict the current and increase its force, causing it to scour the entrance. The attraction of the canal was that it avoided the problem of the river's nature, which was to deposit sand at its mouth. The attraction of the jetties was that they seized control of the river's nature.[33]

The bars at the mouth of the river had long been a problem, and both proposals for dealing with them had been discussed in Congress before, without resolution, in part because of costs, and in part because army engineers insisted they could keep the passes open with dredge boats. By 1874, the time had come for a permanent solution to the problem. It may be that ships had gotten larger, their draft deeper. It may also be that

changes in the river valley had exacerbated the problem of sandbar formation. Agricultural expansion increased the sediment load of the river, but
levees forced the river to carry more of it to the passes. The primary motive
in 1874 for definitively solving the problem was the desire of New Orleans
merchants and army engineers to break the stranglehold of the towboat
association.[34]

Half a dozen towboat companies joined in association to maintain
the bars that were their livelihood and to force nonaffiliated companies
out of business. Without towboats, ocean vessels could not get over the
bars between New Orleans and the open water of the Gulf of Mexico as
these bars shifted daily. Towboats were powerful enough to dislodge ships
that got hung up on the sand. The towboat association could easily close
the Port of New Orleans and did so regularly to protect its monopoly.
Whenever maverick operators appeared, or when a ship's captain dared
enter the river on his own, the towboats would place vessels on the bar
and block the river. Whenever army dredges succeeded in removing the
bars, towboats would position large vessels in the river mouth to slow
the current and hasten the formation of a new bar. By 1874, frustrated
New Orleans merchants demanded a canal. Congress was tired of wasting
appropriations on dredging. The obstruction of the mouth of the river,
declared Senator Joseph R. West of Louisiana, "throws an embargo upon
the entire grain crop of the West." No one denied that keeping the mouth
of the Mississippi River open was the responsibility of the central government, and that doing so was in the nation's interest, as Senator West's
remark highlighted.[35]

The debate over the Fort Saint Philip Canal and the jetties subsumed
the problem of the towboat association. Remove or skirt the sand bars
and the association would dissolve. But which plan? The discussion was
almost entirely personal. Andrew Atkinson Humphreys of the Army
Corps of Engineers wanted to dig a canal. James Buchanan Eads, an
independent contractor, proposed to construct jetties. Their personalities
could not have been more different. Eads was a salesman-entrepreneur;
Humphreys was a soldier-bureaucrat. Humphreys thought Eads unsci-
entific, unprofessional, and undisciplined, which he was. Eads thought
Humphreys pedantic, conservative, and imperious, which he was. In 1874,
Eads was constructing a bridge across the Mississippi River at St. Louis,
using an innovative design of steel. Humphreys opposed the design at
the outset but was overruled by Congress. With the bridge nearly completed, he ordered Eads to dismantle it, on the grounds that it was too

low for steamboats. Eads appealed to Congress, which again overruled Humphreys. In 1874 the bridge opened.[36]

When Eads presented Congress with a plan to construct jetties to remove sand bars permanently from the mouth of the southwest pass of the river, Humphreys explained to Congress that jetties would not work. Eads pointed to other rivers where jetties had been used successfully, while Humphreys lectured on differences between these rivers and the Mississippi. Eads, at last, made Congress a business offer it could not refuse: he would build the jetties, and if they did not deepen the channel sufficiently to permit traffic to enter and exit the river freely, he would not accept a cent from Congress. If he failed, Congress could authorize a canal and all the nation would lose was a little time. Both men had their supporters in Congress. The businessmen of New Orleans, many of whom were speculating in swamp land real estate in the vicinity of the proposed canal, and their representatives, Senator Joseph R. West and Representative Jason Hale Sypher, favored a canal, as did Senator James Alcorn of Mississippi. Eads's strongest support came from a Missouri delegation grateful for his St. Louis bridge. Humphreys insisted on further studies and surveys, until he had all the data. West just wanted the problem solved as quickly as possible. When he realized Humphreys was not yet prepared to begin digging a canal, he threw his support behind Eads and the jetties. No bill dealing specifically with the mouth of the Mississippi River passed Congress that spring. Instead, West offered an amendment to a general appropriations bill for harbors and rivers that would establish a commission of engineers to study both proposals. Like the levee commission, it would consist of government and civilian engineers.[37]

As the flood waters receded at the end of June 1874, President Grant appointed two Mississippi River commissions, one to determine how best to open the river's mouth, the other to propose a means for permanently reclaiming the floodplain. The commissions cost little in appropriations, but they represented a reversal in federal policy. In 1874, the central government took charge of supervising all projects to improve the Mississippi River, whether for commerce and navigation, or protection from flooding.[38]

The next year, the commission to study the mouth of the Mississippi made a tour of Europe and then reported in favor of Eads's jetty proposal. Suddenly, Humphreys and his Corps of Engineers appeared very much out of step with the world. Congress authorized Eads to begin work, although at the south pass rather than the southwest pass that he favored.

There had been some objections to striking a deal with a single entrepreneur, but the fact that failure would cost the government nothing put it to rest. There were some members of Congress who insisted that jetties were experimental and untested, but the commission's report on European successes eased most minds. In the end, the debate was not about the river but about Humphreys, whose animosity for Eads blinded him to twenty-five years of engineering. His days as the army's—as the nation's—chief engineer were numbered.[39]

Over the next four years, as work on the jetties proceeded, Humphreys would not leave Eads alone. He withheld sounding data vital to demonstrating the success of the jetties, and then spread rumors that the jetties were not deepening the channel. Concerned investors began to withdraw support, leaving Eads short of cash. As it had when Humphreys obstructed work on the bridge, Congress intervened, ordering Humphreys to stay clear of all business pertaining to the mouth of the Mississippi River. In the spring of 1879, it was clear that the jetties had worked. The channel, only seven-and-a-half feet deep when construction began, was over twenty-six feet deep. In July, Congress officially declared the jetties a success. The next day Humphreys resigned.

The improvements at the mouth of the river brought immediate effects. New Orleans overnight became a major market for western grain, with some predicting that the city might even challenge Chicago as the metropolis of the mid-continent. At the New Orleans Industrial and Cotton Centennial Exposition, held in the winter of 1884–1885, the subject of discussion was Nebraska corn, not Louisiana cotton. However, the railroads proved very capable of competing with the river for trade. They cut their rates, regained their market share, and took western grain elsewhere, principally to Chicago. New Orleans remained a cotton town.[40]

In January 1875, the levee commission recommended that Congress appropriate $1.5 million to Louisiana and $500,000 to Mississippi and Arkansas each, to repair existing flood control structures. The commission estimated that permanent reclamation of the alluvial valley would cost $40 million minimally and would require a long-term role for the federal government in the control of water in the lower valley. But when a delegation representing the three states met with President Grant to ask for his endorsement of the commission's recommendations, the president refused, although not for constitutional or budgetary reasons. The previous year, outbursts of racial violence in New Orleans and Vicksburg had forced Grant to send in troops to restore order. As the *New York Times* reported, the president told the delegation that "he had always desired to aid in promoting the happiness and prosperity of all the people of the South, but at the same time he felt that the acts of violence so constantly occurring would preclude all aid from the General Government." Grant ignored the levee commission's recommendations for the remainder of his time in office. The negotiations that settled the disputed presidential election of 1876, putting Rutherford B. Hayes in the White House and formally ending Reconstruction, brought new hope for federal aid for levees, but a majority in Congress refused it. Meanwhile, severe flooding continued to plague the people of the lower Mississippi Valley. Not until June 1879 did an act of Congress establish the Mississippi River Commission (MRC) and commit the federal government to aiding the lower valley states in their efforts to control Big Muddy.[41]

By 1879, the success of Eads's jetties demonstrated that federal aid for river navigation improvements could be beneficial. Moreover, with the plight of the freedmen no longer dividing Congress, southern congressmen at last convinced a sufficient number of northern colleagues to support a Mississippi River improvements bill. In a speech on behalf of the commission, Louisiana's Randall Gibson declared that "the river is the property of the National Government, held for the benefit of the whole country.... It is clearly within the constitutional power and duty of the Government, as well as promotive of the interest of the people of the whole country, that these vast regions should be protected from the devastations of the river by a uniform system of levees." As Gibson and others pointed out, Eads's jetties were working, and levees would work similarly, to force the power of the river to scour and deepen the entire channel. Levees, they cried, improved commerce and navigation and could therefore be constitutionally funded by the federal government. The river thus became the property of the national government, as Gibson claimed, but it was not to be held for the benefit of all Americans. With the end of Reconstruction, followed by the disfranchisement of African American Southerners, the Mississippi River became the possession of whites, who used federal resources to act against the interests of many black residents of the Mississippi Valley.[42]

The lower valley's African Americans had no place within the MRC's understanding of the river. They simply disappeared, as disfranchised people tend to do, into the landscape. In other parts of the country, army engineers often faced resistance from local landowners and laborers who believed they were getting short-changed by the so-called improvements.

The rationalization of water control and distribution is difficult in a democracy in which all citizens are supposed to have equal access to public resources. By 1879, democracy in Louisiana and Mississippi was being curtailed. The Corps of Engineers, the MRC, and the politicians who paid them knew whom they had to please. The levees were built because the former slaves who might have opposed them, because they lived on the edges of the plantations that were targets of flood relief, could not. Levees led ultimately to the destruction of the edges, enabling cotton fields to consume what remained of the forest and wetland. With no place left to hide, hunt, and fish, laborers had to work on the plantations.[43]

As for who was to provide the labor for constructing the levees, legislation was vague: levees were to be built "by hired labor or otherwise." The unspecified "otherwise" could have included soldiers placed at the disposal of army engineers. More likely, it intended to refer the matter of who was to labor on the levees to local authorities and landowners, who could use convicts, alleged vagrants snatched from street corners, and farm laborers dragooned from nearby plantations. However they were gathered, black men comprised the vast majority of laborers on the levees, while white men owned the vast majority of acreage protected by the levees.[44]

All sides in the debates over levees, jetties, canals, and flood relief assumed that water and land ought to be kept separate. All four measures addressed the problems that arose when water and land mixed. All sides, too, apparently agreed that private interests might hold land but that the general public owned the Mississippi River. However, on the floodplain, where does land end and water begin? Who owns the space between land and water? There was legal precedent for considering the batture, the banks that are covered when the river is high and exposed when the river is low, as public property, but it was never invoked. Had it been, planters might have been told they were squatting on public land. Once the levees were in place, however, the batture all but vanished, like so many other edges and places in-between. Even before the levees were constructed the batture had become invisible, along the river where people could only see land and water and no place between.[45]

Despite their opposition, Humphreys and Eads both believed water and land ought not to mix. Their proposals for improving the mouth of the river, whether by jetties or by canal, were quick fixes to an isolated problem. Neither one cared how several thousand miles of river up from the mouth contributed to the problem. Nor did they ask what new problems might arise from the construction of a canal or jetty. Those who continued

FIGURE 8.1 Levee workers in Plaquemines Parish, 1935. During Reconstruction, the federal government decided against a program of land distribution to former slaves and against federal aid for flood control, for similar constitutional reasons. The end of Reconstruction released many in Congress from a sense of constitutional restraint, and the federal government began to offer regular aid for flood control. African American men, most of whom did not own land that stood to benefit from flood control, provided much of the labor for federally supervised levee construction from 1879 and the establishment of the Mississippi River Commission up into the mid-twentieth century. (Courtesy of the Library of Congress.)

to offer hydrological solutions to flood control were roundly ignored. Ironically, Eads's jetties apparently proved scientifically that levees could solve all problems with the river. Humphreys's legacy was the levees-only policy that guided flood control on the Mississippi River for the next 115 years, but it was Eads's success that convinced Congress to adopt that policy. Levees and jetties were analogous. Therefore, levees constructed the length of the lower river would work like jetties to force the river to rid itself of snags and bars. Southern advocates of federal aid for levees appeared scientifically astute and could no longer be written off as partisan and sectional. The analogy was false, however, and the establishment

FIGURE 8.2 An African American tenant family's home sits in the shadow of the Mississippi River levee near Lake Providence, Louisiana, in this 1840 photograph by Marion Post Walcott for the Farm Security Administration. The land around the home is dry and treeless. Big Muddy rolls past on the opposite side. The marshy edges that earlier separated dry farmland from the river, where many farm laborers hunted and fished, were in the twentieth century replaced by the sharp line of the levee. (Courtesy of the Library of Congress.)

of the MRC had more to do with politics than science. "Redemption" of the South for whites, and redemption of the flood plain for cotton and sugar—the same word was used in both contexts—were two parts of the same national project. Into the Far West, engineers took a science proven in the Mississippi Valley and used it to "improve" rivers and reclaim land for white settlers, and from nature and Native Americans. Out of the West came grain, brought to St. Louis by rail, from which it was shipped to the port of New Orleans and from there to the world. The assertion of white supremacy in the South and the West demanded the assertion of control over the river that connected all regions into an American continental empire.[46]

Congress appropriated $50 million and handed oversight of the budget to the MRC. The 1881 River and Harbor Act permitted direct federal assistance for levee construction, putting design and construction in the hands of the army engineers, on the grounds that levees improved navigation. Still, some planters demanded more federal flood control protection. "The Gov't should do something to protect us from water," Daniel Thompson of St. Mary's Parish demanded. "New England has had her days of protection until they can *go alone* and we should be allowed the same chance for a few years, when I am sure we can stand alone too." By century's end, walls constructed of willow branches, concrete, and earth separated the river from its floodplain. Not until the flood of 1917 did Congress at last drop all pretenses that levees were for commerce and navigation only and not for flood control. The Flood Control Act of 1917 provided for up to $45 million, with matching funds to come from each state, "for controlling the floods and for the general improvement of the Mississippi River." Once built, the states would maintain the levees.[47]

FIGURE 8.3 By the start of the twentieth century, earthen walls separated the river from the floodplain, and water from people. To avoid constitutional questions about using federal aid to protect private property, the levees were said to be needed in the interest of improving navigation. In this image taken ca. 1910, the packet Kate Adams steams past Friar's Point, Mississippi, elevated above the town by a swollen river contained by levees maintained by the Mississippi River Commission and the US Army Corps of Engineers. Not until 1917 did legislation begin to refer to levees as flood control devices. (Courtesy of the Mississippi Department of Archives and History.)

On April 16, 1927, the Mississippi River broke through the levee at Dorena, Missouri, not far below Cairo. Three days later and on the same side of the river, the levee at New Madrid gave way. On April 21, the river broke through at Mounds Landing, near Greenville, Mississippi, killing over 100 African Americans as they piled sandbags under the pointed guns of the National Guard. On April 29, dynamiting commenced at the Caernarvon levee, in Plaquemines Parish, to relieve pressure on the levee at New Orleans, but at the cost of the livelihood of downriver rice farmers and muskrat trappers. By the end of the month, water inundated 26,000 square miles and displaced over 1 million refugees. The 1927 flood was, and by some measures remains, the nation's greatest natural disaster, remembered in photos, songs, and film.[48]

The flood should have made it apparent to all that the levees-only policy had failed miserably, but that is not quite what happened. In 1928,

FIGURE 8.4 In 1927 the levee broke near Greenville, Mississippi, flooding the city and surrounding countryside. The levees put in place by the US Army Corps of Engineers, under the supervision of the Mississippi River Commission, made for less frequent but more catastrophic floods. (Courtesy of the Mississippi Department of Archives and History.)

Congress appropriated funds for the reconstruction of the levees, including the section intentionally blown at Caernarvon, and committed itself to
a new long-term project, which became known as the Mississippi River
and Tributaries Project, or Project Flood. The new project reviewed and
revised the levees-only approach, with the MRC agreeing to build the
Bonnet Carré Spillway in Louisiana and the Bird's Point-New Madrid
floodway in Missouri, both of which would permit the controlled release
of water from the Mississippi to relieve pressure on levees. Eventually,
engineers added a third spillway, at Morganza, Louisiana. The act also
authorized research into ways "proper forestry practice" might reduce
flooding. These adjustments to the system were intended to make the
levees work, not to replace them. Indeed, there were to be no outlets on
the east bank of the river—in the Delta in Mississippi—nor were any outlets to interfere with the project of "raising, strengthening, and enlarging
the levees on the east side of the river." The levee line was to be extended
north to Cape Girardeau. Reservoirs placed along Mississippi River tributaries were intended to help with flood control, but also with problems of
erosion and siltation that came from the mingling of land and water. For
some, spillways and reservoirs signaled the end of the levees-only policy;
nevertheless, flood control still meant barricading land from water, and
once the Corps entered into the business of draining land, which it did
after 1944 and the passage of yet another flood control act, its investment
in levees and dry land was absolute. Civil engineers such as Walter Carey,
who spent many years with the Second New Orleans Engineer District
advocating the use of asphalt rather than concrete in revetment construction, never gave up searching for the perfect levee.[49]

The initial appropriation for Project Flood was $325 million, an amount
some, including Senator Joseph Ransdell of Louisiana, considered inadequate. Estimates of the true costs of the project ran to $1 billion, four
times what had been spent on flood control in all the preceding years
and 1 percent of the annual gross domestic product (GDP) for the United
States at that time. Engineers promised that the Mississippi River would
never flood again, and for the most part they delivered, although flooding
tributaries caught them by surprise. In 1932, the toll in property damage
caused by Tallahatchie River overflow nearly equaled the Delta's losses
of 1927. Politicians, engineers, and assorted other experts still tended to
see flood events as disconnected and not part of a hydrologic system or
riverine environment that included the entire lower valley. Project Flood
exacerbated problems along the tributaries. Nevertheless, in the decade

after the inception of Project Flood, Congress spent on it an additional $312 million. With the Flood Control Act of 1950, the amount spent on the project had, as predicted, surpassed the billion dollar mark. By that time, too, hundreds of millions more had been earmarked for specifically designated tributaries, to dry the entire lower valley one leak at a time.[50]

Project Flood brought federal authority, dollars, and employees into small, impoverished southern towns, transforming places such as Vicksburg, Mississippi, headquarters for the Mississippi River Commission and the Mississippi River Experiment Station. By securing the land against the water of Big Muddy, it prepared the way for several federal agencies concerned with agriculture, including the Works Progress Administration and the Farm Security Administration of the Depression-era New Deal, and the Department of Agriculture.[51]

With the Flood Control Act of 1928 the federal government assumed the authority to take possession of any lands needed for easements, rights of way, and so forth. Landowners would receive compensation minus the equity appreciation in their lands coming from the improvements. Henceforth, Congress and states might debate who should pay what proportion of the cost of flood control, but there was no longer any debate about which level of government was in charge. Private property was to be confiscated, and it was to be developed to protect private property and national interests.[52]

Once again, the plight of thousands of propertyless African Americans living in the lower valley was ignored. The flood of 1927 might have served as an opportunity to use federal funds for levees to address problems of race, class, and poverty. However, the federal government and valley landowners stood shoulder to shoulder, never more visibly than when Herbert Hoover, the Republican secretary of Commerce and soon-to-be president, visited the scene of the disaster during the height of the flood and promised southern white Democrats he would bring them relief. The flood might have served as an opportunity to rethink social and environmental policy. Instead, Hoover, the MRC, and the Corps of Engineers decided to rebuild the levees, to make them bigger and stronger. When asked by a reporter if it was really possible to control the Mississippi River, Hoover replied: "Sure! If we can take care of a normal flood, we also can take care of a super-flood. To control the Mississippi is not a difficult engineering job. It's merely a matter of financing." Several congresses and presidents provided the financing, enough so that ten years after the flood of 1927 the *New York Times* could declare the lower valley both dry and white.

The valley is safe, the *Times* declared, safe "as the Valley has never before known safety since the white man entered it." It made no mention of the people who built the white man's levees to protect the white man's plantations, working fourteen hours a day for only ten cents an hour. In 1929 the federal government purchased land near New Orleans containing three African American cemeteries. Army engineers laid out the Bonnet Carré spillway over two of them, and placed a section of levee over another.[53]

Ownership of dry land separated whites from blacks, rich from poor. Levees propped up Jim Crow as surely as they segregated land and water. It was not politically feasible to understand the river as anything other than a giant stream to be walled off from the land. The MRC, the Army Corps of Engineers, the Congress, and President Hoover responded to the disaster by rededicating themselves to fighting the river with more massive earthen and concrete structures, to keep the water out and the laborers in.[54]

Drought, Disease, and Other Symptoms of a Pathological Landscape

"WATER SCARCE," REPORTED the *Daily Picayune*, on the situation in Concordia Parish, the same parish that had been mostly underwater when Jacob Bieller settled there ninety years earlier. In 1899, drought hit the lower valley hard. In May, cotton plant growth was well behind schedule in Concordia and elsewhere. Dry soil was stunting sugarcane in St. Mary Parish and potatoes in St. Landry Parish, where people faced a shortage of drinking water. By June, rice planters in St. Bernard Parish were pumping river water over the levee and into their fields to save their crops. Farmers everywhere dread seasons of drought, but the drought of 1899 was felt especially severely in what had historically been the wettest region of the state, the parishes near the Mississippi River. It was the fifth drought in eight years.[1]

The drought of 1896 had been much worse. That year the entire state suffered, along with large portions of Mississippi, Arkansas, and Texas. Upland areas were hardest hit. Farm income dried up with the cotton, leaving families with no means for purchasing food. Those who normally provided for themselves saw their corn wither in the field. Louisiana's rice harvest fell by two thirds. Cattle pastures turned brown, and herders had no supplementary feed. By the late fall, livestock began to starve, and by winter, so did people. In November, the Louisiana legislature appropriated $65,000 in emergency funds to buy corn for people and livestock, but by the end of December it was clear that much more was needed. Reports estimated that three fourths of the residents of the drought-stricken regions of Louisiana were without any means of support. Committees formed to seek food donations from across the nation.[2]

It was well known that poorly constructed levees could cause floods, but no one anticipated that levees could cause drought. In May 1893, the river broke through levees in East Carroll and St. Charles Parishes, and seeped under but did not collapse levees in other places. Several tributaries also backed up and onto farm land. Even so, 1893 was also a drought year. That people could suffer droughts and floods in the same year indicated that the lower valley's environmental transformation had gone horribly wrong.[3]

Levees enabled the lower valley states to reorganize the geography of agriculture. Dry land crops such as corn, cotton, and sugar replaced wetland rice in counties and parishes along the river. This in the turn created opportunites for rice planting in the parishes west of the flood plain, in Calcasieu and Acadia Parishes especially. As cotton moved onto the floodplain, rice moved out and west. Louisiana's southwestern plain was flat and firm, perfect for mechanized rice farming. Tractors and harvesters could move through wet fields without becoming immobilized by mud, which helped make Louisiana the nation's leading producer of rice. The only drawback to farming rice on the southwestern plain was the lack of a reliable, natural means of flooding fields. The plains had to be irrigated artificially with expensive canals and pumps that the state subsidized and which were put into place according to the specifications of state extension agents. The wetlands too moved west.[4]

During the drought years of the 1890s, the only crop to fare well was the rice crop along the river. In 1892, for example, drought reduced the crop on the southwestern plain by 20 percent to 25 percent, but along the river the yield held steady. As the *Daily Picayune* explained, "farmers in the river section had an abundance of fresh water for their crops, and the drought did not materially affect the growing rice," whereas the crop that reached market in Acadia and Calcasieu Parishes was "a great disappointment to the farmers who raised it." However, by the end of the decade, few acres along the river were devoted to rice. Reported the *Daily Picayune*, "Owing to the placing of much of the former rice lands in sugar cane, because of the successful competition of the Calcasieu district in the rice business, comparatively little rice has been produced along the river and Bayou Lafourche for a couple of years back." As a new century began, rice fields were spreading upriver, in Arkansas, but that was only because the engineers had not gotten there yet and the land was still wet.[5]

Much of the lower valley's wetland had been made dry and its dry land made wet. Pumps kept rice wet on the southwestern plain, while levees kept cotton and sugarcane dry near the river. During dry years, farmers along the river suffered because levees deprived their soil of a good spring soaking. In times of drought, indeed, even in times of flood, farmers on the floodplain relied on irrigation pumps to lift water over the levees that kept the land dry and that also raised the risk of disastrous flooding. In its natural state, when it annually spilled across the floodplain, moistening the land for the summer, Big Muddy was a lower, slower, and more creative force, leveling out the vicissitudes of drought and flood. Levees created a situation that guaranteed more frequent and severe floods and droughts, sometimes simultaneously.[6]

The droughts and floods of the 1890s were not the only symptoms of a pathological landscape created by landowners and state-sanctioned experts who banished the river from the land as they transformed the lower valley environment for dry agriculture. The deadly diseases for which the lower valley became justly famous offered another sign of environmental dysfunction. Certain diseases, such as malaria, have long been associated with water, especially with standing water. However, in the valley, diseases such as malaria and yellow fever became more deadly as the wetlands were dried. The Mississippi River's natural pattern of advancing and retreating over the valley kept water moving. However, with levees and drainage ditches, the total water surface area was reduced, but the remaining water still sat.

Europeans thought wetlands released noxious and deadly miasmas, which were in reality the odor of decaying organic matter. They cited health as the reason for draining swamps, and some feared planting wet crops such as rice. One visitor to the lower valley noted, in summer "comes heat; then miasmas that rise from wet expanses of rice culture. Planter and family must retreat to higher ground or risk fevers that claim many a victim." Neither the swamp water nor the fumes emanating from it caused illness; the micro-organisms and the mosquitoes that carried them made people sick.

Of course, the lower valley had always had an abundance of mosquitoes, which breed on water. The life of a priest in early eighteenth-century Louisiana could be hard for any number of reasons, "but the greatest torture," wrote Father Poisson, "is the mosquitoes," which have caused "more swearing since the French came to Mississippi than had been done before that time in all the rest of the world." Many decades later, one visitor to the valley, who was skeptical of its agricultural potential, observed that the region's one guaranteed bumper crop was stinging insects. Governor Laussat and his wife used to retire early every night, "to screen ourselves against the mosquitoes, which, at sunset, swarm down from the horizon into every nook and cranny of the apartments." Mosquitoes turned Laussat's living room into a "torture chamber." "Only a passion for cards and a body toughened by habit can render such discomfort endurable." In New Orleans, it was said, mosquitoes carried a brick bat under their wings. Ironically, drying the valley for agriculture created a more optimal environment for the two species that carried deadly disease.[7]

Of the many species of mosquito native to the lower Mississippi Valley, one, *Anopheles quadrimaculatus*, proved capable of carrying malaria, which may have arrived first with Hernando de Soto. The disease could have played a role in reducing the most densely clustered agriculturalists Soto encountered in the Delta of present-day Mississippi and across the Mississippi River in present-day Arkansas. It appears not to have had any effect on settlements downriver, perhaps because they were less attached to agriculture. If the virus arrived with the Spanish, it is likely that it soon died out, to be reintroduced by later European arrivals. Regardless of when malaria arrived in the valley, it became part of the natural environment as agriculture transformed the environment and created breeding habitat for *anopheles*. The disease may have been endemic in the plantation districts around New Orleans in the eighteenth century. In the nineteenth century, it spread upriver wherever people were clearing forests and draining land for agriculture. Agriculture brought more people into the floodplain and closer to the mosquitoes that carried malaria.[8]

From Africa to Asia to southern Europe, the connection between rice cultivation, mosquitoes, and malaria has been strong. The French brought that combination to the lower Mississippi Valley. In the nineteenth century, cotton plantations may have provided an even better environment for malaria. "Wet" cultivation of rice tended to keep water moving, at least where ditches were properly maintained. Cotton, ostensibly a dry crop, was typically planted in fields that lacked the sophisticated irrigation systems of rice fields. Moreover, earthen barriers designed to keep river water permanently off the land also trapped summer rain waters as well as what river water managed to surmount or leak through levees. In the valley at certain times of the year, cotton fields were often quite wet. Water trapped on what was supposed to be dry land sat still, escaping only through evaporation and percolation. In addition, all the human additions to the land made for perfect mosquito breeding ground, from furrows and wheel ruts that held water, to various containers. The result was more people, more mosquitoes, and more malaria to take the lives of the constitutionally weak, which in the context of plantation development meant the overworked and underfed. Malaria contributed to the high death rate among enslaved African Americans in the cotton plantation districts of the mid-nineteenth century lower valley.[9]

The other disease associated with the valley, and with New Orleans especially, was yellow fever. It would strike in July—"Yellow fever comes during the season known as 'dog days,'" wrote the last French governor—with passengers or sailors inbound from Havana, Vera Cruz, Kingston, and other tropical ports, and rage until the weather cooled in late October. It would not entirely disappear until December frosts. During the colonial era, the winters in the lower Mississippi Valley were enough to kill the virus, but yellow fever epidemics were an annual event from 1840 to 1880 in New Orleans. The only sustained period without an outbreak occurred during the years of the Civil War, which interrupted international trade and travel.[10]

Other diseases took more lives than yellow fever—tuberculosis, for example—but more slowly, over more time, and more quietly. About one half of those who contracted yellow fever died in agony, their lips, gums, nose, and stomach ulcerated and bleeding, their head and body aching and shaking with chills. Their livers failed, turning their complexions to yellow, and they vomited black, partially digested blood. Then, after about a week of excruciating pain, they died of blood poisoning. Africans and African Americans indicated an inherited resistance thought to be a legacy of their ancestors' long association with the disease in Africa. The epidemics were clearly urban phenomena, so everyone who could do so fled the city and business halted.

In the summer of 1853, residents of New Orleans observed that the mosquitoes seemed especially bothersome. Then the fever hit. As many as 40,000 people became sick. Between 9,000 and 11,000 died. City leaders did what they could to keep the epidemic from interfering with commerce, but when 75,000 of its 100,000 citizens evacuated, the matter was out of their hands. Fleeing people took the virus with them. That summer, yellow fever hit Natchez and Vicksburg particularly hard. The scene was repeated in 1878, when yellow fever swept the entire lower valley from New Orleans to St Louis.[11]

Like malaria, yellow fever was associated with a particular species of mosquito, the *Aedes aegypti*, which was not native to North America and came on ships from overseas. The insect preferred urban environments, the driest spaces within the lower valley, and disdained the wetlands of the floodplain. There is some evidence that this mosquito liked sugar and may have been attracted to sugar mills and processing factories.[12]

The circumstances had to be just right for yellow fever epidemics. The transformation of the lower valley into cotton plantations accelerated the growth of New Orleans and secondary cities up the valley, creating urban mosquito habitat. As the volume of trade and travel increased between New Orleans and places overseas where yellow fever was endemic, and between New Orleans and other valley cities, so too did chances increase for yellow fever to return every summer. In the two decades before the Civil War, business between New Orleans and tropical ports multiplied, to the point that many in the South dreamed of annexing these places to the United States and expanding an empire of slaves and plantations. After war and emancipation those hopes faded, as did the business connections and the threat of yellow fever. Between the election of Abraham Lincoln in 1860 and the discovery of a vaccination for yellow fever in the 1930s, there were only two outbreaks as deadly as those that occurred regularly in the twenty years before Lincoln's election. The last of the horrifying epidemics struck in the summer of 1878. The epidemic of 1905 took far fewer lives, yet it is remembered because it came after fifteen fever-free summers and because it was the last. Although opportunity for importing the yellow fever virus declined, with changes in trade patterns and possibly with the advent of steam ships, the non-native mosquito that transmitted the disease persisted in New Orleans and the lower valley's growing urban environments.[13]

Agriculture and urbanization expanded mosquito habitat; they also reduced habitat for other animals. Forest clearing and fragmentation affected bird populations, especially the flycatchers that consumed mosquitoes. Swamp drainage and water control left fewer and fragmented habitats for fish and amphibians, which had also kept mosquito populations down. Percy Viosca, a Louisiana biologist working in the 1920s, was convinced the problem with mosquitoes had gotten worse over the centuries, and he attributed it to deforestation, water control, and agriculture. Before the twentieth century, few understood the relationship between standing water, mosquitoes, and disease. Benjamin Latrobe, developer of New Orleans's first waterworks, observed mosquitoes breeding in wells and cisterns, and advocated hiding water in pipes to reduce their numbers. Sadly, before he could make further observations he contracted yellow fever and died.[14]

In addition to drought and disease, other unintended side effects accompanied the drying of the lower Mississippi Valley. Clearing hardwood forest left the region's higher areas and upland edges more vulnerable to forest fires. The trash left in clearings provided kindling for the sparks of locomotives and lightning. Absent the forest canopy, the ground dried out and vegetation burned more quickly and easily. In the 1920s, official reports claimed that nearly 50 percent of the total forest area in the state of Mississippi burned annually. Unofficial estimates ran to 90 percent. Frequent fire hindered forest regeneration, as did soil erosion, which became a serious problem where the land sat exposed to summer downpours. In the wetlands of the river delta around New Orleans, cypress clearing led to erosion of coastal marshes and to increased salinity of marsh water. Saltwater killed what cypress the logging companies left behind and made it impossible for the trees to return. The cypress forests cut a century ago in the coastal marshes have mostly not regenerated, leaving the coast exposed to summer hurricanes that contribute to erosion. Forests have returned on their own in many places, but this takes time. An abandoned field in the lowest reaches of the valley will grow into a young forest of wax myrtle as a first stage of regeneration in about twenty-five years. A forest with greater plant diversity, and so with greater overall adaptability and survivability, regenerates more slowly.[15]

The hastening of coastal erosion as a consequence of Mississippi River levees was first noted by Elmer Corthell, an engineer who had worked with James Eads. In an 1897 article, Corthell warned that the sea was claiming the delta, not, as some believed, because ocean levels were rising but because levees had interfered with the process of sediment accumulation. Levees also created an erosion problem farther up the valley. In the 1920s, agents with the Delta Branch of the Mississippi Agricultural Experiment Station noted that the soil was giving out after decades of farming. By keeping the river off the land, levees deprived it of its annual blanket of rich sediment. Rain easily washed topsoil away from cleared land, but there was no longer an annual flood of sediment to replace what rain washed away. Big Muddy had made the valley not through erosion, but through deposition. Over thousands of years the great river filled the valley and built the Louisiana coastline with soil it carried across much of North America. The levees ended that, and for the first time in its history the lower Mississippi Valley experienced annual net losses of topsoil—in recent times and in some places at a rate of several tons per acre. The famously rich soil of the lower valley, which had encouraged agriculture and levees in the first place, was impoverished by agriculture and levees. Before the mid-twentieth century, farmers were supplementing the soil with expensive fertilizers. In a monumental break with the geophysical and environmental past, engineers had succeeded in reversing the valley's hydrological process from depositional to erosive, and in turning water into a destructive and impoverishing rather than a creative and enriching force on the land.[16]

South American water hyacinth was introduced into Louisiana in the 1880s as an ornamental plant but spread into the wild. It actually impeded erosion by firming up river and coastal banks. However, it also crowded out native plant and animal species, and clogged waterways and plantation drainage ditches. To stem the rapid growth of the hyacinth—in one year, twenty-five plants can produce 2 million—some hoped another import, the nutria, a South American vegetarian muskrat, might be of some use. Imported in the 1930s by fur farmers and others, such as E. A. McIlhenny of Avery Island, an heir to the Tabasco Sauce fortune, nutria quickly made their way into the wild. In some places, state officials intentionally intro- duced them as agents to control hyacinth. Once in the wild the rodents rapidly multiplied. By 1957 their number reached perhaps 1 million and continued to grow, their proliferation assisted by the over-hunting of alli- gators. Nutrias eat just about anything green, consuming up to 25 percent of their body weight in swamp vegetation per day. For over half a century they have been eating away Louisiana's wetlands. They have also been known to forage in fields of rice and sugarcane. In recent times, a resur- gent alligator population in lower valley swamps has promised to keep the nutria population in check. Meanwhile, the Louisiana Department of Wildlife and Fisheries has worked with the Louisiana Culinary Institute to turn ragondin, as nutria meat is called, into a popular food.[17]

The spread of agriculture destroyed habitat for all sorts of living crea- tures, including wolves, cougars, and black bears. It also created habitat for animals that preyed on the crops in the fields, from imported nutrias to native quails and bobolinks. But most troubling to farmers were the insects. Armies of cotton lice, worms, and boll weevils advanced with agri- culture across the valley.[18]

Deforestation, swamp drainage, and erosion affected micro-climates. As fields dried out, the ground shrank and sank, sometimes falling four feet below its original level. Sunken fields pooled rainwater and were more susceptible to frost. The clearing of wetland for sugar lowered ground temperatures, which shortened the growing season and reduced the range of sugarcane in Louisiana. It also shortened the mosquito season: more mosquitoes in the summer, but an earlier frost in autumn and end to the malaria season. The lower valley's marshlands were expansive composts filled with decaying vegetable matter, from which warm methane bubbles percolated up and into the atmosphere. Eventually, drained land stopped emitting gas, but in newly deforested and drained marshes littered with kindling, methane was known to escape from the ground in the mid-day heat of the Louisiana summer and ignite spontaneously, setting the ground ablaze. This phenomenon, the result of cleaning, draining, and drying the valley, has been attributed to voodoo, witchcraft, and in more recent times to UFOs.[19]

The drying of the floodplain had unintended consequences for the human population and for transportation. Dry land made railroads feasible and practical. Railroads competed with riverboats, and railroad towns competed with river towns for the business of shipping cotton. Many river towns died. By 1910, over 1,000 miles of track networked over the Delta. Train depots could be placed downtown, whereas river landings were often some distance from town centers and had a habit of moving unexpectedly when Big Muddy shifted course. The town of Rodney faded to a ghost town when the river abandoned its wharf and when railroads made the relocation of its wharf unnecessary. In 1876, the river abandoned Vicksburg, too, although engineers eventually constructed a canal to redirect the Yazoo River past Vicksburg and put the town back on the water; by then, however, Jackson had developed into a railroad center that eventually supplanted Vicksburg as the state's commercial center.[20]

But it was the railroad towns away from the river and its natural and man-made levees that really began to grow at the end of the nineteenth century. In former wetlands all across the lower valley, railroad towns such as Clarksdale in Mississippi, Monroe in Louisiana, and Brinkley in Arkansas surpassed many older Mississippi River towns as centers of commerce and society. Railroads also accelerated growth of a few river towns that successfully integrated rail and water transportation networks. The port of Greenville, Mississippi, became a local railroad hub, with two lines terminating near its wharf. Mississippi's unofficial commercial center was Memphis, at the intersection of Big Muddy, the Illinois Central Railroad, and after the 1892 opening of the first Mississippi River bridge in the lower valley, the St. Louis and San Francisco Railroad. Interregional railroads, such as the Illinois and Frisco lines, eventually drove many steamboat companies out of business. Downriver from Memphis, bridges were more difficult to build. By 1930, when Vicksburg got its bridge, it had been eclipsed by Memphis. There was no bridge at New Orleans until 1935. However, New Orleans was an exception. It was an ocean port, an advantage Memphis lacked. Railroad companies, including two transcontinental lines, could not ignore New Orleans, although they had to ferry their cars across the river. Nevertheless, if the river interrupted rail connections, the railways came between the cities and their river, when they captured from steamboats much of the cotton trade, and then when they captured the riverfront. By 1885, depots, warehouses, and five sets of double tracks separated Jackson Square, the heart of New Orleans, from the levee. Across the lower valley, railroads accelerated the removal of timber and the spread of agriculture, as timber companies shipped logs by rail and then sold their cut-overs to farmers and agribusinesses. By separating land and water, levees began a process of reorganizing space and nature within the valley, a process railroads completed, with the unintended consequence of killing many riverside towns and indeed making the river itself apparently irrelevant.[21]

Whenever people pushed the valley's wet nature out of sight and out of mind, it had a way of returning, often unexpectedly and unpredictably. Thus Big Muddy remained relevant to human life and history in the lower Mississippi Valley, despite having been banished from the land by levees and drainage ditches. The droughts, the mosquitoes and the deadly diseases they carried, the plagues of insects that ravished cotton crops, the swamps that spontaneously burst into flames, all were symptoms of a repressed river on the "wet" side of the levee making its presence known to all on the "dry" side from which the river had been expelled. One way or another, everyone felt Big Muddy's absence.

Big Muddy returned to the valley most visibly and forcefully as water, when it broke through the levee and invaded dry farmland and cities. The human response to the river's intrusion was to push it back by building higher levees, and to continue to treat the symptoms of the pathology, rather than the pathology itself, by draining land where it was too wet, irrigating it where it was too dry, dusting it with DDT and other chemicals where it was too pestilential and infertile. In the lower Mississippi Valley, people given little or no choice in the matter—slaves, tenants, convicts, soldiers, immigrants, the poor—expended much energy in this endeavor. Significant contributions came too from scientists and engineers, government agents and taxpayers, and of course, a wide array of machines, from plows and dredge boats to bulldozers and crop-dusters—and most of all, from the levees, floodways, and drainage ditches that together comprised the lower Mississippi River system. In time, the pathological condition of a repressed landscape demanded too much energy to be sustained and the symptoms began to take over.[22]

The flood of 1927 was perhaps the most severe symptom of the pathological landscape that the dried lower Mississippi Valley had become. Through the programs and constructions of the Mississippi River and Tributaries Project, the Army Corps of Engineers and the Mississippi River Commission regarded that flood, as they had all others, as the primary problem, rather than as a symptom of a much more profound disorder. Not surprisingly, more floods followed, in 1929, 1932, and 1935. In 1937, the levee at the Bird's Point-New Madrid Spillway failed to open as originally designed and had to be dynamited to save Cairo, Illinois, from inundation. The Mississippi reached dangerous heights in 1944, 1945, and 1950. The flood of 1973 was nearly as bad as that of 1927, necessitating the opening of the Bonnet Carré Spillway to relieve pressure on the levee at New Orleans. When the Old River Control Structure at Shreve's Cut-off nearly collapsed, engineers opened the Morganza Spillway for the first time, forcing the temporary relocation of 1,200 people from the Atchafalaya basin. Over 2,000 deer drowned in the basin, much to the chagrin of the Louisiana Wildlife and Fisheries Commission, which had sponsored the development of the emergency easement as a wildlife preserve. In 1975, 1979, and 1983, high water again strained but did not break the levee system in the lower valley. Then, in the summer of 1993, Big Muddy broke through barriers in its middle and upper regions, flooding 31,000 square miles and causing $16 billion in property and crop damage. Although the lower valley did not flood, the disaster encouraged many, including many within the Army Corps of Engineers, to reconsider its century-old approach to river management.[23]

With the establishment of the Wetlands Reserve Program, a federally sponsored initiative to help private landowners restore wetlands, the approach to flood control has taken a new turn. The pathology, rather than the symptom, is at last receiving attention and treatment. In a few places, Big Muddy is interacting with its floodplain as it did before it was pushed off the land and repressed behind the levees. Although agriculture remains predominant in the region's economy, it is industrialized and far less labor intensive. Large plantations and farms remain, but they are incorporated and largely emptied of people. Moreover, other industries compete with agriculture. With fewer people, there are fewer voters. Since 1993 it has become politically feasible to consider tearing down the levees, at least in some places, and allowing the Mississippi to have its way.[24]

In the spring and early summer of 2011, engineers carefully detonated explosives embedded in the levee at Bird's Point and opened the spillway gates at Bonnet Carré and Morganza. The cities of Cairo and New Orleans were saved, and to that extent the flood control system successfully held back the highest water since 1927. However, tributaries backed up and spilled over in Arkansas, Illinois, Kentucky, Missouri, and especially in the Delta in Mississippi. In all, controlled and uncontrolled flooding inundated over 2 million acres of farmland, forced the evacuation of tens of thousands of people, and caused over $6 billion in damages. As engineers confessed to a strategy of flooding rural areas to save urban areas, which elicited lawsuits from those who were being sacrificed to save others, it became clear that the cry of "never again" that followed the 1927 flood had been replaced by a frank statement of "sometimes, in some places."[25]

Many now understand that when more river water is permitted to wet the valley, floods are less dangerous. Similarly, other symptoms of the valley's pathological condition that first appeared after it was dried for agriculture, and which for much of the twentieth century were mistakenly regarded as problems rather than as symptoms of an underlying illness, are now being treated with water. Wet fields of fish and rice are replacing dry fields of cotton. No longer is water so scarce in the lower Mississippi Valley.

10

Cotton, Chemicals, Catfish, Crawfish

THE HIGH WATER of the 1927 flood coincided very nearly with the height of the cotton kingdom in the lower valley, as acreage devoted to cotton production in Louisiana, Mississippi, and Arkansas reached an all-time high in 1929 and then began a steady decline. That decline was particularly pronounced in the Delta in Mississippi, the region perhaps most devastated by the flood. Nearly 40 percent of Delta land planted with cotton in 1930 had by decade's end been abandoned or given over to other crops. By 2007, the total land in the Delta planted with cotton was a mere 25 percent of the cotton land in its peak year. Other crops, soybeans especially, sustained agricultural growth for a time, but by midcentury across the valley, total farm acreage was again on the decline. Moreover, since the 1930s the valley's total farm population has dropped, down 78 percent by 1970, down nearly 50 percent in the Delta by the end of the century. At the same time, average farm size has quadrupled. Since 1930 productivity has also increased fourfold.[1]

Ironically, flood control projects designed to open land to agriculture coincided with agriculture's contraction. By the end of 1928, federal and state governments had spent millions of dollars on flood control and committed to many millions more, primarily to keep the lower valley dry for agriculture— and yet by that time the heyday of dry land agriculture was passing. The flood control act of 1944 authorized the Corps of Engineers to drain swamps and dry the land sufficiently to keep large machines, such as mechanical cotton harvesters, from sinking into the mud. Machines replaced people and encouraged migration from rural areas to cities, such as Memphis and Chicago, and to other regions of the country. Drying the land facilitated mechanization that in turn "dried up" the farm laboring population. When falling agricultural prices continued to undermine the achievements of industrialized, intensified production, landowners looked for new ways to make a living. Many turned to rice, others to catfish or crawfish. By the 1970s, the levees of Project Flood, built to keep land dry for cotton and other dry land crops, guarded wetland rice fields and ponds of fish from the river. By the end of the twentieth century, partially completed flood control projects, such as the Big Sunflower River Maintenance Project and the Yazoo Pump, an ambitious proposal to pump water trapped behind levees in the southern end of the Delta over the giant embankments and into the river, were either stalled or were being actively dismantled as groups of conservationists, hunters, and fishers successfully challenged the wisdom of drying the land—wildlife habitat, they called it—for a shrinking number of farmers. Instead, they demanded that large areas of the valley be restored to their original wet state.[2]

The lower Mississippi Valley's transformation back into wetland—from a dried land back to a wet land—began when several historic trends combined to threaten the cotton economy. First, the global price of cotton fell. The First World War in Europe was good for American cotton farmers because it drove agricultural prices upward. In 1919 the price of baled cotton peaked at 35 cents per pound, plunged during the Depression years, and did not recover until the next war. By the time the price peaked again, in 1950, at about 40 cents per pound, programs intended to help farmers when prices were low had restructured agriculture in the lower valley. Second, the price of labor increased. Beginning in the 1920s, with the closing of the doors to immigrants from overseas, African American laborers began to leave the South for jobs in industry in the North and eventually on the West Coast. They were joined by thousands of white laborers, especially during the Great Depression. The Great Migration accelerated during World War II. In 1910 the average annual wage for a farm laborer in the United States was $526. Wages rose during the First World War, peaking at $1,326 in 1920. By 1933, in the depths of the Great Depression, the figure was down to $454. Thereafter farm wages began to rise, and by 1948 the average annual wage for farm labor was $2,558. From 1920 to 1950 the price of cotton increased 15 percent; meanwhile, the price of farm labor increased over 90 percent. Third, the costs of sustaining agriculture began to increase, as the valley's soil required ever more applications of fertilizer.[3]

Lower valley farmers shared many problems with farmers across the South. From Texas to Georgia the federal government addressed the crisis on southern farms and plantations with programs designed to stabilize prices, reduce labor costs, and restore the soil. The ultimate goal was to free the South from its long-time dependency on cotton and manual labor. Federal agencies introduced new crops. They subsidized mechanization, which in the lower valley necessitated draining and drying, to make the ground sufficiently firm for heavy machinery. They restructured the system of land tenure, driving sharecroppers off the land in what amounted to an enclosure movement. They reconfigured networks of credit and marketing. They applied tons of chemical pesticides and fertilizers to the land. In all, an agricultural revolution occurred across the South. In one important respect, however, the lower Mississippi Valley was unique. When the federal government undertook to stop the flooding once and for all and at the same time to revolutionize agriculture, it worked at cross purposes.[4]

Men had made fortunes in the lower valley off a combination of rich land and cheap labor. As the price of labor rose and the land became less productive, landowners sought help from chemicals. According to the US Department of Agriculture, farmers nationwide doubled what they spent on fertilizer and pesticide, measured as a percentage of total production expenses. In 1910, fertilizers and pesticides accounted for 4.5 percent of production expenses. By 1980 the figure stood at 9.8 percent. Most of the increase in expenditures occurred after mid-century and went toward pesticides, although chemical defoliants were popular where they enhanced the efficiency of mechanical harvesters. In 1980, American farmers added over 11 million tons of nitrogen fertilizer and 300,000 tons of chemical pesticides to their soil and crops—enough for three piles each the size of the Great Pyramid of Egypt. They added several more pyramid-size piles of phosphates. Between a third and a half of all the fertilizer applied in the United States landed on southern farms, including those of the lower valley states of Mississippi, Louisiana, and Arkansas. Twenty-six percent of the insecticides used on American farms went into southern agriculture, two thirds of it—about 11,000 tons in 1966 and about 16,000 tons in 1971, or about one pound of insecticide per forty-five pounds of cotton—onto fields in Louisiana, Mississippi, and Arkansas.[5]

Segregated from the river, the richest land in the world had to be supplemented with fertilizers. Drained and deforested, the valley presented itself as one large field with few barriers to the insects that invaded, and so farmers turned to chemical pesticides. Most of the chemicals eventually found their way into the river, contaminating it and its inhabitants, which only made its segregation from land and people all the more urgent.

In the first years of the twentieth century, the boll weevil arrived in the valley, en route from Mexico to Georgia. At first it appeared as an

unstoppable army waging scorched earth warfare. It threatened the entire
cotton kingdom, its economy and its social and racial hierarchy. Yet, years
after its arrival, cotton cultivation in the valley expanded and production increased. The insect left Mississippi's Delta relatively untouched.
Downriver, in Concordia Parish, panicked farmers acted preemptively,
giving up cotton for rice. However, after a few years, when the weevil had
advanced to Alabama, they regained their composure and returned to
planting cotton. The weevil was a pest, and yet the lower valley presented
it with too many environmental obstacles for it to become the ravaging
force many had feared. In the valley and in the Delta especially, the battle
over the weevil was less man versus nature and more man versus man,
a contest between black laborers and tenant farmers who saw the weevil
as presenting an opportunity to upset the social order and white plantation owners who privileged their scientific knowledge of the insect as a
means of holding onto their privileged social position. The weevil caused
far more real damage to older and poorer plantation districts elsewhere in
the South, especially those of the Southeast, which people abandoned by
the thousands. No chemical weapon kept insects at bay like a good flood,
and the lower valley experienced good floods regularly, until the walls of
Project Flood began to take shape. In addition, cotton plants matured
quickly in the fertile soil of the valley, their blossoms forming often ahead
of the life cycle of destructive insects. However, by closing the land to
the river, Project Flood exposed Delta cotton to the predations of the boll
weevil and other insects. Flood control structures encouraged the expansion of agriculture in the valley, until the region was nearly one giant cotton field. Into the 1920s, a patchwork of field, forest, and marsh, all of
which periodically flooded, had helped keep insect populations down and
insect predator populations up. Minor floods could bring short-term costs
to income and peace of mind, but they were a fact of life for farmers in the
valley. Over the long term they enriched the soil, enabling plants to mature
quickly so they could better withstand insects. By the 1950s that patchwork
was gone, the flooding had ceased, and the soil was less productive. And
so it was that forty years after the boll weevil's arrival in the lower valley, it
and many other pests suddenly appeared as a serious threat to the livelihood of Delta cotton farmers. They found help in the form of nitrogen-
based fertilizers and synthetic pesticides, DDT most famously.[6]

Widely used by armies on all sides of the conflict in World War II, primarily for delousing, after 1945 DDT (Dichloro-Diphenyl-Trichloroethane)
served on the front lines of a new war, one waged by the USDA and its

extension agents on farms across America. Pesticides were not new. Many southern farmers had applied with mixed results organic insecticides made of soap, oil, or pepper, as well as more dangerous inorganic compounds. Paris Green, an arsenic and copper compound used as a rat killer in the sewers of Paris, was probably the most commonly used inorganic pesticide. In powdered form it was applied with burlap bags that when shaken over targeted plants released a toxic dust. In 1922, the first experiments with aerial applications of calcium of arsenate began near Tallulah, Louisiana. However, DDT and other synthetic pesticides mixed with oil and sprayed from trucks and airplanes represented a whole new type of warfare against insects.[7]

The experts who solved the problem of flooding created the problem of insects for a different set of experts to address. The two groups of experts worked separately, engineers on flood control, agricultural entomologists on insect control, never imagining that their problems might be linked. As the river apparently became less dangerous to humans, the land became more so, although landowners, chemical companies, and USDA experts did what they could to brush aside mounting evidence of health and environmental risks from pesticide use. The Mississippi River had not really become less dangerous, only apparently so because it flooded less frequently. Chemicals applied to the land eventually ended up in the water and the danger was merely resituated, from the water itself to the toxic sediment it carried. Toxic river water had to be treated before it could safely be used in many agricultural practices, but the expense of doing so was more than farmers could bear. To avoid river water that was loaded with toxic agricultural runoff, farmers throughout the valley began to irrigate their fields with water pumped from underground aquifers. Since 1920, the water level in the Sparta or Middle Claiborne Aquifer beneath the intersection of Mississippi, Louisiana, Arkansas, and Tennessee— the Greater Memphis area—has dropped in some places by more than 360 feet. The levees of Project Flood have both encouraged the taking of water from and impeded the flow of water into the aquifers.[8]

Project Flood was also about navigation, keeping water in the river in the interest of shipping. While the USDA and other agencies used chemicals to make plants grow on the land, the Army Corps of Engineers used chemicals to kill plants in the water. Until 1947, engineers had relied on mechanical means of cutting water hyacinths and other aquatic plants from channels in the lower Mississippi River delta; after that year, they, along with Tulane University chemical scientists, began experimenting with chemical herbicides. The next year, engineers began applying six to eight pounds of 2,4D to each acre of water clogged with hyacinth, but to no avail. Over the next few years they experimented with dosage levels. In 1951, engineers mixed 2,4D with 2,4,5T; combined in equal proportions, these become Agent Orange, the infamous chemical defoliant used by the US Army in the jungles of Vietnam in the 1960s. The chemical combination proved lethal to just about everything but its intended target, the water hyacinth. In 1953, a helicopter spraying over Morganza Bay accidentally killed rice crops. Farmers sued for $11 million in damages but settled for $350,000. Engineers increased the dosage and began spraying after the July rice harvest. Despite lack of success and tragic mishaps, engineers such as Walter Carey insisted that herbicides were "a new weapon in its [the Army Corps of Engineers'] never-ending battle with the aquatic plants growth, water hyacinth and the alligator weed, which infest the sluggish streams, bayous and lakes of the gulf states and cause damages, under several different heads, totaling many millions of dollars annually." Carey's use of the word "infest" suggested that the plants did not belong in the water, that they sickened the water. Hyacinth had long been a nuisance, but it became a more serious problem with the development of the petrochemical industry near New Orleans during and after World War II. Channel construction for oil pipelines disturbed native plant life, creating openings for water hyacinth to spread, more rapidly when chemical fertilizers intended for agriculture ran into the Mississippi River. The causes of hyacinth's "infestation" belied the separation of water and land that was assumed by farmers and engineers alike. Chemicals sprayed on land fed plants in water; chemicals sprayed on water killed plants on land.[9]

Chemicals such as DDT and 2,4D acted within and in accordance with the natural environment and its processes. Where they ended up depended not just on the men who applied them, but on the ways water, wind, and land interacted in the lower Mississippi Valley. Herbicides worked on land not simply because of the properties of the chemical, but also because of the nature of the plants and the soil that received them. Chemists, engineers, farmers, and other experts attributed their success at terrestrial plant control to chemicals, and so when they applied the same chemicals in a similar fashion to aquatic plants, they were surprised to get different results. Their response to failure was to increase the dosage of poisons, as if aquatic plants were merely terrrestrial plants in water.[10]

Chemical herbicides, pesticides, and fertilizers, together with mechanical planters and harvesters, crop hybrids, and other introductions to cotton cultivation, did succeed intentionally in raising output per acre. But the costs of chemicals and machines were high. Many landowners abandoned farming and left the valley, selling out to corporate agribusinesses with greater capital resources. Among those who stayed were some who tried their hand at other crops, such as fish and rice.

The commercial fishery on the lower Mississippi River has a long history, dating back to the French colonial period when native peoples, lower class French, and Africans, in cooperation and in competition, supplied the New Orleans market with fresh fish. In the nineteenth century, a fleet of flatboats stayed on the river all summer, their crews hauling in tons of catfish and buffalo fish for sale locally as food and oil. In 1889, over 400 men worked as commercial freshwater fishers in Arkansas, Mississippi, and Louisiana, landing 1,936 metric tons of catfish, buffalo fish, gar, bowfin, paddlefish, and other popular and abundant species. As late as the 1950s, the annual commercial catch from the lower valley was large, although it supplied a mostly regional market. Including tributaries and the estuaries at the river's mouth, the catch averaged about 8,000 metric tons, including most of the 1,400 metric tons of wild channel catfish marketed annually in the United States. The commercial market for crawfish was smaller, about 40 metric tons, but the business was well established.[11]

In the second half of the twentieth century the transformed river and floodplain began to have a visible effect on the region's fish populations. As early as 1927, Louisiana biologist Percy Viosca warned that the levees were impoverishing one of the world's richest freshwater ecosystems by depriving it of the life-sustaining nutrients brought annually by Big Muddy. Noting the positive effects on the environment of that year's otherwise disastrous flood, Viosca hoped that the renewed efforts to control the river, which were sure to come in the flood's aftermath, might be implemented in ways that would not further harm the lower valley's aquatic life. Instead, engineers and policy makers responded to the flood with the giant levees of Project Flood, which proved more damaging to the freshwater ecosystem than Percy or anyone else at that time could have imagined. The new and improved levees separated water on the dry side of the levee—lakes, streams, and remaining swamps—from the water of Big Muddy so thoroughly that by the 1960s the flood pulse pattern that Viosca hoped might be restored no longer had any effect on the lower valley's fish population, which adapted to a wetland ecosystem utterly disconnected from the Mississippi River. Moreover, the levee barrier between people and the river encouraged the dumping of dangerous pollutants into the water system without regard for life within it, or for human safety, falsely trusting that toxic water would be kept separate. As Big Muddy became a sewer, the fish that inhabited the river, which had been a vital food for valley people since before Hernando de Soto, became, in the minds of many consumers, dirty, carcinogenic, and inedible.[12]

The toxins dumped into the river had a way of returning, in floodwaters that broke through or topped levees, and that backed up tributaries and spilled into lakes and ponds full of fish. They also returned in the flesh of the fish caught from the river and consumed by people who might or might not have known where the fish came from. Finally, levees encouraged more clearing of wetland hardwood forests, primarily for agriculture, which destroyed fish habitat, but which also encouraged construction of fish ponds that were vigilantly protected from the surrounding natural environment, although this separation inevitably broke down.

In the 1960s, the annual commercial catch in the lower valley fell 25 percent. It recovered somewhat in the 1970s, and in 1973 fishermen landed 12,000 metric tons, the industry's biggest haul ever. That year the US Fish and Wildlife Service reported sufficiently high levels of DDT and chlordane in wild catfish to issue consumption advisories. Thereafter, the total catch fell until in 1977 the National Marine Fisheries Service stopped collecting statistics for the commercial catch in the Lower Mississippi River basin as a region, and instead measured the annual freshwater catch for the entire state of Louisiana. In 2000, about 1,500 fishers worked Louisiana's fresh waters, hauling in a catch of about 6,500 metric tons, of which catfish comprised slightly more than half, bowfin, buffalo, shad, gar, and carp the rest. As for the state of Mississippi, the catch fell to such low levels that in 1976 state and federal agencies ceased bothering to count it.[13]

At the dawn of the twenty-first century, farm-raised fish dominated the market. The reason given by several studies was "society's perception of the river" as "highly contaminated by a wide variety of compounds." Recent efforts to improve water quality generally in the lower valley and in the Mississippi River specifically have done little to improve Big Muddy's toxic reputation, and occasional EPA advisories warning that DDT and toxaphene levels remain high in many waters have not helped. Several lakes near the river are completely closed to fishing. Consequently, few commercial fishers, especially those hoping for catfish, work the lower river anymore. Those who do so sell their catch at discounted prices to "ethnic" markets, so-called because they are patronized by lower income immigrants and people of color who have to stretch their dollars, since corporate or chain markets catering to more affluent and better educated shoppers reject them. Few fish from the river will pass safety inspections. In the Delta, the self-proclaimed catfish capital of the world, people eat wild fish at their peril. But the pond-raised catfish industry has flourished.[14]

Consumer apprehensions about toxic fish dated to the early 1960s and a series of spectacular fish kills—5 million dead fish in 1963–1964. Scientists who investigated quickly ruled out natural causes of the kills and suspected pesticides. The argument over who was to blame, the companies that produced the chemicals or the farmers who applied them, did little to ease concerns about the health of the river. In 1964, a Public Health Services report identified the Velsicol plant at Memphis as the primary culprit, although individual farmers contributed to the fish kills through improper handling, storage, disposal, and application of endrin and other chemicals. The public expressed its greatest concern, not for the health of the fish, nor for the health of the commercial fishery and the welfare of the people who made their living off of it, but for the health of consumers. As Denzel Ferguson, a professor at Mississippi State University predicted in 1967, "the time may come when we will be more concerned over the fish that survive a pesticide kill than over those that are killed." Indeed, the fish kills set off a cancer scare that persists to this day, although it must be said that not everyone was worried: vendors sold dead and dying catfish found belly up on the surface of the river to unaware, incautious, or very hungry consumers.[15]

With agriculture struggling despite chemical additives, and with the commercial fishery dying in part because of chemicals, many farmers saw an opportunity to farm fish. However, the emergence of fish farming as a major industry in the lower Mississippi Valley was the final death knell for commercial fishing, which simply could not compete. The failure of Louisiana's "Eat Wild Catfish" campaign in the 1990s was telling. In 2000, Louisiana fish farmers produced nearly ten times as much catfish in ponds as commercial fishers took from the state's rivers, lakes, and bayous. In Mississippi, the imbalance between farmed and wild fish at grocery store counters was even greater. With such quantities of pond-raised catfish, the price per pound fell so far that commercial fishing no longer paid, even if the commercial fisher had a buyer for his toxic river fish.[16]

The modern aquaculture industry in the lower Mississippi Valley began in the mid-twentieth century amid the struggles of the southern cotton economy. In 1950 the state of Louisiana, eager to shore up agriculture, undertook to study the life cycle of the crawfish, with an eye to raising it in ponds. Elsewhere in the valley, farmers experimented with raising catfish. As several old-time fish farmers recalled for a freelance Web journalist at the Catfish Festival held annually in Dumas, Arkansas, "As the price of fish went up, the lowly catfish started to look like a pretty marketable alternative and commercial fishermen started netting them from the rivers. Eventually some folks connected one more dot and decided that if they could grow catfish on their own land in conveniently sized ponds they wouldn't have to invest in a boat and they wouldn't have to worry about another fisherman beating them to their favorite fishin' hole." With the dry land economy failing, the lower Mississippi Valley was poised to return to its greatest resource, water, to rebuild its economy and way of life. Yet the falling price of cotton turned cotton farmers into fish farmers, who were quite different from fishers. By raising fish in ponds, landowners intended to supplement farm income, not to change careers. So successful were they at turning fishing into a form of husbandry analogous to agriculture that fish farming repeated the environmental problems that helped undermine agriculture in the first place.[17]

Historically, wherever farmers have had access to rivers and lakes they have supplemented their diet and sometimes their incomes with fish. In the lower valley, the turn to pond fish cultivation was almost accidental, and also quite natural. "Fishing is a part of the very life and being of many in Mississippi," wrote Mississippi State Supreme Court Justice Robertson in a case involving a fishing hole, in which he invoked over a dozen regional writers and poets on the meaningfulness of the cherished pastime of fishing. When rivers flooded cattle ponds and cotton fields, ruining crops and pasture but leaving behind fish, and when hungry crawfish destroyed rice crops, farmers found an alternative source of food and income.[18]

A fine line separates the farmer with a cattle pond full of catfish from the catfish farmer. Vernon Hammett crossed that line sometime in the late 1950s when he began to market fish taken from ponds on his Deer Creek plantation, just north of Greenville, Mississippi. Hammett is credited with being the first commercial catfish farmer in Mississippi, which came to be the leading state in aquaculture. But if it had not been Hammett, it would have been someone else, perhaps Turner Arant. Arant built a pond on his farm and stocked it with catfish for his children's pleasure. By 1965, he was in the catfish business. Across the Mississippi River, in Arkansas, Edgar "Chip" Farmer and others were already raising buffalo fish in their cattle ponds and rice fields and selling them to supplement farm income. In Louisiana, it was rice planters who turned to crawfish farming. In the

1950s, Tommy Herpin helped supplement his family's meals by gathering baskets of crawfish from the fields of his grandfather's Atchafalaya Basin rice farm, and by the 1960s the Herpins sold them for cash. Since the colonial era, rice planters had sought to keep crawfish out of their fields, because the fish ate young plants. By the mid-twentieth century, farmers such as the Herpins were responding to market demands for fish by flooding fields following the rice harvest, to encourage a second crop that would feed crawfish.[19]

The term "farm-raised" is quite familiar to early twenty-first-century consumers. Salmon may be farmed, but they are not raised on farms, that is to say, on the land, by farmers who ride tractors. However, in the lower valley, catfish and to a lesser extent crawfish are raised almost as if they were plants. In 1969, a Department of the Interior news release drew attention to the emerging business of catfish farming in the South, which was fast becoming "an integral part of agricultural operations." The document refers to fish food as fertilizer and to the feeding of catfish as "fertilization of water," as if ponds were fields and fish were cotton. The troubled agricultural economy stimulated the nation's largest aquaculture industry, in part by destroying the river and lake fisheries, and then by imagining fish as plants and water as farmed acreage. When cotton farmer Vernon Hammett hired commercial fishermen to fish his ponds, he revealed his inexperience in his new business. However, when he (and the Department of the Interior and the USDA) began to think of fish as a crop to be harvested, like cotton, he was back on dry land. Hammett, Farmer, Arant, and others effectively pulled fish up onto the land, turning fish into a crop, fishing into farming, ponds into fields, and ultimately, water into land. They abstracted the catfish from its natural environment, reimagined it as a crop, then solidified the abstraction. As one Arkansas extension agent put it, "Fish ponds are just like other agriculture, just wetter."[20]

The process of transforming fish into a crop and fishing into farming involved a shift from fish polyculture to monoculture. In the first years of aquaculture in the lower Mississippi Valley, catfish, buffalo, bass, sunfish, crappie, and crawfish were often raised together, as in the wild. Moreover, they were often raised in ponds planted with rice. Vegetarian buffalo and crawfish ate weeds and rice stubble. Catfish and bass ate crawfish and fry. However, differences in market value of fish species encouraged cultivation of some at the expense of others. The rising price of crawfish relative to catfish made them too expensive to be used as fish food. Buffalo were difficult to market. They were easy and inexpensive to raise in large numbers but were not as familiar as catfish to consumers outside the region and did not freeze well. Game fish such as bass were difficult to raise in numbers large enough to make them marketable. By 1960, fish farmers were concentrating on either crawfish or channel catfish. Local consumers with a taste for the other fish found in the Mississippi River caught it themselves or bought it from the vendors of the region's shrinking commercial catch.[21]

It was only a matter of time before fish farming began to reproduce some of the environmental problems associated with industrialized agriculture. Pond construction, like field preparation, altered flood patterns, often resulting in civil suits between neighbors. Pond effluent was a problem. It was always polluted, often in excess of regulatory limits for suspended solids, nitrogen, and phosphorus. According to a 1999 Southern Regional Aquaculture Center report, catfish pond effluents "generally have higher concentrations of nutrients and organic matter than natural stream waters but much lower concentrations than municipal and industrial wastewater." Inorganic fertilizers leached from fish feed made of grain and accumulated in the pond water, and in some cases they were added directly to the water to encourage growth of natural foods. Untreated, effluents full of fertilizers disrupt river and lake ecologies, stimulating algae blooms; when these die and decay, they cause hypoxic conditions that kill fish.[22]

A second problem came from algae within the ponds, more specifically, blue-green algae, cyanobacteria that produced geosmin and 2-methylisoborneol (2-MIB), which tainted the flavor of the fish and rendered it unmarketable. Blue-green algae outbreaks were treated with diuron, a substituted urea herbicide rated by the EPA as a class III toxin. It is mildly toxic to people, moderately toxic to fish, and highly toxic to aquatic invertebrates. Used widely to control weeds in cotton and sugarcane fields, diuron was then applied to a new "crop," catfish.[23]

The best way to reduce pollution to the surface water system from pond effluent was to drain ponds as infrequently as possible. The best way to reduce blue-green algae was to drain ponds as often as possible. Fish farmers, who drained their ponds every year to minimize the problem with blue-green algae and the need for applications of diuron, dumped high concentrations of nitrogen and phosphorus into the water system, contributing to wild fish kills. Farmers who reused their pond water to minimize effluent discharge inevitably faced an algae problem, which they treated with diuron. When the pond was eventually drained, the algae may have been neutralized with the herbicide but at the cost of adding another toxin to the water system, one that disrupted river and lake ecologies at the beginning of the food chain by killing aquatic invertebrates.

Both problems—effluents high in fertilizer and fish tainted by blue-green algae—were consequences of fish monoculture, and more generally of thinking of fish as crops and ponds as fields. In rivers and lakes, and in ponds designed to replicate river and lake ecologies, fish food was reproduced naturally, as were herbicides and animal consumers of cyanobacteria. But fish in ponds were different, at least to farmers and agricultural extension agents.

Crawfish farming thus far has fared better. Since the 1930s, when various government agencies proposed it as an alternative to agriculture, the business has grown steadily. Wild crawfish, unlike catfish, did not present consumers with any apparent cause for concern. People associated them with wetlands rather than with the river. A crawfish pond, especially if combined with rice, was like a marsh. Both wild and farm-raised crawfish regularly topped lists of fish and shellfish that were safe to eat and eco-friendly. Wild crawfish were taken from wetlands that were cleaner than rivers and that filtered out toxins. The dirtier Big Muddy and its fish became, the cleaner crawfish swamps and ponds seemed to be.[24]

Between 1998 and 2005, the number of Louisiana crawfish farms increased from 498 to 605, and the total value of the state's industry grew from $9 million to $20 million. Crawfish were raised in shallow ponds where they lived off natural voluntary vegetation. The fish were taken in traps that were hauled into boats, just as in the wild. A growing number of farmers harvested a crop of rice along with crawfish, after which the rice sprouted a second crop on which remaining crawfish fed. In the winter months the rice died, but as it decayed it fed a variety of insect larvae that served as crawfish food. In spring, fields were drained, which reduced rice weevil populations, and while the crawfish dug into burrows the farmer planted a new crop of rice. The combination of crawfish and rice cultivation could be so efficient that organic matter collected to an excess and ponds had to be drained and left fallow, during which time they were often planted with soy. Pond-raised crawfish proved far less susceptible to disease and parasites than did catfish, making pesticides unnecessary. Keeping the water well oxygenated could be difficult, but not unmanageable. The costs of raising crawfish together with rice were minimal, that is, once the farmer had made the initial investment in pond construction. The greatest single problem came from predators. Every year raccoons, mink, and birds made off with a portion of the harvest. In response, some farmers experimented with hunting as a sideline business. Just as the crawfish ponds attracted ducks, the ducks and other birds attracted hunters. What the landowner lost in rice and crawfish to predators he partly regained in fees and admission prices charged to hunters.[25]

The business of crawfish farming succeeded to the extent that it incorporated natural ecological processes. Crawfish culture was profitable because, for the most part, it mimicked fishing in the wild. There were exceptions—for example, on farms that made extensive use of chemical defoliants or pond bottom-churning machines known as crawlers. Nevertheless, crawfish farming offered a model for aquaculture, one the catfish industry has recently begun to follow. At the same time, the health of the wild crawfish industry offered a model for restoring other wild fisheries.[26]

In contrast, catfish farming suffered from its similarity to agriculture. Catfish were crops planted in flatbottom ponds that were measured in acres and kept free of invading plants and animals. They were fertilized rather than fed, and they were treated with pesticides and herbicides. Predators were shot at, poisoned, and scared away with noisemakers and other modern scarecrows. The fish were made to grow at a uniform rate to a uniform size and then they were harvested with tractors and trucks. Farmers sought assistance from agricultural extension agents at nearby agricultural schools who dispensed advice based on the logic of agricultural economics. In this manner, according to a report produced by the Department of Agricultural Economics at the Mississippi State University, the catfish industry became "one of the most important agricultural activities" in the lower Mississippi Valley.[27]

In the first decade of the twenty-first century, a growing number of catfish farmers and extension agents, frustrated by the rising costs of feed, pesticides, and herbicides and by the falling price of their crop, began experimenting with raising catfish along with crawfish, buffalo fish, and paddlefish, all of which are indigenous to the lower valley, as well as carp and tilapia, which are imports. Some advocated an integrated multitrophic aquaculture (IMTA), the cultivation of several species from different levels of a shared ecological system, including fish, shellfish, plants, plankton, and insects in a manner that mimicked their relationship in nature. Some experimented with constructing marshes that integrated natural vegetation with catfish so as to enhance water purity and aeration naturally, rather than mechanically and chemically. Results were mixed. The primary obstacle to successful polyculture was the lack of a market

FIGURE 10.1 After decades of drying the lower valley for agriculture, aquaculture suggests a return to an older tradition of living off the wet environment. However, catfish farmers often regarded their business as a form of agriculture, building ponds on dry land apart from the river and wetlands, fertilizing ponds with fish food made of grain, applying pesticides and herbicides, and harvesting fish with tractors. Fish farming often replicated many of the environmental problems associated with dry land agriculture in a natural wetland. (Courtesy of Jimmy Avery, National Warmwater Aquaculture Center, Mississippi State University.)

for the other fish raised in ponds. Carp were effective agents for maintaining grass and other vegetation in ponds. Buffalo fish fed off plankton, insects, and plant detritus, helping to maintain water purity. But with only a limited market for them, farmers had to remove and destroy many of them. In addition, regulations restricted the use of carp because they were not indigenous. However, there were ways of regulating their populations. Carp require running water to reproduce, so they did not reproduce well in catfish ponds. Big-mouth buffalo/black buffalo hybrid fish cleaned ponds but could not reproduce. Paddlefish were marketable for meat and caviar but were far more sensitive than catfish to water conditions, especially to oxygen levels. Researchers learned that in wild settings, crawfish facilitate catfish breeding, most likely by providing essential amino and fatty acids to the female catfish that consume them. If the natural relationship between crawfish and catfish was to be replicated in ponds, it was necessary to construct ponds that mimicked the flood pulse of the river floodplain, which decades of levees and drainage had prevented. Successful aquaculturists learned to think of themselves as fishers rather than as farmers, and to think of ponds as wetlands rather than as dry fields.[28]

"It is certainly sad that nobody in the family is following the yearly course of planting cotton and seeing it through the harvest," wrote Margaret Jones Bolsterli in 2008, of the demise of her family's farming business. Where for five generations there had been rows of tall cotton there now are "catfish ponds dug out of the richest land in the world." "Now our connection with the land in that particular way is gone…[and] nobody will even remember it. (Do catfish really count?)" If catfish are to count, they will have to count in new ways. Cotton connected Bolsterli and her people to dry land. Catfish will connect future generations to wet land. It may seem ironic that catfish ponds are dug out of such rich land, and yet it was the Mississippi River that made the land rich in the first place. A far greater irony is that few saw the richness until the land was dried, planted, and impoverished, at least ecologically. Raising catfish suggests a means of restoring the Arkansas Delta, and much of the lower valley, to a former state of wet richness.[29]

Counting catfish and richness requires new metrics appropriate for a business built on fish and water. For example, the netting or seining of several species of fish necessitates their sorting and separation before they can be marketed or returned to the pond. This is considered a prohibitive cost, but only if fish are thought of as plant crops. To be sure, it would be expensive to harvest corn, cotton, and soy from the same field. Yet fishers on the seas and the Great Lakes, as well as those few who remain on the Mississippi River and its tributaries, separate fish all the time. "Species suitable for polyculture with channel catfish must provide increased profits for the farmers—an obvious point that is often lost when discussing catfish polyculture," wrote biologist Craig Tucker and aquaculturalist John Hargreaves. There may be more than one way to account for profits, and more than one way to count catfish.[30]

Faced with stiff competition from foreign producers of catfish and other species, such as tilapia, innovations in production would help if they reduced the costs of fighting the natural environment. Multi-trophic aquaculture, for example, may hold the key to stemming the rising costs of feed, which have driven many farmers out of business. However, such a calculation can be made only if the lower Mississippi Valley is first reimagined as a wetland. The industry is struggling while catfish farms "dry up," in the words of one journalist, in the heat of high grain prices and overseas competition. Should they succeed, the lower valley will begin to resemble the valley before it was remade for agriculture.[31]

There are 250,000 water acres of catfish and crawfish ponds in the lower Mississippi Valley. There are nearly 2 million acres planted in wet rice, some of which overlap with crawfish acreage. Ten percent of the lower valley's 22 million acres are devoted to wet rice and aquaculture, most of it subsidized though direct payments, tax credits, and tariffs. The acres given to wet rice and aquaculture have increased the valley's total wetland by nearly 40 percent, bringing it to well over 8 million acres. At the beginning of the early twenty-first century, far more of the lower valley floodplain sat underwater for at least part of the year than at any time since the nineteenth century. Though not intended as such, subsidies for rice and aquaculture have paid for a tremendous conservation project. These millions of new acres, what might be called working wetlands, have provided habitat for birds traveling the Mississippi flyway. Rice and crawfish wetlands are helping to filter pollutants and sediment from water and to stem the damage caused by decades of agricultural erosion.[32]

The emergence in the lower valley of an economy based on wetlands is reminiscent of earlier days, when the Plaquemine people harvested fish, shellfish, and small game in floodplain marshes, when the people of Pacaha kept large ponds full of all sorts of fish, when French colonists first adapted to the wet environment by planting rice. History in the lower Mississippi Valley, it would appear, is coming full circle. However, much of the new working wetland remains disconnected from the Mississippi River. It sits on the floodplain but is kept apart from the floodplain ecosystem. In early modern Europe, and in colonial America, farmers integrated polycultural fish ponds into the agroecological cycle, or perhaps they integrated agriculture into the aquaecological cycle. It is hard to tell the difference because the line between land and water and between farming and fishing was so thoroughly blurred. Artificial and natural ponds caught field runoff, which fertilized aquatic plants that fed fish, and which farmers later scooped from pond bottoms to spread on their fields to fertilize crops. Sometimes they drained and dried ponds, planted them with a crop they might or might not have harvested, re-flooded them, and reintroduced fish. Such practices crossed the Atlantic.[33]

Aquaculture in the present-day lower Mississippi Valley stands in stark contrast to past practices. Catfish ponds are kept apart and indeed require

protection from the surrounding natural environment, and in their isola-
tion they transform the perception of natural bodies of water and fish. A
pond catfish, because it is carefully isolated from the environment, is sold
as a delicious, healthy, economical, surface-eating fish, in contrast to the
river fish that is effectively transformed into a foul, unhealthy, impractical
bottom feeder. Pond water is thought of as clean and controlled; river water
is dirty and uncontrolled. Aquaculture is like agriculture, ponds are fields,
and fish are crops harvested by farmers who ride tractors and apply chemicals; fishing of the sort fishers do, in rivers, lakes, and "natural" ponds is
another business entirely, although fish farmers send large portions of
their dirty and often toxic runoff into the river. Fishponds in earlier times
integrated land and water. In the lower valley of the twentieth and twenty-
first centuries, they reinforce the separation of land and water.[34]

The new wetlands of rice and fishponds might again connect land and
river if rice and fish farm subsidies were to become subsidies for environmental conservation and ecological protection through wetland rice
cultivation and fishpond construction and management. It might, too, be
possible to think of pond fishing as an extension of, rather than a threat to,
swampland, lake, and river fishing. This appears to be the approach taken
with recreational fish pond construction and management. Commercial
aquaculture, however, exists within an economic structure completely
separate from that of commercial fishing, with its own subsidies, agencies, objectives, business models, and marketing strategies. Both methods
could compete within a common structure, so long as they were practiced
in ways that considered and respected the entire lower valley ecology. At
present, they pit the wet half of that ecology against the dry half.[35]

Like aquaculture, wet rice cultivation offered cotton planters and other
growers an alternative to dry land farming, especially if they thought of
rice as a wetland plant and not an irrigated dry land crop. Rice has long
been a transitional crop, a wetland crop that enabled landowners to dry
the land, thereby turning rice into an irrigated dry crop that was often
replaced with a truly dry crop such as cotton or sugar. Between 1955 and
1975, in the northeastern parishes of Louisiana along the river, rice planting expanded from 7,500 acres to 60,000 acres. Across the river in the
Mississippi-Yazoo Delta, rice planting expanded from almost nil to over
130,000 acres.[36]

Into the early twenty-first century, dry land farming persisted in the
valley, but only by full mechanization and heavy use of chemicals. Cotton
fields were planted with genetically altered Round-Up Ready seed, which

FIGURE 10.2 Catfish ponds in the vicinity of Belzoni, Mississippi, in the Delta, are reintroducing water to the lower Mississippi Valley, albeit in a rectilinear fashion. Despite efforts to keep the ponds separate from the surrounding environment, wetland water, plants, and animals intrude, and water and fish from the ponds escape, making the ponds an important component of the larger wetland environment. (Courtesy of NASA, Landsat.)

produced plants able to endure heavy doses of herbicides and pesticides. There was no need to prepare fields with plows that turned the soil to kill weeds. There was no need to chop and hoe through the summer months, as slaves and sharecroppers had been required to do. The soil was poisoned with chemicals that killed everything but the cotton. Chemicals and genetics and machines succeeded in raising production in the valley to three bales per acre, triple what it was mid-nineteenth century. The cost of human labor was reduced to about one man-hour per bale. Yet the price of cotton continued to fall—in 2004 it was where it had been in the 1980s—while the costs of seed and machines increased. Landowners struggled to make a profit, even with government subsidies. Much of the lower valley continued to lose population because new methods of agriculture required few laborers, and because the new methods were still not reliably profitable. From suburban Baton Rouge to suburban Memphis, nearly every county and parish along both sides of the river had fewer people than twenty years earlier. Some sold out when offered prices they could not refuse; others walked away when faced with debts and mortgages they could not pay. Much of the land ended up in incorporated and well-funded agribusinesses. Land abandoned and unwanted by farmers and agribusiness, often because it was too wet for mechanized production, was in some places taken over by the US Fish and Wildlife Service, the Mississippi Game Commission, the Louisiana Freshwater Fish and Game Commission, or some other conservation agency, to be assembled into large parcels for bottomland hardwood forest restoration. In some places, depopulation permitted the dismantling of levees, over the objections of the few remaining and disregarded landowners. Restoration projects represented a new sort of agriculture. Readmission of water onto the land had to be carefully controlled to protect hardwood seedlings planted in former fields where there were no mature trees to shelter them. But because reforested areas require half a century to mature, voters and politicians could not easily see the progress of conservation. Nevertheless, population decline changed the political landscape in ways that mirrored other rural areas in the nation.[37]

The ongoing debate over the so-called Yazoo Pump may be a harbinger of the lower valley's future. At issue is a decades-old plan to install a giant pump capable of removing water from a 4,000 square mile area at a rate of 14,000 cubic feet per second from the South Mississippi-Yazoo Delta just north of Vicksburg, including all of Issaquena and Sharkey counties and parts of Warren, Yazoo, and Washington Counties. Flooding in this region has always been a problem for farmers, exacerbated by the construction of the levees along the Mississippi and Yazoo rivers. The levees kept river water off the land but they trapped rainwater on what was supposed to be the dry side of the embankments. The 1941 Flood Control Act never mentioned pumps, although the Mississippi River Commission at that time recommended them, but the act did allow that "the Chief of Engineers may, in his discretion, from time to time, substitute therefore combinations of reservoirs, levees, and channel improvements." Whether the vague phrase authorized a pump was and remains an open question.[38]

In 2000, about 1,600 people lived in Issaquena County, down from the twentieth-century high of over 10,000. About 5,500 people lived in Sharkey County, down from its peak of more than 15,000. About 65 percent of these residents were African American, most of whom were officially unemployed and living off welfare or were engaged in "below the radar" economic activities. The rate of out-migration increased following the welfare reforms of the 1990s. One third of the remaining population of Issaquena County lived below the poverty line. The county's per capita income was the second lowest in Mississippi, one of the nation's poorest states. Conditions in Sharkey County were not much better. Many of those who were recognizably employed made their living as farm laborers, planting and harvesting corn, cotton, and soybeans. Others made their living fishing, hunting, and planting marginalized crops, including marijuana. Whites owned most of the farmland. In Issaquena County, some 100 whites, about 6 percent of the county population, owned 98 percent of the farmland. However, Delta politicians, black and white, have seen their political influence diminish as populations have declined. In the South Delta, white businessmen and black politicians joined forces to speak on behalf of the Yazoo Pump Project. For white businessmen, the pump would protect their existing landholdings and allow them to bring more acres into production, qualifying them for federal agricultural subsidies available for farmers on marginal, in this case flood-prone, land. For black politicians, the pump would protect the lives, homes, and jobs of their constituents and would perhaps stem the flow of out-migration before congressional district apportionments were revised. Beyond the Delta, concern was with the expense of a project that would protect so few people in an economically marginal place. Meanwhile, conservation organizations sought to give growing populations of bears and birds priority over declining numbers of people.[39]

Regardless of which side wins, victory in the debate over the Yazoo Pump will bring extinction and loss. Deforestation, draining, and flood control transformed much of the wetland environment that had existed in the Delta before the Civil War. Alligators, ivory-billed woodpeckers, and black bears disappeared along with the wetlands and cypress forests. However, deer, grouse, and turkey populations grew, at least for a time. If built, the Yazoo Pump would drain between 67,000 and 200,000 acres of wetland, creating more habitat for deer and turkey, less habitat for black bears and pondberry plants. It would also make large-scale, mechanized cultivation more feasible, so it would not likely stem the trend of population out-migration, adding urgency to the question: Who is the pump supposed to protect? In an effort to appease critics, the Army Corps of Engineers has plans to reforest 55,000 acres of farmland that would remain too wet to farm very productively even with the pump installed. The plan amounts to destroying wetland here and recreating wetland there. As other reforestation efforts around the lower valley have shown, a mere fragment of wetland forest brings little benefit, especially to large territorial animals such as black bears. Regardless of reforestation plans, fields will be abandoned as people leave, and in time, water, trees, and perhaps even some bears will return. Those content to farm and hunt and live on a small scale might make homes in the renewed wetland, living off the grid, out of sight of authorities. One natural environment and one sort of resident would replace another.

It all depends on the levees that line the Mississippi and Yazoo rivers, which simultaneously keep water off and on the land. Neither side has proposed tearing them down. The levees sustain conflicting dreams of economic and ecological recovery. Both have their champions. The National Audubon Society, the National Wildlife Federation, and the great grandson of Theodore Roosevelt have publicly opposed the pump. They are countered by representatives of local hunting clubs who favor the pump and a reduction in wetland: "there is absolutely nothing about South Delta flooding that enhances wildlife habitat for game or non-game species. Who in the world would think that flooding is good for nesting turkeys or whitetail deer during the spring when animals are most vulnerable to predation and in need for their hatch and fawn drop?" Champions of the pump point to the economic benefits of a revitalized agriculture, although any benefits will necessarily favor landowners, who are mostly white. Opponents, who are predominantly white and affluent, are prepared to offer buyouts to those who will be flooded, but again, buyouts favor white landowners. For the majority of South Delta residents, who are poor and black, the debate over the Yazoo Pump asks them to choose between maintaining a status quo of poverty or leaving to make way for restored wetlands.[40]

In February 2008, the Environmental Protection Agency overruled the Army Corps of Engineers and for the time being halted plans to begin construction of a pump. As the population of the South Delta declines and the region loses political relevance, chances fade that it will ever be constructed. Even if no final decision is ever made, political paralysis favors the pump's opponents. The whole idea of drying the wettest place in the Delta, once the wettest place in the lower valley, to plant cotton and soybeans is anachronistic and increasingly untenable. Yet abandoning the pumps implies abandoning agriculture and giving the entire area over to water, birds, fish, and conservationists, which many are loath to do. No one seems to have sought a middle ground. Rather than a pumped out cotton field or a wet conservation area empty of people but for a few sportsmen, wetlands with embanked rice fields and fish ponds could be built. That would be something on which sportsmen, conservationists, landowners, and tenant farmers might be able to work together. Landowners, engineers, and extension agents might follow the example of the rice fields first built by the French in the lower valley.[41]

Throughout the lower Mississippi Valley, time favors those who wish to see the flood plain restored. As people leave, as levees and other flood control infrastructure age and incur increasing maintenance costs, it becomes more possible to imagine a day when the levees will be abandoned, if not outright torn down, and the land will become wet once again, except for scattered urban islands. Valley residents might conceivably adapt their economy to a re-wetted valley by planting rice or raising fish, or perhaps by distancing themselves from direct interaction with the natural environment through investment in tourism, gaming, and high-tech industries. The decision not to construct the Yazoo Pump may come to mark the end of an era when the valley was kept dry at all costs. However, that may depend on the outcome of the debate over the reconstruction of New Orleans, post–Hurricane Katrina, which involves many of the same issues, institutions, and organizations, but also many more people and much more of the nation's wealth and resources.[42]

Nature's Return: Hurricane Katrina and the Future of the Big Muddy

WHEN HURRICANE KATRINA struck Louisiana in the early morning of August 29, 2005, a repressed wet nature returned to the lower Mississippi Valley with a vengeance. The storm center passed over Plaquemines Parish, southeast of New Orleans, as it moved across the delta and toward the Mississippi Coast. Winds averaging 125 miles per hour and blowing in a counterclockwise circle whipped up a storm surge of twelve feet or more that inundated coastal beaches and marshes from the south and pounded the levees and walls along Lake Pontchartrain from the north. At first, the city's barricades withstood assault from surrounding waters, while pumps removed the six to ten inches of rain that had fallen overnight. Coastal Mississippi lay in ruins, a storm surge of twenty-seven feet having swept away structures for miles inland, but New Orleans apparently had survived more or less intact. In the daylight after the storm, New Orleans, it seemed, was dry. But in fact the city's walls had not held. Some had been topped and toppled during the storm, others gave way later that day. By evening, 80 percent of New Orleans was inundated. Over 800 city residents were dead or dying, many in their homes where they were trapped in attics and swallowed by water in some places twenty feet deep.[1]

In the immediate aftermath of the storm, before the water had begun to recede, with thousands of people still stranded in the Superdome and at the convention center, inquiries began into the full extent of the disaster and the reasons for it. Most of the city was abandoned when commissions and task forces convened to take up the matter of rebuilding New Orleans. The questions asked by all—What went wrong? How do we rebuild so as to prevent another such natural disaster?—took as given two words: natural and disaster.

Measured in human costs, it is hard to see the aftermath of Hurricane Katrina as anything but disastrous. Thousands died, tens of thousands lost their homes, and the Gulf Coast lost billions of dollars in property damage and business. But was it a natural disaster? Hurricanes are as natural to the Gulf of Mexico as sand beaches and oysters. They are disasters only when they disrupt human life. The rest of nature is rather well adapted to hurricanes and flooding, and indeed, would be hard-pressed to sustain itself were the storms to stop. Hurricane winds and rains flush and replenish wetlands; increase food supplies for many species of fish, shellfish, and birds; thin coastal forests, especially of old and ailing trees; and moisten the soil for younger ones. Their long-term effect on coastal erosion is minimal; indeed, they may play an important role in the formation of barrier islands, which help prevent erosion. While some plants and animals experience significant declines in numbers following storms, they tend to recover quickly. Many animals experience population booms, only to decline until the next major storm begins the cycle anew. While thousands of individual animals and plants die in major storms, collectively, the coastal biotic community, minus people, is either largely unaffected or actually benefits from severe storms.[2]

To many it seemed obvious, that the 2005 flood, while disastrous, was not truly natural because people had created the conditions that made it possible. People built the faulty levees that high seas easily toppled. People constructed the Mississippi River Gulf Outlet (MRGO) that funneled the tidal surge into low-lying wards. People meddled with the coastal environment, causing its erosion and degradation, thereby depriving New Orleans of a natural barrier to the most destructive effects of hurricanes. People built and paved over wetlands, which consequently dried up and caused the city to sink. People put housing developments in low-lying districts. People fashioned and implemented policies that kept the city, particularly its hotel and restaurant businesses, dependent on a cheap labor force that could only afford to live in the lowest lying districts. The list of human causes of the disaster goes on.[3]

The discussion of causes and consequences of the Katrina disaster, which for the most part addressed issues specific to New Orleans and the city's recent past, provides a unique opportunity to bring environmental history to bear on a critical present-day environmental question: Can twenty-first century Americans adapt themselves to their environment, as past generations did, rather than always seeking to adapt the environment to suit them? It is clear that the struggle to keep New Orleans dry cannot be sustained. In the days after Hurricane Katrina, New Orleans and the surrounding delta were as wet as they have ever been, despite billions of dollars and immeasurable quantities of human energy expended since the construction of the first French levee to make and keep that patch of ground dry.

What happened in late August 2005 was, in one respect, nothing new or unique. Hurricane Katrina developed over the ocean during the time of year when hurricanes are most expected. It hit a coastline that has been hit by hurricanes many times before and flooded a city that has been flooded many times before. And yet, this completely expected event caught New Orleans and the nation off guard. Paradoxically, the event was both entirely predictable—indeed, many did predict it—and yet completely unexpected because such disasters brought by hurricanes and floods are not sup- posed to happen in the United States.[4] The residents of New Orleans, like Americans generally, imagine that people and their cities stand apart from the natural world. A hurricane or a flood can only be understood, there- fore, as the sudden and disastrous intrusion of the natural world into the human world. Such intrusions are typically explained in two ways: they are the result of natural forces extraordinarily powerful and completely unpredictable. Alternatively, they are the result of human failure to secure the barriers between people and nature. Recently, a third explanation, a combination of the two, has been proffered: human alterations of natural environments have upset nature's balance, causing nature to strike back with tremendous force.[5]

All three explanations could be heard in the days and weeks following hurricane Katrina. President George W. Bush invoked the first when he told a television audience "I don't think anybody anticipated the breach of the levees." Levee failures had in fact been predicted by several agencies, including the National Infrastructure Simulation and Analysis Center and the Federal Emergency Management Agency, both within the Department of Homeland Security, and their reports of pending disaster were provided to the White House, at which point critics of the president invoked the second explanation and blamed his administration for failing to heed the warnings. Those invoking the third explanation took aim mostly at the Army Corps of Engineers and at Congress, which funds Corps projects. A New York Times editorial, headlined "Nature's Revenge," demanded that Congress appropriate $70 million for levee construction and repairs it had earlier cut from Corps appropriations, but also recognized that the flooding was largely caused by the lower Mississippi Valley's network of levees: "Indeed, the evidence is indisputable that systematic levee-building along the Mississippi upstream of New Orleans has blocked much of the natural flow of silt into the delta. That, in turn, has caused the delta to subside and made the city and its environs even more vulnerable to the waters of the Gulf of Mexico, which itself has been rising." Each explanation assumes the inherent separation of people and nature, land and water, dry and wet. When the unexpected did happen, and especially after it turned out not to be so unexpected, then a host of people, beginning with the president, were blamed for allowing land and water to mix, as if that were unnatural. The *Times* editorial board, like many who came before, saw no easy solution to the contradiction between demanding more money for more levees to prevent flooding and simultaneously arguing that levees ultimately contributed to flooding.[6]

It is true that human-induced environmental changes have made New Orleans more vulnerable to flooding.[7] It is also true that technology has sustained the city for the last several decades by keeping the Mississippi River from turning into the Atchafalaya, because changing course, abandoning one channel for another, is what the river does. New Orleans may be sinking because of short-sighted engineering projects, but with or without them the city would be sinking, or sunk, anyway. The Louisiana Coast is a graveyard of dead and buried deltas. At the end of the nineteenth century, before Project Flood disconnected the river from the floodplain, one engineer calculated that the delta sank naturally at a rate of one foot every twenty years. By that reckoning, New Orleans, which is nearly three centuries old, has sunk fifteen feet on its own. That the city still exists owes entirely to engineers. It is also true that the same technology that has simultaneously sustained New Orleans and made it more vulnerable to hurricanes and floods has given its residents a false sense of security, a feeling that they can be kept securely isolated from the wet environment that surrounds them.[8]

Land and water are not and never have been inherently separate in the lower Mississippi Valley. In this place, the mixing of land and water, of wet and dry, is irrepressible. The residents of New Orleans and of the lower Mississippi Valley used to live with floods and not think of them as disastrous. No sooner had the French moved their colonial capital to the newly surveyed town of New Orleans than a hurricane leveled the place. No sooner had they completed a levee than the Mississippi River inundated them. Over time, the engineers added to the levees, making them taller, wider, and longer, but the flooding and high winds continued. "We are here in July," Louisiana Governor Carondelet wrote in 1797 to the commandant of a fort below New Orleans, and "thus you begin to take precautions against hurricanes." The governor reminded the officer to close some gutters, and most important, to remove his powder to where it would be out of reach of flood waters, because flooding was inevitable. In the city, residents learned to build two-story homes, to have refuge in times of flood. Across the lower delta and all around the valley, people built homes on stilts. Everyone expected floods, and for good reason.[9] Since 1800, New Orleans has endured a major flood on average once every seven or eight years. All the levees, drainage canals, and pumps did not stop the flooding, although they did raise expectations and thereby worsen the catastrophe when water returned to the city's neighborhoods. To be sure, the source of flooding changed over time. Levees somewhat successfully sealed the city off from the river but left it vulnerable to flooding from the backside and to rain which collected in the city's center. Whereas the greatest threat used to be the river, more recently rain and storm surges of hurricanes bring inundation. One way or another, water always returns. Yet, at some point in the second half of the nineteenth century, in the face of regular flooding, city residents began to imagine that New Orleans could be made permanently dry. After the 1927 flood, they came to expect and even demand it.[10]

The people of New Orleans in the past had a different relationship with the wet delta environment, even in the midst of disaster, which is how many residents of New Orleans experienced the 1849 flood, as a disaster. While many silently wondered how they would feed themselves and pay their rent, some blasted the "criminal imbecility of the public authorities." A public debate broke out over whether landlords could hold tenants who had abandoned flooded buildings legally responsible for breaking the terms of their leases. The local press referred to the flood, or at least to the crevasse at Sauvé's plantation, as the scene of disaster. They also called it "terrible," an "inconvenience and a discomfort," a "distressing" and "serious matter," its effects "enormous," "detrimental to health," and "severely felt," primarily in the form of damage to furniture and inflated vegetable prices at market.[11]

Still, it must be asked what New Orleanians of a century and a half ago meant by disaster. Newspaper accounts from 1849 stand in stark contrast to television images from New Orleans in 2005: elderly women sitting in propped up rocking chairs, knitting, their houses surrounded by three feet of water; elderly men catching catfish from their front porches; young gentlemen rowing young ladies about on outings and sightseeing excursions through city streets; children racing bare-legged, laughing and shrieking as they push each other into the deepest pools, and, to the concern of one reporter, knocking water moccasins unconscious with sticks and stones and then playing with them. All the while, business in the city continued as well as possible under the circumstances. People trudged to and from work and market in outwear made of India rubber, what the locals called *caoutchouc*, and in waterproof "California" boots, named for the California gold-rushers who wore them when they panned for gold. Under the heading "Yachting in the Inundated District," the *Daily Delta* observed that few had left the city, none who had upper stories, and that everyone was resigned to the flood, some even facing it with smiles. This disaster was one of rather different proportions from those of more recent history, not only in terms of material and physical consequences but also in the way it was perceived. One observer recorded, "The people of New Orleans, though doomed to a sort of amphibious existence, are not overwhelmed by the flood that threatens to submerge them. On the contrary, they bear the inconveniences of the present situation with a most commendable spirit, and exhibit a faculty of adapting themselves to circumstances."[12]

In their reaction to periodic flooding, the people of nineteenth-century New Orleans resembled the Native Americans who picked up and moved to higher ground when the water rose, returning when the water receded, and who told Bienville that a place only knee deep in water in late spring was a habitable place. There was little expression of entitlement to a life apart from water and free of disaster. There were no expressions of fear, and no outrage at having been abandoned by the nation, even though it competed in the national press with news of revolutions in Europe, fires that destroyed much of St. Louis, Missouri, and Watertown, New York, and riots and cholera in New York City. President Zachary Taylor, caught up in the politics of slavery and the western territories, only vaguely knew of the flood when, in May of the next year he and his son purchased a plantation ten miles up the Mississippi from the site of Sauvé's crevasse.[13]

Fear and outrage were omnipresent following Hurricane Katrina: fear of death, ruin, looting, race war, abandonment, and outrage at government of all levels. Most palpable was the deep fear of water, its silent, steady rise; its power to destroy property and take human life; its stench;

its toxicity. Oddly, perhaps, the hurricane itself did not frighten the city, which might explain in part the lack of disaster preparation. Hurricanes last but a few hours, during which time one can only hunker down or get out of the way. The flood that followed caught many by surprise, stranding them for days, much as in 1849.[14]

During the earlier flood, people lived, worked, and played in it. Some died, many suffered pain, many more suffered inconvenience and discomfort. But most, it seems from the press reports, accepted the wet circumstances in which they found themselves and made the best of it because what else could they do in a place they knew was always potentially and occasionally actually very wet? The water was surely cleaner then than it is today, with no oil, gasoline, or chemicals, although in 2005 threat of toxins in the water was greatly exaggerated, whereas in 1849 the water would have had much more animal and human excrement. Disease, cholera especially, was a serious concern then. When the water at last receded, the city government removed silt deposits and sprinkled soggy streets and sidewalks with lime to improve odor and preserve health. In 1849, the people of New Orleans lived with water, expected it, and dealt with it, thereby minimizing disaster. In 2005, water was a foreign intruder within city limits, and it overwhelmed people, which made for disaster. Measured in terms of inundation levels, the floods were comparable, but they could not have been regarded more differently.[15]

The term "natural disaster" is rather new. In 1886, during the public discussion of the Charleston earthquake, people began to speak of the event more as a "natural disaster," for which humans could not be held accountable, and less as an "act of God," which suggested divine retribution for unrepentant human sinners. Still, the term was uncommon. The *New York Times* did not use it in stories on the Flood of 1927 or on Hurricane Betsy in 1965.[16]

In the United States, the modern idea of disaster was clearly defined by the Disaster and Relief Act (1950), as events both natural and manmade of such exceptional proportions that they can only be planned for and prevented, and in their unfortunate event, be cleaned up by the federal government. The 1950 act was the culmination of a historical process that created a constitutional need to imagine disasters. The more the federal government got involved in the natural disaster relief business, the more it got involved in the business of managing nature, which created greater disasters that demanded still greater relief. The reorganization of the relationship between water and land in the lower valley on a massive

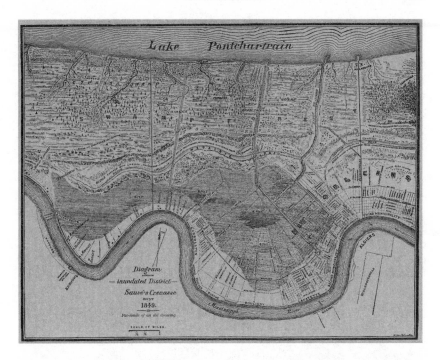

FIGURE 11.1 New Orleans, 1849, showing the inundated area. Water broke through an upriver levee and flooded the lowest areas in the center of the city. Neighborhoods along the river, upon the natural levee, remained dry. From George E. Waring Jr., comp., *Report on the Social Statistics of Cities*, United States Census Office, Part II, 1886.

scale led to the 1927 flood, which in turn led to the 1950 act, and then to the establishment of FEMA in 1979.[7]

It is not the case that earlier generations experienced floods and hurricanes as natural disasters but had yet to think of the term; they experienced such events differently, as not so extraordinary or unavoidable. In 1816, as he prepared a report for the New Orleans City Council, Benjamin Latrobe investigated flood control efforts in central Europe and concluded that whatever New Orleans decided to do, it would only be postponing the inevitable. Either the city could abandon its flood control efforts entirely and live with frequently but relatively mild inundations, or it could build levees that would keep the city dry most years but which would one day fail with catastrophic consequences. Latrobe advised the latter course.

Latrobe did not suggest abandoning the city. Until Katrina, that idea was inconceivable, but no longer; the costs of keeping New Orleans dry rise while the city's contributions to the nation's wealth fall. However, New

FIGURE 11.2 New Orleans, September 6, 2005, showing the inundated area. Water broke through in several places, including through the retaining walls along the 17th Street Canal, in the upper center in a suburb built since 1849. As in 1849, water collected in low-lying areas in the center of the city. The Upper and Lower Ninth Wards, also built since 1849, are to the right. They were inundated when water forced by high winds up the Mississippi River Gulf Outlet breached the walls of the Industrial Canal. (Courtesy NASA Earth Observatory)

Orleans post-Katrina appears to be following Latrobe's advice yet again and building better flood control structures that will postpone but not prevent future floods. "Rebuilding the familiar" is a typical response to disaster. Thus far, the strategy of reinforcing barriers between wet and dry has not worked, indeed, has probably made the situation more dire. As historical geographer Craig Colten has explained, New Orleans has for decades been losing its adaptive resilience, as new and improved water control structures built in the wake of floods, rather than protect the city, have facilitated urban development farther onto low-lying areas, making the city ever more vulnerable to inundation. Thus, the response to each hurricane has left New Orleans less prepared for the next hurricane.

Katrina, a smaller storm than 1965's Hurricane Betsy, was so devastating in large part because of control structures put in place after Betsy. Disaster, it seems, has become more inevitable over time. [18]

The other option Latrobe proposed, to abandon flood control efforts and live with inundations, has received little serious attention, because doing so would mean to consider rebuilding the unfamiliar: a city that is not a dry place. Instead of asking "How do we continue to keep New Orleans dry?" residents of New Orleans might ask "Is it possible to live with periodic flooding, to see the city as naturally, but not disastrously, wet?"

Venice, the city of canals, is famously wet. In December 2008, it was inundated by the worst flood in over twenty years. The city's residents responded with portable, elevated sidewalks and rubber boots. Artwork and archives were secured. Buildings sustained little damage. Indeed, a debate broke out in city hall over whether a flood control scheme, planned decades ago and dubbed Project Moses, was worth the expense, with the mayor of Venice arguing it was not. Meanwhile, kite-surfers played in St. Mark's Square.[19]

St. Petersburg, Russia, the Venice of the North, is built on over forty islands that comprise the Neva River delta. A massive flood control structure, designed to prevent Baltic Sea waves and tides from backing up the Neva and flooding St. Petersburg's many bridges, has never been completed, and probably never will be because it is so expensive and because Petersburgers have learned to live with frequent, unpredictable flooding. They never venture from home without contingency plans. At any time the bridges may close, stranding them in whatever quarter of the city they happen to be. Inconvenience due to water is a fact of life in St. Petersburg.[20]

Louisiana is often compared to the Netherlands, over half of which lies below sea level. Rotterdam, the country's second largest city and one of the world's busiest ports, like New Orleans lies mostly below sea level. Also as with New Orleans, nearly half the area of municipal Rotterdam is water, not dry land. The Dutch have long struggled against water in the Rhine-Meuse-Scheldt delta, but a disastrous flood in 1953 led to implementation of its current program for water management, a term the Dutch prefer over flood control. The program, Project Delta, is an engineering system of dykes and storm surge barriers, the largest of which has sluice gates that are closed only during severe weather conditions, thereby allowing marine life to pass through the barrier and estuarial fishing to continue. The system also incorporates human landscapes—farmland and city parks—that serve as reservoirs if needed. This means that people have to be prepared for the intrusion of water into their "dry" places. Louisiana Senator Mary Landrieu visited the Netherlands and contrasted that nation's approach to water with that of her own. "Instead of pumping all the water out of a 17th Street Canal like we do, they'll drain the water into a retaining lake within their community," she said. "Maybe one day, that area looks like a plaza and the next day, there's six feet of water in a landscape that's an integral part of the city." With limited amounts of dry land, the Dutch have adapted by designing and constructing floating homes. The Netherlands have become a world leader in hydroponic agriculture, a method of soil-less agriculture that produces in small greenhouses, allowing even those who live in floating homes and have no dry backyards, to raise their own vegetables.[21]

One need not look so far afield to find examples of how the people of New Orleans, and residents of the lower Mississippi Valley generally, might adapt themselves to a wet environment. In 1973 a serious flood threatened the entire valley. Engineers opened spillways at Bonnet Carré and for the first time at Morganza. Water rushed into the valley too suddenly for wildlife populations, the number of dead animals for many a vivid memory of the flood. But New Orleans was saved, as were most residential areas in the lower valley. The middle valley was not so fortunate. Suburbs at the confluence of the Missouri and Mississippi Rivers were swamped. St. Charles County, Missouri, outside St. Louis, was especially hard hit. Over 5,000 people evacuated. A combination of levees caused the river to rise eight feet higher than it had sixty-five years earlier, when the same total volume of water had flowed through the area. In the aftermath of the 1973 flood, many called for more and higher levees. Instead, the federal government invoked the 1968 National Flood Insurance Act. By 1975 the government had subsidized over 2,000 policies in St. Charles County. According to the terms of the act, the county had to introduce a program of land use regulation to minimize flood damage and reduce the costs of the insurance program. Rather than stop the flooding, flood insurance, in the words of environmental historian Ted Steinberg, "allowed inundation to become a way of life." After 1973, whenever the county flooded, residents waded to work or school in boots or else went by boat. When the water receded, they totaled the damage to furniture, appliances, and floors and filed a claim.[22]

The insurance program had its problems, most notably, with mobile homes, but in 2008, a flood-swollen Mississippi River broke through the levee at St. Charles, inundating a soccer field and a sod farm, but no homes. Since 1993, FEMA has spent $56.3 million to move people and infrastructure out of the rural areas of the floodplain. In that same time, the Corps of Engineers has spent $2.2 billion to protect 28,000 new homes in the sprawling suburbs of St. Louis built on the floodplain. Nevertheless, the program is showing lurching signs of success. The Army Corps of Engineers considered abandoning the broken levee and allowing a large portion of St. Charles County to return to wetland, albeit, a wetland empty of people.[23]

The homes in St. Charles County might have been elevated, which along with other measures, such as federally guaranteed insurance, might have enabled residents to adapt to periodic inundation, as many in fact were doing before the buyout program, with boots, waders, and rowboats. But officials working on the problem of St. Charles County devoted far more attention to keeping people dry than to enabling those who wished to stay to live wet. When a better levee was deemed too expensive, the only dry alternative was to move people out of wet areas. Some consider living with water as "third world living," a permanent condition of poverty deemed unacceptable in the United States. Whereas flood insurance was thought to perpetuate poverty at the taxpayers' expense, the buyout program was viewed as socially uplifting. Whether or not the buyout program has on the whole been good for individual families is difficult to assess. One presumes that wherever the families are living now, they are drier, even though they may be living in housing they cannot afford, at a greater distance and travel cost from their work places.[24]

There were calls for something like a buyout program for the New Orleans neighborhoods hardest hit by the floods that followed Hurricane Katrina. Yet many people, black and white, wished to return to their home neighborhoods. In the absence of a program aimed at moving people out of the lowest sections of New Orleans, the only alternatives considered seriously were better levees and water pumps to keep the city dry, or else succumbing to something like third world living. The former will inevitably fail, because eventually the water will return. The latter has been no more acceptable in post-Katrina New Orleans than it was in St. Charles County, Missouri, in 1993.

It turns out that one can be dry and poor, as large sections of St. Charles County and New Orleans were before they were flooded. As the Dutch showed, it is possible to be wet and well off. There is no necessary correlation between flooding and poverty. In 1849 and in 2005 and in all the floods in between, the poorest neighborhoods of New Orleans were hardest hit. After Katrina, images from the Lower Ninth Ward vividly reinforced the association of water with poverty. In the news media, the wood frame and clapboard houses of the Lower Ninth Ward crowded out the brick structures of the more affluent but devastated Lakeview neighborhood. They were newsworthy because they were shocking, so third world.[25]

No place has upended the assumed relationship between economic development, wealth, and the dry life like the country of Bangladesh, the very sort of place many probably had in mind when they compared New Orleans after Katrina to the third world. The giant Ganges-Brahmaputra delta that comprises most of the country of Bangladesh may be the wettest place on earth. During severe floods, as much as two thirds of the country can go under water temporarily. But Bangladesh at the start of the early twenty-first century was not wet the way it used to be. Much of the water from the Ganges River was diverted to serve irrigation needs in neighboring India, leaving large parts of Bangladesh short of fresh water. And yet, the country was drowning. In 1998, 2004, and 2007, it suffered floods larger and more deadly than usual. The river's annual deposit of sediment was greatly reduced, which hastened a process of coastal erosion, much as in Louisiana. Making matters worse, by 2050, at least 17 percent, maybe more, of the country's dry landmass will permanently submerge beneath salt water because of rising ocean levels, displacing over 30 million people, unless they somehow adapt to an increasingly wet, increasingly salty environment. Adaptation is precisely what Bangladesh intends to do. By 2010, residents of the chars, small islands in the river deltas, were placing their homes upon earthen mounds that rose more than three feet above the high water mark, developing ever-more varieties of flood and pest-resistant rice, practicing hydroponic agriculture free of fertilizers and pesticides in gardens that floated on the river, collecting fresh rainwater off the surface of heavier sea water, learning to farm saline-tolerant plants and to husband ducks, crabs, and other wetland creatures. These and other "adaptation initiatives" were supported by a group of government agencies in Bangladesh and the United Kingdom, along with the World Bank and several local and international nongovernmental organizations (NGOs) that implemented the world's first strategic action plan—the Chars Livelihood Project (CLP)—to deal with rising ocean levels caused by global warming. According to environment minister Raja Debashish Roy, "Bangladesh has always had floods, cyclones and disasters. People are used to dealing with such changes. We have a history of dealing with challenges. We are mentally equipped for climate change, but we do need support to prepare for it." Neither Roy nor anyone else advocated this acceptance without addressing the problems of delta erosion. The government of Bangladesh negotiated water rights with the government of India. There were discussions on the feasibility of levees and floodwalls able to withstand cyclone winds and tidal surges. Still, in May 2009, in the wake of a severe cyclone that toppled weak embankments, Ainun Nishat, a water resources engineer and his country's representative to the International Union for Conservation of Nature, pointed out that rain, floods, cyclones, and tidal surges were natural happenings in Bangladesh and "we must remain prepared to live with them." There are even signs that communities that have adapted to rising water levels have lowered their rates of poverty.[26]

By the turn of the twenty-first century the most developed nations were becoming more vulnerable to catastrophic flooding, while the least developed were become less vulnerable. Still, there remained a contradiction in the discussion of post-Katrina New Orleans: development, which has meant drying the land, was considered an underlying cause of the flood, because it altered the floodplain, causing the city to sink and the coastline to erode; the proposed solution to the problem was further development, that is to say, further drying. Five years after Katrina, there was still no serious discussion of how New Orleans might be "developed" into a wet city.

In some ways, this development was already under way in parts of the lower Mississippi Valley when Katrina hit. The exodus of people from the valley, as well as federal, state, and nonprofit agency buyout programs made possible the opening of parts of the flood plain to the river, as water storage areas. The largest such program was initiated along the Ouachita River in Morehouse Parish, where the Baron de Bastrop received his grant of land from the Spanish governor Carondelet, and which since the 1960s had been a sprawling soybean operation. Engineers started dismantling levees thirty feet high so that twenty-five square miles of wetland could be restored.

Wetland restoration is one example of a nonstructural approach to flood control. So are wet rice cultivation and aquaculture. Of course, they could be just as problematic as dry agriculture, if managed as such. Ideally, rice fields and fish ponds could become river water storage areas. Rice fields designed to mimic marshes could clean floodwater before returning it to the river. Wetland restoration incorporated into aquaculture could provide clean water for its own ponds, ending the need to draw on a diminishing aquifer. Reluctant rice farmers and aquaculturalists might be persuaded to incorporate the river into their businesses, if the river were cleaner to begin with. Measures might be taken toward cleaning the river by severely restricting the use of chemical fertilizers and pesticides. Dirtier rivers than the Mississippi have been cleaned up. The multibillion dollar restoration of the Rhine River through sewage and industrial waste control and the reincorporation of the floodplain into the river's hydrological system—the re-wetting of the flood plain—was declared a modern miracle when, after a thirty-year absence, Atlantic salmon returned. A cleaner Mississippi River might even resurrect a commercial fishery, making the ponds unnecessary. Such ideas may seem far-fetched, but this is a region where not very long ago few could imagine anything other than cotton and soy in drained and dried fields, worked by the hands of poor tenant farmers and share-croppers in the shadows of giant levees. Not so much further back in time, French were eating rice raised behind very small levees, or no levees at all, and eating fish and shellfish taken from nearby rivers and lakes.[27]

As for New Orleans, there has never been a shortage of good ideas put forward by residents and urban planners who believed that maintaining a "dry" city in the midst of the Mississippi River delta was asking for trouble. Many of those ideas have gotten more play since Katrina. For example, the Urban Land Institute has recommended, among other things, the creation of more green space that can double as water reservoirs during floods, as well as a light rail system that would help commuters and provide fast, safe, and inexpensive means of evacuation. The Bring New Orleans Back Commission embraced both ideas and highlighted them in its final report. Others have pushed the city to become more bicycle friendly and to increase housing density by building up, onto higher ground, and into upper stories. Many upper stories in the French Quarter go unused but could provide comfortable and dry living and office space, as they did for the French.[28]

Yet many of the ideas proposed for New Orleans offer little or nothing to address the city's troubled relationship with its wet environment. Many residents see very little in these ideas that specifically addresses the serious problems they faced in 2005. Proposals often amount to little more than a reshuffling and a downsizing of dry space. Those who have a place in the old city, no matter how tenuous, want to hold onto it, and many are pushing for the reconstruction of New Orleans as it was. Their political representatives are responding because reconstructing New Orleans as it was pre-Katrina—rebuilding the familiar—is the path of least resistance to the most votes.

The false dichotomy of wet versus dry lies at the heart of a public debate over New Orleans's footprint. On one side are those who believe the city as a developed urban space should be reduced in area, so that some places can be restored to wetland that will help protect the remaining areas from future hurricanes and floods. Some insist a smaller urban space will necessitate a significant permanent reduction in population; others say that need not happen if density is increased. All who advocate a smaller footprint are prepared to turn more land back to nature and to huddle people in what dry land remains. People on dry land, nature on wet land: the dichotomy persists. It is the same dichotomy imagined by those who seek to rebuild the familiar, putting people inside bigger, stronger levees that will keep the water out. There is, as yet, no concept of urban development and settlement on undrained, unhardened, unfilled wet land.[29]

If New Orleans is to be sustained, it will be through a combination of water manipulation and water acceptance. Nature always takes its course. Repressed one place, it returns somewhere else. City blocks abandoned since Katrina are rapidly reverting to impenetrable jungles like those Iberville described over three centuries ago, thickets of saplings and vines harboring snakes, alligators, and small mammals, and shrouding the ruins of a city built in denial of nature. It is not necessary, as some have argued, to tear down the levees and "let the water decide" which neighborhoods to rebuild, not if homeowners are prepared to live with water. The Lower Ninth Ward will continue to be protected by levees. Nevertheless, new homes in the neighborhood are raised five to ten feet off the ground, built of wind and water resistant materials, and in some cases outfitted with solar panels and water recycling systems, so that residents can remain in them during hurricanes and floods, even with municipal utilities off line. Many new homes are equipped with escape hatches in their roofs, which more than any other feature indicates a new acceptance of the natural environment. In the old way of thinking, a flood was considered unlikely and evacuation was a last resort; to this new mind-set, evacuation is merely one of several ways of normalizing floods and storms. In the summer of 2008, the homes passed a small but important test when the flood waters of Hurricane Gustav rose over bottom porch steps, keeping residents indoors for several hours. A proposal to divert the river below New Orleans, sending it westward, so that it might rebuild the delta, offers another example of how the river might be manipulated but not controlled or repressed, to the advantage of the delta's human population.[30]

FIGURE 11.3 An old French plantation home built well off the ground in case of flood. In more recent times, homes in and around New Orleans have been built near ground level and relied on levees to keep them safe from water. (Photograph by Kerri McCaffety, 2711 Ursulines Ave., New Orleans, La., 70119.)

As the people of New Orleans look to the future, they might also look back to 1849 and before, when city residents lived with water rather than away from it and in fear of it. Like once thriving but now abandoned mining towns, and the towns that once dotted the Plains during the heyday of railroads and ranching, the river towns of the lower Mississippi are products of a historical moment, when the valley was dried to make way for modern agriculture. That moment, that 150-year episode in a 7,600-year-long history of human settlement in the lower Mississippi Valley, is near its end. Those that survive the end of modern agriculture will do so by adapting to what comes next. What is coming next, for New Orleans and the lower Mississippi Valley, is water, and they must adapt.[31]

New Orleans would not be the first town to vanish beneath the Mississippi's water. There is a scene in Mark Twain's *Life on the Mississippi* in which a passenger expresses his plan to disembark at Napoleon, Arkansas. He is informed that the town no longer exists: "There *isn't* any Napoleon any more. Hasn't been for years and years. The Arkansas River burst through it, tore it all to rags, and emptied it into the Mississippi." "Carried the *whole* town away?" asks the astonished passenger, "banks,

FIGURE II.4 (Continued).

FIGURE 11.4 Homes in New Orleans built since Hurricane Katrina indicate a return to earlier architectural traditions, with modifications, including water recycling systems and solar energy panels. (Photographs by author.)

churches, jails, newspaper offices, courthouse, theater, fire department, livery stable—*everything?*" Everything, he is told, and in just fifteen minutes. Twain comments, "it was an astonishing thing to see the Mississippi rolling between unpeopled shores and straight over the spot where I used to see a good big self-complacent town twenty years ago. Town that was county seat of a great and important county; town with a big United States Marine hospital; town of innumerable fights—an inquest every day; town where I had used to know the prettiest girl, and the most accomplished in the whole Mississippi Valley; town where we were handed the first printed news of the *Pennsylvania*'s mournful disaster a quarter of a century ago; a town no more—swallowed up, vanished, gone to feed the fishes; nothing left but a fragment of a shanty and a crumbling chimney!"[32]

New Orleans is not finished yet. But the people of the lower Mississippi Valley must accept and adapt to the Big Muddy river that runs through it. To fix only one problem, that of a sinking New Orleans and delta, or

FIGURE 11.5 In May 2011, Big Muddy rose to near record heights. In New Orleans, people fished on the flooded batture between the river and the levee, much as city residents fished from their homes in 1849. On one hand, flood control measures worked. Although many rural areas flooded, more heavily populated urban centers remained dry. On the other hand, the flood reminded all valley residents that they live in a naturally wet environment. (Courtesy of John McCusker and *The Times-Picayune*.)

an eroding coastline, or a flood-prone valley with its chemically bolstered farmland, or the polluted river will be to replicate the approach taken by engineers going back at least to Shreve and Humphreys, probably before, to the engineers who urged Spanish Governor Gayoso to straighten the river. The future of New Orleans, like its past, is tied to the future of the entire valley. Five centuries ago the people of the lower Mississippi Valley lived in its wet environment because they had no choice, if that was where they wished to live. After three centuries of struggle to dry the valley, it may be that Americans in the twenty-first century also have no choice.

Notes

INTRODUCTION

1. H. N. Fisk, *Geological Investigation of the Alluvial Valley of the Lower Mississippi River* (Vicksburg, Miss.: U. S. Army Corps of Engineers, Mississippi River Commission, 1944). Roger T. Saucier, "A Contemporary Appraisal of Some Key Fiskian Concepts with Emphasis on Holocene Meander Belt Formation and Morphology," *Engineering Geology* 45 (1996): 67–86. Roger T. Saucier, *Geomorphology and Quaternary Geologic History of the Lower Mississippi Valley* (Vicksburg, Miss.: US Army Corps of Engineers, for the Mississippi River Commission, Waterways Experiment Station, 1994).

2. J. C. Kammerer, "Largest Rivers in the United States," U. S. Geological Survey (USGS), accessed December 23, 2011, http://pubs.usgs.gov/of/1987/ofr87-242/. My calculation assumes new, low-flow toilets of 2.5 gallons per flush. "Spatial Patterns of Sediment Concentration in the United States," USGS, accessed December 23, 2011, http://co.water.usgs.gov/sediment/conc.frame.html. W. H. Durum, S. G. Heidel, and L. J. Tison, "World-Wide Runoff of Dissolved Solids," *International Association of Science Hydrology* 51 (1960): 618–628, accessed December 23, 2011, http://iahs.info/redbooks/a051/051078.pdf. W. Kenneth Hamblin and Eric H. Christiansen, *Earth's Dynamic Systems*, 10th ed. (Upper Saddle River, N.J.: Prentice Hall, Pearson Education, 2004), 304. Colin Thorne et al., "Current and Historical Sediment Loads in the Lower Mississippi River, Final Report to the United States Army" (Nottingham: School of Geography, University of Nottingham, 2008), accessed March 28, 2012, www.dtic.mil/cgi-bin/GetTRDoc?AD=ADA486343. Thorne et al. find that while the Mississippi River's sediment load was almost certainly higher in the nineteenth century, data permit only a very rough estimate of its volume. They also conclude that for the period since 1960, for which there are good data, the volume of sediment has

remained stable, with slight declines in sediment load, measured as parts per million, offset by increases in water discharge.

3. On river width and depth: Mississippi River Navigation Charts, Navigable Waterways, sheet 5 (1998), U. S. Army Corps of Engineers, Mississippi Valley Division, accessed December 23, 2011, www.mvd.usace.army.mil/Gis/nav-book/html/navwater.htm. Since 1928 the Army Corps of Engineers has been authorized to maintain a channel depth of 12 feet, although that has yet to be achieved. On surface velocity see: River Velocity Data for Baton Rouge and New Orleans, U. S. Army Corps of Engineers, accessed December 23, 2011, www.mvn.usace.army.mil/eng/edhd/watercon.asp#. On thickness of alluvial deposits: J. Kerry Arthur and Eric W. Strom, "Thickness of the Mississippi River Alluvium and Thickness of the Coarse Sand and Gravel in the Mississippi River Alluvium in Northwestern Mississippi," Water-Resources Investigations Report 96-4305 (1998), USGS, accessed December 23, 2011, http://ms.water.usgs.gov/ms_proj/eric/delta/index.html.

On topsoil: USDA Soil Survey of Leflore County, Mississippi, 1995, accessed December 23, 2011, www.docstoc.com/docs/1105712/Soil-Survey-of-Leflore-County-Mississippi; Mississippi Online Soil Survey Manuscripts, USDA, accessed December 23, 2011, http://soils.usda.gov/survey/online_surveys/mississippi/. Topsoil in the Delta, in northwestern Mississippi, is deeper than anywhere else, but it is often exaggerated by reports that confuse all alluvial deposits, which are hundreds of feet thick but mostly clay, sand, and gravel, with tillable soil. Only the top layer of 20 inches, which soil surveys classify as deep, is especially rich, and it is followed by 20–40 more inches of good soil before there is too much sand and clay.

4. Of the 1.2 million square miles that comprise the entire Mississippi River basin, over 17,000 square miles, an amount equal to one third the total area of the state of Louisiana, are covered with hard surfaces for automobile usage and urban development. Jonathan Foley et al., "Land Use, Land Cover, and Climate Change Across the Mississippi Basin: Impacts on Selected Land and Water Resources," in Ruth DeFries, Greg Asner, and Richard Houghton, eds., *Ecosystems and Land Use Change*, Geophysical Monograph Series, Vol. 153 (2004): 249–262. Foley et al. report that 45,284 square kilometers, or 17,484 square miles in the Mississippi Basin are urban areas. The area of the state of Louisiana is about 52,000 square miles. The figures appear somewhat higher in Ruben N. Lubowski, "Major Uses of Land in the United States, 2002," USDA Economic Research Service, *Economic Information Bulletin* No. 14 (May 2006), accessed December 23, 2011, www.ers.usda.gov/Publications/EIB14/. Lubowski reports urban land within the lower valley "Delta States" at 3,600 square miles. He also reports 17,000 square miles of "special use" land, of which perhaps 10 percent was rural roads and highways. Measured another way: in the year 2000 there were 3,951,098 miles of road in the United States of which over 36 percent were in the Mississippi

River drainage area. Put another way, there were 61,000 square miles of paved land in the country, 36 percent of which amounts to 21,960 square miles. The total area of the state of Mississippi is 48,430 square miles. Federal Highway Administration Highway Statistics 2000, accessed July 11, 2008, www.fhwa. dot.gov/ohim/hs00/hm20.htm. Lester R. Brown, "Paving the Planet: Cars and Crops Competing for Land," Earth Policy Institute, February 14, 2001, accessed July 11, 2008: www.earth-policy.org/Alerts/Alert12.htm. Ari Kelman describes how human-made levees redefined boundaries between wet and dry, which in time became naturalized in the minds of residents of New Orleans. See Ari Kelman, "Boundary Issues: Clarifying New Orleans's Murky Edges," *Journal of American History* 94 (December 2007): 695–703.

5. Richard Campanella, *Bienville's Dilemma: A Historical Geography of New Orleans* (Lafayette: Center for Louisiana Studies, University of Louisiana at Lafayette, 2008), 77–91. For an interesting study that re-thinks the role of mud in history, see Steven Stoll, *Larding the Lean Earth: Soil and Society in Nineteenth-Century America* (New Haven: Yale University Press, 2002). In thinking about mud as a substance, rather than as a composite of two substances, dirt and water, I have learned from Bruno Latour, *Pandora's Hope: Essays on the Reality of Science Studies* (Cambridge, Mass.: Harvard University Press, 1999), who imagines substances not as essential and transcendent, able to stand alone, but as rooted in historical and cultural context, from which they get their meaning as substances.

6. Rodney James Giblett, *Postmodern Wetlands: Culture, History, Ecology* (Edinburgh: Edinburgh University Press, 1996), 13. Uncanny is Giblett's word for wetlands. Arnold G. van der Valk, *The Biology of Freshwater Wetlands* (New York: Oxford University Press, 2006), 1–12.

7. Michael D. Blum and Harry H. Roberts, "Drowning of the Mississippi Delta Due to Insufficient Sediment Supply and Global Sea-Level Rise," *Nature Geoscience* 2 (June 2009): 488–491.

8. Robert W. Harrison and Walter M. Kollmorgen, "Drainage Reclamation in the Coastal Marshlands of the Mississippi River Delta," *Louisiana Historical Quarterly* 30 (April 1947): 654–709. US Army Corps of Engineers and the Louisiana Department of Natural Resources, "Coastal Wetlands Planning, Protection, and Restoration Act: The Bayou LaBranche Marsh Creation Project," brochure (1994). D. Malakoff, "Death by Suffocation in the Gulf of Mexico," *Science* 281 (1998): 190–192. M. T. Driscoll and H. L. Schramm, Jr., "Relative Abundance of Catfishes in Main Channel and Secondary Channel Habitats in the Lower Mississippi River," abstract of paper presented before the Southern Division of the American Fisheries Society Midyear Meeting, San Antonio, 1997. John Sibley, "The Journal of Dr. John Sibley, July–October, 1802," *Louisiana Historical Quarterly* 10 (1927): 480, 481. James A. Allen and Virginia R. Burkett, "Salt Tolerance of Southern Baldcypress," US Geological Survey, National Wetlands Research Center (June, 1997), accessed December 23, 2011, www.nwrc.usgs.

gov/factshts/fs92_97.pdf. The 2005 Census of Aquaculture reported that nearly half of all farmed oysters (Eastern and Pacific) of food size produced in the United States were produced in Louisiana, and nearly 90 percent of all farmed Eastern oysters of food size were produced in Louisiana. See US Department of Agriculture, Census of Aquaculture, Table 17: Mollusk Production and Sales by Species, by Size Category, by State and United States: 2005, accessed July 16, 2008, www.agcensus.usda.gov/Publications/2002/Aquaculture/. Increasingly, the off-bottom or suspended oyster farming method is replacing the clutch reef method, in part because it allows oyster farmers to adapt quickly to changing water quality conditions. See Elizabeth Coleman, *The Gulf Oyster Industry: Seizing a Better Future* (Silver Spring, Md.: National Sea Grant College Program, National Oceanic and Atmospheric Administration, 2003).

9. Thorne et al., "Current and Historical Sediment Loads." John R. Barbarino et al., "Heavy Metals in the Mississippi River," Contaminants in the Mississippi River, US Geological Survey Circular 1133, ed. Robert H. Meade (Reston, Va., 1995), accessed December. 23, 2011, http://water.usgs.gov/pubs/circ/circ1133/heavy-metals.html. Ronald C. Antweiler, Donald A. Goolsby, and Howard E. Taylor, "Nutrients in the Mississippi River," Contaminants in the Mississippi River, US Geological Survey Circular 1133, ed. Robert H. Meade (Reston, Va., 1995), accessed December 23, 2011, http://pubs.usgs.gov/circ/circ1133/nutrients. html. C. Facemire et al., "Impacts of Mercury Contamination in the Southeastern United States," *Water, Air, and Soil Pollution* 80 (1995): 923–926. Craig E. Colten, "Too Much of a Good Thing: Industrial Pollution in the Lower Mississippi River," in Craig E. Colten, ed., *Transforming New Orleans and Its Environs: Centuries of Change* (Pittsburgh: University of Pittsburgh Press, 2000), 141–159. Mississippi River/Gulf of Mexico Watershed Nutrient Task Force, "Reassessment of Point Source Nutrient Mass Loading to the Mississippi River Basin," November 2006, accessed December 23, 2011, http://epa.gov/owow/msbasin/pdf/point_source_loading_assessment.pdf.

10. Richard White, *The Organic Machine: The Remaking of the Columbia River* (New York: Hill and Wang, 1995), argues that we need to come to terms with rivers and the people who work them—he writes specifically of the Columbia River—as whole systems, as organic machines.

11. For a similar argument on how we as a nation have turned our rivers against us by severing them from the total environment, see Ellen E. Wohl, *Disconnected Rivers: Linking Rivers to Landscapes* (New Haven: Yale University Press, 2004).

CHAPTER 1

1. Roger T. Saucier, *Geomorphology and Quaternary Geologic History of the Lower Mississippi Valley* (Vicksburg, Miss.: US Army Corps of Engineers, for the Mississippi River Commission, Waterways Experiment Station, 1994). Although

commonly referred to as De Soto, scholars now consider the correct short version of Hernando de Soto to be Soto.

2. Arnold G. van der Valk, *The Biology of Freshwater Wetlands* (New York: Oxford University Press, 2006). Lyle S. St. Amant, *Louisiana Wildlife Inventory* (New Orleans: Louisiana Wildlife and Fisheries Commission, 1959). Milton B. Newton, Jr., *Louisiana: A Geographical Portrait* (n.p., 1987). Emile S. Gardener and James M. Oliver, "Restoration of Bottomland Hardwood Forests in the Lower Mississippi Alluvial Valley, USA," in John A. Stanturf and Palle Madsen, eds., *Restoration of Temperate and Boreal Forests* (Boca Raton, Fla.: CRC Press, 2005), 235–252. Marvin D. Jeter and G. Ishmael Williams, Jr., "Environmental Setting and Variability," in M. D. Jeter, J. C. Rose, G. L. Williams, Jr., and A. M. Harmon, eds., *Archeology and Bioarcheology of the Lower Mississippi Valley and Trans-Mississippi South* (Fayetteville, Arkansas: University of Arkansas Press, 1989), 3–16. Bruce D. Smith, "Predator-Prey Relationships in the Southeastern Ozarks: AD 1300," *Human Ecology* 2 (1974): 31–43. Kathleen Du Val, *The Native Ground: Indians and Colonists in the Heart of the Continent* (Philadelphia: University of Pennsylvania Press, 2006), 60.

3. David Ewing Duncan, *Hernando de Soto: A Savage Quest in the Americas* (Norman: University of Oklahoma Press, 1997), 210, 401. Charles Hudson, *Knights of Spain, Warriors of the Sun: Hernando de Soto and the South's Ancient Chiefdoms* (Athens: University of Georgia Press, 1997), 39–47.

4. D. R. Lowery, M. P. Taylor, R. L. Warden, and F. H. Taylor, *Fish and Benthic Communities of Eight Lower Mississippi River Floodplain Lakes,*" Lower Mississippi River Environmental Program Report 6 (Vicksburg: Mississippi River Commission, 1987). H. L. Schramm, Jr., "Status and Management of Mississippi River Fisheries," in R. Welcomme and T. Petr, eds., *Proceedings of the Second International Symposium on the Management of Large Rivers for Fisheries,* Vol. 1 (Bangkok: Food and Agriculture Organization of the United Nations, Regional Office for Asia and the Pacific, 2004), 301–334. G. Lucas and M. Powell, "Survey of the Fishery Resources of the Oxbow Lakes of the Mississippi River, 1987 to 1991," *Freshwater Fisheries Report No. 109* (Jackson: Mississippi Department of Wildlife, Fisheries and Parks, 1992). Thomas E. Dahl, *Wetlands Losses in the United States 1780's to 1980's* (Washington, D.C.: U.S. Department of the Interior, Fish and Wildlife Service, 1990), accessed October 6, 2010, www.npwrc. usgs.gov/resource/wetlands/wetloss/index.htm.

5. Elvas claims the march to Quizquiz took seven days, Ranjel claims nine days, and Biedma claims twelve days. Lawrence A. Clayton, Vernon James Knight, Jr., and Edward C. Moore, *The De Soto Chronicles: The Expedition of Hernando de Soto to North America in 1539–1543,* 2 vols. (Tuscaloosa: University of Alabama Press, 1993), 1:111–114, 122, 238, 299. Hudson, *Knights of Spain,* 274–277. Jeffrey P. Brain, "Introduction: Update of De Soto Studies since the United States De Soto Expedition Commission Report," in John R. Swanton, *Final Report of the*

United States De Soto Expedition Commission (reprint ed.; Washington, D.C.: Smithsonian Institution Press, 1985), xxxiii–xxxvi. Hudson locates Soto's crossing of the Mississippi River at Walls, Mississippi, just south of Memphis. Brain puts the location farther south, at Friar's Point, Mississippi.

6. Jerald T. Milanich, ed., *Spanish Borderland Sourcebooks*, Vol. 11, *The Hernando de Soto Expedition* (New York: Garland, 1991), 121–137, 141. Duncan, *Hernando de Soto*, 405. Clayton, *De Soto Chronicles*, 1:118, 205–206, n. 195. Hudson, *Knights of Spain*, 297–298.

7. Milanich, *Spanish Borderland Sourcebooks*, 11:121–137. Hudson, *Knights of Spain*, 293–303.

8. Milanich, *Spanish Borderland Sourcebooks*, 11:122, 132–133, 253, 449. Clayton, *De Soto Chronicles*, 1: 123, 241. Mark A. Rees, "Coercion, Tribute, and Chiefly Authority: The Regional Development of Mississippian Political Culture," *Southeastern Archaeology* 16 (Winter 1997): 113–133.

9. On disease among indigenous peoples prior to the arrival of Europeans, see Jerome C. Rose, Barbara A. Burnett, and Anna M. Harmon, "Disease and Ecology in the Lower Mississippi Valley and the Trans-Mississippi South," *International Journal of Osteoarchaeology* 1 (September 1991): 241–245, and Clark Spencer Larsen, Margaret J. Schoeninger, Dale L. Hutchinson, Katherine F. Russell, and Christopher B. Ruff, "Beyond Demographic Collapse: Biological Adaptation and Change in Native Populations of La Florida," in David Hurst Thomas, ed., *Columbian Consequences*, Vol. 2, *Archaeological and Historical Perspectives on the Spanish Borderlands East* (Washington: Smithsonian Institution Press, 1990), 409–428.

10. Timothy R. Pauketat, *Ancient Cahokia and the Mississippians* (New York: Cambridge University Press, 2004), 42. William E. Doolittle, "Permanent vs. Shifting Cultivation in the Eastern Woodlands of North America Prior to European Contact," *Agriculture and Human Values* 21 (2004): 181–189.

11. Pauketat, *Ancient Cahokia*.

12. William Cronon, *Changes in the Land: Indians, Colonists, and the Ecology of New England* (New York: Hill and Wang, 1983), 44. Charles Hudson, *The Southeastern Indians* (Knoxville: University of Tennessee Press, 1976), 272–277. Bruce D. Smith, "Predator-Prey Relationships in the Southeastern Ozarks: AD 1300," *Human Ecology* 2 (1974): 31–43. Kenneth B. Tankersley, "Bison and Subsistence Change: The Protohistorical Ohio Valley and Illinois Valley Connection," in Dale R. Croes, Rebecca A. Hawkins, and Barry L. Isaac, eds., *Research in Economic Anthropology, supplement 6, Long-Term Subsistence Change in Prehistoric North America* (Greenwich, Conn.: JAI Press, 1992), 103–130. Jay K. Johnson, Susan L. Scott, James R. Atkinson, and Andrea Brewer Shea, "Late Prehistoric/ Protohistoric Settlement and Subsistence on the Black Prairie: Buffalo Hunting in Mississippi," *North American Archaeologist* 15 (1994): 167–179. Jay K. Johnson, "From Chiefdom to Tribe in Northeast Mississippi: The Soto Expedition as a

Window on a Culture in Transition," in Patricia Galloway, ed., *The Hernando de Soto Expedition: History, Historiography, and "Discovery" in the Southeast* (Lincoln: University of Nebraska Press, 1997), 295–312. Jay K. Johnson, "The Chickasaws," in Bonnie G. McEwan, ed., *Indians of the Greater Southeast: Historical Archaeology and Ethnohistory* (Gainesville: University Press of Florida, 2001), 85–121. Gayle J. Fritz, "Native Farming Systems and Ecosystems in the Mississippi River Valley," in David L. Lentz, ed., *Imperfect Balance: Landscape Transformations in the Precolumbian Americas* (New York: Columbia University Press, 2000), 225–249. Patricia Galloway, *Choctaw Genesis 1500–1700* (Lincoln: University of Nebraska Press, 1995), 27–66. Hiram F. Gregory, Jr., "Maximum Forest Efficiency: Swamp and Upland Potentials," *Southeastern Archaeological Conference Bulletin* 3 (1965): 70–74. John H. House, "Evolution of Complex Societies in East-Central Arkansas: An Overview of Environments and Regional Data Bases," in Neal L. Trubowitz and Marvin D. Jeter, eds., *Arkansas Archeology in Review*, Research Series No. 15 (Fayetteville: Arkansas Archaeology Survey, 1982), 37–47. Tristram R. Kidder, "Timing and Consequences of the Introduction of Maize Agriculture in the Lower Mississippi Valley," *North American Archaeologist* 13 (1992): 15–41. Jon Muller, "The Kincaid System: Mississippian Settlements in the Environs of a Large Site," in Bruce D. Smith, ed., *Mississippian Settlement Patterns* (New York: Academic Press, 1978), 270. Bruce D. Smith, *Middle Mississippian Exploitation of Animal Populations*, Anthropological Papers, Museum of Anthropology University of Michigan, no. 57 (Ann Arbor: University of Michigan, 1975). Bruce D. Smith, "Variation in Mississippian Settlement Patterns," in Bruce D. Smith, ed., *Mississippian Settlement Patterns* (New York: Academic Press, 1978), 480–485.

13. David L. Lentz, "Anthropocentric Food Webs in the Precolumbian Americas," in David L. Lentz, *Landscape Transformations in the Precolumbian Americas* (New York: Columbia University Press, 2000),111. B. Smith, "The Origins of Agriculture in the Americas," *Evolutionary Anthropology* 3 (1995): 174–184. Bruce D. Smith and Westley Cowan, "Domesticated Chenopodium in Prehistoric Eastern North America: New Accelerator Dates from Eastern Kentucky," *American Antiquity* 52 (1987): 355–357. Hugh D. Wilson, "Domesticated Chenopodium of the Ozark Bluff Dwellers," *Economic Botany* 35 (1981): 233–239. David L. Asch and Nancy B. Asch, "Chenopod as Cultigen: A Re-evolution of Some Prehistoric Collections from Eastern North America," *Mid-Continental Journal of Archaeology* 2 (1977): 3–45.

14. Jeffrey Brain, "Late Prehistoric Settlement Patterning in the Yazoo Basin and Natchez Bluffs Regions of the Lower Mississippi Valley," in Bruce D. Smith, ed., *Mississippian Settlement Patterns* (New York: Academic Press, 1978), 331–368. According to archaeologist Jeffrey Brain, population growth, intensified agriculture, and climate change contributed to what he terms "ecological fatigue" within Mississippian settlements. See also Galloway, *Choctaw Genesis*, 67–94; Smith,

"Variation in Mississippian Settlement Patterns," 483, 485; Johnson et al., "Late Prehistoric/Protohistoric Settlement and Subsistence on the Black Prairie," pp. 167–179. On fifteenth- and sixteenth-century climate change and its effects on agriculturalists, see D. A. Hodell, M. Brener, and J. H. Curtis, "Climate Change," in David L. Lentz, *Landscape Transformations in the Precolumbian Americas* (New York: Columbia University Press, 2000). Brian Fagan, *The Little Ice Age: How Climate Made History 1300–1850* (New York: Basic Books, 2000); Keith R. Briffa and Timothy J. Osborn, "Seeing the Wood from the Trees," *Science* 284 (1999): 926–927; D. W. Stahle et al, "Tree-Ring Data Document 16th Century Megadrought over North America," *Eos, Transactions, American Geophysical Union* 81 (2000): 121.

15. Gayle J. Fritz, "Native Farming Systems," in David L. Lentz, ed., *Imperfect Balance: Landscape Transformations in the Precolumbian Americas* (New York: Columbia University Press, 2000), 237, 238. Gayle J. Fritz, "Paleoethnobotanical Information and Issues Relevant to the I-69 Overview Process, Northwest Mississippi," in Janet Rafferty and Evan Peacock, eds., *Time's River: Archaeological Syntheses from the Lower Mississippi River Valley* (Tuscaloosa: University of Alabama Press, 2008), 299–343.

16. In 1804–1805, George Hunter and William Dunbar and speculated that it may have been built for flood control purposes. See William Dunbar and George Hunter, *The Forgotten Expedition, 1804–1805: The Louisiana Purchase Journals of Dunbar and Hunter*, Trey Berry, Pam Beasley, and Jeanne Clements, eds. (Baton Rouge: Louisiana State University Press, 2006), 18–19, 190, 196. Winslow M. Walker, *The Troyville Mounds, Catahoula Parish, La.* Bureau of American Ethnology Bulletin 113 (Washington, D.C.: Smithsonian Institution, 1936).

17. David Leeming and Jake Page, *The Mythology of Native North America* (Norman: University of Oklahoma Press, 1998), 107–109. John R. Swanton, *Indian Tribes of the Lower Mississippi Valley and Adjacent Coast of the Gulf of Mexico*, Bureau of American Ethnology Bulletin 43 (Washington, D.C., 1911), 323–324. Milanich, *Spanish Borderland Sourcebooks*, 11:161, 444. Charles Hudson, *Knights of Spain*, 341. Ann Vileisis, *Discovering the Unknown Landscape: A History of America's Wetlands* (Washington, D.C.: Island Press, 1997), 23. James Taylor Carson, "Sacred Circles and Dangerous People: Native American Cosmology and the French Settlement of Louisiana," in Bradley G. Bond, ed., *French Colonial Louisiana and the Atlantic World* (Baton Rouge: Louisiana State University Press, 2005), 65–82. Dave Aftandilian, "Frogs, Snakes, and Agricultural Fertility: Interpreting Illinois Mississippian Representations," in David Aftandilian, ed., *What Are the Animals to Us? Approaches from Science, Religion, Folklore, Literature, and Art* (Knoxville: University of Tennessee Press, 2007), 53–86.

18. John Andrew Prime, "Graves Indicate Human Settlements Here 3000 Years before Pyramids," (September 11, 1999), accessed December 27, 2011, http://home.earthlink.net/~japrime/oldbones.htm. See also Joe W. Saunders et al.,

"A Mound Complex in Louisiana at 5400–5000 Years before the Present," *Science* 277 (September 19, 1997): 1796–1799. Amelie A. Walker, "Earliest Mound Site," *Newsbriefs* 51 (Archaeological Institute of America, 1998), accessed December 27, 2011, www.archaeology.org/9801/newsbriefs/mounds.html. Tristram R. Kidder and Gayle J. Fritz, "Subsistence and Social Change in the Lower Mississippi Valley: The Reno Brake and Osceola Sites, Louisiana," *Journal of Field Archaeology* 20 (Fall 1993): 281–297. Gayle J. Fritz, "Multiple Pathways to Farming in Precontact Eastern North America," *Journal of World History* 4 (1990): 387–435. Gayle J. Fritz, "Levels of Native Biodiversity in Eastern North America," in Paul E. Minnis and Wayne J. Elisens, eds., *Biodiversity and Native America* (Norman: University of Oklahoma Press, 2000), 225–233.

19. Jon L. Gibson, *Poverty Point: A Terminal Archaic Culture of the Lower Mississippi Valley* 2nd ed., Anthropological Study Series, no. 7 (Baton Rouge: Department of Culture, Recreation and Tourism, Office of Cultural Development, 1996). Jon L. Gibson, *The Ancient Mounds of Poverty Point: Place of Rings* (Gainesville: University Press of Florida, 2001), 79, 81.

20. Gibson, *Poverty Point*, 32. Timothy Earle, "The Evolution of Chiefdoms," in Timothy Earle, ed., *Chiefdoms: Power, Economy, and Ideology* (Cambridge: Cambridge University Press, 1991), 1–15. Kenneth M. Ames, "Myth of the Hunter-Gatherer," *Abstracts* 52 (Archaeological Institute of America, 1999), accessed December 27, 2011, www.archaeology.org/9909/abstracts/hunter.html. Patricia Galloway, *Choctaw Genesis*, 68–69; Vincas P. Steponaitis, "Location Theory and Complex Chiefdoms: A Mississippian Example," in Bruce D. Smith, ed., *Mississippian Settlement Patterns* (New York: Academic Press, 1978), 417–453.

21. Mark A. Rees and Patrick C. Livingood, *Plaquemine Archaeology* (Tuscaloosa: University of Alabama Press, 2007), in particular the contributions to the volume by Lori Roe, Ian W. Brown, Marvin D. Jeter, and Tristram R. Kidder.

22. Gayle J. Fritz, "Keepers of Louisiana's Levees: Early Mound Builders and Forest Managers," in *Rethinking Agriculture: Archaeological and Ethnoarchaeological Perspectives*, ed. Tim Denham, José Iriarte, and Luc Vrydaghs, One World Archaeology Series, Vol. 51 (Walnut Creek, Calif.: Left Coast Press, 2007), 189–209. Clayton, *De Soto Chronicles*, 1: 120. On the transition from hunter-gatherer to agriculturalist, see Allen W. Johnson and Timothy Earle, *The Evolution of Human Societies: From Foraging Groups to Agrarian State* (Stanford: Stanford University Press, 1987), 16–18; Kenneth M. Ames, "Myth of the Hunter-Gatherer." Marvin Harris, *Cannibals and Kings: Origins of Cultures* (New York: Random House, 1977). Bruce D. Smith, "Origins of Agriculture in Eastern North America," *Science* 246 (December 22, 1989), 1566–1571. B. Smith, "The Origins of Agriculture in the Americas," *Evolutionary Anthropology* 3 (1995): 174–184.

23. Kidder, "Timing and Consequences of the Introduction of Maize Agriculture," p. 34.

24. Bruce D. Smith, "Resource Resilience, Human Niche Construction, and the Long-Term Sustainability of Pre-Columbian Subsistence Economies in the Mississippi River Valley Corridor," *Journal of Ethnobiology* 29 (2009): 167–183. On lower valley peoples and the ivory-billed woodpecker, see Alfred M. Bailey, "Ivory-Billed Woodpecker's Beak in an Indian Grave in Colorado," *Condor* 41 (1939): 164. Mikko Saikku, "'Home in the Big Forest': Decline of the Ivory-Billed Woodpecker and Its Habitat in the United States," in Timo Myllyntaus and Mikko Saikku, eds., *Encountering the Past in Nature* (Athens: Ohio University Press, 2001), 94–140. Jerome A. Jackson, *In Search of the Ivory-Billed Woodpecker* (Washington, D.C.: Smithsonian Books, 2004). Shepard Krech III, *Spirits of the Air: Birds and American Indians in the South* (Athens: University of Georgia Press, 2009).

25. William G. McIntire, *Prehistoric Indian Settlements of the Changing Mississippi River Delta* (Baton Rouge: Louisiana State University Press, 1958), 38–43. Fritz, "Levels of Native Biodiversity," 237. Fritz, "Multiple Pathways to Farming," 387, 435. Julia E. Hammett, "Ethnohistory of Aboriginal Landscapes in the Southeastern United States," in Paul E. Minnis and Wayne J. Elisens, eds., *Biodiversity and Native America* (Norman: University of Oklahoma Press, 2000), pp. 248–299. Mikko Saikku, *This Delta, This Land: An Environmental History of the Yazoo-Mississippi Floodplain* (Athens: University of Georgia Press, 2005), 67–70. Tristram R. Kidder, "The Rat that Ate Louisiana: Aspects of Historical Ecology in the Mississippi River Delta," in W. Balée, ed., *Advances in Historical Ecology* (New York: Columbia University Press, 1998), 143. Tristram R. Kidder, "Making the City Inevitable: Native Americans and the Geography of New Orleans," in Craig E. Colten, ed. *Transforming New Orleans and Its Environs: Centuries of Change* (Pittsburgh: University of Pittsburgh Press, 2000), 9–21. Milanich, *Spanish Borderland Sourcebooks* 11:271. Father Vivier, "Letter from Father Vivier of the Society of Jesus, to a Father of the same Society, November 17, 1750," Jesuit Relations, accessed March 3, 2012,

26. Kathleen Du Val, *The Native Ground: Indians and Colonists in the Heart of the Continent* (Philadelphia: University of Pennsylvania Press, 2006), esp. chapters 2 and 3. Marvin Jeter, "From Prehistory through Protohistory to Ethnohistory in and near the Northern Lower Mississippi Valley," in Robbie Ethridge and Charles Hudson, eds., *The Transformation of the Southeastern Indians, 1540–1760* (Jackson: University of Mississippi Press, 2002). Robbie Ethridge and Sheri M. Shuck-Hall, eds., *Mapping the Mississippian Shatter Zone: The Colonial Indian Slave Trade and Regional Instability in the American South* (Lincoln: University of Nebraska Press, 2009). Galloway, *Choctaw Genesis*, 307–309, 348–349. Fred B. Kniffen, Hiram F. Gregory, and George A. Stokes, *The Historic Indian Tribes of Louisiana, from 1542 to the Present* (Baton Rouge: Louisiana State University Press, 1987), 44–61. Jeffrey P. Brain, *Tunica Archeology*, Papers of the Peabody Museum of Archaeology and Ethnology, Harvard University, 78 (Cambridge,

Mass., 1988). Brain, "Late Prehistoric Settlement Patterning," 331–368. Marvin T. Smith, "Aboriginal Population Movements in the Postcontact Southeast," in Robbie Etheridge and Charles Hudson, eds., *The Transformation of the Southeastern Indians* (Jackson: University of Mississippi Press, 2002), 3–20. Vincas P. Steponaitis, "Contrasting Patterns of Mississippian Development," in Timothy Earle, ed. *Chiefdoms: Power, Economy, and Ideology* (Cambridge: Cambridge University Press, 1991), 193–228.

27. Galloway, *Choctaw Genesis*, 131–143. Ann F. Ramenofsky and Patricia Galloway, "Disease and the Soto Entrada," in Patricia Galloway, ed., *The Hernando de Soto Expedition History, Historiography, and "Discovery" in the Southeast* (Lincoln: University of Nebraska Press, 1997), 259–279. Ann F. Ramenofsky, *Vectors of Death: The Archaeology of European Contact* (Albuquerque: University of New Mexico Press, 1987), 59–71. Daniel H. Usner, Jr., *American Indians in the Lower Mississippi Valley: Social and Economic Histories* (Lincoln: University of Nebraska Press, 1998), 37. Paul T. Kelton, "The Great Southeastern Smallpox Epidemic," in Robbie Etheridge and Charles Hudson, eds., *The Transformation of the Southeastern Indians* (Jackson: University of Mississippi Press, 2002), 21–37. Paul T. Kelton, *Epidemics and Enslavement: Biological Catastrophe in the Native Southeast 1492–1715* (Lincoln: University of Nebraska Press, 2007), 59–69. Robert L. Blakely and Bettina Detweiler-Blakely, "The Impact of European Diseases in the Sixteenth-Century Southeast: A Case Study," *Midcontinental Journal of Archaeology* 14 (1989): 73.

28. Galloway, *Choctaw Genesis*, 52–53, 352–353; Brain, "Late Prehistoric Settlement Patterning," 331–368.

29. Duncan, *Hernando De Soto*, 419–424. Hudson, *Knights of Spain*, 341–398. Brain, "Late Prehistorical Settlement Patterning," 360; Brain, *Tunica Archaeology*. Brain, "Introduction," xliii–xlvi. Galloway, *Choctaw Genesis*, 308–309. Jeter, "From Prehistory through Protohistory," 177–223.

CHAPTER 2

1. Claiborne A. Skinner, *The Upper Country: French Enterprise in the Colonial Great Lakes* (Baltimore: Johns Hopkins University Press, 2008), 25–65. W. J. Eccles, *France in America*, rev. ed. (East Lansing: Michigan State University Press, 1990), 90–91.

2. James S. Pritchard, *In Search of Empire: The French in the Americas, 1670–1730* (Cambridge: Cambridge University Press, 2004), 7. Daniel H. Usner, Jr., *American Indians in the Lower Mississippi Valley: Social and Economic Histories* (Lincoln: University of Nebraska Press, 1998), 41–42.

3. The river's delta is not to be confused with the Delta, the popular name for the floodplain of northwestern Mississippi, which is typically spelled with a capital "D." Julie K. Cronk and M. Siobhan Fennessy, *Wetland Plants: Biology and Ecology*

(Boca Raton: Lewis Publishers, 2001), 37, 51–52. C. R. Kolb and Van Lopik, "Depositional Environments of the Mississippi River Deltaic Plain, Southeastern Louisiana," in M. L. Shirley and J. A. Ragsdale, eds., *Deltas* (Houston, Tex: Houston Geological Society, 1966), 17–62. William T. Penfound and Edward S. Hathaway, "Plant Communities in the Marshlands of Southeastern Louisiana," *Ecological Monographs* 8 (1938): 1–56. G. H. Lowery, *The Mammals of Louisiana and Its Adjacent Waters* (Baton Rouge: Louisiana State University Press, 1974). A. W. Palmisano, "Habitat Preference of Waterfowl and Fur Animals in the Northern Gulf Coastal Marshes," in R. H. Chabreck, ed., *Proceedings of the Second Coastal Marsh and Estuary Management Symposium* (Baton Rouge: Louisiana State University, Division of Continuing Education, 1972), 163–190. Christopher Neill and Linda A. Deegan, "The Effect of Mississippi River Delta Lobe Development on the Habitat Composition and Diversity of Louisiana Coastal Wetlands," *American Midland Naturalist* 116 (October 1986): 296–303.

4. James M. Coleman, "The Dynamic Changes and Processes in the Mississippi River Delta," *Geological Society of America Bulletin* 100 (1988): 999–1015. Antoine Simon Le Page du Pratz, *The History of Louisiana* (reprint of 1774 edition; New Orleans: Harmonson, 1947), 114. The Fork, better known as Bayou La Fourche, was very likely the River of the Ouachas that Iberville noted in 1699 but which he thought flowed into the Mississippi from the west. During spring flood, Iberville may have had trouble discerning which way the water was flowing. Pierre Le Moyne d'Iberville, *Iberville's Gulf Journals*, Richebourg Gaillard McWilliams, trans. and ed. (University: University of Alabama Press, 1981), 58.

5. Hervé Gourmelon, *Le Chevalier de Kerlérec, 1704–1770: L' affaire de la Louisiane* (Rennes: Les Portes du Large, 2003), 105. Thomas Hutchins, *An Historical Narrative and Topographical Description of Louisiana, and West-Florida* (Philadelphia, 1784), 33. Georges-Henri-Victor Collot, *A Journey in North America, Containing a Survey of the Mississippi, Ohio, Missouri, and Other Affluing Rivers*, 2 vols. (Paris, 1826), 2:103, 122, American Journeys Collection, Document AJ-088B, Wisconsin Historical Society Digital Library and Archives, www.americanjourneys.org. Kolb and Lopik, "Depositional Environments," 17–62. Francis P. Shepard and Harold R. Wanless, *Our Changing Coastlines* (New York: McGraw-Hill, 1971), 198–207. Recent research on Louisiana coastal erosion is available from the United States Geological Service online, accessed February 6, 2004, www.lacoast.gov/cwppra/projects/mississippi/. On the sinking of Fort de la Balise, see E. L. Corthell, "The Delta of the Mississippi River," *National Geographic* 8 (December 1897): 351–354.

6. "Mississippi River Sediment Plume," March 5, 2001, 10:55 A.M. local time, accessed February 1, 2004, http://earthobservatory.nasa.gov/Newsroom/NewImages/images.php3?img_id=4720. La Salle sailed in late December. The sediment plume would have been greater in spring, when this image was taken. Pierre Clément de Laussat, the official who presided over the transfer of Louisiana to

the United States in 1803–1804, noted as he sailed into New Orleans in March 1803 that the color of the sea had changed. Laussat, *Memoirs of My Life*, Robert D. Bush, ed., Agnes-Josephine Pastwa, trans. (Baton Rouge: LSU Press, 1978), 11. Anuradha Mathur and Dilip da Cunha, *Mississippi Floods: Designing a Shifting Landscape* (New Haven: Yale University Press, 2001), 136.

7. Henri Joutel, *The La Salle Expedition to Texas: The Journal of Henri Joutel 1684– 1687*, William C. Foster, ed., Johanna S. Warren, trans. (Austin: Texas State Historical Association, 1998), 66. Jean-Baptiste Minet, Journal de Jean-Baptiste Minet, pt. 2, p. 17, R7971-0-7-F, Library and Archives of Canada, Ottawa, accessed March 3, 2012, http:// data2.archives.ca/e/e083/e002069785.jpg.

8. Enríquez Barroto, "The Enríquez Barroto Diary," in Robert S. Weddle, Mary Christine Morkovsky, and Patricia Kay Galloway, eds., *La Salle, Mississippi, and the Gulf: Three Primary Documents* (College Station: Texas A & M University Press, 1987), 190, 191, 192. Laussat also noted the trees that brushed up against his ship as he approached the Mississippi. Laussat, *Memoirs of My Life*, 11.

9. Bernard Romans, "Maps of East and West Florida," drawn 1774, published 1781. Library of Congress, Geography and Map Division, Washington, D.C., accessed February 1, 2004, http://hdl.loc.gov/loc.gmd/g3931p.ar16220b.

10. "Gulf of Mexico" (1989), National Oceanic and Atmospheric Administration, Department of Commerce, National Ocean Service, Silver Springs, Maryland, accessed February 1, 2004, http://historicalcharts.noaa.gov/historicals/preview/ image/411-6-1989.

11. The classic, full biography of La Salle remains Francis Parkman, *La Salle and the Discovery of the Great West* (London: John Murray, 1869). On the "fatal error" and misunderstood currents, see pages 315, 321. La Salle left Canada with an astrolabe that was too small to be accurate, and he broke his only compass en route downriver to the Gulf. This and the other problems historians have offered in explaining La Salle's failure to find the mouth of the Mississippi River are discussed in Weddle, Morkovsky, and Galloway, eds., *La Salle*, 8, 10, 43, 56, 80–81, 93. Robert S. Weddle, *The Wreck of The Belle, the Ruin of La Salle* (College Station: Texas A & M University Press, 2001). Joutel, *Journal*, 32, 65, n.18, 97, 98. Peter H. Wood, "La Salle: Discovery of a Lost Explorer," *American Historical Review* 89 (April 1984): 294–323. Jean Delanglez, ed., *The Journal of Jean Cavelier: The Account of a Survivor of La Salle's Texas Expedition, 1684–1688* (Chicago: Institute of Jesuit History, 1938). Louis de Vorsey, Jr., "The Impact of the La Salle Expedition of 1682 on European Cartography," in Patricia K. Galloway, ed., *La Salle and His Legacy: Frenchmen and Indians in the Lower Mississippi Valley* (Jackson: University Press of Mississippi, 1982), 60–78. Gilles Havard and Cécile Vidal, *Histoire de L'Amerique Française* (Paris: Flammarion, 2003), 72.

For decades, silver was an obsession for Louisiana administrators and investors. See Iberville's Prospectus (1698), The Historic New Orleans Collection, New Orleans, Louisiana. Etienne Veniard De Bourgmont, "Exact Description of Louisiana," Marcel Giraud, ed., Mrs. Max W. Myers, trans., *The Bulletin of the Missouri Historical Society* 15 (October 1958): 12, 16. Crozat, "Mémoire sur la Louisiane," fevrier 11, 1716, Archive Nationales, Paris, microfilm copy in The Historic New Orleans Collection. Jacques Gravier, "Relation of Journal of the Voyage of Father Gravier, of the Society of Jesus, in 1700, from the Country of the Illinois to the Mouth of the Mississippi River," *Relations*, 65:156, accessed March 28, 2012, http://puffin.creighton.edu/jesuit/relations/relations_65.html.

12. Joutel, *Journal*, 65. Jean-Baptiste Minet, "Journal of Our Voyage to the Gulf of Mexico," Ann Linda Bell, trans., in Robert S. Weddle, Mary Christine Morkovsky, and Patricia Galloway, eds., *La Salle, the Mississippi, and the Gulf: Three Primary Documents* (College Station: Texas A & M University Press, 1987)" 93.

13. Isaac Cox, ed., *The Journeys of Réné Robert Cavelier Sieur de La Salle*, 2 vols. (New York: A. S. Barnes, 1905), 1:25, 145, 146. La Salle, "Memoir of the Sieur de La Salle Reporting to Monseigneur de Seignelay the Discoveries Made by Him under the Order of His Majesty," in Joslin Cox, ed., *The Journeys of Réné Robert Cavelier Sieur de La Salle*, 2 vols. (New York: A. S. Barnes, 1905), 1:203. Nicolas de La Salle, *The La Salle Expedition on the Mississippi River: A Lost Manuscript of Nicolas de La Salle, 1682*, William C. Foster, ed., Johanna S. Warren, trans. (Austin: Texas State Historical Association, 2003), 115, 116. Jean-Baptiste Minet, "Voyage Made from Canada Inland Going Southward in 1682," Ann Linda Bell, trans., in Robert S. Weddle, Mary Christine Morkovsky, and Patricia Galloway, eds., *La Salle, the Mississippi, and the Gulf: Three Primary Documents* (College Station: Texas A & M University Press, 1987), 55–56. Minet, "Journal of Our Voyage," 98–99, 106, 108. Jean-Baptiste Minet, Journal de Jean-Baptiste Minet, R7971-0-7-F, Library and Archives of Canada, Ottawa, accessed March 3, 2012, www.collectionscanada.gc.ca/pam_archives/index.php?fuseaction=genitem.displayEcopies&lang=eng&rec_nbr=2395451&title=Journal%20de%20Jean-Baptiste%20Minet%20[document%20textuel].&ecopy=e002069705&back_url=%28%29

14. Robert S. Weddle, *Spanish Sea: The Gulf of Mexico in North American Discovery 1500–1685* (College Station: Texas A & M University Press, 1985), 100, 193, 223. Jerald T. Milanich, ed., *Spanish Borderland Sourcebooks*, Vol. 11, *The Hernando de Soto Expedition* (New York: Garland, 1991), 261.

15. Minet, "Voyage Made from Canada," 66. Minet, "Journal of Our Voyage," 99. Jean-Baptiste Louis Franquelin, "Carte de la Louisiane ou des voyages du Sr. De La Salle" (1684), copy in the Library of Congress Geography and Map Division, Washington, D.C., accessed March 28, 2012, http://hdl.loc.gov/loc.gmd/g3300.ct000656. Wood, "La Salle: Discovery of a Lost Explorer," 310.

16. Minet, "Journal of Our Voyage," 122.

17. Nellis M. Crouse, *Lemoyne d'Iberville: Soldier of New France* (Baton Rouge: Louisiana State University Press, 2001), 155–195.

18. Compare the two maps by Guillaume Delisle, *L'Amerique septentrionale* (1700), first state, acc no. 1985.230, The Historic New Orleans Collection, New Orleans,

and *L'Amerique septentrionale*, (1700), second state, David Rumsey Historical Map Collection, San Francisco, accessed March 28, 2012, www.davidrumsey.com/ luna/servlet/detail/RUMSEY~8~1~2921~300057:L-Amerique-Septentrionale--Dressee-.

19. Iberville's Prospectus (1698). Iberville, *Iberville's Gulf Journals*, 56.

20. Maurice Ries, "The Mississippi Fort, Called Fort de la Boulaye," *Louisiana Historical Quarterly* 19 (October 1936): 829–899. Crouse, *Lemoyne d'Iberville*, 207–209.

21. Nicolas de La Salle, *The La Salle Expedition*, 102, 120. Zenobius Membré, "Narrative of La Salle's Voyage down the Mississippi," in Isaac Cox, ed., *The Journeys of Réné Robert Cavelier Sieur de La Salle*, 2 vols. (New York: A. S. Barnes, 1905), 1:137. Paul du Ru, *Journal of Paul du Ru, Missionary Priest to Louisiana*, Ruth Lapham Butler, ed. (Fairfield, Wash: Ye Galleon Press, 1997), 6, 18, 20, 38.

22. John Gilmary Shea, ed. *Early Voyages Up and Down the Mississippi, by Cavelier, St. Cosme, Le Sueur, Gravier, and Guignas* (Albany, N.Y.: Joel Munsell, 1861), 86. Father Vivier, "Letter from Father Vivier of the Society of Jesus, to a Father of the same Society," in *Relations*, 205, accessed March 28, 2012, http://puffin. creighton.edu/jesuit/relations/relations_69.html. Father Julien Binneteau, "Letter of Father Julien Binneteau, of the Society of Jesus, to a Father of the same Society, from the Illinois country, [January,] 1699, in *Relations*, 71, accessed March 28, 2012, http://puffin.creighton.edu/jesuit/relations/relations_65.html. Crozat, "Mémoire sur la Louisiane, February 11, 1716, Archive Nationales, Archives Coloniales, ser. C 13 A, microfilm copy in the Historic New Orleans Collection, Williams Research Center, New Orleans. Iberville's Prospectus (1699). Minet, "Voyage Made from Canada," 47. Unauthored, untitled memoir (1717?), Archives Nationales, Archives Coloniales, ser. C 13 A, microfilm copy in the Historic New Orleans Collection, Williams Research Center, New Orleans.

23. Howard Morphy and Frances Morphy, "The Spirit of the Plains Kangaroo," in Tim Bonyhady and Tom Griffiths, eds. , *Words for Country: Landscape and Language in Australia* (Sydney: University of New South Wales Press, 2002), 102–123.

24. Charles Hudson, *Knights of Spain, Warriors of the Sun: Hernando de Soto and the South's Ancient Chiefdoms* (Athens: University of Georgia Press, 1997), 284, 339.

25. "Mississippi," *American Heritage Dictionary*, 4th ed. (New York: Houghton Mifflin, 2000). An online dictionary of Ojibwa words can be found at www.nativetech.org/ shinob/ojibwelanguage.html. The earliest reference to the "Messipi" River I have found is in 1666, in the Jesuit Relation of Claude Jean Allouez, "Of the Mission to the Nadouesiouek," *Relations*, 51:112, accessed March 28, 2012, http://puffin.creigh-ton.edu/jesuit/relations/relations_51.html. On the changing name of the river on European maps, see, for example, Diego Ribero, *Map of America*, 1529 (Rio del Spiritu Santo); Nicholas Sanson, *fils's Amerique Septentrionale*, 1674 (Rio del Spiritu Santo); Vincenzo Coronelli *America Settentrionale*, 1688 (Mechissipi, Mississippi,

Colbert, Grande Riviere); Guillaume Delisle, *Carte de la Louisiane et du cours du Mississippi*, 1718 (Mississippi, Riviere S. Louis). Eccles, *France in America*, 90–94.

26. Richard White, *The Middle Ground: Indians, Empires, and Republics in the Great Lakes Region, 1650–1815* (Cambridge: Cambridge University Press, 1991).

27. Ru, *Journal*, 5, 67–69. Iberville, *Iberville's Gulf Journals*, 116. Gravier, *Relations*, 65:167.

28. Gravier, *Relations*, 65:149. Ru, *Journal*, 30, 34, 53.

29. Poisson, "Letter from Father du Poisson, Missionary to the Akensas, to Father ***," October 3, 1727, *Relations* 67:297, accessed March 28, 2012, http://puffin.creighton.edu/jesuit/relations/relations_67.html. Gravier, *Relations*, 65:161.

30. Iberville, *Iberville's Gulf Journals*, 116. Ries, "The Mississippi Fort."

31. Gravier, *Relations*, 65: 160–161.

32. Bienville to Pontchartrain, February 25, 1708, in Dunbar Rowland, A. G. Sanders, and Patricia Galloway, eds., *Mississippi Provincial Archives, French Dominion*, Vols. 1–3 (Jackson: Mississippi Department of Archives and History, 1927), Vols. 4–5 (Baton Rouge: Louisiana State University Press, 1984), 3:122.

33. H. Sophie Burton and F. Todd Smith, *Colonial Natchitoches: A Creole Community on the Louisiana-Texas Frontier* (College Station: Texas A & M University Press, 2008), 5–6.

34. Iberville, *Iberville's Gulf Journals*, 113–114. Hubert to the Council, October 1717, *Mississippi Provincial Archives, French Dominion*, 2:237, 241, 252. General Correspondence of Louisiana, Letters of the Company of Louisiana, written at Paris, December 1721, *Mississippi Provincial Archives, French Dominion*, 2: 254.

CHAPTER 3

1. D'Artaguette to Pontchartrain, May 1712, Dunbar Rowland, A. G. Sanders, and Patricia Galloway, eds., *Mississippi Provincial Archives, French Dominion*, Vols. 1–3 (Jackson: Mississippi Department of Archives and History, 1927), Vols. 4–5 (Baton Rouge: Louisiana State University Press, 1984), 2:63, hereafter cited as *MPAFD*. Crozat,, "Mémoires sur la Louisiane," n.d. [1713–1715?], Paris, Archives Nationales, Archives Coloniales: Correspondance à l'arrivée en provence de la Louisiane, Tome 1, articles C13A, 1 à 37, microfilm copy in the Historic New Orleans Collection, hereafter cited as AC. Etienne Veniard de Bourgmont, "Exact Description of Louisiana," Marcel Giraud ed., Mrs. Max W. Myers, trans., *The Bulletin of the Missouri Historical Society* 15 (October 1958): 18. Marcel Giraud, *A History of French Louisiana*, Vol. 2, *Years of Transition, 1715–1717*, Brian Pearce, trans. (Baton Rouge: Louisiana State University Press, 1993), 134. Crozat, "Mémoires sur la Louisiane," fevrier 11, 1716, AC. "Arret du Conseil de Marine sur les mesures prises par Crozat en vue de revitailler la Louisiane en farine et en riz," juillet 28, 1716, AC. Gwendolyn Midlo Hall, *Africans in Colonial Louisiana: The Development of Afro-Creole Culture in the Eighteenth Century*

(Baton Rouge: Louisiana State University Press, 1992), 122. Jeffrey Alan Owens, "Holding Back the Waters: Land Development and the Origins of Levees on the Mississippi, 1720–1845," 3 vols. (Ph.D. diss., Louisiana State University, 1999), 1:111–112. On rice left in the husks for storage and shipping, see Judith A. Carney, *Black Rice: The African Origins of Rice Cultivation in the Americas* (Cambridge, Mass.: Harvard University Press, 2001), 146; C. Wayne Smith and Robert H. Dilday, eds., *Rice: Origin, History, Technology, and Production* (Hoboken, N.J.: John Wiley, 2003), 294, 546.

2. John Gilmary Shea, ed., *Early Voyages Up and Down the Mississippi, by Cavelier, St. Cosme, Le Sueur, Gravier, and Guignas* (Albany, N.Y.: Joel Munsell, 1861), 151. Jacques Gravier, "Relation of Journal of the Voyage of Father Gravier, of the Society of Jesus, in 1700, from the Country of the Illinois to the Mouth of the Mississippi River," *Relations*, 65:129, 132, quotation p. 125, accessed March 31, 2012, http://puffin.creighton.edu/jesuit/relations/relations_65.html. Nicolas de La Salle, *The La Salle Expedition on the Mississippi River: A Lost Manuscript of Nicolas de La Salle, 1682*, William C. Foster, ed., Johanna S. Warren, trans. (Austin: Texas State Historical Association, 2003), 114. *Journal of Paul du Ru, Missionary Priest to Louisiana*, Ruth Lapham Butler, ed. (Fairfield, Wash.: Ye Galleon Press, 1997) 11, 13, 23, 34.

3. *Iberville's Gulf Journals*, Richebourg Gaillard McWilliams, trans. and ed. (University, Alabama: University of Alabama Press 1981) 111, 134. Du Ru, *Journal*, 55. Gravier, *Relations*, 65:161. Marcel Giraud, *A History of French Louisiana*, Vol. 1, *The Reign of Louis XIV, 1698–1715*, Joseph C. Lambert, trans. (Baton Rouge: Louisiana State University Press, 1974), 101.

4. Peter A. Coclanis, *The Shadow of a Dream: Economic Life and Death in the South Carolina Low Country 1670–1920* (New York: Oxford University Press, 1989), 133, notes that rice was "by far the least significant" of the staples produced in the Americas for the European market. As a food, and as a means of adapting European methods of agriculture to American wetlands that were later planted with more valuable export commodities, rice was very significant. This was especially the case in Louisiana. See Coclanis, "Distant Thunder: The Creation of a World Market in Rice and the Transformations It Wrought," *American Historical Review* 98 (October 1993): 1070–1072; Mildred Kelly Ginn, "A History of Rice Production in Louisiana to 1896," *Louisiana Historical Quarterly* 23 (April 1940): 544–588.

5. Patrick Lavelle and Alister V. Spain, *Soil Ecology* (New York: Springer, 2002), 43. Julie K. Cronk and M. Siobhan Fennessy, *Wetland Plants: Biology and Ecology* (Boca Raton. Fla.: Lewis Publishers, 2001), 29, 34, 173, 253.

6. Antoine Simon Le Page Du Pratz, *L'Histoire de la Louisiane*, 3 vols. (Paris, 1758), 2:8, 3:346. J. F. Dumont de Montigny and Jean-Baptiste Le Mascrier, *Mémoires Historiques sur la Louisiane*, 2 vols. (Paris: J. B. Bauche, 1753), 1:15. Lauren C. Post, "Domestic Animals and Plants of French Louisiana as Mentioned in the

Literature, with Reference to Sources, Varieties, and Uses," *Louisiana Historical Quarterly* 16 (October 1993): 575–576. Lewis Cecil Gray, *History of Agriculture in the Southern United States to 1860*, 2 vols. (Gloucester, Mass.: Peter Smith, 1958), 1:66. Sam B. Hilliard, "Antebellum Tidewater Rice Culture in Southern Carolina and Georgia," in James R. Gibson, ed., *European Settlement and Development in North America: Essays on Geographical Change in Honour and Memory of Andrew Hill Clark* (Toronto: University of Toronto Press, 1978), 94, 110.

7. Gravier, *Relations*, 65:165. By the eighteenth century the average French family consumed about eight pounds of bread a day. In Paris, white bread was a marker of elite status. Susan Pinkard, *A Revolution in Taste: The Rise of French Cuisine* (Cambridge: Cambridge University Press, 2009), 200. In light of these statistics, it is hard to disagree with Bertie R. Mandelblatt's claim that flour "was an unequivocal marker of Frenchness." See Mandelblatt, "'Beans from *Rochel* and Manioc from *Prince's Island*': West Africa, French Atlantic Commodity Circuits, and the Provisioning of the French Middle Passage," *History of European Ideas* 34 (December 2008): 418.

8. McWilliams, *Fleur de Lys and Calumet*, 20. Gravier, *Relations*, 65, 161.

9. Fernand Braudel, *Civilisation and Capitalism, 15th–18th Century*, 3 vols., Siân Reynolds, trans. (New York: Harper and Row, 1979), 1:110. Fernand Braudel, *The Mediterranean and the Mediterranean World in the Age of Phillip II*, Siân Reynolds, trans. (Berkeley: University of California Press, 1995), 1:69. H. G. Koenigsberger and George L. Mosse, *Europe in the Sixteenth Century* (London: Longman, 1977), 31. Romano, "Italy in the Crisis of the Seventeenth Century," in Peter Earle, ed., *Essays in European Economic History 1500–1800* (Oxford: Oxford University Press, 1974): 192. Jeffrey Alford and Naomi Duguid, *Seductions of Rice* (New York: Artisan, 1998), 317, 338, 340–341. Emmanuel Le Roy Ladurie, *Peasants of Languedoc*, John Day, trans. (Urbana: University of Illinois Press, 1974), 81, 82. Christopher Morris, "Wetland Colonies: Louisiana, Guangzhou, Pondicherry, and Senegal," in Christina Folke Ax, Niels Brimnes, Niklas Thode Jensen, and Karen Oslund, eds., *Cultivating the Colonies: Colonial States and Their Environmental Legacies* (Athens: Ohio University Press, 2011), 135–163. Guillaume Tirel dit Taillevent, *Le Viandier*, avant-propos et notes par Le Baron Jérôme Pichon, George Vicaire, et Paul Aebischer (Lille: Lehoucq, 1991), 19, 59, 92–93, 106, 122, 233. Terence Scully, ed. and trans., *The Vivendier: A Fifteenth-Century French Cookery Manuscript* (Totnes, Devon: Prospect Books, 1997), 73. Francois Pierre de la Varenne, *Le Cuisinier françois*, n.d., published in English as Francis Peter de la Varenne, *The French Cook* (London, 1654), 17, 159, 221. François Massialot, *Le Cuisinier Roial et Bourgeois* (Paris, 1691; reprint edition, Limoges: René Dessagne, 1980), 126, 181, 394. André Viard, *Le Cuisinier Impérial* (Paris, 1806; reprint edition, Paris: Champion-Slatkine, 1985). See also *Le Ménagier de Paris* (1393), by an unknown author, Jérome Pichon, ed., in 1846 for La Société des Bibliophiles

François, accessed March 31, 2012, www.pbm.com/~lindahl/menagier/. Three seventeenth-century cookbooks in Gilles Laurendon and Laurence Laurendon, eds., *L'art de la cuisine française au XVIIe siècle* (Paris: Payot & Rivages, 1995), 137, 416. D. Eleanor Scully and Terence Scully, *Early French Cookery: Sources History, Original Recipes and Modern Adaptations* (Ann Arbor: University of Michigan Press, 1995), 261. There is reason to believe that jambalaya, a rice dish associated with Louisiana cuisine, was originally French. See Andrew Sigal, "Jambalaya by Any Other Name," *Petits Propos Culinaires* 84 (2007): 101–119. The word jambalaya doesn't appear in print in the United States until 1881, in Abby Fisher, *What Mrs. Fisher Knows about Old Southern Cooking* (San Francisco, 1881). The potato, introduced into France in the 1500s, did not become popular until the nineteenth century. See Susan Pinkard, *A Revolution in Taste: The Rise of French Cuisine* (Cambridge: Cambridge University Press, 2009), 20, 201.

10. Le Page du Pratz, *History of Louisiana*, 166. Hachard, *Relation du Voyage*, 26. Dumont de Montigny and Le Mascrier, *Mémoires*, 1:15, 31–32.

11. Laurendon and Laurendon, *L'art de la cuisine française*, p. 573. Jean-Anthelme Brillat-Savarin, *The Physiology of Taste*, Anne Drayton, trans. (New York: Penguin, 1994), 72. Pinkard, *A Revolution in Taste*, 22, 106, 270. Pinkard notes that sauces thickened with a roux of flour were uncommon before the late eighteenth century or later, after milling, storing, and distribution methods were improved and households found freshly ground flour easily available so that they did not have to keep it stored for long. In Louisiana, roux did not become essential to Creole cooking until well after the French departed.

12. Allan Gallay, *The Indian Slave Trade: The Rise of the English Empire in the American South, 1670–1717* (New Haven: Yale University Press, 2002), 308–311. Le Page Du Pratz, *L'Histoire de la Louisiane*, I, 82–83, 118. My estimate of 200 enslaved Indians is intentionally high. Censuses indicate 159 enslaved native men and women for 1726. By 1832 there were fewer than 100. Any census was likely to undercount, however. Daniel H. Usner, Jr., *Indians, Settlers, and Slaves in a Frontier Exchange Economy: The Lower Mississippi Valley before 1783* (Chapel Hill: Institute of Early American History and Culture, University of North Carolina Press, 1992), 46–59. Gilles Havard and Cécile Vidal, *Histoire de L'Amerique Française* (Paris: Flammarion, 2003), 162–164. Jennifer M. Spear, " 'They Need Wives': Métissage and the Regulation of Sexuality in French Louisiana, 1699–1730," in Martha Hodes, ed., *Sex, Love, Race: Crossing Boundaries in North American History* (New York: New York University Press, 1999), 35–59. Thomas N. Ingersoll, *Mammon and Manon in Early New Orleans: The First Slave Society in the Deep South, 1718–1819* (Knoxville: University of Tennessee Press, 1999), 9, 18–20. Crozat, "Mémoire sur La Louisiane," n. d. (1713–1717?), AC, C 13 A. Crozat, "Mémoires sur la Louisiane," fevrier 11, 1716, AC, C 13 A. Blume, *German Coast.* "Extract of Census of Inhabitants in the Colony of Louisiana,

January 1, 1726, habitation sur la droite en descendant le fleuve depuis les Tonicas. Les Bayagoulas concession de M. Paris Duvernay," The Rosemonde E. and Emile Kuntz Collection, Special Collections, Howard-Tilton Memorial Library, Tulane University, New Orleans. Poisson, "Letter," *Relations*, 67:279–283. Hall, *Africans in Colonial Louisiana*, 60, 175. "Mémoire des directeurs de la Compagnie," AC, C 13 A. 1720, fevrier 06/Nouvelle-Orléans, AC (Canada), G 1, RC 7067. On slavery and race in French North America, see Guillaume Aubert, "'The Blood of France': Race and Purity of Blood in the French Atlantic World," *William and Mary Quarterly* 61 (July 2004): 439–478; Juliana Barr, "From Captives to Slaves: Commodifying Indian Women in the Borderlands," *Journal of American History* 92 (June 2005): 19–46; Marcel Trudel, *L'Esclavage au Canada: Histoire et Conditions de l'Esclavage* (Québec: Presses de l'Université Laval, 1960); Brett Rushforth, "'A Little Flesh We Offer You': The Origins of Indian Slavery in New France," *William and Mary Quarterly* 60 (October 2003): 777–808. Jennifer M. Spear, *Race, Sex, and Social Order in Early New Orleans* (Baltimore: Johns Hopkins University Press, 2008). On slaves as a part of an exploitable nature, like plants and animals, see Laura Hollsten, "Knowing Nature: Knowledge of Nature in Seventeenth Century French and English Travel Accounts from the Caribbean" (Ph.D. dissertation, Åbo Akademi University, 2006). Hollsten, "Controlling Nature and Transforming Landscapes in the Early Modern Caribbean," *Global Environment* 1 (2008): 80–113.

13. Carney, *Black Rice*, 9–68. Koenigsberger and Mosse, *Europe in the Sixteenth Century*, 31. Romano, "Italy in the Crisis of the Seventeenth Century," in Peter Earle, ed., *Essays in European Economic History 1500–1800* (Oxford: Oxford University Press, 1974), 192. Alford and Duguid, *Seductions of Rice*, 317, 338, 340–341, 370–371.

14. Le Page Du Pratz, *History of Louisiana*, 166, 277–278, 366. Hachard, *Relation du Voyage*, 26. Emily Clark, ed., *Voices from an Early American Convent: Marie Madeleine Hachard and the New Orleans Ursulines 1727–1760* (Baton Rouge: Louisiana State University Press, 2007), 80. Dumont du Montigny and Mascrier, *Mémoires*, 1:15, 95–103. Carney, *Black Rice*, 114–117. Pinkard, *Revolution in Taste*, 200. Mandelblatt, "'Beans from *Rochel* and Manioc from *Prince's Island*,'" 422. Alford and Duguid, *Seductions of Rice*, 370–371. Ibrahima Seck, "The Relationship between St. Louis of Senegal, Its Inhabitants, and Colonial Louisiana," in Bradley G. Bond, ed., *French Colonial Louisiana and the Atlantic World* (Baton Rouge: Louisiana State University Press, 2005), 282.

Corn appeared in nineteenth-century Creole cuisine most often as a breading for fried oysters and fish, and as mock fried oysters (corn fritters). On corn in Louisiana cuisine, see Lafcadio Hearn, *La Cuisine Creole* (New Orleans: F. F. Hansell, 1885), 84–85. Le Page Du Pratz, *History of Louisiana*, 274. Célestine Eustis, *Cooking in Old Créole Days: La Cuisine Créole à l'Usage des Petits Ménages* (New York: R. H. Russell, 1904), 106.

15. On food production and consumption and class relations in Louisiana, see Daniel H. Usner, Jr., "'The Facility Offered by the Country': The Creolization of Agriculture in the Lower Mississippi Valley," in David Buisseret and Steven G. Reinhardt, eds., *Creolization in the Americas* (College Station: Texas A & M University Press, 2000), 35–62.

16. Périer to Maurepas, December 10, 1731, *MPAFD*, 4:107. Henry P. Dart, "The Career of Dubreuil in French Louisiana," *Louisiana Historical Quarterly* 18 (April 1935): 269–275.

17. Le Page Du Pratz, *Histoire*, 3:346. Giraud, *History of Louisiana*, Vol. 5, *The Company of the Indies, 1723–1731*, Brian Pearce, trans. (Baton Rouge: Louisiana State University Press, 1991), 192. Gray, *History of Agriculture*, 2:66. Throughout much of the eighteenth century South Carolina rice planters endeavored to control river and swamp waters in a similar manner. By the end of the century, however, they harnessed the power of coastal tides to control irrigation of fields, a technique not used in Louisiana. See Joyce E. Chaplin, *An Anxious Pursuit: Agricultural Innovation and Modernity in the Lower South, 1730–1815* (Chapel Hill: University of North Carolina Press, for the Institute of Early American History and Culture, 1993), 228–232. Sam B. Hilliard, "Antebellum Tidewater Rice Culture in South Carolina and Georgia," in James R. Gibson, ed., *European Settlement and Development in North America: Essays on Geographical Change in Honour and Memory of Andrew Hill Clark* (Toronto: University of Toronto Press, 1978), 91–115.

18. De La Tour planted a crop of indigo in 1723 that was "entirely destroyed by the flood which overflowed his lands from the rear." "De la Chais to the Directors of the Company of the Indies, September 1723," *MPAFD*, 2:322. Carlos Trudeau, "Plan de l'habitation de Don Bertran Gravier [1794]," Historic New Orleans Collection, Williams Research Center, New Orleans. Pierre Clément de Laussat, *Memoirs of My Life*, Robert D. Bush, ed., Agnes-Josephine Pastwa, trans. (Baton Rouge: Louisiana State University Press, 1978), 62–63, 68, 70, 86.

19. "Superior Council of Louisiana to the General Directors of the Company of the Indies, February 1725," *MPAFD*, 2:402. Petition of Chaperon, 1759 Janvier 18, French Land Grants, p. 17, Tulane University Special Collections, Jones Hall, Tulane University, New Orleans. Giraud, *History of French Louisiana*, 5:195.

20. Henry P. Dart, ed. and trans., "Ceard's Case 1724," *Louisiana Historical Quarterly* 5 (April 1922): 155–171. "Records of the Superior Council of Louisiana," *Louisiana Historical Quarterly*, 1 (1918): 224–257. Dart, "The Career of Dubreuil," 269–275. Father Poisson, "Letter from Father du Poisson," October 3, 1727, *Relations*, 67: 279. Gary B. Mills, "The Chauvin Brothers: Early Colonists of Louisiana," *Louisiana History* 15 (Spring 1974): 127.

21. Robert W. Harrison, *Alluvial Empire: A Study of State and Local Efforts toward Land Development in the Alluvial Valley of the Lower Mississippi River, including Flood Control, Land Drainage, Land Clearing, Land Forming*, 2 vols. (Little Rock,

Ark.: Pioneer Press, for the Economic Research Service, US Department of Agriculture, 1961), 1:53–54. In 1727 and 1743, the Superior Council in New Orleans, the colonial government, issued official edicts requiring the construction of levees from below New Orleans to Cannes Brulées, a stretch of about fifty miles. See Giraud, *History of French Louisiana*, 5:193, 194, 206, 208–209. It is important to note that the French levees were too small to affect flooding patterns down the entire 600 miles of lower valley; however, the fifty or so miles of levees in the vicinity of New Orleans did cause localized floods of short duration, by diverting water into fields not yet behind earthen walls and by reducing the capacity of the swamps back of the fields to absorb water quickly, as the concession managers at Tchoupitoulas and St. Reyne learned. Owens, "Holding Back the Waters," 1:72, 149. The Company of the Indies ordered levee construction that relied on techniques dating from the 1660s and the construction of the Canal du Midi in France. That canal also failed to end flooding. See Chandra Mukerji, "Stewardship Politics and the Control of Wild Weather: Levees, Seawalls, and State Building in 17th-Century France," *Social Studies of Science* 37 (February 2007): 127–133.

22. Noting that settlers needed to keep slaves occupied year round, the Council in New Orleans encouraged company directors to facilitate a timber trade with St. Domingue. See Council to the Directors, August 1725, *MPAFD*, 2:494. Le Page Du Pratz, *History of Louisiana*, 217. John Hebron Moore, "The Cypress Lumber Industry of the Lower Mississippi Valley during the Colonial Period," *Louisiana History* 24 (1983): 25–47. Giraud, *History of French Louisiana*, 5:142–143. Périer to the Abbé Raguet, August 1728, *MPAFD*, 2:616. Hilliard, "Antebellum Tidewater Rice Culture in South Carolina and Georgia," 98. Elsewhere in the French empire, observers expressed concern with deforestation. See Richard Grove, *Green Imperialism: Colonial Expansion, Tropical Edens and the Origins of Environmentalism, 1600–1860* (Cambridge: Cambridge University Press, 1996).

23. Craig E. Colten, "Cypress in New Orleans: Revisiting the Observations of Le Page du Pratz," *Louisiana History* 44 (Fall 2003): 463–477.

24. Father Vivier, "Letter from Father Vivier," November 17, 1750, *Relations*, 69:211. "De la Chaise to the Directors of the Company of the Indies, September 1723," *MPAFD*, 2:310, 344, "October 1723," *MPAFD*, 2:377. The Company urged the construction of more mills: "Mémoires des directeurs de la Compagnie," Septembre 15, 1720, AC, C 13 A. Dumont describes a rice mill in New Orleans, although it never worked properly and was soon abandoned. Dumont du Montigny and Mascrier, *Mémoires*, 1:30. On the need for more and better rice mills, see *MPAFD*, 2:587. Berquin-Duvallon, *Travels in Louisiana and the Floridas, in the Year 1802*, John Davis, trans. (New York: Riley, 1806), 15–16. Moore, "Cypress Lumber Industry of the Lower Mississippi Valley during the Colonial Period," 590. Giraud, 5:193–194. Owens, "Holding Back the Waters," 1:70.

25. Chaplin, *An Anxious Pursuit*, 228.

26. Louis Houck, ed., *The Spanish Regime in Missouri*, 2 vols. (Chicago: R. R. Donnelly, 1909), 2:11. John Joyce to David Hodge and D. Ross, May 6, 1784, Turnbull-Bowman-Lyons Family Papers, Special Collections, Hill Memorial Library, Louisiana State University, Baton Rouge. Post, "Domestic Animals and Plants," 571. Dart, "The Career of Dubreuil," 285, 286. Jack D. L. Holmes, "Indigo in Colonial Louisiana and the Floridas," *Louisiana History* 8 (Fall 1967): 330–349. Kenneth H. Beeson, Jr., "Indigo Production in the Eighteenth Century," *Hispanic American Historical Review* 44 (May 1964): 218. Wailes (B. L. C.), Diary Typescripts, April 5, 1853, Mississippi Department of Archives and History, Jackson.

27. Holmes, "Indigo in Colonial Louisiana," 344–349. Post, "Domestic Animals and Plants," 574. Wailes, Diary, April 5, 1853.

28. Dart, "Career of Dubreuil," 275, 279, 286. *MPAFD*, 5:118, 119, 261. Rochemore claimed that the Jesuits had experimented with sugar in 1742 but Dubreuil's efforts were the first to succeed, in 1758. Thomas Hutchins, *An Historical Narrative and Topographical Description of Louisiana, and West-Florida* (Philadelphia, 1784), 38. By 1762, according to Hutchins, Mississippi River planters were harvesting and milling sugar. John Sibley, "The Journal of Dr. John Sibley, July–October, 1802," *Louisiana Historical Quarterly* 10 (1927): 477, 478, 483. Laussat, *Memoirs*, 52. Post, "Domestic Animals and Plants," 579. James Pitot, *Observations on the Colony of Louisiana from 1796 to 1802*, Henry Pitot, trans. (Baton Rouge: Louisiana State University Press), 73, 77. John B. Rehder, *Delta Sugar: Louisiana's Vanishing Plantation Landscape* (Baltimore: Johns Hopkins University Press), 41–44. Iberville, *Gulf Journals*, 112, describes Louisiana's first governor's failed attempts to raise sugar. For other early attempts at sugar, before Dubreuil's success, see Hervé Gourmelon, *Le Chavalier de Kerlérec, 1704–1770: L' affaire de la Louisiane* (Rennes: Les Portes du Large, 2003), 144–145. The Spanish regime halted sugar production in Louisiana, out of deference to other Spanish sugar-producing colonies.

29. Ingersoll, *Mammon and Manon*, 6. Post, "Domestic Animals and Plants," 571. Christopher Morris, *Becoming Southern: The Evolution of a Way of Life, Warren County and Vicksburg, Mississippi, 1770–1860* (New York: Oxford University Press, 1995), 25.

30. Dart, "The Career of Dubreuil," 286. Sibley, "Journal," 490, 496. Pitot, *Observations*, 118. Post, "Domestic Animals and Plants," 576–578.

31. "Records of the Superior Council of Louisiana," *Louisiana Historical Quarterly*, 8 (1925): 290, 293, 487; 9 (1926): 140, 292, 293. Jennie O'Kelly Mitchell and Robert Dabney Calhoun, "The Marquis de Maison Rouge," *Louisiana Historical Quarterly* 20 (April 1937): 301. Carl J. Ekberg, *French Roots in the Illinois Country: The Mississippi Frontier in Colonial Times* (Urbana: University of Illinois Press, 1998), 213–238. *MPAFD*, 2: 617. Post, "Domestic Animals and Plants," 567–568, 571.

32. Georges-Henri-Victor Collot, *A Journey in North America, Containing a Survey of the Mississippi, Ohio, Missouri, and Other Affluing Rivers*, 2 vols. (Paris 1826), 2:175. François Marie Perrin du Lac, *Travels through the two Louisianas, and among the savage nations of the Missouri: also, in the United States, along the Ohio, and the adjacent provinces, in 1801, 1802, & 1803: with a sketch of the manners, customs, character, and the civil and religious ceremonies of the people of those countries* (London: Printed for R. Phillips by J. G. Barnard, 1807), 84, 85, 86, 96. Laussat, *Memoirs*, 62, 63, 64, 68, 70. Sibley, "Journal," 480. Correspondencia de oficio de D. Bernardo de Galvez, Gobernador de Luisiana y Florida Occidental, March 2, 1780, Archivo General de Indias, Papeles Procedentes de Cuba, Legajo 2, documents 121b-121h, folders 272–278, microfilm copy, Hill Memorial Library, Louisiana State University, Baton Rouge. Rice remained the most important subsistence crop in the lower valley below Baton Rouge through the nineteenth century, when Louisiana began to develop a commecial rice agriculture. See Gray, *History of Agriculture*, 2:723. In 1839, the lower parishes of Louisiana produced 3.6 million pounds of rice, all of it consumed in Louisiana. By comparison, South Carolina produced 60.6 million pounds, and Georgia 12.4 million pounds, most of it exported. US rice exports for 1840 amounted to 61 million pounds. Department of State, *Compendium of the Sixth Census* (Washington: Thomas Allen, 1842), 192, 204, 240.

33. Périer to Maurepas, August 1730, *MPAFD*, 4:38. Bienville and Salmon to Maurepas, March 1734, *MPAFD*, 3:637–638. In the "excessive heat" of June, 1738, laborers made makeshift repairs to levees and fields of indigo and rice damaged by floods. See "Louboey au ministre," juin 30, 1738, AC, C13A.

34. Owens, "Holding Back the Waters," 1:72, 76–77, 188, 256, 290. Robin de Logny quoted on p. 171.

CHAPTER 4

1. Baron Marc de Villiers, "A History of the Foundation of New Orleans (1717–1722)," Warrington Dawson, trans., *Louisiana Historical Quarterly* 3 (April 1920): 157–251. Tristram R. Kidder, "Making the City Inevitable: Native Americans and the Geography of New Orleans," in Craig E. Colten, ed., *Transforming New Orleans and Its Environs: Centuries of Change* (Pittsburgh: University of Pittsburgh Press, 2000), 19.

2. Conrad M. Widman, "Some Southern Cities (in the U.S.) about 1750," *Records of the American Catholic Historical Society of Philadelphia* 10 (June 1899): 202. "Records of the Superior Council of Louisiana," *Louisiana Historical Quarterly*, 1 (1918): 109. De Villiers, "Foundation of New Orleans," 190, 195. Marcel Giraud, *A History of French Louisiana*, Vol. 5, *The Company of the Indies, 1723–1731*, Brian Pearce, trans. (Baton Rouge: Louisiana State University Press, 1991), 206. Shannon Lee Dawdy, *Building the Devil's Empire: French Colonial New Orleans*

(Chicago: University of Chicago Press, 2008), 81. Richard Campanella, *Bienville's Dilemma: A Historical Geography of New Orleans* (Lafayette: Center for Louisiana Studies, University of Louisiana at Lafayette, 2008), 110. Lawrence N. Powell, *The Accidental City: Improvising New Orleans* (Cambridge, Mass: Harvard University Press, 2012), 43. Heloise H. Cruzat, trans., "Louisiana in 1724: Banet's Report to the Company of the Indies, Dated Paris, December 20, 1724," *Louisiana Historical Quarterly* 12 (January 1929): 125. J. F. Dumont de Montigny and Jean-Baptiste Le Mascrier, *Mémoires Historiques sur la Louisiane*, 2 vols. (Paris: J. B. Bauche, 1753), 2:48–49. Bienville to the Council, February 1, 1723, Dunbar Rowland, A. G. Sanders, and Patricia Galloway, eds. *Mississippi Provincial Archives, French Dominion*, Vols. 1–3 (Jackson: Mississippi Department of Archives and History, 1927), Vols. 4–5 (Baton Rouge: Louisiana State University Press, 1984), 2:404, 3:343, hereafter cited as *MPAFD*. Minutes of the Council of Commerce, July 1721, *MPAFD*, 2:266. Jeffrey Alan Owens, "Holding Back the Waters: Land Development and the Origins of Levees on the Mississippi, 1720–1845," 3 vols. (Ph. D. diss., Louisiana State University, 1999), 1:14, 16, 37–41.

3. Giraud, *French Louisiana*, 5:133. *MPAFD*, 2:233.

4. Jeffrey Alan Owens, "Holding Back the Waters," 1:39–41, 149.

5. Giraud, *French Louisiana*, 5:213–216. Daniel H. Usner, Jr., *Indians, Settlers, and Slaves in a Frontier Exchange Economy: The Lower Mississippi Valley before 1783* (Chapel Hill: Institute of Early American History and Culture, University of North Carolina Press, 1992), 40–41, 115. Dawdy, *Building the Devil's Empire*, 81–82. Marion Stange, "Governing the Swamp: Health and the Environment in Eighteenth-Century Nouvelle-Orléans," *French Colonial History* 11 (2010): 1–22. Craig E. Colten, *An Unnatural Metropolis: Wresting New Orleans from Nature* (Baton Rouge: Louisiana State University Press, 2005).

6. "Records of the Superior Council of Louisiana," *Louisiana Historical Quarterly* 1 (1918): 109; 2 (1919): 339, 464, 407. Jean-Baptiste Bénard de La Harpe, *Historical Journal of the Settlement of the French in Louisiana*, Virginia Koenig and Joan Cain, trans., and Glenn R. Conrad, ed. (1724; reprint, Lafayette: Center for Louisiana Studies, University of Southwest Louisiana, 1971), 18–19, 32–33, 40. Widman, "Some Southern Cities," 205.

7. Hubert to the Council [1717], *MPAFD*, 2:229, 233, 252. Sally Dart, "French Incertitude in 1718 as to a Site for New Orleans, Part I," *Louisiana Historical Quarterly* 15 (January 1932): 37–43, and Dart, "Part II," (July 1932): 417–427, quotation p. 424. In 1717 Father François Le Maire advised that a settlement be established on the Mississippi River as a "buffer against English expansion" and to discourage "all the disorders and scandals" among the Indians. Le Maire, quoted in Daniel H. Usner, Jr., *American Indians in the Lower Mississippi Valley: Social and Economic Histories* (Lincoln: University of Nebraska Press, 1998), 22.

8. Périer and de la Chaise to the Directors of the Company of the Indies, November 1727, *MPAFD*, 2:547, 565. Périer and de la Chaise to the Directors of the Company

of the Indies, August 1728, *MPAFD*, 2: 589–590. General Correspondence of Louisiana, Letters of the Company of Louisiana, written at Paris, December 1721, *MPAFD*, 2:254. Minutes of the Council, New Orleans, January 1723, *MPAFD*, 2:286–288. "Records of the Superior Council of Louisiana," *Louisiana Historical Quarterly* 1 (1918): 250; 6 (1923): 141, 493; 9 (1926): 522; 26 (1943): 181. Salmon au minister, juin 3 et 11, 1739, Paris, Archives Nationales, Archives Coloniales: Correspondance à l'arrivée en provence de la Louisiane, Tome 1, articles C13A, 1 à 37, microfilm copy in the Historic New Orleans Collection (hereafter cited as AC). Usner, *Indians, Settlers, and Slaves in a Frontier Exchange Economy*, 198–201. Christopher Morris, "Impenetrable but Easy: The French Transformation of the Lower Mississippi Valley and the Founding of New Orleans," in Craig E. Colton, ed., *Transforming New Orleans and Its Environs* (Baton Rouge: Louisiana State University Press, 2000), 32.

9. Carl J. Ekberg, *French Roots in the Illinois Country: The Mississippi Frontier in Colonial Times* (Urbana: University of Illinois Press, 1998), 33–34. Cécile Vidal, "Antoine Bienvenu, Illinois Planter and Mississippi Trade: The Structure of Exchange between Lower and Upper Louisiana," in Bradley G. Bond, ed., *French Colonial Louisiana and the Atlantic World* (Baton Rouge: Louisiana State University Press, 2005), 111–133. M. J. Morgan, *Land of Big Rivers: French and Indian Illinois, 1699–1778* (Carbondale: Southern Illinois University Press, 2010), 70–71. H. Sophie Burton and F. Todd Smith, *Colonial Natchitoches: A Creole Community on the Louisiana-Texas Frontier* (College Station: Texas A & M University Press, 2008), 149.

10. Peter Sahlins, *Unnaturally French: Foreign Citizens in the Old Regime and After* (Ithaca: Cornell University Press, 2004). David Bell, *The Cult of the Nation in France: Inventing Nationalism, 1680–1800* (Cambridge, Mass.: Harvard University Press, 2003).

11. Giraud, *French Louisiana*, 5:395–415.

12. Bienville to Cadillac, June 23, 1716, *MPAFD*, 3:214. Minutes of the Council, March 1725, *MPAFD*, 2:421. Patricia Dillon Woods, *French-Indian Relations on the Southern Frontier 1699–1762* (Ann Arbor: UMI Research Press, 1980), 55–63.

13. *MPAFD*, 2:396, 420. Usner, *American Indians in the Lower Mississippi Valley*, 22, 23. Woods, *French-Indian Relations*, 71–78. Claudio Saunt, "'The English Has Now a Mind to Make Slaves of Them All': Creeks, Seminoles, and the Problem of Slavery," *American Indian Quarterly*, 22 (1998): 159–164, describes Creek Indian hostility as a reaction to the growth of plantation slavery in ways that parallel what I see in Louisiana, with French agriculture and Natchez revolt.

14. Usner, *American Indians in the Lower Mississippi Valley*, 65–76. Dumont de Montigny and Mascrier, *Mémoires*, 2:128–208. Antoine Simon Le Page Du Pratz, *L'Histoire de la Louisiane*, 3 vols. (Paris, 1758), 3:230–251. Gordon M. Sayre, "Plotting the Natchez Massacre: Le Page du Pratz, Dumont de Montigny,

Chateaubriand," *Early American Literature* 37 (September 2002): 381–413. Woods, *French-Indian Relations*, 95–109. Allan Gallay, *The Indian Slave Trade: The Rise of the English Empire in the American South, 1670–1717* (New Haven: Yale University Press, 2002), 315–344. The name of the French commandant at Natchez is Chopart in Dumont de Montigny's account, and Chépart in Le Page du Pratz's account.

15. "Records of the Superior Council of Louisiana," *Louisiana Historical Quarterly* 6 (1923): 142, 145–146, 493; 7 (1924):336, 514, 519–520; 8 (1925): 288, 289; 9 (1926):517, 526, 727; 10 (1927):276; 13 (1930):157. "Lettre de Beauharnois au ministre—arrivée de Vinsenne...(1733, juillet, 31)," Ottawa, Archives Nationales du Canada, Archives des Colonies, Série C11A, Correspondance générale, Canada, digital copies of originals in the Centre des archives d'outre-mer, Aix-en-Provence, France, Vol. 59, folios 20–23, accessed January 3, 2012, http://collectionscanada.gc.ca/pam_archives/index.php?fuseaction=genitem. displayItem&lang=eng&rec_nbr=3051271&rec_nbr_list=3051271. "Lettre de Beauharnois au ministre—la petite vérole et...(1733, mai, 30)," Vol. 59, folios 8–9, accessed January 3, 2012, http://collectionscanada.gc.ca/pam_archives/ index.php?fuseaction=genitem.displayItem&lang=eng&rec_nbr=3051268. "Mémoire sur les colonies françaises et anglaises de l'Amérique septen-trionale (1739)," Vol. 72, folios 330–334, accessed January 3, 2012, http:// collectionscanada.gc.ca/pam_archives/index.php?fuseaction=genitem. displayItem&lang=eng&rec_nbr=3068780&rec_nbr_list=3068780,3072107,113 049,4124254,4107375. "News received from Dominica of two ships there which will...(1739, July, 24)," Fonds du Vatican. Archives secretes, Secrétairerie d'État (Segreteria di Stato, Francia), typed abstract of original from private collection, accessed January 3, 2012, http://collectionscanada.gc.ca/pam_archives/index. php?fuseaction=genitem.displayItem&lang=eng&rec_nbr=3069834&rec_nbr_ list=3069834,2810291,2809900.

16. Guy Chet, *Conquering the American Wilderness: The Triumph of European Warfare in the Colonial Northeast* (Amherst: University of Massachusetts Press, 2003).

17. Woods, *French-Indian Relations*, 111–146. Usner, *Indians, Settlers, and Slaves*, 246. Salmon au minister, Novembre 25, 1738, AC. Richard White, *Roots of Dependency: Subsistence, Environment, and Social Change among the Choctaws, Pawnees, and Navajos* (Lincoln: University of Nebraska Press, 1988), 62–67. Kathleen Du Val, *The Native Ground: Indians and Colonists in the Heart of the Continent* (Philadelphia: University of Pennsylvania Press, 2006), 97.

18. "M. de la Galissonière to Count de Maurepas, Quebec, September 1, 1748," "Memoir on the French Colonies in North America," and "Ministerial Minute on Despatches from Louisiana," in *Documents Relative to the Colonial History of the State of New York*, 15 vols., E. B. O'Callaghan, ed. and trans. (Albany: Weed, Parsons, 1856–87), 10:134–136, 220–232, 219–220. M. de la Galissonière, "Mémoire Sur Les Colonies de la France dans l'Amerique Septentionale,"

Mémoires et Documents, Amérique 24, 110–138, Archives of the Ministry of Foreign Affairs, Paris, photocopy courtesy of Paul Mapp.

19. "Déclaration d'avaries de Nicolas Pescay aîné (s), capitaine du Saint-Antoine...(1740, septembre, 17)," Ottawa, Archives Nationales du Canada, Archives départementales de la Gironde, Série 6B- Amirauté de Guyenne; attributions judiciaries, abstract of original document in Fonds des Archives départementales de la Gironde, Bordeaux, France, accessed January 3, 2012, http://collectionscanada.gc.ca/pam_archives/index.php?fuseaction=genitem. displayItem&lang=eng&rec_nbr=3034459&rec_nbr_list=3034459. "Name and type of ship: Elephant. Tonnage: 550. Crew members:...(March 3, 1745)," abstract of original records in the National Archives, Kew, UK, High Court of Admiralty (HCA 32), Prize Court, Papers, miscellaneous ships papers, etc., in Finding Aid MSS 1909, National Archives of Canada, accessed January 3, 2012, http://data2.archives.ca/pdf/pdf001/p000002145.pdf. "Records of the Superior Council," *Louisiana Historical Quarterly*, 14 (1931): 583; 17 (1934): 191; 23 (1940): 616. *MPAFD*, 4: 318–334, 5: 40, 45–50, 182, 188–190, 23: 904. Hervé Gourmelon, *Le Chavalier de Kerlérec, 1704–1770: L' affaire de la Louisiane* (Rennes: Les Portes du Large, 2003), 133. Between 1756 and 1759 several ships left France with supplies, typically wine, brandy, flour, and iron goods, for St. Domingue and Louisiana, but were captured by British ships en route. See the records for the following ships: Saint-Jacques de la Rochelle, captured December 2, 1756; Marie Esther de La Rochelle, captured August 31, 1756; Marguerite de la Rochelle, captured August 26, 1756; Don de Dieu de La Rochelle, captured March 8, 1757; Heureuse, captured August 2, 1759, Finding Aid MSS 1909, National Archives of Canada, accessed January 3, 2012, http://data2.archives.ca/pdf/pdf001/p000002145.pdf

20. "Journal of Captain Harry Gordon, 1766," in *Travels in the American Colonies*, Newton D. Mereness, ed. (New York: Antiquarian Press, 1961), 482–483. Usner, *American Indians in the Lower Mississippi Valley*, 35. Usner, *Indians, Settlers, and Slaves*, 279.

21. Périer quoted in Usner, *Indians, Settlers, and Slaves*, 76. Henry P. Dart, ed. and trans., "Ceard's Case 1724," *Louisiana Historical Quarterly* 5 (April 1922): 167. On French Louisiana as an economic failure, see W. J. Eccles, *France in America*, rev. ed. (East Lansing: Michigan State University Press, 1990), 167; Wood, *French-Indian Relations*, 111–127; Gilles Havard and Cécile Vidal, *Histoire de L'Amerique Française* (Paris: Flammarion, 2003), 90–91. In contrast, some scholars have noted economic growth following the Natchez War and the loosening of central authority. See Usner, *Indians, Settlers, and Slaves*, 76; Dawdy, *Building the Devil's Empire*; Thomas N. Ingersoll, *Mammon and Manon in Early New Orleans: The First Slave Society in the Deep South, 1718–1819* (Knoxville: University of Tennessee Press, 1999), 23; Leslie Choquette, "Center and Periphery in French North America," in *Negotiated Empires: Centers and Peripheries in the Americas, 1500–1820*, Christine

Daniels and Michael V. Kennedy, eds. (New York: Routledge, 2002), 193–206. The argument for bottom-up growth in Louisiana has been made with reference to other French colonial contexts similar to Louisiana. See Philip P. Boucher, "The 'Frontier Era' of the French Caribbean, 1620–1690s," in Daniels and Kennedy, *Negotiated Empires*, 207–234.

22. Vaudreuil to Maurepas, June 4, 1748, *MPAFD*, 4: 318. Guerre avec les Chicachas, mars 24, 1732, AC. "Records of the Superior Council of Louisiana," *Louisiana Historical Quarterly*, 24 (1941): 831. In the late 1760s Choctaws raided Gulf Coast herds frequently. See Thomas Hutchins, *An Historical Narrative and Topographical Description of Louisiana and West-Florida*, (1784; Gainesville: University of Florida Press, 1968), 63. James Taylor Carson, "Native Americans, the Market Revolution, and Culture Change: The Choctaw Cattle Economy, 1690–1830," *Agricultural History* 71 (Winter 1997): 1–18.

23. "Abstracts of French and Spanish Documents Concerning the Early History of Louisiana," *Louisiana Historical Quarterly* 1 (1917): 109. "Records of the Superior Council of Louisiana," *Louisiana Historical Quarterly*, 4 (July 1921): 347–348, 357; 5 (April 1922): 246–247; 5 (July 1922): 385–388, 593–594; 6 (April 1923): 283; 7 (April 1924): 335; 10 (October 1927): 567; 13 (January 1930): 135; 13 (October 1930): 673, 679; 19 (January 1936): 212–225; 19 (July 1936): 768–770; 19 (October 1936): 1087–1088; 22 (January 1939): 229–230, 236, 237; 22 (April 1939): 548–549; 22 (July 1939): 884110.

24. Rochemore to Berryer, December 17, 1760, *MPAFD*, 5:261. Sugar, the writer proclaimed, was the plant "which alone would be sufficient to wipe out the defects that originate from the natural poverty in Louisiana."

CHAPTER 5

1. Bernard Romans, *A Concise Natural History of East and West Florida* (1775; reprint edition, Gretna, Louisiana: Pelican Press, 1998), 224. Rufus Putnam, *The Memoirs of Rufus Putnam*, Rowena Buell, comp. (Boston: Houghton Mifflin, 1903), 47.

2. Wailes (B. L. C.) diary typescript, March 20, 1852, Mississippi Department of Archives and History, Jackson.

3. Putnam, *Memoirs*, 46, 47, 60–61, 99.

4. Wailes, diary typescript, February 27, 1857. Charles S. Sydnor, *A Gentleman from the Old Natchez Region: Benjamin L. C. Wailes* (Durham: Duke University Press, 1938).

5. Two recent histories of the Louisiana Purchase are Jon Kukla, *A Wilderness So Immense: The Louisiana Purchase and the Destiny of America* (New York: Knopf, 2003), and Roger G. Kennedy, *Mr. Jefferson's Lost Cause: Land, Farmers, Slavery, and the Louisiana Purchase* (New York: Oxford University Press, 2003).

6. "Records of the Superior Council of Louisiana," *Louisiana Historical Quarterly* 15 (1932): 670–672; 23 (1940): 616. Daniel H. Usner, Jr., *Indians, Settlers, and*

Slaves in a Frontier Exchange Economy: The Lower Mississippi Valley before 1783 (Chapel Hill: Institute of Early American History and Culture, University of North Carolina Press, 1992), 174.

7. Evaluation of Luis Vilemont Report, May 19, 1799, Mss 350, Historic New Orleans Collection, New Orleans. James Pitot, *Observations on the Colony of Louisiana from 1796 to 1802*, Henry Pitot, trans. (Baton Rouge: Louisiana State University Press, 1979), 77. Daniel H. Usner, Jr., *American Indians in the Lower Mississippi Valley: Social and Economic Histories* (Lincoln: University of Nebraska Press, 1998), 54–55. David Hodge to John Joyce, March 13, 1786, Turnbull-Bowman-Lyons Family Papers, Mss. #4026, Louisiana and Lower Mississippi Valley Collections, Hill Memorial Library, Louisiana State University, Baton Rouge. Christopher Morris, *Becoming Southern: The Evolution of a Way of Life, Warren County and Vicksburg, Mississippi, 1770–1860* (New York: Oxford University Press, 1995), 14–15.

8. Pitot, *Observations*, 70–71. Turnbull and Company Accounts (1779–1804, n.d.), microfilm reel 1, Turnbull-Bowman Family Papers, Mss. #4452, Louisiana and Lower Mississippi Valley Collections, Hill Memorial Library, Louisiana State University, Baton Rouge. Joyce (John) Diary, Mss. #4342, Louisiana and Lower Mississippi Valley Collections, Hill Memorial Library, Louisiana State University, Baton Rouge.

9. Lawrence Kinnaird, ed., *Spain in the Mississippi Valley 1765–1794*, 3 vols. (Washington, D.C.: Government Printing Office, 1946), 3: xvi–xvii, 280–282, 285, 310. Mississippi Provincial Archives, Spanish Dominion, Vol. IV, January 1792–June 1793, RG 26, microfilm roll #33, Mississippi Department of Archives and History, Jackson. David Hodge to John Joyce, July 30, 1786, Turnbull-Bowman-Lyons Family Papers. Dunbar Rowland, ed., *Mississippi Territorial Archives, 1798–18*, Vol.1 (Nashville: Brandon Printing Co., 1905), 226. "Third Spanish Detailed Statistical Report of the Products of St. Louis and Ste. Genevieve, for 1774," 1:92, and "Report of Indian Traders Given Passports by Don Francisco Cruzat, Dated November 28, 1777," 1:139, in Louis Houck, ed., *The Spanish Regime in Missouri*, 2 vols. (Chicago: R. R. Donnelly, 1909). Richard White, *Roots of Dependency: Subsistence, Environment, and Social Change among the Choctaws, Pawnees, and Navajos* (Lincoln: University of Nebraska Press, 1988), 98–105. James Taylor Carson, "Native Americans, the Market Revolution, and Culture Change: The Choctaw Cattle Economy, 1690–1830," *Agricultural History* 71 (Winter 1997): 1–18. Bernard Romans passed through Choctaw territory in the 1770s and observed cultivation in a context of scarce game. Romans, *Concise Natural History*, 56–58. In January 1805, George Hunter encountered several Choctaw in the vicinity of the Ouachita River, west of the Mississippi River: William Dunbar and George Hunter, *The Forgotten Expedition, 1804–1805: The Louisiana Purchase Journals of Dunbar and Hunter*, Trey Berry, Pam Beasley, and Jeanne Clements, eds. (Baton Rouge: Louisiana State University Press, 2006), 188.

10. Thomas Hutchins, *An Historical Narrative and Topographical Description of Louisiana and West-Florida* (1784; Gainesville: University of Florida Press, 1968), 41. Alfred W. Crosby, *Ecological Imperialism: The Biological Expansion of Europe, 900–1900* (New York: Cambridge University Press, 1986). Morris, *Becoming Southern*, 12–13, 26–29, 189–191. Virginia Anderson, *Creatures of Empire: How Domestic Animals Transformed Early America* (New York: Oxford University Press, 2006). William Cronon, *Changes in the Land: Indians, Colonists, and the Ecology of New England* (New York: Hill and Wang, 1983), 51–52. Cattle presented more problems for farmers near New Orleans, where they could do serious damage to levees. Nevertheless, they provided landowners with a means of building capital for further agricultural development.

11. Usner, *American Indians in the Lower Mississippi Valley*, 41–42. Bennett Wall et al., *Louisiana: A History* (Wheeling, Ill: Harlan Davidson, 1997), 79. Don H. Doyle, *Faulkner's County: The Historical Roots of Yoknapatawpha* (Chapel Hill: University of North Carolina Press, 2001), 23–52.

12. "Records of the Superior Council of Louisiana," *Louisiana Historical Quarterly*, 25 (1942): 559–566.

13. Pitot, *Observations*, 52, 65, 69, 107. John Sibley, "The Journal of Dr. John Sibley, July–October, 1802," G. P. Whittington, ed., *Louisiana Historical Quarterly* 10 (1927): 478.

14. Sibley, "Journal," 477, 484, 486, 487. Martyn (Michael) Letter, 1774, Mississippi Department of Archives and History, Jackson. Mrs. Dunbar Rowland (Erin Rowland), ed., *Life, Letters and Papers of William Dunbar of Elgin, Morayshire, Scotland, and Natchez, Mississippi* (Jackson: Mississippi Historical Society, 1930), 23–74. Hutchins, *Historical Narrative*, 38–39.

15. Joseph C. G. Kennedy, comp., *Agriculture of the United States in 1860* (Washington, D. C.: Government Printing Office 1864), 6–9, 66–69, 84–87. The quantity of tilled land peaked during these years in this, the earliest settled region of the state. By century's end, the percentage of "improved" land, as the census called cleared acreage, had begun to fall and currently stands at about 13 percent. Sibley, "Journal," 486. Rachael Edna Norgress, "The History of the Cypress Lumber Industry in Louisiana," *Louisiana Historical Quarterly* 30 (July 1947): 986. Ari Kelman, "Forests and Other River Perils," in Craig E. Colten, ed., *Transforming New Orleans and Its Environment: Centuries of Change*,(Pittsburgh: University of Pittsburgh Press, 2000), 45–63. Measured in cords, the outputs of the early and later saws were, respectively, one half cord per day and nearly 700 cords per day.

16. Rowland, ed., *Life, Letters, and Papers*, 74. Morris, *Becoming Southern*, 30, 212 n28. Cronon, *Changes in the Land*, 116–117.

17. N. M. Surrey, *Commerce of Louisiana during the French Regime, 1699–1763* (New York: Columbia University Press, 1916), 382–384. *MPAFD*, 2: 617. "Records of the Superior Council of Louisiana," *Louisiana Historical Quarterly* 2 (1919): 338–339; 3 (1920): 423; 4 (1921): 237; 5 (1922): 80, 98, 100, 589.

18. "Records of the Superior Council of Louisiana," *Louisiana Historical Quarterly* 3 (1920): 429; 5 (1922): 100, 105–106, 253, 268; 17 (1934): 570. Laura L. Porteous, "Index to the Spanish Judicial Records of Louisiana XXIX," *Louisiana Historical Quarterly* 13 (July 1930): 542–545.

19. "Records of the Superior Council of Louisiana," *Louisiana Historical Quarterly* 17 (1934): 376–377. On clearing as legal indication of possession see Morris, *Becoming Southern*, 19–20, and Cronon, *Changes in the Land*, 54–81. The underlying assumption of flood control is that flooding is a "disturbance," like an earthquake or hurricane. This assumption follows from the notion that land and water are separate ecologies, rather than components in a shared ecology. See Peter B. Bayley, "Understanding Large River-Floodplain Ecosystems," *Bioscience* 45 (March 1995): 153–158.

20. Roscoe R. Hill, *Descriptive Catalogue of the Documents Relating to the United States in the Papeles Procedentes de Cuba Deposited in the Archivo General de Indias at Seville* (Washington, D.C.: Carnegie Institution of Washington, 1916), 299, 332, 474. Duparte to Gayoso, January 24, 1799, Archivo General de Indias, Papeles Procedentes de Cuba, legajo 216, folder 786, microfilm copy, Hill Memorial Library, Louisiana State University, Baton Rouge. Mapa de la parte del Mississippi situada a sur la confluencia del Rouge y Chafalaya, con proyecto de cortar lazo para abreviar la navegación entre Natchez y Nueva Orleans [1796], Archivo General de India, Mapas y Planos, no. 180, microfilm copy, Historic New Orleans Collection, Williams Research Center, New Orleans. Anuradha Mathur and Dilip da Cunha, *Mississippi Floods: Designing a Shifting Landscape* (New Haven: Yale University Press, 2001), 73–75.

21. Pitot, *Observations*, 103, 116–117, 132, 133, 135. Thomas Jefferys, *The Natural and Civil History of the French Dominions in North and South America* (London,1760), 152.

22. Todd Shallat, *Structures in the Stream: Water, Science, and the Rise of the U.S. Army Corps of Engineers* (Austin: University of Texas Press, 1994), 18, 24–26, 42.

23. Carl A. Brasseaux and Keith P. Fontenot, *Steamboats on Louisiana's Bayous: A History and Directory (Baton Rouge: Louisiana State University Press, 2004)*, 63–65. John McPhee, *The Control of Nature* (New York: Noonday 1990), 3–92.

24. Herbert Anthony Kellar, ed., *Solon Robinson, Pioneer and Agriculturalist: Selected Writings*, Vol. 1: *1825–1845*, Vol. 2: *1846–1851*, Indiana Historical Collections, Vols. 21 and 22 (Indianapolis: Indiana Historical Bureau, 1936), 1:467, 2:127.

25. Steven Stoll, *Larding the Lean Earth: Soil and Society in Nineteenth-Century America* (New York: Hill and Wang, 2002), 108–120.

26. Romans, *Concise Natural History*, 82.

27. Richard H. Grove, *Green Imperialism: Colonial Expansion, Tropical Island Edens and the Origins of Environmentalism, 1600–1860* (Cambridge: Cambridge University Press, 1995). Donna Landry, *The Invention of the Countryside: Hunting, Walking and Ecology in English Literature, 1671–1831* (Houndmills, Basingstoke, Hampshire: Palgrave, 2001).

28. Simon Schama, *Landscape and Memory* (New York: Alfred A. Knopf, 1995). Keith Sutton, "Reclamation of Wasteland during the Eighteenth and Nineteenth Centuries," in Hugh D. Clout, ed., *Themes in the Historical Geography of France* (New York: Academic Press, 1977), 252. Shallat, *Structures in the Stream*, 17–20. Chandra Mukerji, *Territorial Ambitions and the Gardens of Versailles* (Cambridge: Cambridge University Press, 1997).

29. Simon-Louis Pierre de Cubières, *Mémoire sur le Cyprès de la Louisiane* (Versailles: P. J. Jacob, 1809).

30. Romans, *Concise Natural History*, 101. Georges-Henri-Victor Collot, *A Journey in North America, Containing a Survey of the Mississippi, Ohio, Missouri, and Other Affluing Rivers*, 2 vols. (Paris: Arthus Bertrand, 1826), 2:150–151.

31. Clarence Edwin Carter, ed., *The Territorial Papers of the United States*, Vol. VI, *The Territory of Mississippi 1809–1817* (Washington, D.C.: Government Printing Office, 1938), 205–207.

32. Pierre Clément de Laussat, *Memoirs of My Life*, Robert D. Bush, ed., Agnes-Josephine Pastwa, trans. (Baton Rouge: Louisiana State University Press, 1978), 49, 69–70. Sibley, "Journal," 480, 481. Romans, *Concise Natural History*, 80–81. George Dougherty, "Plan of Concord: The Plantation and Residence of the Late Major Stephen Minor" (1829), Mississippi Department of Archives and History, Jackson.

33. Usner, *American Indians in the Lower Mississippi Valley*.

34. *New Orleans Bee*, English language edition, May 5, 17, 18, 23, 26, 31 and June 1, 6, 10, 12, 16, 1849, p. 1. *Daily Picayune*, May 10, 1849, p. 1. *Daily Delta*, May 16, 1849, p. 2, May 19, 1849, p. 2.

35. "Southern Medical Reports," *De Bow's Review* 9 (1850): 298. Capt. A. A. Humphreys and Lieut. H. L. Abbot, *Report upon the Physics and Hydraulics of the Mississippi River; upon the Protection of the Alluvial Region against Overflow; and upon the Deepening of the Mouths: Based upon Surveys and Investigations Made under the Acts of Congress Directing the Topographical and Hydrographical Survey of the Delta of the Mississippi River, with Such Investigation as Might Lead to Determine the Most Practicable Plan for Securing It from Inundation, and the Best Mode of Deepening the Channels at the Mouths of the River*, Professional Paper no. 4 (Philadelphia: United States Army, Corps of Topographical Engineers, 1861; reprint edition, Washington: Government Printing Office, 1876), 98–99.

CHAPTER 6

1. Deed of sale, Alonzo Snyder Papers, Mss. 655, Louisiana and Lower Mississippi Valley Collections, Hill Memorial Library, Louisiana State University, Baton Rouge. Carol Young Knight, *First Settlers of Catahoula Parish, Louisiana 1808–1839*, Conveyance Records of Catahoula Parish, LA, Book A, 1808–1839 (1985), 88, 94, 96, 98, 104, 109, accessed January 4, 2012, http://files.usgwarchives.net/la/catahoula/history/settlers/p76-90.txt.

2. J. A. Green, "Governor Perier's Expedition against the Natchez Indians," *Louisiana Historical Quarterly* 19 (1936): 547–577. Jean Filhiol, "Description of the Ouachita in 1786, by Jean Filhiol," H. Wynn Rickey, trans., *Louisiana Historical Quarterly* 20 (April 1937): 476. Jennie O'Kelly Mitchell and Robert Dabney Calhoun, "The Marquis de Maison Rouge, the Baron de Bastrop, and Colonel Abraham Morehouse, Three Ouachita Valley Soldiers of Fortune. The Maison Rouge and Bastrop Spanish Land 'Grants,'" *Louisiana Historical Quarterly* (April 1937): 298, 301. Daniel H. Usner, Jr., *American Indians in the Lower Mississippi Valley: Social and Economic Histories* (Lincoln: University of Nebraska Press, 1998), 89. Samuel Dorris Dickinson, "Don Juan Filhiol at Écore à Fabri," *Arkansas Historical Quarterly* 46 (Summer 1987): 133–155.

3. The following account of the Marquis de Maison Rouge comes from the documents translated and published in Mitchell and Calhoun, "The Marquis de Maison Rouge," 289–462, and other sources where noted.

4. The description of the terrain where Maison Rouge settled comes from Juan Filhiol, the commander of the Spanish Fort, and from William Dunbar, who journeyed up the Ouachita River in 1804. Dickinson, "Don Juan Filhiol at Écore à Fabri." William Dunbar and George Hunter, *The Forgotten Expedition, 1804–1805: The Louisiana Purchase Journals of Dunbar and Hunter*, Trey Berry, Pam Beasley, and Jeanne Clements, eds. (Baton Rouge: Louisiana State University Press, 2006), 25–34.

5. A Spanish map indicates the location of Prairie Ronde, where Bayou Bartholomew empties into the Ouachita River. "Puerto de Ouachta y terrenos de la cuenca del bayú Bartellemy." [1797] Historic New Orleans Collection, Williams Research Center, New Orleans, copy of original from the Archivo General, Sevilla.

6. *US v. Turner*, 52 U.S. 663 (1850). House of Representatives, "Maison Rouge Land Claims," Executive Documents, 27th Congress, 2d Session, Serial Set 403, Vol. 3, Doc. No. 151, accessed April 1, 2012, www.books.google.com/books?id=300FAAAAQAAJ&pg=RA6-PA1&lpg=RA6-PA1&dq=%E2%80%9g CMaison+Rouge+Land+Claims,%E2%80%9D+Executive+Documents&source=bl&ots=suR3_k1Tf1&sig=7NRC_30HTvmW3EJf9HkZRJnLfsI&hl=en&sa=X&ei=K-N4T9DZOqre2QX8ieW1Bg&ved=0CCEQ6AEwAQ#v=onepage&q&f=false.

7. Mitchell and Calhoun, "The Marquis de Maison Rouge," 289–462.

8. A. R. Kilpatrick, "Historical and Statistical Collections of Louisiana—Parish of Catahoula, Part 1," *Debow's Review* 12 (March 1852): 256–275, quotation on p. 258. A. R. Kilpatrick, "Historical and Statistical Collections of Louisiana—Parish of Catahoula, Part 2," *Debow's Review* 12 (June 1852): 631–646.

9. Forshey, Caleb Goldsmith, Diaries, 1838–1879, Mississippi Valley Collection, University of Memphis, 1:12–14; 2:12. Robert C. Reinders, "Dr. James G. Carson's Canebrake: A View of an Ante-bellum Louisiana Plantation," *Louisiana Historical Quarterly* 33 (October 1950): 353–356. Dunbar and Hunter, *The Forgotten Expedition*, 45, 49.

10. Green, "Perier's Expedition, 547–577." Forshey diaries, 1:12. Clarence Edwin Carter, ed., *The Territorial Papers of the United States*, Vol. VI, *The Territory of Mississippi 1809–1817* (Washington, D.C.: Government Printing Office, 1938), 6:211, 569. For a description of the Ouachita basin, including its fertile but wet lowlands interspersed with sandy hills or islands covered with pine, see Dunbar and Hunter, *The Forgotten Expedition*, 49. William Dunbar, "Observations," in Meriwether Lewis et al., *Travels in the Interior Parts of America; Communicating Discoveries Made in Exploring the Missouri, Red River, and Washita, by Captains Lewis and Clark, Doctor Sibley, and Mr. Dunbar* (London: Printed for Richard Phillips by J. G. Barnard, 1807), 83.

11. Eighth Census of the United States, 1860, Population Schedules, Louisiana, Concordia Parish, accessed January 4, 2012, www.archive.org/stream/populationschedu41ounit#page/n391/mode/2up. Jacob Bieller to Alvarez Fisk, February 1828, Alvarez Fisk to Jacob Bieller, May 15, 1828, Jacob Bieller to Alvarez Fisk, August 25, 1828, Snyder Papers. Mikko Saikku, *This Delta, This Land: An Environmental History of the Yazoo-Mississippi Floodplain* (Athens: University of Georgia Press, 2005), 108. In January 1805, William Dunbar traveled on horseback over the road from the mouth of the Tensas to Natchez and described the road's condition in his journal: Dunbar and Hunter, *The Forgotten Expedition*, 196–197.

12. Joseph Bieller to Jacob Bieller, August 21, 1827, Joseph Bieller to Jacob Bieller, June 1, 1828, Enos McKey to Joseph Bieller, July 14, 1830, Joseph Bieller to Jacob Bieller, October, 1830, David Draffin to Jacob Bieller, August 9, 1833, Jacob Bieller to David Draffin, August 21, 1833, Snyder Papers. In 1804, William Dunbar of Natchez journeyed up the Ouachita River, where he observed the Louisiana black bear "does not confine himself to vegetable food; the planters have ample experience of his Carnivorous disposition. He is particularly found of Hog's flesh, but no animal escapes him that he is able to conquer: Sheep & Calves are frequently his prey and he often destroys the fawn when he stumbles upon it." Dunbar and Hunter, *The Forgotten Expedition*, 54, quotation on 61. Louis Hughes recalled that bears in Bolivar County made off with hogs. Louis Hughes, *Thirty Years a Slave, from Bondage to Freedom* (Milwaukee: South Side Printing, 1897), 77. Matthew M. Smith, " 'Women Locked the Doors, Children Screamed, and Men Trembled in their Boots': Black Bears and People in Arkansas," *Arkansas Historical Quarterly* 66 (Spring 2007): 1–17.

13. Dunbar and Hunter, *The Forgotten Expedition*, 15, 45, 51, 52. Rod Giblett, *Postmodern Wetlands: Culture, History, Ecology* (Edinburgh: Edinburgh University Press, 1997).

14. Robert C. Reinders, "Dr. James G. Carson's Canebrake: A View of an Antebellum Louisiana Plantation," *Louisiana Historical Quarterly* 33(October1950): 353–363. Forshey, Diaries, 2:12.

15. Knight, *First Settlers of Catahoula Parish*, 88, 89.

16. Janet Sharp Hermann, *Joseph E. Davis: Pioneer Patriarch* (Jackson: University Press of Mississippi, 1990), 49, 53. Christopher Morris, *Becoming Southern: The Evolution of a Way of Life, Warren County and Vicksburg, Mississippi, 1770–1860* (New York: Oxford University Press, 1995), 141–142.

17. Dunbar and Hunter, *The Forgotten Expedition*, 15. Knight, *First Settlers of Catahoula Parish*, 76. Kilpatrick, "Parish of Catahoula, Part 2," 634–635.

18. Lewis Cecil Gray, *History of Agriculture in the Southern United States to 1860*, 2 vols. (Gloucester, Mass.: Peter Smith, 1958), 1:533. Saikku, *This Delta, This Land*, 116.

19. Joseph C. G. Kennedy, *Population of the United States in 1860; Compiled from the Original Returns of the Eighth Census* (Washington, D.C.: Government Printing Office, 1864), 17, 193, 269.

20. Morris, *Becoming Southern*, 194. Saikku, *This Delta, This Land*, 104. Seventh Census of the United States, 1850, Mortality Schedules for Louisiana and Mississippi available online through the University of Virginia Library Historical Census Browser, accessed January 4, 2012, http://mapserver.lib.virginia.edu/. This census is deeply flawed, and so offers only the roughest sketch of mortality rates. Edward Countryman, "The Price of Cotton: The Demography of Inequality in Mid-Nineteenth Century Mississippi," *Quaderno* 4 (Milan: Dipartimenti di Storia della Societa e delle Instituzione, Universita degli Studii di Milano, 1998), 167–186. The highest mortality in Louisiana recorded by the 1850 census was for New Orleans, where there were approximately thirty-five white deaths per thousand whites. This accounting would have included victims of the devastating flood of 1849, as well as the victims of a cholera epidemic that struck the city and several others around the country that same year.

21. Snyder Papers. It is possible the population of Franklin County was suffering yellow fever, which claimed more deaths among whites than among blacks.

22. In 1850, Joseph's son Jacob, age twenty-five, lived with his overseer. Seventh Census of the United States, 1850, Population Schedules, Louisiana, Tensas Parish, accessed January 4, 2012, www.archive.org/details/populationschedu-0241unix. Marriage Book A, 1847–1868, Concordia Parish, accessed January 4, 2012, http://files.usgwarchives.net/la/concordia/vitals/marriages/marbka.txt.

23. Seventh Census of the United States, 1850, Population Schedules, Louisiana, Tensas Parish. Eighth Census of the United States, 1860, Population Schedules, Louisiana, Tensas Parish. Andrew B. Booth, Records of Louisiana Confederate Soldiers (1920), index by Jan Craven, p. 642, accessed January 4, 2012, http://files.usgwarchives.net/la/state/military/wbts/booths-index/sk-sz.txt.

24. Snyder (Alonzo) Papers, Ledger, 1842–1847, manuscript vol. 3, Louisiana and Lower Mississippi Valley Collections, Hill Memorial Library, Louisiana State University, Baton Rouge. The tree inventory is undated and separated from older entries written on the inside of an account book that is dated 1842–1847. According to the United States Department of Agriculture in 1992, the density

standard for a healthy forest in Louisiana requires that 20 percent of large trees (all those over twenty-four inches in diameter) be at least thirty inches in diameter. Snyder's record does not indicate forest acreage, although the total count of 289 large trees, using the USDA standard, suggests between two and three acres. John S. Vissage, Patrick E. Miller, and Andrew J. Hartsell, *Forest Statistics for Louisiana Parishes—1991*, USDA Forest Service, Southern Forest Experiment Station, Resource Bulletin SO-168, February 1992, p. 4.

25. I have discerned the spread of agriculture through the category in the decennial agricultural censuses, "Improved Acreage in Farms," for each decade from 1850 to 1950, with the exception of 1910 and 1940, and which are available at http://mapserver.lib.virginia.edu/. For county and parish areas, from which I calculated percentage of total area "improved," I relied on the statistics provided by the National Association of Counties Web site: www.naco.org/Pages/default.aspx. Collot, *A Journey in North America*, 2:155. Eugene W. Hilgard field notebooks 1849–1881, Bancroft Library, University of California, Berkeley. Ernst von Hesse-Wartegg, *Travels on the Lower Mississippi, 1879–1880*, Frederic Trautmann, ed. and trans. (Columbia: University of Missouri Press, 1990), 43, 123, 124.

26. Thomas E. Dahl, "Wetlands Losses in the United States 1780's to 1980's," US Department of the Interior, Fish and Wildlife Service, Washington, D.C., 1990. Percy Viosca, Jr., "Louisiana Wet Lands and the Value of their Wild Life and Fishery Resources," *Ecology* 9 (April 1928): 220. Percy Viosca, Jr., *Flood Control in the Mississippi Valley and Its Relation to Louisiana Fisheries*, Department of Conservation Technical Paper no. 4, (New Orleans: Louisiana Department of Conservation, 1928), 4. Robert W. Harrison and Walter M. Kollmorgen, "Drainage Reclamation in the Coastal Marshlands of the Mississippi River Delta," *Louisiana Historical Quarterly* 30 (1947): 656–657, 669, 670, 671.

27. J. D. B. DeBow, *The Seventh Census of the United States: 1850. Embracing a Statistical View of Each of the States and Territories, Arranged by Counties, Towns, Etc.*... (Washington: Robert Armstrong, 1853), 456–460, 482–486. *Eighth Census of the United States, 1860, Agricultural Schedules*, Louisiana, South Carolina, Georgia. *Twelfth Census of the United States, 1880, Agricultural Schedules*, Louisiana. Velma Lea Hair, "History of Crowley, Louisiana," *Louisiana Historical Quarterly* 27 (1944): 1157–1160. Mildred Kelly Ginn, "A History of Rice Production in Louisiana to 1896," *Louisiana Historical Quarterly* 23 (1940): 553, 557.

28. Benjamin L. C. Wailes, *Report on the Agriculture and Geology of Mississippi* (Jackson: E. Barksdale, 1854). Aldo Leopold, *Report on a Game Survey of Mississippi: Submitted to the Game Restoration Committee, Sporting Arms and Ammunition Manufacturers Institute* (Jackson: Mississippi Museum of Natural Science, 1929), p. 36, Leopold manuscript, Mississippi Department of Archives and History, Jackson. Lyle S. St. Amant, *Louisiana Wildlife Inventory* (New Orleans: Louisiana Wildlife and Fisheries Commission, 1959), 39, 43, 116–117.

Reinders, "Canebrake," 360–361. Hesse-Wartegg, *Travels*, 112, 113. Hughes, *Thirty Years a Slave*, 28–30. Saikku, *This Land, This Delta*, 130, 132–133. Steven Stoll, *Larding the Lean Earth: Soil and Society in Nineteenth-Century America* (New Haven: Yale University Press, 2002). Mikko Saikku, "'Home in the Big Forest': Decline of the Ivory-Billed Woodpecker and Its Habitat in the United States," in Timo Myllyntaus, Mikko Saikku, and Alfred W. Crosby, eds., *Encountering the Past in Nature: Essays in Environmental History* (Athens: Ohio University Press, 2001), 94–140.

29. Saikku, *This Delta, This Land*, 133. Richard White, "'Are You an Environmentalist or Do You Work for a Living?': Work and Nature," in William Cronon, ed., *Uncommon Ground: Toward Reinventing Nature* (New York: W. W. Norton, 1995), 171–185. Richard White, *The Organic Machine: The Remaking of the Columbia River* (New York: Hill and Wang, 1995), especially pp. 4–29. William Cronon, "The Trouble with Wilderness," 89, and Cronon, "Saving the Land We Love: Land Conservation and American Values," Keynote Address for the Land Trust Alliance Rally, Madison, Wisconsin, October 17, 2005, www.williamcronon.net/writing/LTA_Plenary.htm.

30. Saikku, *This Delta, This Land*, 31.

31. *Times-Picayune* (New Orleans), April 15, 1938.

CHAPTER 7

1. Meriwether Lewis et al., *Travels in the Interior Parts of America; Communicating Discoveries in Exploring the Missouri, Red River and Washita* (London: Printed for Richard Phillips by J. G. Barnard, 1807) 78, 79.

2. Benjamin L. C. Wailes, *Report on the Agriculture and Geology of Mississippi* (Jackson: E. Barksdale, 1854), 329–332. Wailes's careful description of turtles followed by comments on their edibility closely resembles the descriptions of the soft-shell turtle made by William Bartram three quarters of a century earlier. See William Bartram, *Travels* (New York: Penguin, 1988), 158–159.

3. George P. Rawick, ed. *The American Slave: A Composite Autobiography, Supplement, Series 1*, 12 vols. (Westport, Conn.: Greenwood Press, 1977), 7:770–771.

4. Bruno Latour, *Reassembling the Social: An Introduction to Actor-Network-Theory* (New York: Oxford University Press, 2005), 39.

5. James C. Scott, *Seeing like a State: How Certain Schemes to Improve the Human Condition Have Failed* (New Haven: Yale University Press, 1998).

6. Eugene W. Hilgard field notebooks, June 13, 1859, Bancroft Library, University of California, Berkeley.

7. Lewis et al., *Travels*, 76, 80. Mart Stewart has made a similar point, arguing that there were in the slave south two landscapes, the masters' "landscapes of control and domination" and the slaves' "landscape of subsistence and small profit." Slaves, Stewart argues, "lived closer to the ground" and had a detailed

and practical knowledge of the land, whereas masters talked about the land with "intensive detachment." Mart A. Stewart, "Slavery and the Origins of African American Environmentalism," in Dianne D. Glave and Mark Stoll, eds., *"To Love the Wind and the Rain": African Americans and Environmental History* (Pittsburgh: University of Pittsburgh Press, 2006), 10, 12, 13, 18.

8. Wailes, diary, January 27, 1852; March 11, 1852; June 18, 1852, typescript, Mississippi Department of Archives and History, Jackson. When he commenced his travels in March, Wailes mentioned a servant but gave no name. He mentioned Gabriel as the servant with whom he traveled in a June diary entry. Charles S. Sydnor, *A Gentleman of the Old Natchez Region: Benjamin L. C. Wailes* (Durham, N.C.: Duke University Press, 1938), 183–184. Seventh Census, 1850, Manuscript Slave Schedules, Adams County, Mississippi, accessed January 5, 2012, www.archive.org/details/populationscheduo383unix. The census lists Wailes as in possession of nineteen slaves. One of two, aged nineteen and twenty, are likely to have been Gabriel. On slave hunting guides, see Glave and Stoll, eds., *"To Love the Wind and the Rain,"* 24.

9. Wailes, diary, April 3, 1852; July 13, 1852.

10. Wailes, diary, March 29, 1852, April 3, 1852, July 13, 1852, August 2, 1852, August 3, 1852, August 5, 1852, September 11, 1852. Wailes, *Report*, 284–285.

11. William Dunbar and George Hunter, *The Forgotten Expedition, 1804–1805: The Louisiana Purchase Journals of Dunbar and Hunter*, Trey Berry, Pam Beasley, and Jeanne Clements, eds. (Baton Rouge: Louisiana State University Press, 2006), 12–13. Gwendolyn Midlo Hall, *Africans in Colonial Louisiana: The Development of Afro-Creole Culture in the Eighteenth Century* (Baton Rouge: Louisiana State University Press, 1992), 142–143. Rod Giblett, *Postmodern Wetlands: Culture, History, Ecology* (Edinburgh: Edinburgh University Press, 1997), 206.

12. Rawick, *The American Slave*, supp. ser. 1, 7:770–771; 9:1660, 1742–1743. "Born in Slavery: Slave Narratives from the Federal Writers' Project, 1936–1938," Library of Congress, American Memory, Texas Narratives, Vol. 16, Part 1, 18, 253, Oklahoma Narratives, Vol. 13, 114, accessed April 2, 2012, http://memory.loc.gov/ammem/snhtml/. Lewis, *Travels*, 77, 85. *Isaac Roberts vs. Benj. L. C. Wailes, Guardian of the Heirs of E. H. Covington, dec'd* (1839), Probate Court, minutes book F, p. 62, Chancery Clerk's Office, Warren County Courthouse, Vicksburg, Mississippi. Daniel H. Usner, Jr., "'The Facility Offered by the Country': The Creolization of Agriculture," in David Buisseret and Steven G. Reinhardt, eds., *Creolization in the Americas* (College Station: Texas A & M University Press, 2000), 44. Daniel H. Usner, Jr., *Indians, Settlers, and Slaves in a Frontier Exchange Economy: The Lower Mississippi Valley before 1783* (Chapel Hill: Institute of Early American History and Culture, University of North Carolina Press, 1992), 149–190. Christopher Morris, *Becoming Southern: The Evolution of a Way of Life, Warren County and Vicksburg, Mississippi, 1770–1860* (New York: Oxford University Press, 1995), 5–21.

13. Amy L. Young, Michael Tuma, and Cliff Jenkins, "The Role of Hunting to Cope with Risk at Saragossa Plantation, Natchez, Mississippi," *American Anthropologist* 103 (September 2001): 692–704. Elizabeth M. Scott, "Food and Social Relations at Nina Plantation," *American Anthropologist* 103 (September 2001): 671–691. I am indebted to Evan Engwall for bringing these articles to my attention.

14. Jill-Karen Yakubik and Rosalinda Méndez, "Beyond the Great House: Archaeology at Ashland-Belle Helene Plantation," accessed April 2, 2012, www.crt.state. la.us/archaeology/virtualbooks/GREATHOU/MTGH.HTM. "Born in Slavery," Texas Narratives, Vol. 16, Part 1, 1–2, 157, 308; Mississippi Narratives, Vol. 9, 38. Solomon Northup, *Twelve Years a Slave*, Sue Eakin and Joseph Logsden, eds. (Baton Rouge: Louisiana State University Press, 1968), 152–153. James Patrick Whelan, Jr., "Plantation Slave Subsistence in the Old South and Lousiaiana," in *Plantation Traits in the New World: Studies in Geography and Anthropology*, Roland E. Chardon, ed. (Baton Rouge: Louisiana State University Department of Geography and Anthropology, 1983). Whelan suspected a unique role for fish and game in the diets of Louisiana slaves, which subsequent research is bearing out.

15. Wailes, *Report*.

16. Richard White, " 'Are You an Environmentalist or Do You Work for a Living?': Work and Nature," in William Cronon, ed., *Uncommon Ground: Toward Reinventing Nature* (New York: W. W. Norton, 1995). Richard White, *The Organic Machine: The Remaking of the Columbia River* (New York: Hill and Wang, 1995), 4–29.

17. Edward Teas, Julia Ideson, and Sanford W. Higginbotham, "A Trading Trip to Natchez and New Orleans, 1822: Diary of Thomas S. Teas," *Journal of Southern History* 7 (August 1941): 388. Albert J. Raboteau, *Slave Religion: The "Invisible Institution" in the Antebellum South* (New York: Oxford University Press, 1978), 9–11, 57, 82. Kathleen S. Murphy, "Translating the Vernacular: Indigenous and African Knowledge in the Eighteenth-Century British Atlantic," *Atlantic Studies* 8 (March 2011): 29–48.

18. The Turkey Runner, "The Chase in the South West," *Spirit of the Times* (July 12, 1845). Mark A. Keller, " 'Th' Guv'ner Wuz a Writer': Alexander G. McNutt of Mississippi," *Southern Studies* 20 (1981): 394–411.

19. Hall, *Africans in Colonial Louisiana*, 197.

20. Melvin Dixon, *Ride Out the Wilderness: Geography and Identity in Afro-American Literature* (Urbana: University of Illinois Press, 1987), 18.

21. Lawrence W. Levine, *Black Culture and Black Consciousness: Afro-American Folk Thought from Slavery to Freedom* (New York: Oxford University Press, 1977), 7.

22. Hall, *Africans in Colonial Louisiana*, 119.

23. Michael Fellman, "Card Sharpers and Alligator Horses: Deadly Southwestern Humor," *Huntington Library Quarterly* 49 (Autumn 1986): 307–323.

24. B. I. Wiley, "Vicissitudes of Early Reconstruction Farming in the Lower Mississippi Valley," *Journal of Southern History* 3 (November 1937): 446, 447.

25. Céline Frémaux Garcia, *Céline: Remembering Louisiana, 1850–1871*, Patrick J. Geary, ed. (Athens: University of Georgia Press, 1987), 70. Ira Berlin, Thavolia Glymph, Steven F. Miller, Joseph P. Reidy, Leslie S. Rowland, and Julie Saville, eds., *Freedom: A Documentary History of Emancipation*, Ser. 1, Vol. 3, *The Wartime Genesis of Free Labor: The Lower South* (New York: Cambridge University Press, 1990), 457, 465, 472, 477, 479, 505, 730, 732, 740.

26. Ted Steinberg, *Down to Earth: Nature's Role in American History* (New York: Oxford University Press, 2002), 96.

27. Eric Foner, *Nothing but Freedom: Emancipation and Its Legacy* (Baton Rouge: Louisiana State University Press, 1983), 65–66. Scott E. Giltner, *Hunting and Fishing in the New South: Black Labor and White Leisure after the Civil War* (Baltimore: Johns Hopkins University Press, 2008), 10–44.

28. Janet Sharp Hermann, *The Pursuit of a Dream* (New York: Oxford University Press, 1981).

29. "Born in Slavery," Arkansas Narratives, Vol. 2, Part 4, 6.

30. Elizabeth Fox-Genovese, *Within the Plantation Household* (Chapel Hill: University of North Carolina Press, 1988), 160–161. "Born in Slavery," Arkansas Narratives, Vol. 2, Part 3, 274, Part 5, 53. Elizabeth Blum, "Power, Danger and Control: Slave Women's Perceptions of Wilderness in the Nineteenth Century," *Women's Studies: An Interdisciplinary Journal* 31 (March/April 2002): 247–267. Lewis, *Travels*, 76. Stewart, "Slavery and the Origins of African American Environmentalism," 15. Sharla M. Fett, *Working Cures: Healing, Health, and Power on Southern Slave Plantations* (Chapel Hill: University of North Carolina Press, 2002), 69–72. Amy Young, "Gender and Landscape: A View from the Plantation Slave Community," in Deborah L. Rotman and Ellen-Rose Savulis, eds., *Shared Spaces and Divided Places: Exploring the Material and Spatial Dimensions of Gendered Relations and the American Historical Landscape* (Knoxville: University of Tennessee Press, 2003), 103–134.

31. William Head Coleman, *Historical Sketch Book and Guide to New Orleans and Environs, with Map* (New York: William H. Coleman, 1885), 84. Federal Writers Project, *Guide to New Orleans* (Boston: Houghton Mifflin, 1938), liii. George H. Lowery, Jr., *Louisiana Birds* (Baton Rouge: Louisiana State University Press, 1974).

32. Lyle S. St. Amant, *Louisiana Wildlife Inventory* (New Orleans: Louisiana Wildlife and Fisheries Commission, 1959), 40, 42, 185–187, 261. Aldo Leopold, *Report on a Game Survey of Mississippi: Submitted to the Game Restoration Committee, Sporting Arms and Ammunition Manufacturers Institute* (Jackson: Mississippi Museum of Natural Science, 1929). According to Leopold, the only predatory mammal that could still be found in the settled regions of Mississippi was the bobcat, which, not posing much of a threat to livestock had not been targeted by herders, and which for a while had increased along with the small game off of which it fed—rabbits especially. Leopold's study was commissioned by

the Sporting Arms and Ammunition Manufacturers' Institute, which was concerned about the disappearance of large game. Percy Viosca, Jr., "Louisiana Wet Lands and the Value of Their Wild Life and Fishery Resources," *Ecology* 9 (April 1928): 223. David M. Burdick, Douglas Cushman, Robert Hamilton, and James G. Gosselink, "Faunal Changes and Bottomland Hardwood Forest Loss in the Tensas Watershed, Louisiana," *Conservation Biology* 3 (September 1989): 282–292. James A. Allen and Virginia R. Burkett, "Salt Tolerance of Southern Baldcypress," US Geological Survey, National Wetlands Research Center (June, 1997), accessed December 23, 2011, www.nwrc.usgs.gov/factshts/fs92_97. pdf. Bob Bowker and Theresa Jacobson, "Louisiana Black Bear Recovery Plan" (Jackson, Miss.: United States Fish and Wildlife Service, 1995), 2–7.

33. Abby Fisher, *What Mrs. Fisher Knows about Old Southern Cooking* (San Francisco: Women's Co-operative Printing Office, 1881), 16, 36–37. Abby Fisher was born in or around 1835 in South Carolina to a Frenchman, or so she claimed. One of her children later reported her place of birth as Florida. By 1865 she was married to Alexander C. Fisher, a minister, and living in Mobile, Alabama. In 1877 or so, the Fishers moved to California. Abby was pregnant and gave birth along the way, in Missouri. By 1880 they were living in San Francisco. Fisher, who was illiterate, dictated her recipes to a transcriber, providing us with a rare glimpse of the knowledge possessed by skilled African American cooks. Although the printed recipes are refined, as is the language, there are glimpses of the vernacular in the former slave's advice on how to prepare game, and in such words as "jumberlie," a mistaken transliteration of Fisher's "jambalay[a]." See Patricia E. Clark, "Archiving Epistemologies and the Narrativity of Recipes in Ntozake Shange's *Sassafrass, Cypress & Indigo*," *Callaloo* 30 (Winter 2007): 154–156. A brief but informative biography of Fisher can be found at *Feeding America: The Historic American Cookbook Project*, "Fisher, Abby," Michigan State University, accessed June 5, 2008, http://digital.lib.msu.edu/projects/cookbooks/html/ authors/author_fisher.html. I have supplemented it with information from the 1870 Census for Mobile, Alabama, and the 1880, 1910, and 1920 censuses for San Francisco, California, available at HeritageQuest Online. The case that jambalaya was originally of French origin is made by Andrew Sigal, "Jambalaya by Any Other Name," *Petits Propos Culinaires* 84 (2007): 101–119.

34. Albert James Pickett, *Eight Days in New Orleans in February* (Montgomery, Ala.: Albert J. Pickett,1847), 27. Lafcadio Hearn, *La Cuisine Creole* (New Orleans: F. F. Hansell, 1885). Irma Rombauer, *The Joy of Cooking: A Compilation of Reliable Recipes with a Casual Culinary Chat* (Indianapolis: Bobbs-Merrill, 1936). Rombauer, a St. Louis, Missouri, housewife, wrote what was for decades the standard cookbook in homes across the United States. Early editions included instructions on preparing and cooking squirrel, opossum, and raccoon, beaver, muskrat, and other game, reflecting the hunting traditions of much of the country, but perhaps most especially, the Mississippi and Missouri river valleys.

It also recognized a Depression-era need for self-reliance on the part of many households. Recent editions of *The Joy of Cooking* have dropped many of the original game recipes. Stewart, "Slavery and the Origins of African American Environmentalism," 12. WPA, Mississippi, Supp Ser. 1, VIII, Part 3, 1293. On game and southern cooking, see John Egerton, *Southern Food, at Home, on the Road, in History* (Chapel Hill: University of North Carolina Press, 1993), 171, 248–250.

35. David M. Oshinsky, *"Worse Than Slavery": Parchman Farm and the Ordeal of Jim Crow Justice* (New York: Free Press, 1996), 109, 137.

36. Rawick, ed. *The American Slave*, Mississippi, Supp. Ser. 1, Vol. 7, 447–478. One Delta plantation manager, Henry Crydenwise, listed "Bears, panthers, wild-cats and wolves, besides a variety of less dangerous animals" among those that inhabited the area in the nineteenth century. James C. Cobb, *The Most Southern Place on Earth: The Mississippi Delta and the Roots of a Regional Identity* (New York: Oxford University Press, 1992), 44.

37. "President Roosevelt's Hunt," *New York Times,* June 9, 1902, 1. "President in Camp, Ready for Bears," *New York Times,* November 14, 1902, 2. "One Bear Falls Prey to President's Party," *New York Times,* November 15, 1902, 1. Giltner, *Hunting and Fishing in the New South,* 109–114.

38. William Faulkner, "The Bear," in *Go Down, Moses* (New York: Random House, 1942). The mill town that serves as the base for the hunting party in Faulkner's story is called Hoke. In 1902, several newspapers mistakenly referred to Holt Collier as Hoke Collier. See "President in Camp, Ready for Bears," *New York Times,* November 14, 1902, 2. The bear killed in the presidential hunt was starving. In contrast, William Dunbar described November as the time of year when "the bear is now also in his best state, with regard to the quality of his fur, and the quantity of fat or oil he yields, as he has been feasting luxuriantly on the autumnal fruits of the forest." See Lewis, *Travels,* 85.

CHAPTER 8

1. Albert Stein, "Mississippi Valley. Remarks on the Improvement of the River Mississippi," *De Bow's Review* 8, February 1850, 105–111; 8, April 1850, 335–338; 9, July 1850, 55–66; 9, September 1850, 304–306; 9, October 1850, 353–357: 9, December 1850, 594–601. J. G. Barnard, "Protection of the Low Lands of the Mississippi," *De Bow's Review* 9, July 1850, 90–95; 9, August 1850, 177–184. Duff Green, "Submerged Land. Which Is the Best and Cheapest Method of Reclaiming the Submerged Lands of Louisiana," *De Bow's Review* 9, September 1850, 300–303. Mikko Saikku, *This Delta, This Land: An Environmental History of the Yazoo-Mississippi Floodplain* (Athens: University of Georgia Press, 2005) ,144–150. Zachary Taylor to Richard Taylor, May 9, 1850, typescript, Taylor Papers, Library of Congress. Taylor's letter discusses flooding of his Jefferson County,

Mississippi, cotton plantation, and the effect of the 1849 flood on a sugar plantation he and his son were buying in St. Charles Parish, Louisiana. I am grateful to
my colleague Steven Maizlish for sharing Taylor's letter with me, after he came
across it in the course of researching his forthcoming book on the Compromise
of 1850. "The Flood in the Mississippi," *New York Times*, April 15, 1858, 3. *New
York Times*, [no title], June 19, 1858, 4. Senator John S. Harris of Louisiana,
Congressional Globe, June 2, 1870, 4000. Harris describes the flood of 1857, but
he surely means 1858, there having been no serious flood in 1857. Harris's error
is understandable, as he was a Northerner who moved to Louisiana during the
Civil War and did not witness the 1858 flood firsthand. V. Alton Moody, "Slavery
on Louisiana Sugar Plantations," *Louisiana Historical Quarterly* 7 (1924): 290.
Flood years were 1849, 1850, 1851, 1858, and 1859. See Paul S. Trotter, G. Alan
Johnson, Robert Ricks, and David R. Smith, "Floods on the Lower Mississippi:
An Historical Economic Overview," SR/SSD 98-9, 3-1-98, Technical Attachment,
National Oceanic and Atmospheric Administration (NOAA), accessed January
9, 2012, www.srh.noaa.gov/topics/attach/html/ssd98-9.htm. In addition, there
were numerous local floods, such as one in 1856 that ruined the sugar crop on
the McCollam plantation. J. Carlyle Sitterson, "The McCollams: A Planter Family
of the Old and New South," *Journal of Southern History* 6 (August 1940): 353.

2. Christopher Morris, *Becoming Southern: The Evolution of a Way of Life, Warren
County and Vicksburg, Mississippi, 1770–1860* (New York: Oxford University
Press, 1995), 140. Robert W. Harrison, "Levee Building in Mississippi before the
Civil War," *Journal of Mississippi History* 12 (April 1950): 63. "Southern Medical
Reports," *De Bow's Review* 9 (1850): 297. "Letter and plans from Mr. B. Latrobe on
the means of filling the crevices, June 10, 1816," New Orleans Conseil de Ville;
Letters, petitions, reports, 1804–1835, Vol. 2, No. 607, New Orleans Public Library,
Special Collections, Louisiana Division, New Orleans. Latrobe's approach to
civil engineering was deeply influenced by Heinrich August Riedel and Johann
Albert Eytelwein and their work in the marshlands and flood plains of Silesia.
See Kathryn M. Olesko, "Geopolitics and Prussian Technical Education in the
Late Eighteenth Century," *Actes D'Història de la Ciència I de la Tècnica*, nova
època, 2 (2009): 11–44. Craig E. Colten, *An Unnatural Metropolis: Wresting New
Orleans from Nature* (Baton Rouge: Louisiana State University Press, 2005), 24.

3. Public Acts of the Thirtieth Congress of the United States, Sess. II (1849), Chap.
87. Public Acts of the Thirty-First Congress of the United States, Sess. I (1850),
Chap. 84. Saikku, *This Delta, This Land*, 144.

4. Saikku, *This Delta, This Land*, 144. Todd Shallat, *Structures in the Stream: Water,
Science, and the Rise of the U. S. Army Corps of Engineers* (Austin: University of
Texas Press, 1994), 176–177.

5. Saikku, *This Delta, This Land*, 145–146. Shallat, *Structures in the Stream*, 175–
176. Vileisis, *Discovering the Unknown Landscape: A History of America's Wetlands*
(Washington, D.C.: Island Press, 1997) ,78–80.

6. For example, P. O. Hebert and A. D. Woodridge both served as state engineers for Louisiana, and both expressed serious doubts about the reliance of levees; however, politics rendered any more comprehensive strategy, one involving outlets, impossible. As a consequence, engineers had to attend to a series of local crises, rather than address the river in its entirety. Colten, *An Unnatural Metropolis*, 26–30.

7. Shallat, *Structures in the Stream*, 176.

8. Forshey, Caleb Goldsmith, Diaries, 1838–1879, Mississippi Valley Collection, University of Memphis 2:2. Albert Phenis attributes the assertion to Eads in "Potentialities of Louisiana's Wet Lands," *Manufactures Record* (July 1914): 42, cited in Robert W. Harrison and Walter M. Kollmorgen, "Drainage Reclamation in the Coastal Marshlands of the Mississippi River Delta," *Louisiana Historical Quarterly* 30 (1947): 658.

9. Capt. A. A. Humphreys and Lieut. H. L. Abbot, *Report Upon the Physics and Hydraulics of the Mississippi River; Upon the Protection of the Alluvial Region Against Overflow; and Upon the Deepening of the Mouths: Based Upon Surveys and Investigations Made under the Acts of Congress Directing the Topographical and Hydrographical Survey of the Delta of the Mississippi River, with Such Investigation as Might Lead to Determine the Most Practicable Plan for Securing It from Inundation, and the Best Mode of Deepening the Channels at the Mouths of the River*, Professional Paper, no. 4 (Philadelphia: United States Army, Corps of Topographical Engineers, 1861; reprint edition, Washington, D.C.: Government Printing Office, 1876), 13, 350.

10. Humphreys and Abbot, *Report*, 6, 112–113, 123–132, 135, 371, 395. Humphreys argued that levees raised the water level only briefly, for which they also compensated by shortening the duration of flooding. See page 439.

11. Charles Ellet, *The Mississippi and Ohio Rivers* (1853; reprint edition, New York: Arno and New York Times, 1970), 17, 27, 83–92, 107, 135. R. Thomassy, *Géologie Pratique de La Louisiane* (New Orleans, 1860), xxiv, describes hydrography as the study of water on the earth's surface, and hydrology as the study of the relationship between water on and below the surface. On the question of agriculture in the Far West and flooding in the Mississippi Valley, Ellet was correct, as conservation biologists now understand. See Mark W. Miller and Thomas Nudds, "Prairie Landscape Change and Flooding in the Mississippi River Valley," *Conservation Biology* 10 (June 1996): 847–853.

12. Humphreys and Abbot, *Report*, 14, 15. Ellet, *Mississippi and Ohio Rivers*, 64–77. Thomassy, *Géology Pratique*, 175, argued that the riverbed was rising in its lower reaches from accumulated deposits of sediment.

13. Humphreys and Abbot, *Report*, 96. Thomassy, *Géologie Pratique*, 174–181.

14. Ellet, *Mississippi and Ohio Rivers*, 18, 19. Humphreys and Abbot, *Report*, 154. William Dunbar Jenkins, "The Mississippi River and the Efforts to Confine It in Its Channel," *Publications of the Mississippi Historical Society* 6 (1902): 283–306.

15. Ira Berlin, Thavolia Glymph, Steven F. Miller, Joseph P. Reidy, Leslie S. Rowland, and Julie Saville, *Freedom: A Documentary History of Emancipation*, Ser. 1, Vol. 3, *The Wartime Genesis of Free Labor: The Lower South* (New York: Cambridge University Press, 1990), 384, 447, 449, 451, 739, 837. Céline Frémaux Garcia, *Céline: Remembering Louisiana, 1850–1871*, Patrick J. Geary, ed. (Athens: University of Georgia Press, 1987), 161–162. B. I. Wiley, "Vicissitudes of Early Reconstruction Farming in the Lower Mississippi Valley," *Journal of Southern History* 3 (November 1937): 450. Shallat, *Structures in the Stream*, 193. Eric Foner, *Reconstruction: America's Unfinished Revolution, 1863–1877* (New York: Harper and Row, 1988), 55–57.

16. Willie Lee Rose, *Rehearsal for Reconstruction: The Port Royal Experiment* (New York: Vintage, 1964). William Tecumseh Sherman, *Memoirs*, Michael Fellman, ed. (New York: Penguin, 2000), 609–611. Foner, *Reconstruction*, 68–71. James M. McPherson, *Ordeal by Fire: The Civil War and Reconstruction*, 2nd ed. (New York: McGraw-Hill, 1992), 503–506.

17. Berlin et al., *Freedom*, Ser. 1, Vol. 3: 396, 448–450, 454, 456, 682–683, 699–701, 718, 797. Janet Sharp Hermann, *The Pursuit of a Dream* (New York: Oxford University Press, 1981), 48–60. Foner, *Reconstruction*, 54–60. Steven Hahn, *A Nation under Our Feet: Black Political Struggles in the Rural South from Slavery to the Great Migration* (Cambridge, Mass.: Belknap Press of Harvard University Press, 2003), 79–80.

18. Berlin et al., *Freedom*, Ser. 1, Vol. 3: 561, 563, 568, 569, 841, 887.

19. Daniel W. Hamilton, *The Limits of Sovereignty: Property Confiscation in the Union and Confederacy during the Civil War* (Chicago: University of Chicago Press, 2007), 14–81. On the conservative basis of Republican Reconstruction generally, see Michael Les Benedict, *Compromise of Principle: Congressional Republicans and Reconstruction, 1863–1869* (New York: W. W. Norton, 1974), and Benedict, *Preserving the Constitution: Essays on Politics and the Constitution in the Reconstruction Era* (New York: Fordham University Press, 2006).

20. James M. McPherson, *Drawn with the Sword: Reflections on the American Civil War* (New York: Oxford University Press, 1996), 203–207. McPherson, *Ordeal by Fire*, 504–505.

21. In calling for federal aid for levees, lower valley Republicans sought to reach out to northern colleagues and to divide Democratic opponents. Michael Perman, *The Road to Redemption: Southern Politics, 1868–1879* (Chapel Hill: University of North Carolina Press, 1984), 69–75. See also Mark W. Summers, *Railroads, Reconstruction, and the Gospel of Prosperity: Aid under the Radical Republicans, 1865–1877* (Princeton: Princeton University Press, 1984), and Terry L. Seip, *The South Returns to Congress: Men, Economic Measures, and Intersectional Relationships* (Baton Rouge: Louisiana State University Press, 1983).

22. Mary G. McBride and Ann M. McLaurin, "The Origin of the Mississippi River Commission," *Louisiana History* 36 (Fall 1995): 390–391.

23. Journal of the House of Representatives, 39th Cong., 1st Sess., June 9, 1866, p. 814. *Congressional Globe*, Senate, 39th Cong., 1st Sess., June 11, 1866, p. 3075, July 2, 1866, p. 3522. *Congressional Globe*, House of Representatives, 40th Cong., 1st Sess., July 19, 1867, pp. 738–739. Lillian A. Pereyra, *James Lusk Alcorn, Persistent Whig* (Baton Rouge: Louisiana State University Press, 1966), 74.

24. *Congressional Globe*, House of Representatives, 40th Cong., 1st Sess., July 12, 1867, pp. 615–617.

25. Harris's speech, on which this discussion is based, may be found in *Congressional Globe*, 41st Cong., 2nd Sess., Senate, June 2, 1870, pp. 3999–4002. Howard J. Jones, "Biographical Sketches of Members of the 1868 Louisiana State Senate," *Louisiana History* 19 (Winter 1978): 80–82. On Alcorn's Memphis speech, see Pereyra, *James Lusk Alcorn*, 77. Ari Kelman, *A River and Its City: The Nature of Landscape in New Orleans* (Berkeley: University of California Press, 2003), 127.

26. *Congressional Globe*, 41st Cong., 2nd Sess., Senate, June 2, 1870, p. 3999. Shallat, *Structures in the Stream*, 53. Thomas Hutchins, *An Historical Narrative and Topographical Description of Louisiana, and West-Florida* (Philadelphia, 1784). On Jefferson and the dispute over the New Orleans batture, see Kelman, *A River and Its City*, 33–36.

27. *Congressional Globe*, 41st Cong., 2nd Sess., Senate, June 2, 1870, p. 4002.

28. *Congressional Globe*, 41st Cong., 3rd Sess., Senate, January 11, 1871, pp. 425–426. Harris left the Senate in 1871, eventually moving to Montana. He was replaced by Joseph R. West, who had lived in California and served in the US Army in the New Mexico and Arizona territories. Jones, "Biographical Sketches," 82. "Biographical Directory of the United States Congress," accessed January 9, 2012, http://bioguide.congress.gov/scripts/biodisplay.pl?index=W000303.

29. *Congressional Record*, 43rd Cong., 1st Sess., April 17, 1874, p. 3151, April 21, 1874, p. 3247. On the 1873 yellow fever epidemic in Memphis, see Khaled J. Bloom, *The Mississippi Valley's Great Yellow Fever Epidemic of 1878* (Baton Rouge: Louisiana State University Press, 1993), 77–80.

30. *Congressional Record*, 43rd Cong., 1st Sess., April 21, 1874, pp. 3246–3247. Nathaniel Means, "Sugar Cane, Cotton Fields, and High Water: Building the Louisiana Branch of the Texas and Pacific Railroad," *Louisiana History* 45 (Autumn 2004): 445–461.

31. *Congressional Record*, 43rd Cong., 1st Sess., House of Representatives, April 17, 1874, p. 3151, April 21, 1874, pp. 3241–3247, June 6, 1874, pp. 4650–4658, Senate, June 17, 1874, pp. 5083–5084. *Congressional Globe*, 42nd Cong., 3rd Sess., Senate, February 28, 1873, p. 1930.

32. *Congressional Record*, 43rd Cong., 1st Sess., House of Representatives, April 21, 1874, pp. 3245–3247, June 6, 1874, pp. 4650, 4652, 4657. Perman, *Road to Redemption*, 67, 75.

33. E. L. Corthell, *A History of Jetties at the Mouth of the Mississippi River* (New York: Wiley and Sons, 1881).

34. Kelman, *A River and Its City*, 129–130.

35. *Congressional Record*, 43rd Cong., 1st Sess., Senate, January 22, 1874, p. 831, January 23, pp. 862–865, February 5, 1874, pp. 1215–1219.

36. The story of the personal and professional rivalry between Eads and Humphreys is told most engagingly by John M. Barry, *Rising Tide: The Great Mississippi Flood of 1927 and How It Changed America* (New York: Simon and Schuster, 1997), 21–92.

37. *Congressional Record*, 43rd Cong., 1st Sess., House of Representatives, April 29, 1874, p. 3477. May 11, 1874, pp. 3771–3772, Senate, June 20, 1874, pp. 5293–5297, June 22, 1874, pp. 5366–5367, 5373. Humphreys explained why jetties would not work in a letter and four memoranda, written in 1874 and 1875, and published as Appendix M in the 1876 edition of Humphreys and Abbot, *Report*. Corthell *A History of Jetties*, 37.

38. "Dispatch to the Associated Press," *New York Times*, July 4, 1874, 1.

39. *Congressional Record*, 43rd Cong., 2nd Sess., House of Representatives, February 18, 1875, pp. 1439–1448.

40. Shallat, *Structures in the Stream*, 194–199. Kelman, *A River and Its City*, 135.

41. "Dispatch to the Associated Press," *New York Times*, January 18, 1875, 1. "The President and the South," *New York Times*, January 20, 1875, 1. That year, the lower Mississippi River flooded again, twice, in April and in August. "The Mississippi Floods," *New York Times*, August 5, 1875, 2, and "The Suffering Crops," *New York Times*, August 6, 1875, 1. "The Demands of the South," *New York Times*, February 6, 1876, 6, "Washington. Congressional Topics," February 9, 1876, p. 1, "The New Southern Policy," April 26, 1877, p. 4. C. L. Marquette, "Letters of a Yankee Sugar Planter," *Journal of Southern History* 6 (November 1940): 528–529. McBride and McLaurin, "Origin of the Mississippi River Commission," 395. C. Vann Woodward, *Origins of the New South* (Baton Rouge: Louisiana State University Press, 1951), 35.

42. Matthew Todd Pearcy, "A History of the Mississippi River Commission, 1879 to 1928: From Levees Only to a Comprehensive Program of Flood Control for the Lower Mississippi Valley" (Ph.D. diss., University of North Texas, 1996). Charles A. Camillo and Matthew T. Pearcy, *Upon Their Shoulders: A History of the Mississippi River Commission* (Vicksburg: Mississippi River Commission, 2004). McBride and McLaurin, "Origin of the Mississippi River Commission," 399. Thomassy, *Géologie Pratique*, 150.

43. Jessica B. Teisch, *Engineering Nature: Water, Nature, and the Global Spread of American Engineering Expertise* (Chapel Hill: University of North Carolina Press, 2011), 17–38, argues that British engineers worked with Indian *zamindars* (landlords) and treated Indian laborers as part of the landscape, controlled along with the land and water. Similarly, in the lower valley, wartime "compulsory" free labor and the postwar use of convict and contract labor permitted engineers to manage people as they managed land and water.

44. *Flood Control Act (1917)*, 64th Cong., Sess. II, Ch. 144.

45. On *John Gravier v. Mayor, Aldermen, and Inhabitants of the City of New Orleans* (1807), the so-called batture case, see Kelman, *A River and Its City*, 19–49.

46. John Cowdon, *The Outlet System; Its Effects on the Commercial and Agricultural Industries and Sanitary Conditions of New Orleans and the Mississippi Valley* (New Orleans, 1881). John Cowdon, *In the Senate of the United States…Memorial of John Cowdon on Matters Pertaining to the Improvement of the Mississippi River and Its Tributaries, and Stopping the Overflow of Their Valley Lands, 52d Congress, 2d session, Senate Mis. Doc. No. 38* (Washington, D.C.; Government Printing Office, 1893). Cowdon authored several texts that were critical of the levees-only approach of the MRC. The connection between flood control and navigation in the valley and the development of the West, made a few years earlier, was a commonly held assumption by 1879. Ernst von Hesse-Wartegg, *Travels on the Lower Mississippi, 1879–1880*, Frederic Trautmann, ed. and trans. (Columbia: University of Missouri Press, 1990), 145, 188, and Corthell, *A History of Jetties*, 5, 6, 237–238.

47. *Flood Control Act (1917)*, 64th Cong., Sess. II, Ch. 144. Saikku, *This Delta, This Land*, 149–150, 155. Marquette, "Letters," 542.

48. Histories of the 1927 flood include Pete Daniel, *Deep'n as It Come: The 1927 Mississippi River Flood* (New York: Oxford University Press, 1977); Barry, *Rising Tide*. Songs about the flood include Memphis Minnie and Kansas Joe McCoy, "When the Levee Breaks," 1929; Charley Patton, "High Water Everywhere, Parts 1 and 2," 1929; Randy Newman, "Louisiana 1927," *Good Old Boys*, 1974. Films about the flood include Chana Gazit, Director, *Fatal Flood*, 2001; Bill Morrison, Director, *The Great Flood*, 2011; Pare Lorentz, Director, *The River*, 1938.

49. *Flood Control Act (1917)*, 64th Cong., Sess. II, Ch. 144. 1917. *Flood Control Act (1928)*, 70th Cong., Sess. I, Ch. 569. 1928. "New Orleans' Flood Valve Finished," *Popular Science Monthly* (March 1931): 34. Project Flood is both shorthand for the Mississippi River and Tributaries Project, and the object of the project, which seeks to protect the valley from a "project flood," by which is meant a projected flood of greater magnitude than the flood of 1927. See the Army Corps of Engineers Web page for the project at www.mvn.usace.army.mil/pao/bro/misstrib.htm. Walter Carey Papers, Box 1, personal correspondence, New Orleans Public Library, Special Collections, Louisiana Division, New Orleans.
The 1927 flood is often cited as the end of the levees-only policy. For example see Pearcy, *History of the Mississippi River Commission*; Camillo and Pearcy, *Upon Their Shoulders*; Barry, *Rising Tide*, 399; Saikku, *This Delta, This Land*, 59; Kelman, *A River and Its City*, 191–192.

50. According to Ann Vileisis, $131 million had been spent on levees in the lower valley by the end of 1916. See Vileisis, *Discovering the Unknown Landscape: A History of America's Wetlands* (Washington, D.C.: Island Press, 1997), 82, 134. The Flood Control Act of 1917 authorized $45 million in federal aid to be matched equally

by the states, for a total of $90 million. The Flood Control Act of 1927 authorized an appropriation of $325 million, for a total of $546 million. See the texts of the acts on the Corps of Engineers Web site, accessed January 11, 2012, www.mvd. usace.army.mil/mrc/history/index.php#. Additional figures may be found in John M. Barry, *Rising Tide: The Great Mississippi Flood of 1927 and How It Changed America* (New York: Simon and Schuster, 1997), 402. Subsequent appropriations for flood control are stated in the texts of the flood control acts, accessed January 9, 2012, www.mvd.usace.army.mil/mrc/history/index.php. Matthew T. Pearcy, "After the Flood: A History of the 1928 Flood Control Act," *Journal of the Illinois State Historical Society* (Summer 2002): 172–201. In the decade after the 1927 flood, tributaries inundated the Yazoo-Mississippi Delta twice, in 1932 and 1935. In 1937, the Mississippi rose to heights that challenged the new levee system along the river. The levees held, but the Yazoo backed up at Vicksburg, forcing residents in the southern portion of the Delta to flee their homes. Thomas Fauntleroy, "Delta Folk Push Flood Work Plans," *New York Times*, October 1, 1933, E7. "Mississippi Flood Forms Vast Lake," *New York Times*, January 26, 1935, 19. More floods elicited more calls for money invested in flood control projects. For a congressional debate over an appropriation of $400 million, see "Senate Body Split on Flood Control," *New York Times*, April 19, 1936, 27.

In 1929, the GDP for the United States was $103.6 billion. The estimated costs of flood control projects undertaken in the wake of the 1927 flood reached $1 billion, or about 1.00 percent of 1929's GDP. This was in addition to the billions already spent on flood control by the time of the 1927 flood. In today's dollars, the cost of the project would be over $110 billion, ten times the appropriations for flood control at New Orleans in the five years following Hurricane Katrina. In 2010, the GDP was $14,526.5 billion. Estimated expenditures on flood control in the five years after Hurricane Katrina reached $14 billion, or about 0.10 percent of 2010's GDP. Bureau of Economic Analysis, Department of Commerce, "GDP and Other Major NIPA Series, 1929–2011:II," *Survey of Current Business Online* 91 (August 2011): 181–182, accessed January 9, 2012, www.bea.gov/scb/pdf/2011/08%20August/0811_gdp_nipas.pdf. Sheila Grissett, "Hurricane Season Begins Tuesday with $5.8 Billion of Work Still in Progress," *Times-Picayune*, May 29, 2010, accessed January 9, 2012, www.nola.com/hurricane/index.ssf/2010/05/hurricane_season_begins_tuesda.html.

51. Personal conversation with Gerald E. Galloway, Glenn L. Martin Institute Professor of Engineering, University of Maryland, October 28, 2006. Galloway was commander of the Army Corps of Engineers District in Vicksburg, Mississippi, from 1974 to 1977.

52. *Flood Control Act (1917)*, 64th Cong., Sess. II, Ch. 144. 1917. *Flood Control Act (1928)*, 70th Cong., Sess. I, Ch. 569. 1928, accessed January 9, 2012, www. mvd.usace.army.mil/mrc/history/index.php. After 1928 Congress continued to debate whether the states should pay some of the costs of flood control. See

"Senate Body Split on Flood Control," *New York Times*, April 19, 1936, 27, when the Senate Commerce Committee split over whether to ask states to put up $100 million to match a federal appropriation of $400 million.

53. Hoover is quoted in Kelman, *A River and Its City*, 191–192. James E. Crown, "Lower Valley's Safety Proved by Great Flood," *New York Times*, March 21, 1937, 73. "Negroes Ask Inquiry," *New York Times*, January 9, 1933, 2. "No New Deal Seen for Negro Labor," *New York Times*, January 9, 1934, 13. I am grateful to Edwin A. Lyon, a former senior archaeologist with the Corps of Engineers, New Orleans District, now retired, for bringing to my attention the Cultural Resource Management reports containing information on the cemeteries buried by the Bonnet Carré Spillway. In 1975, excavations to repair a drainage ditch uncovered one of the cemeteries under the spillway. Jill-Karen Yakubik, Herschel A. Franks, R. Christopher Goodwin, and Carol J. Poplin, *Cultural Resources Inventory of the Bonnet Carré Spillway, St. Charles Parish, Louisiana* (1986), copy in US Army Corps of Engineers, New Orleans District and in the National Anthropological Archives, Smithsonian Museum Support Center, Suitland, Maryland. Recent efforts to recover the buried cemeteries are discussed in "Bonnet Carré Spillway Master Plan," US Army Corps of Engineers, 2009, pp. 3–16 and 3–17, accessed January 9, 2012, www.mvn.usace.army.mil/recreation/mp_without_appendices.pdf.

54. Saikku, *This Delta, This Land*, 149–150.

CHAPTER 9

1. *Daily Picayune*, June 7, 1899, 10 (quotation); May 24, 1899, 11.

2. "Many Sufferers from Drought," *New York Times*, August 25, 1896, 7; "Sufferers from Drought," November 29, 1896. "Fearful Drought," *Dallas Morning News*, August 20, 1896, 9; "Louisiana Drouth [sic] Sufferers," January 1, 1897, 1.

3. *Daily Picayune*, May 19, 1893, 1. In 1897, floodwaters also broke through levees near Greenville, Mississippi, and in Madison Parish, Louisiana. *Daily Picayune*, March 30, 1897, 1; April 21, 1897, 1, 2. C. Vann Woodward, *Origins of the New South* (Baton Rouge: Louisiana State University Press, 1951), 270.

4. "The Rice Crop: Its Condition in Louisiana, Georgia, and South Carolina," *New York Times*, August 13, 1889. Pete Daniel, *Breaking the Land: The Transformation of Cotton, Tobacco, and Rice Cultures since 1880* (Champaign: University of Illinois Press, 1986), 39–61.

5. *Daily Picayune*, September 1, 1902, 17; January 27, 1897, 4; May 31, 1909, 12.

6. *Daily Picayune*, June 21, 1906, 13. Frank Uekoetter, "The Magic of One: Reflections on the Pathologies of Monoculture," *Rachel Carson Center Perspectives* no. 2 (2011): 3–20, accessed April 9, 2012, www.carsoncenter.uni-muenchen.de/download/publications/perspectives/2011_perspectives/rcc_issue5_sw.pdf .

7. Father Poisson, "Letter from Father du Poisson, Missionary to the Akensas, to Father ***," October 3, 1727, *Relations* 67:297, accessed April 9, 2012, http://

puffin.creighton.edu/jesuit/relations/relations_67.html. Ernst von Hesse-Wartegg, *Travels on the Lower Mississippi, 1879–1880*, Frederic Trautmann, ed. and trans. (Columbia: University of Missouri Press, 1990), 76, 208. Pierre Clément de Laussat, *Memoirs of My Life*, Robert D. Bush, ed., Agnes-Josephine Pastwa, trans. (Baton Rouge: Louisiana State University Press, 1978), 32. Jacob Bieller to David Draffin, August 21, 1833, Alonzo Snyder papers, Mss. 655, Louisiana State University, Baton Rouge. Rod Giblett, *Postmodern Wetlands: Culture, History, Ecology* (Edinburgh: Edinburgh University Press, 1997), 103–126.

8. Lafferty and Kruis, "How Environmental Stress Affects the Impacts of Parasites," *Limnology and Oceanography* 44 (May 1999): 926. Paul Kelton, *Epidemics and Enslavement: Biological Catastrophe in the Native Southeast 1492–1715* (Lincoln: University of Nebraska Press, 2007), 60–66. There are over thirty species worldwide of *anopheles* capable of transmitting malaria, of which few are better at it than the American *anopheles quadrimaculatus*. J. R. McNeill, *Mosquito Empires: Ecology and War in the Greater Caribbean, 1620–1914* (New York: Cambridge University Press, 2010), 3, 54, 55. By mid-twentieth century, over fifty species of mosquitoes were found in the states of Mississippi and Louisiana. Charles D. Michener, "Mosquitoes of a Limited Area in Southern Mississippi," *American Midland Naturalist* 37 (March 1947): 325.

9. Margaret Humphreys, *Malaria: Poverty, Race, and Public Health in the United States* (Baltimore: Johns Hopkins University Press, 2001), 52. John B. Gerberich, "An Annotated Bibliography of Papers Relating to the Control of Mosquitoes by the Use of Fish," *American Midland Naturalist* 36 (July 1946): 87. McNeill, *Mosquito Empires* 57.

10. Lausset, *Memoirs of My Life*, 41. Kenneth F. Kiple and Virginia H. Kiple, "Black Yellow Fever Immunities, Innate and Acquired, as Revealed in the American South," *Social Science History* 1 (Summer 1977): 419–436. Benjamin H. Trask, *Fearful Ravages: Yellow Fever in New Orleans, 1796–1905* (Lafayette: University of Louisiana at Lafayette, 2005).

11. Margaret Humphreys, *Yellow Fever and the South* (Baltimore: Johns Hopkins University Press, 1999), 2–6. Bloom, *Yellow Fever*, 8–9. Duffy, *Sword of Pestilence: The New Orleans Yellow Fever Epidemic of 1853* (Baton Rouge: Louisiana State University Press, 1966). Trask, *Fearful Ravages*, 37–56. Benjamin Wailes, diary, typescript, August 18, 1853 to August 30, 1853, September 1, 1853 to December 9, 1853, Mississippi Department of Archives and History, Jackson. Mahala Roach, diary, 1, September 24, 1853, Roach-Eggleston Family Papers, Southern Historical Collection, University of North Carolina, Chapel Hill. Ari Kelman, *A River and Its City: The Nature of Landscape in New Orleans* (Berkeley: University of California Press, 2003), 87–118. Kelton, *Epidemics and Enslavement*, 34. Kiple and Kiple, "Black Yellow Fever Immunities," 424–245. According to Kiple and Kiple, in 1820 in New Orleans 84 percent of yellow fever deaths were white

residents, 99.6 percent in 1849, and 100 percent in 1850, most likely because of an inherited resistance to the disease.

12. Khaled J. Bloom, *The Mississippi Valley's Great Yellow Fever Epidemic of 1878* (Baton Rouge: Louisiana State University Press, 1993), 23–30. Humphreys, *Yellow Fever*, 5. S. R. Christophers, *Aedes aegypti (L.), the Yellow Fever Mosquito: Its Life History, Bionomics, and Structure* (Cambridge: Cambridge University Press, 1960). James Goodyear, "The Sugar Connection: A New Perspective on the History of Yellow Fever," *Bulletin of the History of Medicine* 52 (1978): 5–21. McNeill, *Mosquito Empires*, 49–52.

13. Trask, *Fearful Ravages*. Humphreys, *Yellow Fever and the South*, 4. Robert E. May, *The Southern Dream of a Caribbean Empire, 1854–1861* (Baton Rouge: Louisiana State University Press, 1973).

14. Percy Viosca, Jr., "Louisiana Wet Lands and the Value of their Wild Life and Fishery Resources," *Ecology* 9 (April 1928): 223. Trask, *Fearful Ravages*, 18–19.

15. Leopold Manuscript, Mississippi Department of Archives and History, Jackson. James A. Allen and Virginia R. Burkett, "Salt Tolerance of Southern Baldcypress," US Geological Survey, National Wetlands Research Center (June, 1997), accessed December 23, 2011, www.nwrc.usgs.gov/factshts/fs92_97.pdf. Juanda Bonck and W. T. Penfound, "Plant Succession on Abandoned Farm Land in the Vicinity of New Orleans, Louisiana," *American Midland Naturalist* 33 (March 1945): 520–529. Sammy L. King and Bobby D. Keeland, "Evaluation of Reforestation in the Lower Mississippi River Alluvial Valley," *Restoration Ecology* 7 (December 1999): 348–359. Statistics for timberland in Louisiana and Mississippi can be found at www.fedstats.gov.

16. E. L. Corthell, "The Delta of the Mississippi River," *National Geographic* 8 (December 1897): 351–354. Mikko Saikku, *This Delta, This Land: An Environmental History of the Yazoo-Mississippi Floodplain* (Athens: University of Georgia Press, 2005), 133, 241.

17. John Klorer, "The Water Hyacinth Problem," *Journal of the Association of Engineering Societies* 42 (1909): 42–48. William T. Penfound and T. T. Earle, "The Biology of the Water Hyacinth," *Ecological Monographs* 18 (October 1948): 447–472. Spencer C. H. Barrett, "Water Weed Invasions," *Scientific American* 261 (October 1989): 90–97. T. R. Kidder, "The Rat That Ate Louisiana: Aspects of Historical Ecology in the Mississippi River Delta," in W. Balée, ed., *Advances in Historical Ecology* (New York: Columbia University Press, 1998): 142. Shane K. Bernard, "M'sieu Ned's Rat? Reconsidering the Origin of Nutria in Louisiana: The E. A. McIlhenny Collection, Avery Island, Louisiana," *Louisiana History* 43 (2002): 281–293. T. Edward Nickens, "Trying to Show the Door to a Marsh Munching Immigrant from South America," *National Wildlife*, 38 (December/January, 2000), accessed July 15, 2008, www.nwf.org/nationalwildlife/article.cfm?articleId=246&issueId=27.

18. Louis Hughes, *Thirty Years a Slave, from Bondage to Freedom* (Milwaukee: South Side Printing, 1897), 28–30. James Giesen, " 'The Truth about the Boll Weevil': The Nature of Planter Power in the Mississippi Delta," *Journal of Southern History* 14 (October 2009): 683–704. James Giesen, *Boll Weevil Blues: Cotton, Myth, and Power in the American South* (Chicago: University of Chicago Press, 2011), especially chapters 3 and 4.

19. Robert W. Harrison and Walter M. Kollmorgen, "Drainage Reclamation in the Coastal Marshlands of the Mississippi River Delta," *Louisiana Historical Quarterly* 30 (1947): 662–663. Wayne P. Sousa, "The Role of Disturbance in Natural Communities," *Annual Review of Ecology and Systematics* 15 (1984): 353–391. Percy Viosca, Jr., "Spontaneous Combustion in the Marshes of Southern Louisiana," *Ecology* 12 (April 1931): 439–442.

20. Saikku, *This Delta, This Land*, 124, 150

21. Saikku, *This Delta, This Land*, 124, 191–193. John Willis, *Forgotten Time: The Yazoo-Mississippi Delta after the Civil War* (Charlottesville: University of Virginia Press, 2000), 91–113. Kelman, *A River and Its City*, 123, 137.

22. On the energy expended to maintain by artificial means ecological processes where rivers have been disconnected from their surrounding environment, see, for example, Ellen Wohl, *Disconnected Rivers: Linking Rivers to Landscapes* (New Haven: Yale University Press, 2004); Richard White, *The Organic Machine: The Remaking of the Columbia River* (New York: Hill and Wang, 1995). On the extraordinary human costs of drying and planting the lower Mississippi Valley, see, for example, Edward Countryman, "The Price of Cotton: The Demography of Inequality in Mid-Nineteenth Century Mississippi," *Quaderno* 4 (Milan: Dipartimenti di Storia della Societa e delle Instituzione, Universita degli Studii di Milano, 1998), 167–186; Michael Tadman, "The Demographic Cost of Sugar: Debates on Slave Societies and Natural Increase in the Americas," *American Historical Review* 105 (December 2000), 1534–1575. Richard Follett, " 'Lives of Living Death': The Reproductive Lives of Slave Women in the Cane World of Louisiana," *Slavery and Abolition*, 26 (August 2005): 289–304. Pete Daniel, *Toxic Drift: Pesticides and Health in the Post–World War II South* (Baton Rouge: Louisiana State University Press, 2005).

23. Roy Reed, "Engineers Open Spillway in Attempt to Save an Imperiled Mississippi Dam," *New York Times*, April 18, 1973, 93. Stanley A. Changnon, "The Historical Struggle with Floods on the Mississippi River Basin," *Water International* 23 (December 1998): 263–271. Nicholas Pinter, "Environment: One Step Forward, Two Steps Back on U.S. Floodplains," *Science* 308 (April 8, 2005): 207–208. Vileisis, *Discovering the Unknown Landscape*, 341.

24. The Wetlands Reserve Program is defined in the US Code, Title 16, Chapter 58, Subchapter 4, Part 1, Subpart C, section 3837.

25. Christine Hauser, "Flooding Takes an Economic Toll, and It's Hardly Done," *New York Times*, May 18, 2011, A11. *State of Missouri v. U.S. Army Corps of Engineers,*

et al. Missouri, Eastern District Court, April 29, 2011, accessed January 10, 2012, http://docs.justia.com/cases/federal/district-courts/missouri/moedce/1:2011cv 00067/113238/26/.

CHAPTER 10

1. Susan B. Carter, Scott Sigmund Gartner, Michael R. Haines, Alan L. Olmstead, Richard Sutch, and Gavin Wright, eds., *Historical Statistics of the United States Millennial Edition Online* (Cambridge: Cambridge University Press, 2008),: accessed April 13, 2012, http://hsus.cambridge.org/HSUSWeb/toc/hsu- sHome.do. Table Da225-290-Average acreage per farm, by region and state: 1850–1997; Table Da28-92-Farm population, by region and state: 1890–1969; Table Da159-224-Land in farms, by region and state: 1850–1997; Table Da1175- 1204-Indexes of agricultural land and labor productivity, by region: 1939–1990. Richard L. Forstall, ed., "Population of Counties by Decennial Census: 1900 to 1990, Mississippi" (Washington, D.C.: Population Division, US Bureau of the Census, 1995), accessed April 13, 2012, www.census.gov/population/cencounts/ ms190090.txt. Mikko Saikku, *This Delta, This Land: An Environmental History of the Yazoo-Mississippi Floodplain* (Athens: University of Georgia Press, 2005), 237.

2. On appropriations and expenditures, see chapter 8, note 50. On the 1944 act, see Stanley A. Changnon, "The Historical Struggle with Floods on the Mississippi River Basin," *Water International* 23 (December 1998): 263–271. On the direct connection between the mechanization of cotton agriculture and the migration of laborers from the Delta to Chicago, see Nicholas Lemann, *The Promised Land: The Great Migration and How It Changed America* (New York: Random House, 1991), 3–7.

3. Annual summaries for farm expenses since 1973 can be found at USDA National Agricultural Statistics Service, Farm Production Expenditures and Annual Summary, 1973 to 2007, accessed January 11, 2012, http://usda. mannlib.cornell.edu/MannUsda/viewDocumentInfo.do?documentID=1066. For cotton production and prices since 1866, see USDA National Agricultural Statistics Service, Track Records, United States Crop Production, Cotton, pp. 27–30, accessed January 10, 2012, http://usda.mannlib.cornell.edu/usda/nass/ htrcp/2000s/2003/htrcp-04-25-2003.pdf. For fertilizer and farm labor costs since 1910, see USDA, "US Production Agriculture Expenses, All Categories, 1910–2008," accessed January 10, 2012, www.ers.usda.gov/Data/FarmIncome/ FinfidmuXls.htm.

4. Pete Daniel, *Breaking the Land: The Transformation of Cotton, Tobacco, and Rice Cultures since 1880* (Champaign: University of Illinois Press, 1986). For an example of the personal costs, financial and social, of fertilizer borne by strug- gling southern farmers in the early twentieth-century South, see Nate Shaw, *All*

God's Dangers: The Life of Nate Shaw, Theodore Rosengarten, comp. (Chicago: University of Chicago Press, 2000).

5. Richard B. Alexander and Richard A. Smith, "County-Level Estimates of Nitrogen and Phosphorus Fertilizer Use in the United States, 1945 to 1985," US Geological Survey Open-File Report 90-130 (Reston, Va., 1990), accessed April 13, 2012, http://pubs.usgs.gov/of/1990/ofr90130/report.html. Saikku, *This Delta, This Land*, 237. Pete Daniel, *Toxic Drift: Pesticides and Health in the Post–World War II South* (Baton Rouge: Louisiana State University Press, 2005), 99, 110, 111. USDA, "Consumption of Commercial Fertilizers and Primary Plant Nutrients in the United States, 1850–1964, and by States, 1945–64," Statistical Reporting Service, Statistics Bulletin No. 375, Washington, D.C., June 1966, tables 3 and 4.

6. Saikku, *This Delta, This Land*, 132. James C. Giesen, " 'The Truth about the Boll Weevil': The Nature of Planter Power in the Mississippi Delta," *Environmental History* 14 (October 2009): 683–704. Giesen, *Boll Weevil Blues: Cotton, Myth, and Power in the American South* (Chicago: University of Chicago Press, 2011), 73–100.

7. Daniel, *Breaking the Land*, 7, 14–15. Saikku, *This Delta, This Land*, 132. For a description of the application of Paris green, see Shaw, *All God's Dangers*, 224. Eldon W. Downs and George F. Lemmer, "Origins of Aerial Crop Dusting," *Agricultural History* 39 (July 1965): 123–135. On the role of DDT in postwar American foreign policy, see David Kinkela, *DDT and the American Century: Global Health, Environmental Politics, and the Pesticide that Changed the World* (Chapel Hill: University of North Carolina Press, 2011).

8. Brian R. Clark and Rheannon M. Hart, "The Mississippi Embayment Regional Aquifer Study (MERAS): Documentation of a Groundwater-Flow Model Constructed to Assess Water Availability in the Mississippi Embayment," *US Geological Survey Scientific Investigations Report 2009–5172* (Reston, VA.: US Geological Survey, 2009), 2. R. M. Scheiderer and D. A. Freiwald, "Monitoring the Recovery of the Sparta Aquifer in Southern Arkansas and Northern Louisiana," US Geological Survey Fact Sheet 2006-3090 (2006), accessed January 11, 2012, http://pubs.usgs.gov/fs/2006/3090/.

9. Walter Carey Papers, Box 12, Control and Eradication of Water Hyacinth, New Orleans Public Library Special Collections, Louisiana Division, New Orleans.

10. Timothy Mitchell, *Rule of Experts: Egypt, Techno-Politics, Modernity* (Berkeley: University of California Press, 2002), 47. Bruno Latour, *Reassembling the Social: An Introduction to Actor-Network-Theory* (New York: Oxford University Press, 2005), 63–86.

11. Daniel H. Usner, Jr., *Indians, Settlers, and Slaves in a Frontier Exchange Economy: The Lower Mississippi Valley before 1783* (Chapel Hill: Institute of Early American History and Culture, University of North Carolina Press, 1992), 153. Ernst von Hesse-Wartegg, *Travels on the Lower Mississippi 1879–1880*, Frederic Trautmann,

ed. and trans. (Columbia: University of Missouri Press, 1990), 88. Census Office, "Report on Statistics of Fisheries in the United States at the Eleventh Census: 1890" (Washington, D.C.: Government Printing Office, 1894), 8. Stephen P. Risotto and R. Eugene Turner, "Annual Fluctuation in Abundance of the Commercial Fisheries of the Mississippi River and Tributaries," *North American Journal of Fisheries Management* 5 (1985): 565. H. B. Carlander, *A History of Fish and Fishing in the Upper Mississippi River* (Rock Island, Ill.: Upper Mississippi River Conservation Committee, 1954). Harold L. Schramm, Jr., "Status and Management of Mississippi River Fisheries," US Geological Survey, Mississippi Cooperative Fish and Wildlife Research Unit, p. 13, accessed January 11, 2012, www.ibcperu.org/doc/isis/2958.pdf. Teresa Ish and Katy Doctor, "Channel Catfish, U.S. Farmed: Final Report," Seafood Watch, Seafood Report, Monterey Bay, 2005, accessed January 11, 2012, www.mbayaq.org/cr/cr_seafoodwatch/content/media/MBA_SeafoodWatch_USFarmedCatfishReport.pdf. National Marine Fisheries Service, Fisheries Statistics Division, Silver Spring, Md., accessed January 11, 2012, www.st.nmfs.noaa.gov/st1/index.html. C. Greg Lutz, Pramod Sambidi and R. Wes Harrison, "Crawfish Profile," Agricultural Marketing Resource Center, Iowa State University, 2003, accessed January 11, 2012, www.agmrc.org/commodities__products/aquaculture/crawfish_profile.cfm.

12. Percy Viosca, Jr., "Flood Control in the Mississippi Valley in Its Relation to Louisiana Fisheries," Technical Paper No. 4 (New Orleans: Louisiana Department of Conservation, 1928). Risotto and Turner, "Annual Fluctuation in Abundance of the Commercial Fisheries," 566, 567.

13. Risotto and Turner, "Annual Fluctuation in Abundance of the Commercial Fisheries," 565. C. J. Schmitt, M. A. Ribick, J. L. Ludke, and T. W. May, "National Pesticide Monitoring Program: Residues of Organochlorine Chemicals in Freshwater Fish, 1976–79," US Fish and Wildlife Service Resource Publication 152 (1983). LSU Agricultural Center, "Summary, Louisiana Agricultural and Natural Resources," accessed January 11, 2012, www.lsuagcenter.com/agsummary/. Robert Black, Stephanie Hutchison, and Chris Warshaw, *Economic Profile of the Lower Mississippi River Region* (Cambridge, Mass.: Industrial Economics, Inc., 2004), 2–9.

14. Harold L. Schramm, Jr., "Status and Management of Mississippi River Fisheries," 31. Brian D. Leblanc and Rex H. Caffey, "Mississippi River Water Quality: Agriculture and Wetlands," accessed February 15, 2006, www.usawaterquality.org/conferences/2004/posters/LeblancLA.pdf. Ish and Doctor, "Channel Catfish, U.S. Farmed: Final Report." Robert H. Meade, ed. *Contaminants in the Mississippi River, 1987–92*, USGS circular no. 1133 (Washington, D.C., 1995), 109, 113. Mississippi Department of Environmental Quality, "Fish Tissue Advisories" (2001). Current advisories are at www.deq.state.ms.us/mdeq.nsf/page/FS_Mississippi_Fish_Advisories?OpenDocument. USEPA, "Lake

Washington Nutrient Showcase Project," accessed January 11, 2012, www.epa. gov/gmpo/presentations/lmrsbc-lakewashington/lmr-lakewashington.html.

15. Daniel, *Toxic Drift*, 84–100. Ferguson quotation is from page 100. Craig E. Colten, "Too Much of a Good Thing: Industrial Pollution in the Lower Mississippi River," in Craig E. Colten, ed., *Transforming New Orleans and Its Environs* (Pittsburgh: University of Pittsburgh Press, 2000), 150–153. On fear of rivers as conveyors of cancer-causing chemicals, see Sandra Steingraber, *Living Downstream: An Ecologist's Personal Investigation of Cancer and the Environment* (Reading, Mass.: Addison-Wesley, 1997).

16. Louisiana Cooperative Extension Service, LSU Agricultural Center, "Sea Grant Program Lagniappe," 15 (November 15, 1991), 3 accessed January 11, 2012, www.lsu.edu/seagrantfish/pdfs/lagniappe/1991/11-15-1991.pdf. Falling fish prices is a global problem, connecting ocean and land-based aquaculture industries, as well as sea and freshwater commercial fishers. See John P. Volpe, "'Salmon Sovereignty' and the Dilemma of Intensive Atlantic Salmon Aquaculture Development in British Columbia," in C. C. Parrish, N. J. Turner, and S. M. Solberg, eds., *Resetting the Kitchen Table: Food Security, Culture, Health and Resilience in Coastal Communities* (Hauppauge, N.Y.: Nova Science, 2006), 75–86, and John P. Volpe, "Dollars without Sense: The Bait for Big-Money Tuna Ranching around the World," *BioScience* 55 (April 2005): 301–302.

17. Hesse-Wartegg, *Travels on the Lower Mississippi 1879–1880*, 88. Lutz, Sambidi, and Harrison, "Crawfish Profile."

18. Gary Kulik, "Dams, Fish, and Farmers: Defense of Public Rights in Eighteenth-Century Rhode Island," in Steven Hahn and Jonathan Prude, eds., *The Countryside in the Age of Capitalist Transformation* (Chapel Hill: University of North Carolina Press, 1985), 25–50. H. B. Carlander, *A History of Fish and Fishing in the Upper Mississippi River* (Rock Island, Ill.: Upper Mississippi River Conservation Committee, 1954). Ish and Doctor, "Channel Catfish, U.S. Farmed: Final Report." W. Ray McClain, Robert P. Romaire, C. Greg Lutz, and Mark G. Shirley, *Louisiana Crawfish Production Manual*, Louisiana State University Agricultural Center, publication 2637, January 2007, www.lsuagcenter.com/NR/rdonlyres/3AD14F0D-567D-4334-B572-D55D1C55A1F1/34429/pub2637Craw-fishProductionManualLOWRES.pdf. *Dycus v. Sillers* 557 So. 2d 486; 1990 Miss. LEXIS 2438 (Supreme Court of Mississippi, 1990), [online] LexisNexis Academic Universe/State Legal Research/Cases/Mississippi.

19. John A. Hargreaves, "Channel Catfish Farming in Ponds: Lessons from a Maturing Industry," *Reviews in Fisheries Science*, 10 (2002): 499–528. "Catfish Pioneer Hammett Dead at 79," Associated Press State and Local Wire Service, Greenville, Mississippi, January 1, 2002, [online] LexisNexus Academic Universe/Newswire Service, July 12, 2010. "Catfish: A Southern Cultural Icon," accessed July 12, 2010, http://users.aristotle.net/~russjohn/commerce/ctfsh. html. T. L. Wellborn, Jr. "The Catfish Story: Farmers, State Services Create New

Industry," *1983 Yearbook of Agriculture*, J. Hayes, ed. (Washington, D.C.: US Department of Agriculture, 1983), 298–305, accessed January 1, 2012, http://naldr.nal.usda.gov/NALWeb/Agricola_Link.asp?Accession=IND84105124. Chris Kirkham, "Mudbugs Rebound," *Times-Picayune*, February 24, 2007, accessed January11, 2012, www.nola.com/timespic/stories/index.ssf?/base/news-7/1172299678254830.xml&coll=1. Chris Kirkham, "Crawfishers Feel the Pinch," *Times-Picayune*, March 23, 2008, accessed January 11, 2012, www.nola.com/news/index.ssf/2008/03/crawfishers_feel_the_pinch.html.

20. "Catfish Farming on the Rise in the South," News Release, Department of the Interior, Fish and Wildlife Service, Bureau of Sport Fisheries and Wildlife, July 27, 1969. Andy Goodwin et al., "Farm Pond Management for Recreational Fishing," Cooperative Extension Program, University of Arkansas, Pine Bluff, www.extension.org/sites/default/files/w/9/9f/FarmPondManagementforRecreational Fishing.pdf.

21. Thomas Wellborn, Jr., *Catfish Farmer's Handbook* , Publication 1549, Extension Service of Mississippi State University, accessed April 13, 2012, http://aqua.ucda-vis.edu/DatabaseRoot/pdf/1549MIS.PDF. On page 30 Wellborn discusses how to eradicate unwanted fish from ponds with rotenone, fintrol, and other chemicals.

22. Craig S. Tucker, "Characterization and Management of Effluents from Aquaculture Ponds in the Southeastern United States," *Southern Regional Aquaculture Center Publication*, no. 470 (February 1999). Strother E. Roberts, " 'Esteeme a Little of Fish': Fish, Fishponds, and Farming in Eighteenth-Century New England and the Mid-Atlantic," *Agricultural History* 82 (Spring 2008), 143–163. Darin Kinsey, " 'Seeding the Water as the Earth': The Epicenter and Peripheries of a Western *Aqua*cultural Revolution," *Environmental History* 11 (July 2006): 552. *Paul Haworth and David Dawson v. Lester A. L'Hoste, Jr. and Donald W. Eppley* 664 So. 2d 1335; 1995 La. App. LEXIS 3236 (Court of Appeal of Louisiana, Fourth Circuit 1995), [online] LexisNexis Academic Universe/State Legal Research/Cases/Louisiana. *Masonite Corp v. Windham* 48 So. 2d 622; Miss. LEXIS 325; (Supreme Court of Mississippi, 1950), [online] LexisNexis Academic Universe/State Legal Research/Cases/Mississippi.

23. Jim Core and Amy Spillman, "Keeping Catfish on Consumers' Menus," *Agricultural Research*, USDA-ARS (March 2003), accessed March 11, 2006, www.ars.usda.gov/is/AR/archive/mar03/menu0303.pdf. Luis Pons, "New Algicide to Help Keep Catfish Tasting Good," *Agricultural Research*, USDA-ARS (April 2003), accessed March 11, 2006, www.ars.usda.gov/is/AR/archive/apr03/fish0403.pdf. "Diuron," Extoxnet: Extension Toxicology Network Pesticide Information Profiles," accessed March 11, 2006, http://extoxnet.orst.edu/pips/diuron.htm.

24. *One Fish, Two Fish, Crawfish, Bluefish: The Smithsonian Sustainable Seafood Cookbook* (Washington, D.C.: Smithsonian Books, 2003).

25. Southern Regional Aquaculture Center Fact Sheets, accessed January 11, 2012, http://srac.tamu.edu/index.cfm?catid=9. Steve Bandy, "Farming Crawfish,

Rice Balancing Act," *Daily Iberian,* June 14, 2007. USDA National Agricultural Statistics Services, Census of Aquaculture, 2005, Table 14: Crustacean Sales by Species, by State and United States: 2005 and 1998, accessed June 18, 2010, www.agcensus.usda.gov/Publications/2002/Aquaculture/aquacen2005_14.pdf. *West v. G. H. Seed Co.* 832 So. 2d 274; 2002 La. App. LEXIS 2676 (Louisiana Court of Appeals, Third Circuit, 2002), [online] LexisNexis Academic Universe/ State Legal Research/Cases/Louisiana.

26. *El Paso Field Service v. Minvielle* 867 So. 2d 120; 2004 La. App. LEXIS 471 (Court of Appeal of Louisiana, Third Circuit, 2004); *South Lafourche Crawfish Farm, Inc. v. Cajun Flying Service, Inc.* 394 So. 2d 1271; 1981 La. App. LEXIS 3562 (Court of Appeal of Louisiana, First Circuit, 1981), [online] LexisNexis Academic Universe/ State Legal Research/Cases/Louisiana.

27. On the mounting evidence in support of the viability of catfish polyculture, see Donny Ponce-Marbán, Juan Hernández, and Eucario Gasca-Leyva, "Economic Viability of Polyculture of Nile Tilapia and Australian Redclaw Crayfish in Yucatan State, Mexico," European Association of Agricultural Economists 95th Seminar, Civitavecchia, Rome, December 9–11, 2005, accessed January 11, 2012, http://ageconsearch.umn.edu/bitstream/56080/2/Ponce.pdf. Aecio M. D'Silva and O. Eugene Maughan, "Polyculture of Channel Catfish and Blue Tilapia in Cages," *Progressive Fish-Culturist* 54 (1992): 108–111. William A. Wurts, "Sustainable Aquaculture in the Twenty-First Century," *Review in Fisheries Science* 8 (2000): 141–150. Craig Tucker and John A. Hargreaves, eds., *Biology and Culture of Channel Catfish* (Amsterdam: Elsevier, 2004), 187. Kathryn White, Brendan O'Neill, and Zdravka Tzankova, "At a Crossroads: Will Aquaculture Fulfill the Promise of the Blue Revolution?" SeaWeb Aquaculture Clearinghouse (2004), accessed July 13, 2010, www.blueyou.com/pdf_knowledgebase/A%20 Aquaculture/At%20a%20Crossroads%20Will%20Aquaculture%20fulfill%20 the%20Promise%20of%20the%20Blue%20Revolution.pdf. James T. Davis is skeptical of polyculture, in "Crawfish Production," accessed January 11, 2012, http://warnell.forestry.uga.edu/service/library/ats-4/ats-4.pdf. Robert R. Stickney, *Culture of Nonsalmonid Freshwater Fishes,* 2ed. (Boca Raton: CRC Press, 1993), 40–41. Craig Tucker, Jimmy Avery, Carole Engle, and Andrew Goodwin, "Industry Profile: Pond-Raised Channel Catfish," a Review Developed for the National Risk Management Feasibility Program for Aquaculture, Department of Agricultural Economics, Mississippi State University (May 2004), 7.

28. Steven D. Mims and Richard J. Onders, "Polyculture and Reservoir Ranching: Sustainable Aquaculture Strategies for Paddlefish *(Polyodon spathula)* Production," Sustainable Agriculture Research and Education Fact Sheet, accessed April 13, 2012, www.sare.org/Learning-Center/Fact-Sheets/National-SARE-Fact-Sheets/Polyculture-and-Reservoir-Ranching. Mark W. La Salle, Benedict C. Posadas, and C. David Veal, "Use of Constructed Wetlands to Improve Water Quality in Finfish Production" (July 1998), Mississippi State

University, Coastal Research and Extension Center, accessed January 11, 2012, http://coastal.msstate.edu/publish/sk98.pdf. J. H. Tidwell et al., "Growout of Freshwater Prawns in Kentucky Ponds" (2002), Kentucky State University Aquaculture Program. Wurts, "Sustainable Aquaculture in the Twenty-First Century."

29. Margaret Jones Bolsterli, *During Wind and Rain: The Jones Family Farm in the Arkansas Delta, 1848–2006* (Fayetteville: University of Arkansas Press, 2008) xiv, 129.

30. Tucker and Hargreaves, *Biology and Culture of Channel Catfish*, 24, 187–190.

31. David Streitfeld, "As Price of Grain Rises, Catfish Farms Dry Up," *New York Times*, July 18, 2008.

32. Terry Hanson and David Sites, "2005 Catfish Database" (March 2006), Department of Agricultural Economics, Mississippi State University, accessed April 13, 2012, http://msucares.com/aquaculture/catfish/database_05. pdf. "Louisiana Crawfish Harvest Statistics, 1978–2007," Louisiana State University Agricultural Center, accessed January 11, 2012, http://text.lsuag-center.com/NR/rdonlyres/4687F896-C5C5-47D6-A4F4-1F4455760816/46429/ CrawfishHarvestStatistics7807.pdf. "2005 Louisiana Rice Parish Estimates," USDA National Agricultural Statistics Service, June 2006, accessed January 11, 2012, www.nass.usda.gov/Statistics_by_State/Louisiana/Publications/Parish_ Estimates/Rice05.pdf. Arkansas Data, Crops, Rice, 2007, National Agricultural Statistics Service, National Agricultural Statistics Service Web site, www.nass. usda.gov/. See also the statistics for Mississippi and Missouri at the same site. Dan Scheiman, "Arkansas Waterbirds on Working Lands Initiative, Technical Report," National Audubon Society (2007), accessed January 11, 2012, www. audubon.org/bird/waterbirds/pdf/Arkansas_Waterbirds_on_Working_Lands_ Initiative_Jan_2007.pdf. *Paul Haworth and David Dawson v. Lester A. L'Hoste, Jr. and Donald W. Eppley* 664 So. 2d 1335; 1995 La. App. LEXIS 3236 (Court of Appeal of Louisiana, Fourth Circuit 1995), [online] LexisNexis Academic Universe/State Legal Research/Cases/Louisiana. On subsidies, see Bolsterli, *During Wind and Rain*, 123–124.

33. Richard C. Hoffmann and Verena Winiwarter, "Making Land and Water Meet: The Cycling of Nutrients between Fields and Ponds in Pre-Modern Europe," *Agricultural History* 84 (Summer 2010): 352–380. Richard C. Hoffmann, "Aquaculture in Champagne before the Black Death of 1348–1350," in P. Béarez et al., eds., *Archéologie du poisson. 30 ans d'archéo-ichtyologie au CNRS. Hommage aux travaux de Jean Desse et Nathalie Desse-Berset* (Antibes: Éditions APDCA, 2008), 67–82. Donald Jackson, ed., *The Diaries of George Washington*, Vol. I: *1748–65* (Charlottesville: University Press of Virginia, 1976), 256, 259, 264–265, 267, 283. Eighteenth-century New England farmers kept and raised fish in ponds in polyculture and near rivers, so water could be passed through them to keep them oxygenated. They used pond sediment to manure fields, and pond water as a

nutrient-rich emergency irrigation reservoir. See Strother E. Roberts, "'Esteeme a Little of Fish': Fish, Fishponds, and Farming in Eighteenth-Century New England and the Mid-Atlantic," *Agricultural History* 82 (Spring 2008): 143–163.

34. Latour, *Reassembling the Social*, 63–86.

35. Chris Kirkham, "Crawfishers Feel the Pinch," *Times-Picayune*, March 23, 2008. On the promising commercial and environmental future of raising rice and fish together, see WorldFish Center, "Rice-Fish Culture: A Recipe for Higher Production," accessed April 9, 2012, www.worldfishcenter.org/wfcms/HQ/article.aspx?ID=158; World Bank, *Changing the Face of the Waters: The Promise and Challenge of Sustainable Aquaculture* (Washington, D.C.: World Bank, 2007); Barry A. Costa-Pierce and Christopher J. Bridger, "The Role of Marine Aquaculture Facilities as Habitats and Ecosystems," in R. R. Stickney, ed., *Responsible Marine Aquaculture* (Oxfordshire, UK: CABI International, 2002). See also Brian Halweil, "Farming Fish for the Future," WorldWatch Report 176 (Washington, D.C.: WorldWatch Institute, 2008), accessed April 9, 2012, www.worldwatch.org/files/pdf/Farming Fish for the Future.pdf.

36. USDA National Agricultural Statistics Service, for Louisiana and Mississippi, www.nass.usda.gov/Statistics_by_State/Louisiana/index.asp and www.nass.usda.gov/Statistics_by_State/Mississippi/index.asp. S. Locke Breaux, "The Rice Crop along the Mississippi River," *Rice Journal* 6 (January 1903): 25. W. D. Smith, "Handling the River Rice Crop," *Rice Journal* 30 (July 1927): 12–14. For a description of rice planting in Plaquemines Parish, below New Orleans, at the end of the nineteenth century, see Hesse-Wartegg, *Travels on the Lower Mississippi*, 206–210. For one family's experiences with rice in the 1950s, see Bolsterli, *During Wind and Rain*, 6–7, 101–102.

37. Bolsterli, *During Wind and Rain*, 121–123. C. J. Newling, "Restoration of Bottom Land Hardwood Forests in the Lower Mississippi Valley," *Restoration and Management Notes* 81 (1990): 23, 25. US Census Bureau, State and County QuickFacts, Mississippi, Louisiana, and Arkansas counties, accessed April 13, 2012, http://quickfacts.census.gov/qfd/index.html. *Mississippi Sierra Club, Inc. v. Mississippi Department of Environmental Quality*, 819 So. 2d 515; 2002 Miss. LEXIS 174 (Supreme Court of Mississippi, 2002), [online] LexisNexis Academic Universe/State Legal Research/Cases/Mississippi.

38. Army Corps of Engineers, "Yazoo Backwater Reformulation Main Report" (October 2007), accessed April 4, 2008, www.mvk.usace.army.mil/offices/pp/projects/YBR_Report/index.htmL. Flood Control Act of 1941, Public Law 228, 77th Cong., 1st Session, H. R. 4911, "An Act Authorizing the Construction of Certain Public Works on Rivers and Harbors for Flood Control, and for Other Purposes," *accessed July 13, 2010*, www.fws.gov/habitatconservation/Omnibus/R&HA1941.pdf.

39. US Census, National Agricultural Statistics Service, Mississippi (Issaquena and Sharkey Counties), accessed January 11, 2012, www.nass.usda.gov/Statistics_by_State/Mississippi/index.asp. Felicity Barringer, "Death Looms for a Flood-

Control Project," *New York Times*, April 9, 2008. In September 2004, local and state law enforcement agents found $150,000 in marijuana plants "in the woods near a cotton field" in Coahoma County. "Bobo Raid Yields $150,000 Worth of Marijuana, *Clarksdale Press Register*, September 9, 2004, accessed April 13, 2012, www.pressregister.com/article_c98efb9f-226c-5d5e-ad4e-f10b113c05af.html. Theresa Kiely, "Authorities Seize $1.5M in Pot Bureau Arrests Almost Twice as Many as in 1999," *Jackson Clarion-Ledger*, August 3, 2000.

40. Danny Barrett, Jr., "Environmentalists Seek Pumps Veto," *Vicksburg Evening Post*, December 12, 2007. Jim Luckett (PoLuck Hunting Club) and Frank Eakin (Greasy Bayou Hunting Club), "To the Editor: Opponents to Yazoo Pump Putting Out Misinformation," *Greenwood Commonwealth*, December 15, 2007. Bennie Thompson, US Representative, "Yazoo Pump Project Helps All in the Delta," *Jackson Clarion-Ledger*, January 20, 2003. "Yazoo Pump: EPA Recognizes It's a Boondoggle," *Jackson Clarion-Ledger*, February 6, 2008 "Yazoo Pumps, R.I.P.?" *New York Times*, February 26, 2008. American Rivers, "EPA Should Veto the Yazoo Pumps" (2007), accessed Jan.uary11, 2012, www.americanrivers.org/site/DocServer/2007_EPA_Should_Veto_without_auth_arg___2_.pdf?docID=6781. On reforestation efforts in the valley, see S. L. King and B. D. Keeland, "Evaluation of Reforestation in the Lower Mississippi River Alluvial Valley," *Restoration Ecology* 7 (1999): 348–354.

41. On the difficulty outsiders and insiders have understanding each others' position on land use, see Richard White, "Are You an Environmentalist or Do You Work for a Living?" in William Cronon, ed., *Uncommon Ground: Toward Reinventing Nature* (New York: W. W. Norton, 1995), 171–185, and Susan Kollin, *Nature's State: Imaging Alaska as the Last Frontier* (Chapel Hill: University of North Carolina Press, 2001).

42. So long as the commitment remains strong to agriculture and to the Mississippi River as a barge transportation corridor, the restoration of the floodplain will be politically difficult to accomplish. See Gore and Shields, Jr., "Can Large Rivers Be Restored?" *BioScience* 45 (March 1995): 142–151.

CHAPTER 11

1. Douglas Brinkley, *The Great Deluge: Hurricane Katrina, New Orleans, and the Mississippi Gulf Coast* (New York: William Morrow, 2006). "Reports of Missing and Deceased, August 2, 2006," Louisiana Department of Health and Hospitals, accessed January 12, 2012, www.dhh.louisiana.gov/offices/page.asp?ID=192&Detail=5248.

2. William H. Connor et al., "Influence of Hurricanes on Coastal Ecosystems along the Northern Gulf of Mexico," *Wetlands Ecology and Management* 1 (1989): 45–56.

3. For a good summary of the many arguments made by many people who blame Katrina on human mistakes, see Michael Grunwald, "The Threatening Storm,"

Time, August 1, 2007, accessed January 12, 2006, www.time.com/time/specials/2007/article/0,28804,1646611_1646683_1648904,00.html.

4. Marq de Villiers, *The End: Natural Disasters, Manmade Catastrophes, and the Future of Human Survival* (New York: Thomas Dunne, 2008). De Villiers explains how events that cause natural disasters are normal, predictable, and therefore survivable, none more so than hurricanes, and yet paradoxically are regarded as exceptional and unpredictable.

5. Ted Steinberg, *Acts of God: The Unnatural History of Natural Disasters in America* (New York: Oxford University Press, 2000).

6. Joby Warrick, "White House Got Early Warning on Katrina," *Washington Post* , January 24, 2006, A02. "Nature's Revenge," *New York Times*, August 30, 2005.

7. Craig E. Colten and Alexandra Giancarlo, "Losing Resilience on the Gulf Coast: Hurricanes and Social Memory," *Environment* 53 (July–August 2011): 6–19. Lawrence J. Vale and Thomas J. Campanella, *The Resilient City: How Modern Cities Recover from Disaster* (New York: Oxford University Press, 2005).

8. E. L. Corthell, "The Delta of the Mississippi River," *National Geographic* 8 (December 1897): 351–354.

9. Francisco Luis Hector, Baron de Carondelet, New Orleans, July 10, 1797, to Pierre-Joseph Favrot, Plaquemines, Louisiana Purchase and Louisiana Colonial History Collection, Louisiana State Museum, New Orleans. Ernst von Hesse-Wartegg, *Travels on the Lower Mississippi, 1879–1880*, Frederic Trautmann, ed. and trans. (Columbia: University of Missouri Press, 1990), 66, 68, 193.

10. C. G. Forshey, "Rise and Fall of the Mississippi River, at Vidalia, Louisiana," *Concordia Intelligencer*, June 16, 1841, 4. New Orleans flooded by river or by rain in 1816, 1826, 1833, 1849, 1857, 1859, 1867, 1871, 1874, 1882, 1884, 1890, 1892, 1893, 1897, 1903, 1912, 1913, 1922, 1927, 1937, 1947, 1965, 1973, 1979, 1993, and 2005. See R. W. Kates, C. E. Colten, S. Laska, and S. P. Leatherman, "Reconstruction of New Orleans after Hurricane Katrina: A Research Perspective," *PNAS* 103 (October 2006): 14653–14660, accessed January 12, 2012, www.pnas.org/cgi/content/full/103/40/14653. Paul S. Trotter, G. Alan Johnson, Robert Ricks, and David R. Smith, "Floods on the Lower Mississippi: An Historical Economic Overview," SR/SSD 98-9, 3-1-98, Technical Attachment, National Oceanic and Atmospheric Administration (NOAA), accessed January12, 2012, www.srh.noaa.gov/topics/attach/html/ssd98-9.htm. With the similar context of south Florida in mind, Ted Steinberg has noted a "hurricane apathy." Steinberg, *Acts of God*, 89.

11. *Daily Picayune*, May 28, 1849, 1; May 31, 1849, 2; June 3, 1849, 2. *Daily Delta*, May 26, 1849, 2. *New Orleans Bee*, May 17, 1849, 1; May 23, 1849, 1.

12. *The New Orleans Bee*, May 18, 1849, 1. *The Daily Delta*, May 30, 1849, 2. *Savannah* (Georgia) *Republican*, June 9, 1849.

13. *The Daily Picayune*, June 13, 1849, 1. Zachary Taylor to Richard Taylor, May 9, 1850, typescript, Zachary Taylor Papers, Library of Congress.

14. On fear of, even paranoia about, nature, see Mike Davis, *Ecology of Fear: Los Angeles and the Imagination of Disaster* (New York: Metropolitan Books, 1998).

15. *The Daily Picayune*, June 13, 1849, 1. *New Orleans Bee*, June 16, 1849, 1. Amy Wold, "'Toxic Soup' Concerns All Hype? Experts Debate True Risks in N. O.," *The Advocate* (Baton Rouge), February 13, 2006, 1 B. Fred C. Dobbs, "Après le Déluge: Microbial Landscape of New Orleans after the Hurricanes," *PNAS* 104 (May 29, 2007): 9103–9104, argues that the effects of water on the spread of fecal matter and the growth of algae have been much less than expected, and that conditions returned to normal very quickly after Katrina.

16. Steinberg, *Acts of God*.

17. Michelle Landis Dauber, "The Sympathetic State," *Law and History Review* 23 (Summer 2005): 387–442. Kevin Rozario, *The Culture of Calamity: Disaster and the Making of Modern America* (Chicago: University of Chicago Press, 2007). Stanley A. Changnon, "The Historical Struggle with Floods on the Mississippi River Basin," *Water International* 23 (December 1998): 263–271. Chandra Mukerji, "Stewardship Politics and the Control of Wild Weather: Levees, Seawalls, and State Building in 17th-Century France," *Social Studies of Science* 37 (February 2007): 127–133. Mukerji argues that the Katrina disaster demonstrates a lost notion of the common good. In earlier centuries the state used engineering as a means of claiming legitimacy, for example, by protecting its subject from floods.

18. Colten, "Losing Resilience." Kates et al., "Reconstruction of New Orleans," on rushing to "rebuild the familiar."

19. Matthew Weaver, "Venice Sees Worst Flooding in Twenty Years," *The Guardian*, December 1, 2008. John Hooper, "Venice Flood Fails to Damp Down Fight over Sea Walls," *The Guardian*, December 6, 2008. I am grateful to my colleague Sam Haynes, who happened to be in Venice during the flooding, for sharing his experience and photographs with me.

20. Alexey Kraykovskiy, "The Neva River in the Identity, Economy and Culture of 'the Northern Capital' of Russia," unpublished paper presented before the First World Congress on Environmental History, Copenhagen, August 6, 2009, and the discussion that followed Kraykovskiy's presentation.

21. Ian Watson and Alister D. Burnett, *Hydrology: An Environmental Approach* (Boca Raton: CRC Press, 1995), 516–520. Suzanne Goldenberg, "U.S. Urged to Abandon Ageing Flood Defenses in Favour of Dutch System," *The Guardian*, June 5, 2009. Mark Schleifstein, "U.S. Sen. Mary Landrieu: U.S. Should Adopt Netherlands-like Policies for Flood Control," *Time-Picayune*, June 5, 2009. Alix Kroeger, "Dutch Pioneer Floating Eco-homes," BBC News, March 1, 2007, accessed January 12, 2012, http://news.bbc.co.uk/2/hi/europe/6405359.stm.

22. Joe Macaluso, "Atchafalaya Wildlife Threatened by Flooding," *The Advocate* (Baton Rouge), May 15, 2011, 14C. On wildlife and floods, see Uwe Lübken, "'Poor Dumb Brutes' or 'Friends in Need'?" in Dorothy Brantz, ed., *Beastly*

Natures: Animals, Humans, and the Study of History (Charlottesville: University of Virginia Press, 2010), 246–263. Steinberg, *Acts of God*, 97–115.

23. Steinberg, *Acts of God*, 97–115. Federal Emergency Management Agency (FEMA), News Release, "Missouri Flood Buyouts Save Lives, Heartache, Money," September 1, 2008, accessed January 12, 2012, www.fema.gov/news/newsrelease.fema?id=45637. Michael J. Walsh, "Regional Interagency Levee Task Force Monthly Report: Levee Repair and Associated Restoration Projects, Midwest Floods of June, 2008" (October 31, 2008), accessed January 12, 2012, www.iwr.usace.army.mil/iltf/docs/ILTF_Oct_08_Monthly_Report.pdf. Nicholas Pinter, "Environment: One Step Forward, Two Steps Back on U.S. Floodplains," *Science* 308 (April 8, 2005): 207–208.

24. Ted Steinberg describes living in a trailer home in the St. Charles County, Missouri, flood plain as "third world living." Steinberg, *Acts of God*, 108.

25. "People want to know whether a place is a credible first-world city," declared urban historian Joel Kotkin, to a *New York Times* reporter. "What they found in New Orleans was that underneath the gloss and facade of a first-world tourist attraction was a third-world reality." Clifford J. Levy, "Post-Katrina, Bricks and Mortals," *New York Times*, September 18, 2005. "The only difference between the chaos of New Orleans and a Third World disaster operation was that a foreign dictator would have responded better." Matt Wells, "New Orleans Crisis Shames US," *BBC News*, September 4, 2005, accessed April 15, 2012, http://news.bbc.co.uk/2/hi/americas/4210674.stm. See also Adam Nossiter, "'It's like Being in a Third World country': Hospitals in Flood Zone Struggle to Save Lives," *Associated Press*, August 31, 2005; Jeff Koinange, "Katrina: When New Orleans Went from Developed World to Third World," *CNN.com*, August 30, 2006, accessed April 15, 2012, www.cnn.com/2006/US/08/30/btsc.koinange/index.html.

26. Oscar Huh et al., "Ganges-Brahmaputra River Delta, India, Asia," in World Delta Database, George F. Hart and James Coleman, comps. and eds., Louisiana State University, Baton Rouge, 2004, accessed April 15, 2012, www.geol.lsu.edu/WDD/ASIAN/Ganges-Brahmaputra/ganga.htm. Tahmima Anam, "Losing the Ground beneath Their Feet," *The Guardian*, September 4, 2008. John Vidal, "Bangladesh: A Country on the Frontline of Climate Change," *The Guardian*, September 10, 2008. Shahidul Islam Chowdhury, "Weak Embankments Fail to Withstand Tidal Surge: Experts," *New Age* (Dhaka), May 27, 2009. M. Monirul Qader Mirza, Ajaya Dixit, and Ainun Nishat, *Flood Problem and Management in South Asia* (Dordrecht, The Netherlands: Kluwer Academic, 2003). Ainun Nishat, "Freshwater Wetlands in Bangladesh: Status and Issues," in Aninun Nishat et al., eds., *Freshwater Wetlands in Bangladesh: Issues and Approaches for Management* (Dhaka Bangladesh: IUCN-The World Conservation Union, 1993). A. H. M. Rezaul Haq, Tapan Kumar Ghosal, and Pritam Ghosh, "Cultivating Wetlands in Bangladesh," *Leisa India, the Magazine on Low External Input and Sustainable Agriculture*, India Regional Edition (December 2004), 17–19. A. H.

M. Rezaul Haq, Pritam Ghosh, and M. Aminul Islam, "Wise Use of Wetland for Sustainable Livelihood through Participatory Approach: A Case of Adapting to Climate Change," Asian Wetland Symposium, Bhubanaswar, India, February 6–9, 2005, accessed April 15, 2012, http://waswc.soil.gd.cn/subjects/wetlands/Wise%20use%20of%20wetland%20for%20sustainable%20livelihood,%20a%20case%20of%20adapting%20to%20climate%20change%20070831aa.doc. Jan Sendzimir and Szuszanna Flachner, "Exploiting Ecological Disturbance," in Sara J. Scherr and Jeffrey A. McNeely, eds., *Farming with Nature: The Science and Practice of Ecoagriculture* (Washington, D.C.: Island Press, 2007), 214. De Villiers, *The End*, 200–201.

27. Cornelia Dean, "Destroying Levees in a State Usually Clamoring for Them," *New York Times*, June 20, 2009. Marq De Villiers, *Water: The Fate of Our Most Precious Resource* (New York: Mariner, 2001), 166–172.

28. Gary Esolen and Valeri LeBlanc, "Rebuilding New Orleans: Twenty Big Ideas and a Postscript," *MetropolisMag.com* (October 31, 2005), accessed April 15, 2012, www.metropolismag.com/cda/story.php?artid=1619.

29. Coleman Warner, "N.O. Planning Process Puts Residents on Edge," *Times-Picayune*, August 31, 2006. Kates et al,, "Reconstruction of New Orleans," 14653–14660. On Perth, Australia, another city built on a wetland, see Rod Giblett, *Postmodern Wetlands: Culture, History, Ecology* (Edinburgh: Edinburgh University Press, 1997), 56.

30. Nathaniel Rich, "Jungleland," *New York Times Magazine*, March 25, 2012, 32–37. Doug MacCash, "Make It Right Rebuilds the Lower 9th Ward with Designs that Are Both Good-Looking and Built to Last," *Times-Picayune*, September 6, 2008. Gerald Clarke and Harry Benson, "Brad Pitt Makes It Right in New Orleans," *Architectural Digest* (January 2009). Doug MacCash, "Brad Pitt's 'Make It Right' Challenged by Urban Planner Andres Duany," *Times-Picayune*, January 31, 2009. Robert Costanza, William J. Mirsch, and John W. Day, Jr., "Creating a Sustainable and Desirable New Orleans," *Ecological Engineering* 26 (2006): 317–320. Richard E. Sparks, "Rethinking, Then Rebuilding New Orleans," *Issues in Science and Technology* 22 (Winter 2006): 33-39. Cornelia Dean, "Time to Move the Mississippi, Experts Say," *New York Times*, September 19, 2006.

31. Daniel B. Botkin, "What's the Likely Future of New Orleans? History Tells Us What's Likely," April 7, 2007, accessed April 15, 2012, www.danielbbotkin.com/2007/04/07/whats-the-likely-future-of-new-orleans-history-tells-us-whats-likely/.

32. Mark Twain, *Life on the Mississippi* (1883), any edition, end of chapter 32.

Index